To the Hopkins

Hope you'll
always enjoy
Seabuck —

Fredi Perry

Perry Publishing 🔼
PO Box 417
Thompson Falls, MT 59873

© Perry Publishing
Second printing 2005

Library of Congress Control Number: 2005902996
ISBN: 1-892282-07-0

Other books by Fredi Perry
Kitsap County: A History. Co-author. 1977.
(Published by Kitsap County Historical Society)
Kitsap County: Year of the Child. 1979.
(Published by Kitsap County Historical Society)
Port Madison: 1854-1889. 1989.
(Published by Perry Publishing)
Kitsap County: A Centennial History. 1989.
(Published by Perry Publishing)
Seabeck: Tide's Out. Table's Set. (First) 1993.
(Published by Perry Publishing)
Manchester: A Century of Stewardship. 1998.
(Published by United States Navy)
Shelton: The First Century Plus Ten. Co-author 1996.
(Published by Mason County Historical Society)
Sanders County CCC. Co-author 2004.
(Published by Perry Publishing)
Bremerton and PSNY. 2002.
(Published by Perry Publishing)

Cover and title page: Seabeck youth pose for portrait sitting on hay bales.
Winfrey Green, his sister, Ella, and their spouses Christina (Peterson) and
Theo E. Peiser, Seattle photographer. This is a rare, self portrait by Peiser.
(Photo courtesy Marcel Colp.)

Seabeck
Tide's Out. Table's Set.

By Fredi Perry

with

Michael Jay Mjelde and Larry Hill

Victoria Rowe, artist

PREFACE

Do ki batt came first to create, second to change or make the world new and that when it shall become old, he will come a third time to make it over again.

Rev. Myron Eells
The Twana, Chemakum and Klallam Indians of Washington Territory.

The Smithsonian Institute. 1887.

Twana Indians summered around Seabeck for centuries and then watched silently as a small group of men began driving piles and pounding nails in 1857. The tribe's name was lost but many of its legends and history were saved through the writings of Rev. Myron Eells, a Nineteenth Century missionary at Skokomish Reservation. The great lumbering industry was lost, as well, and now only grandchildren are left to tell the stories of those glory days.

The history of Seabeck has always intrigued me. I've collected scraps of paper, photos, listened to stories and wanted to write this history but felt that in a community as small as Seabeck, the financial commitment of publishing a book as major as Seabeck would be impossible. With the assurance of the Seabeck Christian Conference Center Board that publication costs would be guaranteed after a publisher-sponsored pre-publication sale, the project began. The pre-sale was overwhelmingly successful and for that I thank the community.

During a 29-year mill operation, stability in residency and ownership created an atmosphere of community, much like that existing today. Speaking at the Seabeck Community Club, I was struck by the warmth of the members, their interest in the history of the community and their willingness to help see the project through to the end. Their encouragement and support was successful.

It struck me how self reliant so many of the Seabeck families were and are, how very concerned they are about the future of the community and Hood's Canal. I've always jokingly said that if stopped-up and boiled, Hood's Canal would be a gigantic pot of bouillabaisse. While interviewing Joe Emel, he said, in referring to the natural resources, *"Tide's Out; Table's Set"*, a saying probably passed down from one of his progenitors, many of whom settled here in the Nineteenth Century.

Like any other community history, some readers will feel that something significant has been left out. The authors have worked diligently in gathering and writing the story of Seabeck with accuracy and as complete as possible.

Thomas Frederick Gedosch was a major contributor despite the fact that we never met. Gedosch did a thorough and comprehensive economic history of Seabeck for his Masters thesis at the University of Washington. He read every ledger, letter and document preserved in the University of Washington's Special Collections, Washington Mill Company papers. For years I'd tried to find him, then ordered a nation-wide search which turned up a Thomas Frederick Gedosch at the National Archives in Washington, D.C.

Suzanne Anest, curator Kitsap County Historical Society museum, edited the major portions of the book with precise comments and observations, working long nights and weekends. She alerted me to grammatical errors, conflict of information, *demanding* that I elaborate on vague statements.

Ella Olanie, daughter-in-law of Territorial pioneers, dreamed of doing this project. Had word processors and ease of accessing information in this computer age been 30 years earlier, she would have had the great joy I've had in producing this book. Once, 15 or so years ago, I placed an ad in *Yankee* magazine looking for genealogical information on Samuel and Marshall Blinn. Two women responded. Ella traveled to California and Arizona and convinced them to share with us their treasure of family photos and biographical information.

I met Larry Hill, Executive Director of the Seabeck Christian Conference Center, on *Prodigy*, a nationwide computer communications system. He was scanning member names of people who lived in the area and found mine. I think his first message a couple of years ago was something like *"Hey. Why don't we get together and talk about writing Seabeck history sometime."* We did. His wife, Sandy Fowler-Hill, and children, Spencer and Whitney, have contributed much of their "family time" to the history. My family has found me wallowing in paper and sitting in front of the computer for the past year. My granddaughter, Alanna, said to me recently: *"Gramma. Don't write books. Read me books."*

There are hundreds of others who have contributed and to mention one and forget another would create problems. So to everyone, thank you. We did it!

Let us look forward to the Third Century of Seabeck's history with optimism and faith in the men, women and children who live and play on the shores and waters of Hood's Canal. Let's not forget all those who came before us.

Fredi Perry

December 1993.

TABLE OF CONTENTS

Book One ~ In the Beginning
    Indians of Hood's Canal   3-10
    Capt. George Vancouver, 1792   11~ 15
    Lt. Charles Wilkes, 1841   15~ 21
    Edward Clayson, 1866   22~ 30
    Jacob Hauptly, 1872   31~ 35

Book Two ~ The Town of Seabeck
    Washington Mill Company   39~ 67
    Shipbuilding   68~ 76
    Washington Mill Fleet   77~ 82
    Transportation   83~ 98
    Hotels, Saloons and Other Fun   99~ 112
    Store and Post Office   113~ 123
    Schools   124~ 134
    Cemetery   135~ 139

Book Three - After the Fire
    Transition   143~ 147
    Seabeck Christian Conference   148~ 166

Book Four ~ Surrounded by Beauty
 Big & Little Beef, Lone Rock   169~ 184
 Head of the Bay   185~ 189
 Miami Beach   190~ 193
 Scenic Beach   194~ 195
 Maple Beach   196~ 198
 Stavis Bay   199~ 205
 Camp Union   206~ 207
 Starvation Flats   208

Appendix
 Legends - Ah Fong and such   210~ 211
 Ernest Riddell - Seabeck history   212~ 215
 Olympus Lost - Fictional account
   by Agatha (Olanie) Lewis   216~ 223
 Seabeck Census, 1857   224~ 225
 Seabeck Census, 1860   226
 Seabeck Census, 1870   227~ 228
 Maps
   1909 Plat Map   229
   1930 circa Kroll Map - tax   230
   1955 Kroll map - tax   231
 Index   232~ 242
 Patrons   243~ 246

INTRODUCTION

Each year thousands of people from many different organizations come to Seabeck Christian Conference Center for a wide diversity of events and purposes. For some it is spiritual renewal, for others personal growth. Many find it an ideal place to strengthen family bonds. Some seek answers, others come to share knowledge. In addition to food and shelter and stimulating programs, there is a sense of connection and community with those around you and those who have been there before you.

There is a sense of something magical in the feeling that you have somehow transcended time. There is a sense that something is very special here, and in this place wonderful and magical things can happen. Seabeck is a place where the lives of many people have changed forever because of their experience.

In June 1990 The Compassionate Friends came to Seabeck for a weekend retreat. TCF is a nationwide support group for people who have experienced the death of a child. It was an opportunity to spend time with others who shared their tragedy and their grief in an environment of love and mutual support. They come from different walks of life and religious beliefs. They represent all facets of our society. Their common denominator is a sense of loss and need to deal with their grief. The depth of their pain can really only be understood by others who have suffered a similar loss. The bond that develops between them is wonderful and inspirational to watch.

While at Seabeck on this particular weekend, there were the expected number of tears and sometimes laughter. There were ceremonies and discussions and opportunities to remember their lost children and to help each other recover some sense of peace.

There was a wreath on display throughout the retreat. Each parent was encouraged to attach mementos or messages of a lost child to it.

On a beautiful, sunny Sunday morning, with the Olympic Mountains as a backdrop, 100 people filed silently over the wooden-planked bridge leading from the Conference Grounds. At the head of the procession the wreath was carried, a bright collage of flowers, ribbons and scraps of paper. One hundred people gathered at the end of the pier where a small boat waited to carry the wreath out onto The Canal.

The marina consists of a 350-foot long main pier with a number of floating docks and ramps at the end that rise and fall twice daily with the tide. Sometimes the docks are almost even with the pier, sometimes well below.

On this particular morning the tide was well out and the dock where the boat waited was a good 10 to 12 feet below the assembled mourners.

Couples stood together, arms around each other, engrossed in their own thoughts and grief. Every eye seemed close to tears and yet there was a collective sense of strength and resolve to make it through this final ceremony.

As they stood together a woman spoke about death and passage. She related a Native American legend. That legend, she claimed, said that when a body died Eagle would descend to carry the spirit to heaven. As they listened, all eyes followed the wreath and its attachments being carried down the ramp and placed on the boat. As the small boat left the dock and headed out into The Canal, all attention was drawn toward it and the wreath that lay across the transom. Every eye grew a little heavier with tears, every heart grew a little heavier with sorrow.

The bright morning sun that shone from behind blended their individual shadows into a single, dark image on the water. Maybe they were too focused on the boat and too consumed in their thoughts to notice another shadow come from behind and pass directly overhead. The eagle could not have been more than 15 feet over their heads; and as it floated down toward the boat it was suddenly and clearly in full view of everyone. This huge bird, wings extended to their full six-feet span, descended gracefully and effortlessly. Its white head and tail shining brightly in contrast to its dark body.

Everyone watched in amazement and disbelief. The majestic bird swooped down and almost touched the top of the boat, rose again and slowly circled; once, twice, rising higher each time. It broke off its upward spiral and headed across the bay. Tears that had been held so bravely now flowed freely and happily. A sense of wonderment could be heard in a collective gasp. No one moved. No one spoke, nor needed to. After the eagle disappeared over Misery Point, no one was sure if what they had seen was real or not. No one who was there can ever explain exactly what had happened, or what they felt. But all agreed that it was far too meaningful, far too spiritual, far too magical to be just a coincidence.

They remained on the pier until the boat returned. Eventually, as they were able, they drifted back over the bridge. Each life had been changed in some way by the power of that eagle and the magic of a Seabeck Sunday morning. And each of them, as they remember the child they can no longer hold, will also remember the eagle and know that somehow those children also shared that moment.

And a piece of every heart will remain in Seabeck forever.

Larry Hill

December 1993.

Book One

Spring

Dokibatt, the Twanas say, was the creator of all things, making birds, beasts and all lower creatures before he made man. According to them, Dokibatt made the moon and sun, the moon first, and in the night, intending it to be the sun. In the morning it rose, but it shone too hot and caused the water to boil, killing the fish and also many animals on land and did much damage generally. So then he made the sun as it now is to rule the day and condemned the moon to shine at night.

A long time after this, Dokibatt came again to this world because things were not good, and rectified them by changing them. Hence his name which means a changer.

Rev. Myron Eells,
The Twana, Chemakum and Klallam
Indians of Washington Territory.

The Indians

The Indians who seasonally camped in the Seabeck area were part of the Twana tribe. When Dr. William Fraser Tolmie of the Hudson Bay Company estimated Indian tribes living on or near Puget Sound in 1844, he calculated that there were 500 Indians on Hood's Canal, members of the Suquamish and Toando tribe.[1] (Gibbs' pronunciation/spelling differs from modern usage of *Twana.*) Thirteen years later it was estimated that there were 200 Skokomish, 265 To-an-hooch (Twana).

". . . the Toanhooch, occupying the western shore of Hood's Canal, (are) a branch of the Nisqually nation, but their dialect differs greatly from the Skokomish, upon the head of the Canal, who probably number 200. Neither of them have had as much intercourse with the whites as most of the Sound tribes."[2]

The S'Klallam, Twana and Chimakum tribes gathered at Point-No-Point on Jan. 25, 1855. They all were to relocate to a reservation surrounding the Skokomish River and bordered by Hood's Canal. By 1874 the reservation occupied nearly 5,000 acres. It wasn't long before these Indians were all known as *Skokomish.* Few of those told to go to the reservation ever did. The S'Klallams and those Chimakums not previously annihilated remained in small villages near their traditional homes.. (A group of S'Klallam even bought acreage so they could stay on the Strait of Juan de Fuca at a place they called Jamestown.)

The Skokomish land wasn't especially good for agricultural purposes and there was little off-reservation employment.

The Twana (of which the Skokomish were a sub-tribe) had, prior to the Point-No-Point Treaty, held 355,800 acres for which they received 15 cents an acre. The Government, of course, realized its mistake and in 1966 awarded them additional compensation of slightly more than $1 per acre.

Myron Eells prepared a census of the S'Klallam Indians in 1881[3] and reported that there were 476 members enrolled with four at Skokomish, ten at Seabeck and 95 at Port Gamble. The remaining members were in traditional areas along the Strait or assimilated into other tribes.

Myron and Edwin Eells were the sons of Cushing and Myra Eells who came to what we now know as Washington state in 1838. Cushing Eells was a Congregational missionary from New England and worked with the Spokane Indians until he was driven out by the depravations caused by the Whitman Massacre near Walla Walla.

The family settled in the Willamette Valley. Edwin was appointed agent for the Skokomish Indians in 1871 and both his father and brother came as missionaries for The Canal Indians.

Myron was a prolific writer and published, among other books and articles, *Ten Years' Missionary Work at Skokomish, 1874-1884.*[4] In 1985 his notebooks were published[5] and serve as excellent source material for in-depth study of the native people of Hood's Canal.

Eells describes the natives of Hood's Canal as "Twanas, spelled *Too-an-hooch* in their treaty. The S'Klallams pronounce it *Tu-an'-hu.*

"These various pronunciations have been shortened into Twana, now used in all governmental reports.

"It is said to mean a portage, and to be derived from the portage between the head of Hood's Canal and the main waters of the Sound, where the Indian, by carrying his canoe three miles, avoids rowing around a peninsula 50 miles long.

---

[1]Gibbs, George. Executive Document No. 91, US House of Representatives for the 2nd Session, 33rd Congress.

[2]Ibid.

[3]*Puget Sound Argus.* Feb. 18, 1881.

[4] Myron Eells. *Ten Years' Missionary Work Among the Indians at Skokomish, Washington Territory, 1874-1884.* Boston, Congregational Sunday School and Publishing Society. Circa 1886.

[5]Castile, George Pierre. (Editor) *The Indians of Puget Sound: The Notebooks of Myron Eells.* University of Washington Press, Seattle and London; and Whitman College, Walla Walla. 1985.

"These Indians originally occupied both sides of Hood's Canal and were divided into three bands, the Du-hle-lips, Skokomish and Kolsids. The Du-hle-lips lived at the head of the Canal, where a small stream empties into it, now called Du-lay-lip. Fifteen miles below them were the Skokomish, who lived around the mouth of the river of that name, now their reservation. This word is pronounced Ska-ka-bish by the Twanas and Ska-ka-mish by the Klallams. The Americans have changed it to Skokomish, and thus they universally spell the name of the river, reservations, and post office. Dr. Gibbs, in Vol. I, 'Contributions to North American Ethnology,' gives this as the name of the tribe, but it was originally the name of only one band.

"Yet even now, because of its being the name of the reservation and river, these Indians are known fully as well by the name Skokomish to the whites on the Sound as by the name Twana. Skokomish means the 'River People'.

"Thirty miles below this band were the Kol-sids, as pronounced by themselves who lived around the bay of that name and the mouth of the Dos-wail-opsh River. Their name is now variously spelled by the whites: Colcins, Colcene, Colseed and Quil-cene.

"These three bands were not always at peace, but sometimes waed petty war with each other. For 20 years, however, they have mostly been collected on the same reservation, have been on good terms with one another, and have intermarried, so that the band distinctions are rapidly becoming obsolete. Yet, when the older Du-hle-lips have the reservation for fishing they are apt to go to their old waters, and the same is true of the Kol-sids."

Eells states that about 30 S'klallams lived opposite Seabeck but had moved to Port Gamble, 20 miles north of Seabeck, where their main dependence for money was from their work at the saw-mill. It is likely that he was referring to Miami Beach although rough hewn cedar shacks were near the Head of the Bay.

Ethnobotany of Indians of Hood's Canal

Alder: The wood is used for firewood and for making dishes, plates, ladles, bailers and masks and for the building of fish-traps and rough houses. The bark is used for medicine, strings, ropes and dyeing.

Barberry: The bark is used for medicine.

Blackberry: The berry is used for food, the juice for paint, the young leaves for tea and the roots for medicine.

Cat-tail rush: The blades for making one kind of basket, for mats, for strings and ropes. The head was formerly used in making blankets.

Cedar: This is the most useful vegetable production of their country, its woods being used for planks for houses, burial inclosures, and the like; for canoes, oars, baby-boards, buoys, spinning wheels, boxes, torches, arrow-shafts, rails, shingles, fish-traps, tamanous sticks, and sails, baby-head covers, springs, bailers, women's skirts, and, when beaten, beds for infants, wadding to guns, napkins, head bands, blankets, and for gambling purposes; the gum and leaves for medicine.

Cherry: The bark is used for strings and medicine.

Cottonwood: Used for fire-wood, bark for medicine and strings and buds for medicine.

Cranberry: The berry is employed for food, the juice for paint, and the young leaves for tea.

Crab apple: The wood is used for wedges, hoes, and fire-wood; the fruit for food, and the bark for medicine.

Currant: The berry for food.

Dogwood: The wood is manufactured into gambling disks and hollow rattles and is used for fuel.

Elder: The wood is made into arrow-heads, used as playthings; bark for medicine, and berry for food.

Fir (red): The wood for firewood, boards, masts, spearhandles, spits and oars; the bark for firewood. The pitch wood is good for torches, fire-pots and kindlings and the latter use it is sold to the whites. The pitch is used for fastening on arrowheads and spearheads and as a cement.

Gooseberry (two varieties): Berry is used for food and juice for paint.

Grass: Used in making and ornamenting baskets of several kinds.

Hazel: The nuts used for food, the wood for rims for snow-shoes, nets and the bark for strings.

Hemlock: The wood serves for firewood and halibut hooks, the leaves for tea and the branches for covers in steaming food.
Huckleberry: Berry is used for food and the juice for paint.
Ironwood: The wood is used for arrow-shafts, arrow and spear heads, and mat needles and the bark for medicine.
Indian onion: The bulb is eaten.
Kelp: Strings and ropes are made from the root.
Kamast (camas): The root is edible.
Laurel: This is used for making spoons, vessels, and fancy work, as it is easily carves; the leaves are medicinal.
Licorice: The root is used for medicine.
Maple: The wood is utilized for hacklers, mat-blocks, paddle oars, bobbins, and blocks for making seines, combs, fish and duck spear-heads, fish clubs, rails and fire-wood. The leaves are used in steaming.
Maple (small variety): The wood for fire-wood.
Moss: Used for wrapping around wood while steaming it to make bows, the whole being buried in the ground.
Nettle: Used for making strings.
Oregon grape, barberry (?): The root and bark are valuable for medicine, the root for dyeing.
Raspberry: The berries used for food and the juice for paint.
Rose: The roots and leaves serve as medicine.
Rush: For making mats and roots for food.
Sallal berry: Berry for food and juice for paint.
Salmonberry: Berry and young shoots eaten.
Skunk cabbage: The leaves used as medicine and the roots for food.
Spruce: Wood is carved and leaves employed medicinally.
Strawberry: The berry is gathered for food.
Thimble cap: The berry and young shoots are good for food.
Vine maple: The wood is burned for fuel.
Willow: The wood is occasionally used for fire-wood and the bark for strings.
Yew: Paddles, bows, and fish-clubs are made from this wood.

Eells lists 12 kinds of beasts: Black bear, grizzly bear, wild cat, dog, deer, elk, muskrat, otter, sea otter, panther, raccoon, wolf. All are used for food or clothing.

Area lumber mills offered employment to the more industrious of the Indians. One of these was John Palmer, a Chimacum, who was born near Port Townsend in 1847 and orphaned at a young age. He was raised by the Port Townsend family of James Seavy and traveled to San Francisco with them where he remained a couple of years. He learned to speak Russian while working aboard a ship about the mouth of the Amoor River in Russian Asia and could read and speak English. He was an interpreter for the Government at Neah Bay and then worked on the Skokomish Reservation where he was an interpreter as he understood four Indian languages.

In February 1881[6] he was working at Seabeck on the slab car at the mill and as he and others were pushing it along, it accidentally became unhooked and turned over. The others got out of the way and called to him, but he either didn't understand or didn't hear them. As the car turned, a long slab struck him on the arm and side and knocked him off the platform to the slabs below. He was struck on his head, crushing in the side. He was the first Indian at the Skokomish reservation to unite with the church, doing so at its organization in 1874. He was buried at Skokomish.

The Duke of York (Chetzamoka), a S'Klallam, was persuaded to move on the Skokomish reservation in 1870. The Duke's family was large. He had a brother, *King George,* who wasn't as comely as The Duke and threatened the whites with extinction. The Duke had a sister with the un-royal name of *O'Wata*[7] who was married to Ewell Brinnon, an early Seabeck millworker and logger for the Washington Mill Company. He was owner of the land at present-day Brinnon, due west of Seabeck. His wife went by the name of Kate. When Kate died, Rev. Myron Eells held the funeral service in Chinook jargon as there was a large group of Indians present.

The Duke practiced polygamy claiming as his two wives, *Jenny Lind* and *Queen Victoria. Jenny Lind* died at Seabeck:[8]

---

[6]*Puget Sound Argus.* Feb. 11, 1881.

[7]Ida Bailey, Brinnon. Letter of June 12, 1993.

[8]*Seattle Intelligencer.* Nov. 30, 1882.

"Jenny Lind, wife number two of the Duke of York, died at Seabeck last week. Jennie Lind and Queen Victoria, the Duke's two wives were rendered famous by J. Ross Browne in Harper's Magazine ten years ago. Jenny Lind was shot six or eight months ago by a soldier at the garrison at Port Townsend. Rev. M. Eells says Jenny was on a spree at Seabeck and fell in a fire and got so badly burned that she died."

Two other prominent authors recognized the presence of the trio. Charles Nordhoff[9] included engravings of the Queen and Duke while Theodore Winthrop[10] portrayed the trio in less than complimentary light in his account of travels in Hawaii and the West:

"The Duke of York was ducally drunk. His brother, King George, was drunk -- royally. Royalty may disdain public opinion, and fall as low as it pleases. But a brother of the throne, leader of the opposition, possible Regent, possible King, must retain at least a swaying perpendicular. King George had kept his chair of state until an angular sitting position was impossible; then he had subsided into a curvilinear droop, and at last fairly toppled over, and lay in his lodge, limp and stertorous."

Winthrop hired the S'Klallam aristocracy to take him from Victoria where he had been visiting with Hudson Bay Company folk to Port Townsend and then to Nisqually. He didn't want to seem too ardent and, as he said, *"the Duke would grow coy. Prices would climb to the unapproachable. Any exhibition of impatience would cost me largess of beads, if not blankets, beyond the tariff for my canoe-hire."*

After agreeing to transport Winthrop, *"One of the Duchesses, only duchessly intoxicated, came forth from the ducal lodge, and urged him to effort."*

It was Jenny Lind or as she called herself *Chin Lin.* The Duke disappeared in his shack and asked: *"Where is my cleanest shirt?"* She responded: *"Nika macook lum; I buy grog with um."* The Duke yelled at her and she sank meekly upon the mud floor and wept while the Duke hit her *"with palm, fist and staff."*

Of course Winthrop intervened. The Duke donned a faded, black frock-coat and a hat, wrinkled with years and battered by world-wandering. Black dress pantaloons of brassy sheen, much crinkled at the bottom, where they fell over moccasins with a faded scarlet instep-piece, completed his costume, according to Winthrop.

Winthrop devoted 18 pages to the trials of the voyage from Victoria to Nisqually. It paints a colorful picture of why some of the women at Seabeck were unamused by the antics of the Duke and his parties.

The Duke of York died in June 1888 at his home near the mouth of Scow Bay, Port Townsned. When he was appointed a Chief in 1854 by Gov. Isaac Stevens, his tribe numbered 2,000. At the time of his death there were less than 200. He was buried in a lot in the Port Townsend Masonic Cemetery with nearly $300 raised for an appropriate burial. At the Point No Point Indian treaty making, he was said to have given several speeches, counseling for peace and harmony. His survivors were Queen Victoria and two sons, The Prince of Wales and George York.[11]

[9]Nordhoff, Charles. *Northern California, Oregon, and the Sandwich Islands. Harper & Brothers. New York. 1877.*

[10]Winthrop, Theodore. *The Canoe and the Saddle or Klalam and Klickatat. John H. Williams. Tacoma. 1913.*

[11]*Seattle Post-Intelligencer.* June 24, 1888.

Queen Victoria
(From Nordhoff)

The Twanas' main camps were on the Western Shore of Hood's Canal, the closest being on Dabob Bay. Summers were spent wandering other bays and harbors. A few artifacts and midden have been found in the Seabeck area, most of those around Misery Point and Miami Beach.

Many long-time Seabeck residents tell of finding Indian trade beads or watching Misery Point sluff off during heavy rains, exposing skeletal remains. Since the area was inhabited by settlers in 1857, it is estimated that at least 20 feet of Misery Point has eroded and with the erosion, several skeletons fell to the beach below. None have been seen for decades, however.

Hudson Bay Company men often portaged the narrow strip of land between Allyn and Belfair while traveling between Fort Vancouver and Victoria. There was one unfortunate group of travelers in 1828 who paid handsomely for their mistreatment of the Indian guides. Of course every story has two sides.

The Hudson Bay Company report stated that the murder of the men including Alexander McKenzie by natives of Hood's Canal was unprovoked and was for the sake of

their clothing and guns. *"They had dances among themselves to celebrate the deed and sent us (*The Hudson Bay Company) *word to come and revenge it, that they were ready."*[12]

The Indians' side of the murder of the men was written by Mary Ann Lambert[13]. She wrote that four men with backpacks stopped at the Indian village of *Nuf-kay'it* (Port Gamble) and communicated with the Indians that they wanted to be conveyed to Fort Langley. They offered to pay any volunteers and two young men agreed.

The following morning the group departed in a large canoe. Along the way, the Hudson Bay Company men frequently hit and kicked the boys. After reaching Vancouver Island, the young men were told to wait while the company men went about their business. They returned a week later, bringing an Indian woman as an additional passenger.

When they returned to *Nuf-kay 'it,* the Chief asked for the promised money. One of the white men responded that he wouldn't pay as the boys were worthless. They then threw on their backpacks and headed south, on foot, along The Canal.

The Indians, quite understandably, were angry and they decided to follow the men and attack. They found them camped beyond the second spit (now known as Dead Man's spit on the Trident base) at a spring. When all were sleeping, the Indians attacked and killed them all except the woman who was captured and taken prisoner. One of the Indians who was considered a trouble-maker searched the pockets of the dead men and took pocket knives, watches and other things.

Chief Trader Alexander McLeod in the summer of 1829 returned to avenge the murder and killed 27 Indians and burned their village with artillery of the *Cadboro.*

Myron Eells wrote an Indian legend pertaining to the three spits:[14]

---

[12]Letter from John McLoughlin to Hudson Bay Company. July 10, 1828.

[13]Lambert, Mary Ann (Vincent). *Dungeness Massacre and Other Regional Tales",* 1961.

[14]*Seattle Post-Intelligencer.* Oct. 17, 1884.

These were formerly three brothers, but Do-ki-batt changed them into their present condition. He found the Indians gambling with their disks and told them it was not good. He took their disks of wood and threw them into the water, but the sticks came back to the Indians. He threw them into the fire, but they came out. He threw them away as far as he could, but again they came back. Thus he threw them away five times and every time they returned and so at last he allowed them to keep these for sport, as they had conquered him, the only thing which did.

* * *

Edward Clayson immortalized Jack Clams and his wife, Sally Smashrocks, residents of Seabeck.[15] Jack, according to Clayson, was both indolent and independent. When the tide was out, old Sally would go out on the sand with a short stick, dig up a mess of clams, smash them between two rocks and dinner was ready.

In the course of time, they began to acquire a taste for *Boston muck-a-muck* (American food) so Jack had to go to work.

"The old Indian liked flour and sugar and fruit, but he cared little for beef, pork or butter. But when his taste for civilized products began to tempt him, then he had to work."

Edward Clayson built a ten-pin alley at Seabeck in 1873 at the Bayview Hotel and he hired Jack to work at the new entertainment facility as he had previously employed him in the kitchen and in splitting firewood, or peeling potatoes or cleaning fish. His usual pay was *"four bits"*. Opening day was the Fourth of July and Jack showed up at 10 a.m. He was getting paid $2 a day to set pins. Jack worked setting up pins for two or three games. Then he quit. He came strolling down the alley in a very leisurely manner with an expression of disgust upon his face.

He explained: *Klaxta o'coke!* (What's this?)

---

[15]Edward Clayson. *Historical Narratives of Puget Sound; Hoods Canal, 1865-1885.* R. L. Davis Printing Co., c.1911. P. 95.

Mika halo nanitsh (Don't you see, Clayson retorted.)

Nawitka nika delate nanich, o'coke delate cultus mamok. Ecta mika he-he, Boston-man delate hyas pilton. (Yes, I truly see this truly useless work. What are you laughing at? American truly big fools.)

Chinook "jargon" developed between Indian tribes who did not have a common language. With white contact, the jargon was enlarged upon with addition of French and English words. The developing "language" was used throughout the Pacific Northwest to communicate. Clayson was said to have been highly proficient in its use. Clayson used the jargon freely and his book is full of the language. Fortunately he translates much of it. Several dictionaries have been produced giving the various words used between the two groups in communicating.

If one understands a few basic words like *hyas* (large, great, big) and *tyee* (chief), they can then be put together: *hyas tyee* (great chief). One can even guess at meanings: *waum* (warm). There's been a tavern near Gig Harbor named *Hi-yu He-He* for years. That was the first jargon I'd ever heard. It was fun to say, and it wasn't until years later that I learned its meaning: big laugh.

Actually the language has been incorporated into our Northwest vocabulary: *tillicum* (friend), *skookum* (big, powerful), *klootchman* (woman) and place names: *Enetai* (across), *Alki* (in a little while), *Tukwila* (hazelnut).

Potlatch

Clayson tells of the Indian tradition of the potlatch, the great gift-giving practice of the Indians of Puget Sound. Clayson called it a *"great fair where somebody gives to everybody."* [16]

The greatest Potlatch held on Hood's Canal was around 1878 and it was given by Old Sam and his wife, Betsy of Seabeck. Clayson wrote: *"They lived in the most frugal manner, saving every cent of money they ever earned. It cost them in reality nothing to live, for old Betsy used to wash clothes for as many of the families as possible and save*

---

[16]Ibid. Pg. 54.

every cent, as she always took home with her to her slab shanty from every family she worked for sufficient broken victuals for herself and Sam -- much more, in fact, than the two could use. Her clothing as that of Old Sam was from the old clothes thrown away by the white people.

"These two old Indians saved all their 'chickerman' (money) - - the savings of many long years - - until they had over $4,000. They then gave a Potlatch, inviting all their friends, by word of mouth, for some 150 miles around to come at a certain time in the fall and enjoy themselves and receive gifts.

"Very little money is given away at a Potlatch - - the gifts are principally highly colored calicos, blankets, trinkets, flour and sugar.

"When an Indian takes his family to a Potlatch, the big canoe is launched. This family carriage is used only upon great events.

"At this great Potlatch given by old Sam and Betsy of Seabeck, a reporter for the New York Times was sent all the way from New York to write it up. He was a very clever writer. After describing the customs, actions and general enjoyments of the Indians, he devoted about a column to Old Jenny, the Squaw who was brought up in the slab shanty of old Sam and Betsy from her birth.

"Many a high-flown dame in New York at that period would have paid a large sum of money for such a write-up in such a paper, placed, as it was in such a conspicuous position in the paper.

"Jenny, the squaw, as she was always called by everybody in Seabeck, worked for the families in Seabeck at their domestic hearth since she was five years of age and being naturally gifted she was one of the cleverest women in town by the time she was 17 years of age, making, as she did, all her own clothes, consisting of the most fashionable dresses, hats and feathers. She was a good dressmaker, milliner, housekeeper and cook; learned it all through constant association with the families of Seabeck.

"When this Potlatch was over old Sam and his squaw Betsy returned to their shanty and to their accustomed drudgery at Seabeck, with peacefulness of mind and a composure of heart such as is realized by a *few good Christians after giving liberally to charity or to that of a Mohammed who has returned from a pilgrimage to Mecca."*

Thomas Talbot Waterman

While at the University of Washington from 1918-20, Thomas Talbot Waterman worked as an Associate Professor of Anthropology. The University set aside $200 per annum to be expended on an ethnographic survey of the state.[17] Waterman spent his off hours and summers wandering Puget Sound shorelines with Native Americans who spoke and understood the Salish languages.

His work, yet unpublished, is detailed. Often he recorded Indian names for the flora. Other times he jotted down information on traditional native villages or small geographic features such as creeks, small bays.

He was the youngest of ten children (B. April 23, 1885 Hamilton, Missouri; D. Jan. 6, 1936 Honolulu) of an Episcopalian clergyman. Destined by family tradition for a clergyman's career, he was graduated from the University of California in 1907 with Hebrew as his major subject. His philological studies led him into a course in experimental phonetics and he accompanied his professor on a field trip as assistant in recording California Athabascan dialects. This experience was decisive in diverting him from divinity to anthropology.[18]

He was much published, the author of four books, innumerable magazine articles. He contributed notes and monographs to the Museum of American Indian, Heye Foundation, much of which pertained to Puget Sound area Indians.

He was a student and teacher of phonetics. His handwritten notes with phonetic spellings from Hood's Canal are difficult to translate, even more difficult to pronounce.

---

[17]Thomas Talbot Waterman. Indian Notes and Monographs, No. 59. *Notes on the Ethnology of the Indians of Puget Sound, Museum of the American Indian, Heye Foundation.*

[18]*American Anthropologist.* Vol. 39, No. 3, July-September 1937.

Harrison Eastman visited Seabeck in the 1870s and sketched at least two
views of Indian encampments. Many of his sketches were later turned into paintings
although if a painting has been produced from this sketch, it has not been located.
(Copy of copy from Washington State Historical Society, Tacoma.)

But the words and meanings will be following as closely as possible.

Lagoon north of Stavis Bay. *Cte'u.* Was spearing something. Waterman thought that people went there to spear flounders.

A long, straight beach leading to Point Misery (with a tiny lagoon entering the shoreline). *Tux ta! i yu'b.* Not translated.

Point Misery: *X adq!bed.* (Not translated.) The Indian word given by Wilkes in the form Scabock (whence Seabeck) I cannot identify.

Lagoon and flat at the head of Seabeck Bay: *Tu sd E'be-deb.* A myth recounts that certain people here were dancing on planks placed on the ground. The sound *de'bEdEb*, from which the place derives its name represents the thumping of their feet.

The small promontory in the present town of Seabeck. *L TLka'a baq w,* said to mean "suckling." This term is given

by Costello in the form *L-ka-bak-hu.* Not translated.

Little Beef Harbor. *Tatq!a'tsa,* the diminutive of the word for Beef Harbor.

(Big) Beef Harbor. *Q!etsak.* This term is said to refer to the fact that some certain individual "did not wipe himself."

Big Beef Creek. *Sploa'lqe.* "Flatus water". A curious myth concerning the origin of this name is exactly parallel to a myth concerning a locality on White River. It is characteristic of the region that a certain myth spreads and is often very carefully localized in several different places.

(Near) **Lone Rock.** *Ctea'oks.* The suffix indicates a promontory, while the remainder of the name means "a place where a trail descends." The term refers to the old trail which led from this point, probably closer to Anderson Landing, over the hills to Dye's Inlet near the town of Silverdale. (Waterman identifies this as an old village site.)

10

Vancouver and Wilkes
Explore Canal

Relationship with Indians Differs

Of all the voyages to the Pacific Northwest, the two we're most familiar with are those of Captain George Vancouver, 1792, and Lt. Charles Wilkes, 1841. Each performed scientific map making and each left names to endure. AND, for our purposes, they were the earliest who explored Hood's Canal.[19] Vancouver for the British and Wilkes for the United States. Many accounts have been published of each man's work. But the interesting point of the excerpts from the journals is the change in attitude of the Indians in the 49 years between Vancouver and Wilkes' cruises.

What could have caused this? There were some troubles between the Hudson Bay Company men and the Indians on the Canal in 1828.[20] There were increasing contacts with interlopers and conflict between countries over possession of certain northwest land.

But that's up to speculation. By the way, it rained when both men sailed The Canal.

Vancouver's Exploration and Naming of Hood's Canal

Vancouver had been an officer with Captain Cook and he was eager to follow up on Cook's good work. Great Britain later based its claim on that land north of the Columbia River partly upon the voyages of British navigators, including Vancouver.

Vancouver sailed from England April 1, 1791, wintered in Hawaii and reached the Strait of Juan de Fuca April 30, 1792. All along the Strait of Juan de Fuca, he named points of interest: Mt.

Baker (to the northeast), Protection Island, New Dungeness, Port Townshend (sic), Marrowstone Point.[21]

May 9, 1792

Captain Vancouver, with the yawl (*Pinnace*), Lt. Peter Puget with the launch of the *Discovery* and "Master" James Johnstone directing the *Chatham's* cutter set out with five days' provisions to explore from Port Discovery a southerly body of water. Vancouver took the western shore, Puget the middle and Johnstone the eastern shore.

Vancouver's two vessels: the sloop-of-war *Discovery* and the armed tender *Chatham* were left at Port Discovery to be overhauled and refit. The notion that it rains all the time in the Pacific Northwest was a rumor started by both Vancouver and Wilkes. Although both men were in the Northwestern waters in May, it rained!

On May 9 and 10 Puget writes: *"it blew strong, was extremely dark with a perfect torrent of Rain"* and *"we were detained by this tempestuous Weather till the 10th"*. He also grounded his small vessel and had to wait for the tide to get off. He was happy that no Indians bothered them as the guns were wet and offered them no protection.

May 10, 1792

Vancouver encountered some Indians waiting for their approach and they expressed no fear and bartered. Vancouver gave them medals, beads, knives and other trinkets.

Vancouver described a high perpendicular bluff which was named because of the rotten weather, Foulweather Bluff.

Vancouver's journal seems dry in comparison to Puget's. Puget describes the Indians in detail, flora and fauna. *"The Country was greatly beautified by the advanced State of the Spring, every*

---

[19]Vancouver called this body of water Hood's Channel and Canal. Those who live on the waters may call it Hood Canal or The Canal. The author will try and be consistent and call it Hood's Canal.

[20]See chapter on Indians.

---

[21]Edmond S. Meany. *Vancouver's Discovery of Puget Sound.* Macmillan, 1907 and George F. Cotterill. *The Climax of a World Quest.* Olympic Publishing Co., Seattle. 1927.

tree appeared in Blossom & these small projecting Points in particular were every where covered with a Sort of Pale Crimson Flower." (He probably saw rhododendron or salmonberry.)

May 11, 1792

On May 11, Vancouver named Hazel Point *"in consequence of its producing many of those trees."* In Archibald Menzies' *Journal of Vancouver's Voyage* there is a record of *Corylus californica (Hazelnut)* at Hannon Point, May 10, 1792. No other reference to Hannon Point has been found. Vancouver noted that the channel divided into two branches, one nearly due north, the other southwest. They spent the night in Dabob Bay.

Puget wrote: *"We crossed the Inlet after Breakfast after Determining the non existence of any Eastern passage in this Branch to the one we had left off Yesterday Afternoon -- The Weather had now regained its usual Serenity that we were enabled to make great Progress. -- & After a hard Days pull we Stopped for our Nights Quarters about five Miles to the Southward of a Smoak from which we had no Visitors."*

May 12, 1792

Puget wrote: *"After being greatly tormented by Musquito's and Flies &c we left our Quarters early & continued the further investigation of this Branch: Seeing a Smoak on the Western Shore we pulled in & landed at a Small Village where we found a few Indians under two or three Miserable Sheds, or Huts preparing Clams and Fish for the Winter Season /as was supposed/ -- From them we bought a Small quantity of each for which they took any Article we offered -- The stench of this Place was Intolerable, though close to a fine fresh Water Run, yet the Indolence of the Inhabitants appear so great; that the filth is left close to the Habitations, which if carried but a few yards would be swept away into the Stream*

"They willingly disposed of the Bows and Arrows, some of which were barbed with Iron -- This gave rise to various Conjectures, but it was generally supposed that either Europeans had before visited this Tribe or they must have some Mercantile Communication with those situated near the Sea.

"From this Village we kept to the opposite Shore, to visit some more Indians collected on a Point which forms part of the Banks & Entrance of a Fresh Water Run.   There we found People of all

ages & Descriptions to the Amount of Forty or Fifty, they beheld the approach of the Boats without the least Apprehension or evident Signs of Fear. -- They immediately on our Request began a barter for Fish or whatever Articles we wished for in their Possession. The Conduct of these People impressed me with an high Idea of their Honesty, for whatever they had to barter, was suffered to be taken away, without an Exchange & it would be sometimes ten Minutes or a Quarter of an Hour before the person returned from the Boats with the Things he intended to give. Yet this Delay did not cause any murmuring or Discontent on the Contrary they appeared perfectly well satisfied of our friendly Intentions. -- Surely then, if these People behave with such Confidence to Strangers, may we not infer, that Innate Principles of Honesty actuated their Conduct on this Occasion? Some have attributed that Confidence to Fear of the largeness of the Party, that they were glad to receive whatever we offered in Exchange, as they expected, their Property to be wrested from their Possession. -- however I am willing to allow them Credit for Appearances & say they differ in Character from the General Body of their Neighbours, who by Report of former Visitors [seem to be?] most arrant Rogues -- The Women are not distinguishable by any Effeminacy or Softness of Features, they are nearly in appearance similar to the Men, & those we noticed, were discovered by suckling some Children -- They wear their Hair long which is Black & as filthy as the Men's but are most decently covered with Garments as no part of the Body is visible, but the Heads Hands & Feet; some were solicited to grant favors but they refused I believe for want of more Secret Opportunity, nor did the Men appear at all jealous of the Liberties taken with their Women -- Having now finished our Visit we began returning along the Opposite or Eastern Shore & about two Miles from these Friendly Indians we pitched our Tents for the Night. -- nor did a Single Canoe attempt to follow us."

On Saturday, May 12 Vancouver wrote that they were running low on provisions as they had only taken enough for five days. *"Our sportsmen had been unable to assist our stock; and the prospect of obtaining any supplies from the natives was equally uncertain. The region we had lately passed seemed nearly destitute of human beings. The brute creation also had deserted the shores; the tracks of deer were no longer to be seen; nor was there an aquatic bird on the whole extent of* the canal;[22] animated nature seemed nearly exhausted; and her awful silence was only now and then interrupted by the croaking of a raven, the breathing of a seal, or the scream of an eagle. Even these solitary sounds were so seldom heard, that the rustling of the breeze along the shore, assisted by the solemn stillness that prevailed, gave rise to ridiculous suspicious in our seamen of hearing rattlesnakes, and other hideous monsters, in the wilderness, which was composed of the productions already mentioned, but which appeared to grow with infinitely less vigour than we had been accustomed to witness.

"Having very pleasant weather, and a gentle favorable breeze, we proceeded, and passed several runs of fresh water. Near one of the largest we observed our latitude at noon to be 47 degrees 27'; (Lilliwaup) and once again had the pleasure of approaching an inhabited country. A canoe, in which there were three men, went alongside the launch, and bartered a few trifles for beads, iron, and copper, but declined every invitation from us to come on shore. From Mr. Puget I learned, that they appeared to be very honest in their dealings, and had used their utmost endeavors to prevail on the party in the launch to attend them home, which he understood to be at the distance of about a league,[23] and for which they seemed to make the best of their way, probably to acquaint their friends with the approach of strangers. Soon after we had dined, a smoke was observed near the supposed place of their residence; made, as we concluded, for the purpose of directing us to their habitations, for which we immediately set off, agreeably to their very civil invitation.

"An idea during this excursion had occurred to us, that part of the brute creation have an aversion to the absence of the human race; this opinion seemed now in some measure confirmed, by the appearance for the first time during the last three days, of several species of ducks, and other aquatic birds. I do not, however, mean absolutely to infer, that it is the affection of the lower orders of the creation to man, that draws them to the same spots which human beings prefer, since it is highly probable that such places as afford the most eligible residence in point of sustenance to the human race, in an uncivilized state, may be, by the brute creation, resorted to for the same purpose.

---

[22]Vancouver has just used the word "Canal" for the first time.

[23]A league is any of various units of distance from 2.4 to 4.6 miles.

"The habitations of our new friends appeared to be situated nearly at the extremity of this inlet, (Skokomish) or where it appeared to take a very sharp turn to the S.E. still favoring our hopes of returning by the great eastern arm. These, however, vanished on landing, as we found its S.W. direction terminate in land, apparently low and swampy, with a shoal extending some distance from its shores, forming a narrow passage to the south-eastward into a cove or bason (sic) which seemed its termination also in that direction.

Vancouver's Map of Kitsap and Mason Counties

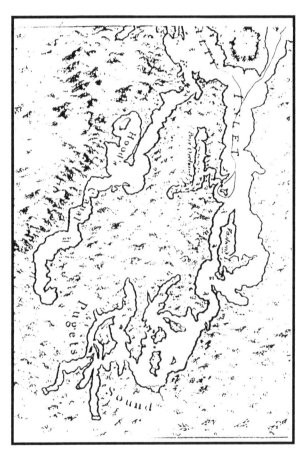

"Here we found the finest stream of fresh water we had yet seen; from the size, clearness and rapidity of which, little doubt could be entertained of its having its source in perpetual springs. Near it were two miserable huts with mats thrown carelessly over them, protecting their tenants neither from the heat nor severity of the weather; these huts seemed calculated to contain only the *five or six men then present, though previously to our quitting the boats we supposed a greater number of persons had been seen; those were probably their women, who on our approach had retired to the woods.*

"These good people conducted themselves in the most friendly manner. They had little to dispose of, yet they bartered away their bows and arrows without the least hesitation together with some small fish, cockles, and clams; of the latter we purchased a large quantity, a supply of which was very acceptable in the low condition of our stock. They made us clearly to understand, that in the cove to the S.E. we should find a number of their countrymen, who had the like commodities to dispose of; and being anxious to leave no doubt concerning a further inland navigation by this arm of the sea, and wishing to establish, as far as possible, a friendly intercourse with the inhabitants of the country, which, from the docile and inoffensive manners of those we had seen appeared a task of no great difficulty, we proceeded to a low point of land that forms the north entrance into the cove. There we beheld a number of natives, who did not betray the smallest apprehension at our approach; the whole assembly remained quietly seated on the grass, excepting two or three whose particular office seemed to be that of making us welcome to their country.

"These presented us with some fish, and received in return trinkets of various kinds, which delighted them excessively. They attended us to their companions, who amounted in number to about sixty, including the women and children.

"We were received by them with equal cordiality, and treated with marks of great friendship and hospitality. A short time was here employed in exchanges of mutual civilities. The females on this occasion took a very active part. They presented us with fish, arrows, and other trifles, in a way that convinced us they had much pleasure in so doing. They did not appear to differ in any respect from the inhabitants we had before seen; and some of our gentlemen were of opinion that they recognized the persons of one or two who had visited us on the preceding Thursday morning; particularly one man who had suffered very much from the small pox. This deplorable disease is not only common, but it is greatly to be apprehended is very fatal amongst them, as its indelible marks were seen on many; and several had lost the sight of one eye, which was remarked to be generally the left, owing most likely to the virulent effects of this baneful disorder. The residence of these peo-

ple here was doubtless of a temporary nature; few had taken the trouble of erecting their usual miserable huts, being content to lodge on the ground, with loose mats only for their covering.

"Little doubt existed of the cove terminating its navigation. To ascertain this, whilst I remained with these civil people, Mr. Johnstone was directed to row round the projection that had obstructed our view of the whole circumference of the cove, which is about two miles; and, if it were not closed, to pursue its examination. Our former conjectures being confirmed,[24] on his return we prepared to depart; and, as we were putting off from the shore, a cloak of inferior sea otter skins was brought down, which I purchased for a small piece of copper. Upon this they made signs that if we would remain, more, and of a superior quality, should be produced; but as this was not our object, and as we had finished our proposed talk sooner than was expected this morning, to the no small satisfaction of our whole party, we directed our course back towards Port Discovery, from which we were now about 70 miles distant.

"A fresh northwardly wind, and the approach of night, obliged us to take up our abode about two miles from the Indians, some of whom had followed us along the beach until we landed, when they posed themselves at the distance of about half a mile, to observe our different employments; at dark they all retired, and we neither heard nor saw anything more of them."

May 13, 1792

Vancouver: *"Early on Sunday morning the 13th, we again embarked; directing our route down the inlet, which, after the Right Honorable Lord Hood[25] I called Hood's Channel;[26] but our progress homeward was so very slow, that it was Monday afternoon, the 14th, before we reached Foulweather Bluff."*

Of May 13, Puget writes: *"Early next morning Sunday 13th of May we set out again on our Return to the Ships & as we were now certain*

---

[24] James Johnstone should be blamed for not pursuing the waterway, not Vancouver.

[25] Named after the Right Honorable Lord Hood. Vancouver named many places *channels* in his journal, but wrote them down as *canals* on his charts.

[26] Edmond S. Meany. *Vancouver's Discovery of Puget Sound. Binfords & Mort. Portland. 1942.* There were cousins named Samuel Hood but "our" Samuel was educated as a sailor, entered the navy as captain's servant. An excellent biography appears Pp. 110-11.

of the Continent as far as the Rendezvous Point, we only stopped for our Meals -- The Pinnace having pulled ahead in the Evening, and night having set in made us apprehensive we had already missed her, we however continued on close in by the Shore & about Ten found them on a Narrow Spit of Low Land, from this Situation the Tide very near floated us out, but it was too late to recede as the Tents & things were already on Shore. The Water came close up which we were glad to see was its height.[27]

Those published accounts of Vancouver's expedition on Hood's Canal do not mention where or how he spent the night of May 13, 1792. Was he at Seabeck?

Wilkes Didn't Get to Seabeck; Lt. Case Did the Leg Work

Lt. Charles Wilkes, as commanding officer of the first United States government-sponsored nautical exploration, spent two years in preparation, four years sailing and surveying and countless years later in writing journals and defending the cost and productivity of the expedition.

As the man in charge, he had to face several critical tests, the most insurmountable, perhaps was that other officers in the party held superior Naval ranks and resented Wilkes' lowly rank.

There were nine scientists in the party. The squadron which left Hampton Roads in 1838 and consisted of six vessels sailed to Madeira, went on to the Cape Verde islands, South American, entered the Antarctic, visited Tuamoti Islands, touched New South Wales, saw Hawaii and The Philippines and, of course, visited the Pacific Northwest -- a grueling four years.

In Wilke's journal, there are several examples of disagreements with crew members. He was strict, disagreeable, rather arrogant and authoritarian. No fanfare was given when the group returned to Washington, DC. His career was plagued by problems associated with the expedition.

Despite all the problems, Wilkes led his ships around the world and collected important scientific and cultural data, charted previously uncharted waters and was careful to detail.

It was Wilkes (not Vancouver) who discovered that Bainbridge was an Island and that Hood's Canal didn't end at the big bend even though Vancouver supposedly charted the waters.

A good-natured group, lacking Wilkes himself, surveyed Hood's Canal. A launch, first cutter and two boats of the *Vincennes* were placed under the command of Lt. Augustus Case to survey Hood's Canal. Robert and Dawn Hansen, Seabeck residents, studied microfilm documents of the Wilkes' journals and Case's journal and made notes on various place names and locations from maps that they saw. The originals are in the United States Naval Academy, Annapolis and photocopies are located at the Kitsap County Historical Society and Mason Historical Society, made available by Irene Davis.[28]

The party entered Pacific Northwest waters, steering round Cape Flattery on April 30, 1841. They departed three months and two days later on August 2.

Those ships entering Puget Sound went to Nisqually where they were greeted by those Hudson Company Bay people in residency. Then Wilkes charted the work directing one group to Eastern Washington, his group south to the Columbia and the Case party to Hood's Canal. From the Case Journal:[29]

May 22, 1841: At 6:45 a.m. commenced work. At 12. landed on a sand point some three miles within the head of The Canal, & for & obtained angles. At 1:20 the boats joined ours and we pulled round a point near by, hoping to find good shelter & water, but were disappointed & compelled to pull some two miles further before we found both. Landed on the W shore & encamped near some lodges of Suquamish.

May 23, 1841: Employed through this day, making obs. for Lat. Long. etc & inking in our work. Soil in the neighborhood of the camp thin and sandy.

May 24, 1841: At 6:40 a.m. commenced work. At 12:30 landed in Harbour B on the

---

[27]This is either at Seabeck or Stavis.

[28]Irene Davis' photocopies of the Case journal are on file at the Kitsap County Historical Society Museum and the Mason County Historical Society.

[29]United Statex Exploring Expedition journals and atlas.

East Shore & commenced its survey. At 6:30 landed the tents on the eastern Point near a run of fresh water & pitched them. At 5:30 the boats returned. This evening found our bread to be getting short and placed all hands on an allowance of 6 biscuits per day.

May 25, 1841: At 6:30 commenced sounding the Channel, which we found to be narrow but deep. At 9:30 completed the survey. This harbour could be difficult for larger vessels to enter except at high water when they would find it easy with the channel buoyed. When inside the points there is plenty of room & good anchorage. Water can be obtained in abundance near the East Pt. Continued the survey up The Canal. At 3, landed in harbour C on the W. shore & chained off a base. Encamped in our Sunday station.

May 26, 1841; At 7 commenced the survey of the Harbour, at 11 completed it, and continued the work up The Canal. Harbour C affords good anchorage & is well protected from the southerly winds by a the of considerable extent & bare at low water. Water can be obtained without difficulty. At 4140 landed at Browns Point, obtained angles & encamped. At 6:45 the boats joined me. The officers of the Avril Pilot reporting they had not seen the signals. Soon after our tents were pitched a party of Suguamish (sic) visited us, bringing salmon in for sale.

May 27, 1841: At 7 send Midshipmen. May & Colvo to the yesterday's station to measure base etc. - Mr. Totten & myself being employed the most of the day getting obs. for 2 quarter altitudes, etc etc -- The soil in the vicinity of the camp was much richer than any I have yet seen.

May 28, 1841: At 7 - Continued the survey work in the Canal. At 1:30 took position on the E shore near a salmon fishery to find for base - then crossed the Canal to the mouth of *Nimko-lo-wap* creek. Sent Mr. May in a canoe to explore it. (The entrance being to shoal for our boats). Mr. May found deep water about 200 yards inside the mouth & was informed by some Indians he met that it was some distance inland - I did not deem a further examination necessary (as the water was quite dry at low

water) crossed to the East shore & encamped in D harbour.[30]

The next harbour is that of Scabock. It lies on the eastern side of the Canal, directly south of Nukolowap Point, distant from it 3 miles. It is one of the most convenient anchorages in the Canal. Its shape is triangular; its shore is bordered by a sand-beach, from which the hills rise: these are well-covered with wood. The distance between the two points, (Samum and Wikat) is one mile; it [harbor] is also a mile deep towards the southwest. Near its head is an extended sand-flat, dry in places at low water. The watering-place can be approached by boats at half tide: the landing is on the southwest side at Makak Point.[31] The best anchorage is near the centre of the harbor, Samum Point bearing northwest, with a gray sandy bottom.

May 29, 1841: Survey'd the harbour. Found it to afford good anchorage & well protected from all winds except the North. Water can be obtained in any quantity from the creek at the head.[32] A part of Scocomish (sic) Indians visited our camp, bring venison, salmon, etc. for sale. -

May 30, 1841: Employed inking in our work, making obs. for Lat & Long - A party of Toandos & Scocomish visited us - Reduced the allowance of bread to 3 biscuits per day. The land in the vicinity of our camp was lower than usual & swampy, and thickly wooden - The soil is rich black loam.

May 31, 1841: At 7, Commenced work. Crossed to the northern shore & took position on - point called *Takutska*, so as to allow the boats to take second position before leaving - the Canal at this place branches into two arms. One turning sharp to the north and the other continuing to the S.W. along the base of the Mount Olympus range of mountains - The banks of the Canal from the entrance to this place, have generally ranged from 30 to 100 feet high - formed of

---

[30]Seabeck Harbor or Scabock as charted on the maps per Robert Hansen.

[31]On Wilkes chart is Makak Landing, about where the Seabeck store is now. Sanum Point is no known as Misery Point and Wikat Point, north of Seabeck, per Robert and Dawn Hansen.

[32]Seabeck (or Slaughter) Creek per Robert Hansen.

stratified clay, with a light gravely soil, and thickly covered with the different species of pines - At this place the northern & western shores assumed a bold & rocky appearance and the soil darker - and much richer, beingan alluvial deposit from the mountains - The Eastern shores continuing of the same character as those below. Worked up the Northern Arm - At 5 P.M. encamped in a small bight called *Zalalched*_on the east shore. At 8:20 P.M. a very large & brilliant meteor was seen bearing from us N by W (?) W, shooting in a diagonal direction nearly to the earth when it burst like a rocket - A long zig zag trail was left by it, which continued of a brightness nearly equal to the moon until 8:50 when it gradually disappeared.

June 1, 1841: At 7. Commenced work, continuing up the Arm. At 10 landed in a small harbour called *Hoostsen* on the West Shore - Surveyed it & obtained observations for equal altitudes etc - Encamped on the East Shore We were now in the district of the *Toandos* - a small Tribe - by their own account mustering 150 fighting men. They generally reside among the mountains and are much the largest & best looking men we have yet me - The land in the vicinity of our camp similar to A below the arms -

June 2, 1841: At 7. Continued the work up the northern arm - by midday we had reached the head of it - the island at this place on Vancouver's chart, we found to be a tongue of land running out some two or three miles & forming two good Harbours - The eastern called *Dabop* [sic] and the western *Col-su-ed*. After completing the survey of *Dabop* pulled round into *Col-su-ed* & landed near some lodges of Suquamish -

June 3, 1841: Rainy weather - At 8:30 it appeared to be clearing - Started for the head of the bay to measure base but was obliged to return, without doing anything. The Rain setting in & continuing through the day, attended by heavy S.E. gales.

June 4, 1841: Showery - Survey the bay - Found it to afford every protection from the wind, and good holding ground in from 8 to 10 fathoms muddy bottom - One large and several small creeks empty into the head of the bay - which would answer well for milling purposes - They have

formed an extensive mud flat which it would be necessary to stake or buoy in case this harbour was much used -

June 5, 1841: Run a few lines of soundings in the mouth of this harbour & then pulled for the S.W. cove - At meridian a heavy rain commenced - landed on the W shore opposite *Tskutska Point* & pitched our tents. About a mile distant from us a large creek called the *Tlopish* emptied into the Canal - which would answer well for mills - Near it were a few lodges of Toandos, containing about fifty employed fishing for salmon which they took in numbers and of a superior quality -

June 6, 1841: Easterly winds and rainy throughout the day - Employed inking in our work. A few Toandos visited our camp, bringing Salmon, etc. for sale.

June 7, 1841: As soon as the weather permitted this morning commenced the survey of the S.W. arm. Encamped on the South Shore -

June 8, 1841: Commenced raining. At 10:30 the weather clearing continued the survey up the Canal. Passed a large creek on the West Shore, which would answer well for mills - The soil in its neighborhood an alluvial deposit from the mountains.

Encamped on the East Shore, which was fast becoming lower as we approached the head of the Canal - the soil, banks etc the same as that below. A small party of Clalams [sic] visited us.

June 9, 1841: At 7 continued the work up the Canal. Pitched our tents on the East shore - A few Toandos & Scocomish Indians visited us bringing salmon, venison etc for sale.

June 10, 1841: At 7 Started up the Canal. At 3 we landed at *Melim Point* on the West shore, near a Scocomish village - On opening the Theodolite at this place missed the vertical eye piece - Made a search for it but without success - and as I had heretofor been particular in seeing it in the box, was convinced one of the Indians must have picked it up. I strongly suspected a woman who sat on the box of having it, but she looked so innocent & joined so readily in the search, that I did not have her blanket examined. Offered two blankets for its recovery & dispatched the men to my

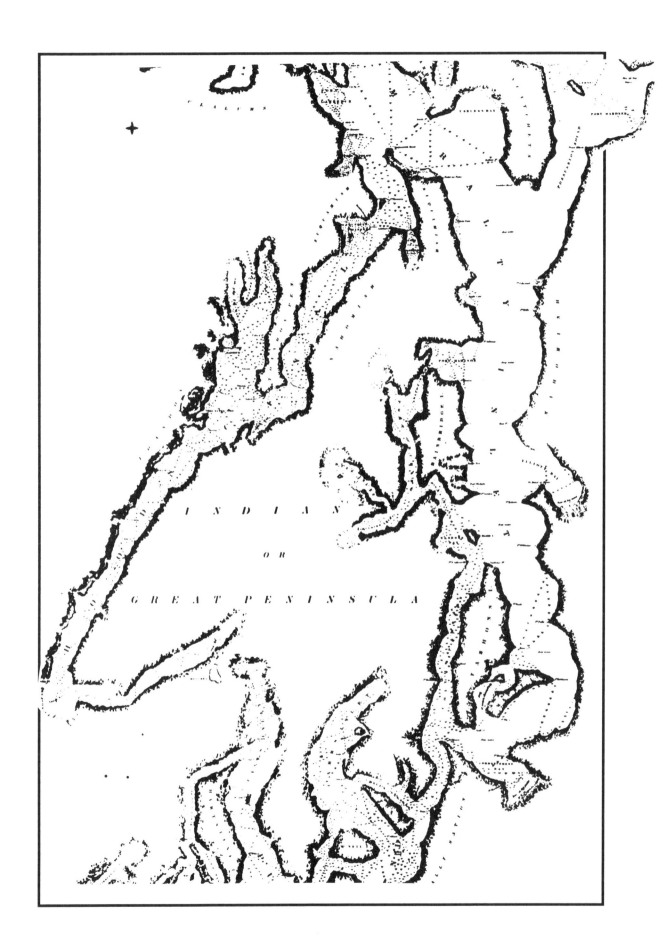

last station to search for it there - at dark they returned without it.

I had been fearful for some time that it would be lost, as the box was scarcely ever opened without it falling out. I had once stowed it in my calabash but afterwards replaced it, on account of using it at night occasionally. That is, it had escaped loss nearly three years it would continue so to do -

This place was the end of the Canal, according to Vancouver's Survey, who had sketched it as a bay. Instead of terminating however it took a sharp turn & continued to the N & E - On the south side of the bay empties a large creek, by which the Indians communicate with the Columbia - The creek is broad but shoal & has formed a large mud flat in that part of the bay -

This district is inhabited by the Scocomish - a Tribe by their own & the Toandos account mustering 150 fighting men. They resemble the Toandos in appearance & appeared to be in close alliance with them.

The mountain range on the West shore had gradually sloped down into low land similar to that below the forks, thickly wooded, & soil good - The East shores low and swampy and not so thickly wooded as those below - The East shores low and swampy and not as thickly wooded as those below.

Pitched our tents on the south shore near some Scocomish lodges -

June 11, 1841: At 7:30 commenced work on turning up the Canal - The land very low and thickly wooded. Encamped on the West shore near a run of fresh water - Our Camp was visited by a large party of Indians, belonging to the different tribes we have met.

June 12, 1841: At 7:30 continued the survey up the Canal. I this morning engaged a couple of Indians to go to Nasqually with a letter to return with a canoe load of bread. When all ready for a start they were persuaded by an old man not to go for price agreed on, and I determined not to send them, trusting I should get others willing to go, at *Chilanatchus* (the portage).

At Meridian had arrived at the head of the Canal and finished its survey - A creek about 60 yards wide empties into the head of it & has formed a flat near two miles down, quite bare at low water. This creek is from 3 to 4 feet deep about a half mile from its mouth - Land flat & wooded, with here & there a clear space - The soil is mixed sand & vegetable mould.

At 1 encamped on the East Shore - Walked over the Portage to Puget's Sound, a distance of about two & a half miles, over a rough & hilly road - On my return got an Indian to take Kellim (Cox of the Arvil) & Io the interpreter to Nasqually & return with a load of bread despatched them immediately - On the shore opposite our camp found the board houses belonging to to the Scocomish. A large party of Indians pitched their lodges near us. Served out the last allowance of bread -

June 13, 1841: Rainy. Employed inking in our work. At 3 P.M. Io the interpreter returned, having left Kellim at the landing with ten days bread for all hands. Sent the men over for it -

June 14, 1841: Immediately after breakfast this morning started down the Canal on my return to the ship - At 3 P.M. reached *Neelim* bay. Made a few lines of soundings to show the land flat on the eastern shore. Encamped at Neelim Point.

June 15, 1841: Rainy weather - At 7 continued down the Canal searching the different points where I had used the Theodolite for the lost eye-piece but without success. At 6 P.M. landed on the N shore of C harbour & pitched our tents.

June 16, 1841: Rainy - the plotting of this harbour did not come in satisfactorily and I determined to re-examine it, but was unable to do anything during the day on account of the rain.

June 17, 1841: Finished the re-examinations of C harbour. At 2:15 started down the Canal. At 3:30 passed into Admiralty Inlet & encamped near our camp of May 19th - Found here a large party of Suquamish - building canoes and winter dwellings.

June 18 - 22, 1841: Passed Bainbridge and began survey of Puget Sound.

June 23, 1841: At 5:30 a canoe boarded me, bringing orders from Capt. W(ilkes) to dispatch Mr. May in the *Pilot* to the ship with the Theodolite & some asimuth observations made in Hood's Canal. Made signal for him to join company - & on his doing so started him immediately for the ship - Encamped on the W shore in harbour F.

June 24, 1841: At 7 A.M., commenced the survey of harbour E. At 2:30 finished & was about leaving when I saw a boat pulling towards me from the Ship. Landed & waited for him. He proved to be the   under charge of Lt. Budd, who brought orders for me to transfer the charge of the party to him & take charge of one of the light boats & proceed to Hood's Canal in search of the lost eye piece.

June 25, 1841: This morning started for Hood's Canal in the *Pilot*. At sunset stopped on the N point of Port Orchard & passed the night -

June 26, 1841: Immediately after breakfast continued down the inlet. At 3 P.M. passed into the Canal and at sunset encamped in C harbour. Few but few Indians and they extremely shy.

June 27, 1841: Continued up the Canal. At 2 P.M. landed at ***Quatsap*** point, the place I had last used the eyepiece, and commenced the search going from station to station up to Nellim Point without find(ing) it - Stopped for the night.

June 28, 1841: Started down the Canal on my return to the ship, overhauling the stations again as I passed in searching. Then I recollected that Mr. Totten had the Theodolite at one camp near ***Bunsap*** Point, went back & searched the place. At Sunset stopped about 3 miles south of Buntsap point & passed the night -

June 29, 1841: A short time after sunrise went to Bunstsap to give it another overhaul, before returning to the ship - while here a canoe with 3 Tuandos landed & on learning what I was looking for, they instantly said it was among the Scocomish & gave a full account of its having been picked up at Nellim Station, where the Theodolite was opened by a woman who was sitting near. Got one of the men to go with me to the village where they had seen it, & I continued up the Canal.

At 2 P.M. landed at Neelim & the men went over to the Chief there saying he could get it. The Chief was absent, on his return I took his gun & I told him I should keep this until the eye piece was brought me - After getting something to eat he started for a village a short distance inland, saying it was there. While he was away a couple of Toando hunters landed in a canoe & I seized the gun of one and attempted to get the other but the warrior to strong for me - The Chief now returned saying the woman who had the eye piece was down the Canal. The Toando went to see her & about 9 P.M. returned saying she had gone up the river - Hauled off about 4 & a mile from the shore & passed the night.

June 30, 1841: At daylight the Chief started down the Canal in a canoe - While getting breakfast I saw eight canoes filled with men come out of the river & pull towards us. This I did not like and directed the men to hurry. As soon as they got through pulled out into the bay when the canoes all headed on me - At this time the Toando I had in the boat wished to be landed, and on my refusing to put him on shore gave me to understand I had better prepare my arms. I now descried several more canoes coming out of the river, & I determined not to wait for them, as it was evident they intended no good & my party was too small and to far from the ship to content with them. So made sail down the Canal. The canoes pulled after me a short distance, until finding they were losing ground gave up the chase & went to the village I had left - The Toando hunters followed us down & I told them at Quatsap I could   & the Chief's gun. About 25 miles down the Canal met the Chief returning. He said he had been to the ***Tlopish*** village learning a girl had something like this like the eye piece (which proved to be a cologne bottle.) I gave him his gun & was about leaving when appeared a part of his word he had said nothing of. Vis. Collect warriors - a canoe had been pulling of the coast of the Canal which now boarded us. It contained 5 of the largest & most muscular men I have seen, armed with guns & knives - After speaking to the Chief they followed us down & landed at some bay six or eight miles below. This was a convincing point that they had assembled above for no good. Although satisfied the eye piece was astray concluded I had better return to the ship, as my party was too small to attempt anything like force. At sunset stopped in the E shore about three miles South of C harbour & passed the night -

July 2, 1841: After breakfast continued my course toward the ship. At Meridian passed through the Narrows & at 3:30 P.M. got alongside - Made my report to the Captain & officers, and offered to go risk the Launch & cutter & the crews & get the eye-piece. This Capt. Wilkes declined prefer-ring to send a message to the Tribes & tell them if the eye piece was not returned he would come with the ship & destroy the towns etc.

Case estimated there were 400 Toandos on Hood's Canal and 400 Scocomish and 1,800 S'Klallams. He also estimated that there were 800 Tsugamish (Suquamish) on Admiralty Inlet.

Also keeping a journal on the Canal portion of the expedition was Lt. George M. Colvocoresses.[33] His brief review of the trip:

"[On July 3] we reported our return from the so-called Hood's Canal, having been absent from the ship upwards of three weeks; it was found to be an arm of Puget Sound . . . We fell in with Indians almost every day, and had considerable intercourse with them in the way of trade --- they supplying us with venison and fish, and we giving them in exchange powder, fish-hooks, red paint, and cotton handkerchiefs. The venison, in particular, was sold very cheap --- five of the ordinary musket charges of powder being the price of a whole carcass.

"Though these Indians seemed to under-stand each other, they informed us that they belonged to different tribes. One party called themselves Squamish,(sic) another Socomish, and a third party Toandos. The Squamish appeared to be the most numer-ous, and, according to their own account, could muster 200 fighting men. The Toandos were the best-looking, and they assured us that they inhabited the mountains and were now paying a visit to their friends the Socomish. All these tribes, in their habits and manner of living, re-semble those about Nisqually. On leaving the ship

we were warned to be on the watch for them, as they were arrant thieves, but I am not aware that they ever attempted to take anything from us, ex-cept one of the eye-pieces belonging to the Theo-dolite. This seemed to excite their attention more than anything else connected with the expedition, and they frequently asked us if it could speak, and whether it had not something to do with the "Great Spirit".[34] The women are not very good-looking, and the whole burden of domestic occupation is thrown upon them.

"They have no permanent settlements; and there were several families who followed us wherever we went, and became familiar with some of the sailors. The men possess muskets, spears, and bows, and arrows. The bows are short and small but have great elasticity, and when in their hands will do good execution.

"The Canal does not terminate where Vancouver's chart would lead one to suppose, but extends ten miles further to the northward and eastward, and approaches within two miles of the waters of the Puget Sound, from which point we communicated with the Vincennes, the second week out, and obtained a fresh supply of bread and other provisions." [35]

---

[33]Lt. Geo. M. Colvocoresses, U.S. Navy. R. T. Young Publisher, New York. 1853.

---

[34]The eye-piece was finally recovered through the kindness of Mr. Anderson, principal agent of the Hudson's Bay Company at Nisqually, by threatening the tribe who had it, the Skokomish, with the destruction of their villages and canoes, if they did not give it up by a certain day.

[35]This position is often called the portage and goes from near Belfair to Allyn. It is the only piece of land keeping the greater Kitsap Peninsula from island status.

Edward Clayson
Mouthpiece of Seabeck

While Vancouver and Wilkes recorded their explorations objectively, Edward Clayson was subjective everytime he dipped his pen.

"Edward Clayson commented on what he saw in crisp, unvarnished English. A spade to him is a spade and not a meat ax. Knowing Clayson, you will either admire him or condemn him. He will return you the same compliment and thirteen eggs to the dozen, too." [36]

If ever a man lived at Seabeck who could kill, with words, it was Edward Clayson, known to thousands of Northwest residents, later, as *"The Patriarch"*. The term referred to his editorship of *The Patriarch*, a Seattle newspaper.

Clayson was driven by a need to go down in history as an author and, even in death, he promised to become a legend: He chiseled his tombstone inscription in Chinook Jargon, a language he tried to promote, a combination of Northwest Coast Indian languages, French and some English.

Besides his work at *The Patriarch*, he was editor, publisher and sole financial backer of his one-issue newspaper published at Seabeck, the first in the County. A few copies of one of his books, *Historical Narratives of Puget Sound, Hood's Canal, 1865-1885,* are prized by Seabeck residents. Glenn Adams, Ye Galleon Press, Fairfield, Washington republished the title in 1969, limiting the edition to 170 copies. Adams states in the forward, biographical sketch of Clayson:

"I would like to be able to tell you, proudly, that Edward Clayson's book is important to civilization, to culture in general terms, to the United States of America, to the colorful and scenic Pacific Northwest, to the state of Washington, to the Hood Canal area.

Edward Clayson
(Victoria Rowe, artist.)

"As each man must live by his own conscience, it is my considered opinion that Edward Clayson's book was badly written and wretchedly printed. It offers little that is constructive and much that is not. Run off the press in the original edition of 1911, it is a product of the 20th century, but the writing is more typical of the rabid, colorful and not always reliable journalism of the 1860 to 1900 period."

Clayson waged war on the Washington Mill Company management, especially Richard Holyoke whom he constantly refers to as *King Hollyhock*. There is no love lost between the two. Holyoke threw him off a company-owned steamer, tore down the bridge to Clayson's property at the head of the bay, threw insulting remarks his way.

Clayson, however, had the final word by publishing the book and venting his anger.

---

[36] Edmond Meany. *Seattle Post-Intelligencer.* Oct. 20, 1912.

Clayson's obituary[37] gives a concise record of his life and knowing Clayson, he probably wrote it:

Edward Clayson, Sr., editor of the Patriarch and the last veteran on the Pacific coast who participated in the Sweaborg bombardment during the Crimean War, died yesterday morning at the Providence hospital after an illness of several weeks. He was taken to the hospital six days ago.

Among Mr. Clayson's cherished possessions was a silver medal conferred upon him by the late Queen Victoria at the close of the Crimean War.

For more than 49 years Mr. Clayson had been a virile figure in the history of the Territory and State of Washington and in Oregon before coming here.

Enthusiastic
About Chinook

Mr. Clayson who took up a permanent residence at Seabeck, Kitsap county, 49 years ago, had done more to perpetuate the Chinook jargon than any other Washington pioneer. He repeatedly made public addresses in that language and urged its wider use throughout the Northwest.

Besides a widow, he is survived by a daughter, Dr. Esther P. Lovejoy, of Portland, and a son, a resident of Cordova, Alaska.

The body was shipped last night to his daughter at Portland for interment in that city. Mr. Clayson enjoyed vigorous health until last summer. In September, he suspended publication of The Patriarch on account of illness.

Mr. Clayson engaged in the tea importing business before any other person, firm or corporation in the Northwest, thought tea was worth importing. He was United States mail contractor and carrier on Puget Sound. In 1868, using a sloop for this work, for the era of steam boating on Puget Sound had not then commenced.

He was the author of a volume entitled, "Historical Narratives of Puget Sound" also one entitled "The Muck Rake," which he dedicated to Col. Theodore Roosevelt.

Fund of Anecdotes

Mr. Clayson enlivened any gathering he attended with his fund of personal anecdotes and experiences. His short, chubby figure and close-cut gray beard, at last grown white, and his quick, nervous step made him a conspicuous figure for years in Seattle.

"Cumtux," Chinook for "do you understand?" was his favorite expression.

September 19, 1912, an unusual distinction was conferred on Mr. Clayson, by the mayor and council of Vancouver, BC when on the occasion of the visit to that city of the Duke of Connaught, Mr. Clayson was the only citizen in the State of Washington and probably in the entire Northwest, to receive an official invitation from these authorities to participate in the reception to the duke, held at Stanley park. (He was there as) the only living veteran of the Crimean War left on the Pacific Coast.

Clayson (B. 1839 Kent, England; D. Jan. 2, 1915 Seattle) came to Port Gamble in 1864 and to Seabeck in 1868. He was a logger, rancher, hotel owner, notary and thorn in the side of the mill management.

He was married in Portsmouth, England in 1864 to Ann Mary Quinton (B. circa 1846 England; D. 1923 Portland). Their eldest son, Edward, B. 1865 Portsmouth, England; D. 1944 Portland). Obviously, Mrs. Clayson followed her husband to the Northwest with her infant son. Young Edward managed the Willamette Iron Works in Portland.

Their second son was William (B. 1867 Port Gamble; D. 1949 Portland) spent his adult life in Skagway and Cordova.

Four children were born in Seabeck: Esther (1869-1967, died New York City); Frederick (1872; Murdered 1899 Dawson Trail); Ted (1874); Annie (1881-1963 Ashland, OR). The youngest, Charlotte, was born in Portland in 1884, was married to John Snook, Sr. and lived in Salmon, Idaho. Annie married W. C. Blanchard.

In September 1880, Clayson had shipped off to a Seattle newspaper, a song he composed and sang at the *Bay View Concert Hall*.[38] Parts of it follow:

---

[37]*Seattle Post-Intelligencer.* Jan. 3, 1915.

[38]*Argus.* Sept. 24, 1880.

The whiskey heads and poker sharps
 All know the well you bet.
And if they will but vote for me
 I'll repeal the Gambling Act.
They say, I've got no education
 What does it matter that.
For I have got the ___ to be
 The gentleman from Kitsap.

My countryman, the great DK
 Has caused a great sensation
And after all he proved to be
 Only a speculation.
If he had run a whiskey mill
 With a monopoly at his back
He might have been a bigger fish
 Than the DK of Kitsap.

Now I will conclude my son
 And Hope you'll all see that
If you wish to win
 By selling gin
You must become a Dimmocrat.

And if I get elected
 I'll ape the aristocrat
By standing champagne for the boys
 Like a gintleman from Kitsap.

The D.K. referred to was D. K. Howard and they were at odds over the election for Kitsap Joint Representative. Clayson was running against George F. Raymond, Holyoke's brother-in-law, and the store-keeper. The Republicans even brought in four big-wig politicans in a one week period. When Judge Burke arrived it was amid "booming of cannons" and he was met on the wharf by the band and escorted to the hotel. Holyoke shut the mill down and Burke spoke for three hours.

Three hours? My vote would have gone to Clayson. The November election found 77 voters turning out and they favored Democrats.

Clayson's admiration for Marshall Blinn fills pages of his book. He compared Richard Holyoke and Marshall Blinn:

Marshall Blinn had the determination to make Seabeck a prohibition town and that was his downfall (but) he was consis-

tent and upright. Holyoke was low, cunning and a culprit.

Blinn built a great industrial center. Under Holyoke it went to destruction.

Once Holyoke was injured in a logging accident when the rope hitch slipped, throwing him to the ground. He was struck in the eye, an accident which made him nearly blind. Holyoke was carried back to camp but he came to his senses and ordered the other loggers to lay him down in the shade and go back to work. *"The loggers joked that Holyoke crawled upon his hands and knees a quarter of a mile to camp sooner than let his hired men lose five minutes time at work."*

Another man who Clayson disliked was D. B. Jackson, great grandfather of Washington's former governor and U. S. Senator, Daniel J. Evans. *"Only two men who were physically lazy. They were never seen with their coats off. They were two of the best paid men and they both understood their business. The one was the boss of the saw-mill at Seabeck (Holyoke) and the other was the boss of the shipyard (D. B. Jackson). Two foremen used to justify themselves by saying that they did not hire themselves out to work but to see that others did their work properly."*

On the other hand, Clayson said that Marshall Blinn, always had his coat off and took a hand everywhere that it was needed. *"One of the ships loading at the wharf was taking in some very heavy timber and they were rather short handed on the lumber pile. Marshall Blinn was lifting and helped to get a heavy piece of timber on the rollers and D. B. Jackson was looking on. Said Blinn: 'Mr. Jackson. Give us a lift here for a moment please.' Jackson replied with provoking equanimity in that easy going manner of his: 'Wal. I guess I can spare ye a hand or two from the slab pile if ye want 'em'.*

Blinn made no reply and Jackson walked off.

Jacob Hauptly and Edward Clayson knew each other well. They were neighbors, for a time, at the head of the bay where Clayson kept his hotel and Hauptly the slaughter house. Each left a legacy in words of the history of the people who came to live in this isolated outpost. One was totally objective . . . the other substantially subjective.

Hauptly's work as a cattleman, rancher and butcher was necessary to the survival of the community while Clayson seems to have done nothing but farm, log, import tea, run a saloon and hotel and raise kids.

Clayson mentions Hauptly, only in passing, in his tyrannical book. Hauptly occasionally writes of Clayson in his diary: The two men were often at odds:

July 20, 1880: *E. Clayson sent me a very insulting letter this afternoon.*

July 22, 1880: *Stopped E. Clayson's credit in my shop today.*

Within two years, Hauptly was again mentioning Clayson in his daily journal but the end of the final two months' of Clayson family residency is cryptically written:

Nov. 30, 1882: *Rumored on The Spit today that Mrs. Clayson had left her husband. She went on the steamer* Gem *Tuesday and rumor has it that she is gone to Portland, Oregon.*

Dec. 1, 1882: *Clayson put up notices giving anybody or every body hell that started the rumor about his wife leaving him. The notice was so vulgar that I tore it down.*

Dec. 15, 1882: *Mrs. Clayson returned from Portland on* Phantom.

Feb. 3, 1883: *E. Clayson left about $450 worth of old liquor bills to collect. Did not pay his last months beef bill and by noon he rushed off on horseback for Olympia.*

Feb. 5, 1883: *Clayson family all left Seabeck this morning.*

Nothing more was heard of Clayson until December 1883 when he was fined $27.50 in Portland for riding a horse on a sidewalk.[39] Then his "lodging house" burned in Portland at a loss of $1,200, diminished to $500 by insurance.[40]

The biography of Clayson's eldest daughter, Esther Clayson Pohl Lovejoy (1969-1967) fills pages. She was a remark-able woman who used her education and skills for the betterment of humanity. She was the second woman graduate from the University of Oregon Medical School (MD 1894) and the first woman graduate to devote her lifetime to medicine.

Her first book, *House of the Good Neighbor*, was a result of her investigation of the war plight of women and children in France during World War I. She was the founder and president of The American Medical Women's Association and received international acclaim for her refugee work. She was presented with the Gold Cross of the Legion of Honor of France, the Gold Cross of the Redeemer, Gold Cross of the Order of King George I and the War Cross, all from Greece; the Gold Cross of the Holy Sepulcher from Jerusalem; the Gold Cross of Saint Sava from Yugoslavia; and the White Russian Red Cross of Constantinople. (These are held by the University of Oregon Medical School for permanent public display.)

Dr. Lovejoy was requested to write her life story by the editor of the University of Oregon alumni publication and it was not published but sent to the medical school library archives. The story of Seabeck:

Washington Territory was a forest primeval where births were not registered at the time I was born. The date is a matter of hearsay, but I certainly can remember that in the middle seventies I was living at a logging camp on Hood Canal, one of the terminal branches of Puget Sound, where logs were hauled over a skid road by five yokes of oxen driven by a bullwhacker. There was no law against cruelty to animals and the bullwhacker used an instrument of torture called a goad stick (an oak rod like a billiard-cue with a steel brad in the tip), instead of a merciful bullwhacker, to get the greatest possible pulling power out of the team.

Virgin timber was still standing at the edge of salt water navigable by deep sea vessels. The first sawmills on Puget Sound (started in the fifties) had been operating only a few years and my father was running a logging camp and selling logs at a loss to the Washington Mill Company at Seabeck where Canal loggers assembled for their periodic sprees.

---

[39] *Seattle Post-Intelligencer.* Dec. 6, 1883.

[40] *Seattle Post-Intelligencer.* June 21, 1884.

That little town was the real thing. Now it is only a memory with the few survivors of those fantastic days. Thousands of youngsters from our western universities flock there for their summer vacations. They are as vital as the first generation of loggers, but they belong to another age. The Eagle Saloon has been converted and is used as a headquarters for the YMCA, but nothing more intoxicating than "coke" is sold at the old bar. Attempts are sometimes made to reproduce the original atmosphere, but it can't be done. For sentimental and historical reasons some of the buildings have been preserved and reconstructed, but Seabeck is no more like the old town than the mummy of Rameses II is like that dominant character in his prime.

Fishing was good on Hood Canal, but life was hard and primitive. We belonged to the first families and we hadn't time to grow up with the country. After we failed in the logging business we kept a backwoods hotel, but the years were passing and in search of a soft spot where other pioneers had already worked themselves to death to make a place fit for human habitation, we moved to Portland, Oregon

Esther wrote several letters to Ella Olanie about her life in Seabeck.

Lizzie Rounds was my best friend during childhood in Seabeck. We left there when I was thirteen years old. I am sorry she did not write because if we had corresponded we could have recalled many interesting things connected with that old town which was active in our day.

In addition to the sawmill, there was shipbuilding that brought to Seabeck some interesting men. The Canal loggers always came to Seabeck for their periodical sprees. Many of the millmen boarded at the Company cookhouse which had a dance hall for Saturday night dances above it. The shipwrights boarded at the Bayview Hotel where I worked from the time I could walk until I left that town. Lizzie sometimes worked with me.

I recall one day when Lizzie and I were picking blueberries on the hill between Seabeck and Stavis Bay. The blueberries were thick on that hill and we were operating on the opposite slope. Returning to Seabeck with our buckets full, the first thing we

glimpsed was the big flag flying at half-mast at the Bayview Hotel.

Somebody was dead! Somebody had been killed in the mill or drowned in the bay.

We ran down the hill, jumping logs and making the best possible speed until we reached the hotel and demanded: "Who is dead?"

It was James A. Garfield, President of the United States, and we were so relieved because he was not a personal friend of ours like the folks who lived at Seabeck. The date was September 1881.[41]

In another letter to Mrs. Olanie[42], Dr. Lovejoy noted:

"Some years ago I wrote a story regarding my own family in Seabeck at a time when a certain publishing company was asking for stories of the Northwest. The only stories they would examine were those that had been passed upon favorably by literary committees of the Universities of Washington or Oregon and both of these universities passed upon my material favorably. However it was not accepted by the publisher and some day when I get time I will dig it up and have it published, in which case you will be able to get my slant on Seabeck and many of the things I can personally remember."

That manuscript, oh how valuable, has not been located.

Clayson is noted in Kitsap County as the first newspaper editor. His *Rebel Battery* waged war against the mill company. Only one copy survived and the Washington State Library copied it on microfilm. That copy follows:

---

[41] Esther Clayson Pohl Lovejoy letter to Ella Olanie. Feb. 19, 1959.

[42] Ibid. Oct. 26, 1959.

THE REBEL BATTERY.

Volume I. SEABECK, KITSAP COUNTY, W. T., OCTOBER, 1878. Number 1.

THE REBEL BATTERY

PUBLISHED OCCASIONALLY AT

SEABECK, KITSAP COUNTY, WASH. T'Y.

EDWARD CLAYSON, Sole Editor and Proprietor.

Single Copy . . . . Fifty Cents.

THE REBEL BATTERY will be devoted principally to the interests of the settlers and loggers of Hood's Canal.

SALUTATORY.

In introducing ourselves to the public, we wish to be distinctly understood that we have neither the education, nor the ability necessary to conduct a newspaper, nor do we aspire to be considered as making any such attempt. Having never followed any other occupation but that of a laboring man, and having never attended school since we were eleven years of age, we fully realize our inability to assume the position of an editor, consequently we cannot justly claim the attention of the public generally. It is only those who have been subjected to the influences which we propose to expose, who can fully realize the situation, and to whom we can look for support. It does not, in our estimation, require much of an education, or ability as a writer, to publish a few plain truths. The title which we have assumed for our little sheet, THE REBEL BATTERY, etc., does not imply that we intend to rebel against any lawful authority but, on the contrary, we shall always endeavor to be a good, law-abiding citizen; but we wish to be considered as rebellious, in the extreme, to the tyranny, persecution and indignity which we have been subjected to for the past ten years, and shall ever be ready to open the ports of THE REBEL BATTERY and give a broadside to the tyrannical oppressors who would make the whole of Hood's Canal nothing more than a penal colony, with its headquarters at Seabeck; with its Governor and staff of officers with unlimited power to dictate whatever terms they chose to their subjects.

We don't expect to be of sufficient importance for the press of the country to notice, unless it be to hold us up to the ridicule of the country as presuming too much; as an amateur in the business, we naturally expect to be ridiculed by the old scholars who can wield a more powerful pen, or would endeavor to make capital by defending tyrannical despot.

The Washington Mill Company

CONTRASTED WITH OTHER MILL COMPANIES ON PUGET SOUND, AND THE MANNER IN WHICH THEY GOT RICH SO FAST.

Washington Mill Co., indeed, we wonder every American within the range of at least one hundred miles of Seabeck don't rise with indignation and protest against the name of Washington being prostituted in any such manner. It would be far more appropriate to name the concern after Boss Tweed, as they have certainly followed more in the steps of Boss Tweed than those of Washington; we have been in this town over ten years and know just what we are talking about. This concern known as the Washington Mill Co., have got rich principally by theft, and about the only talent which their agent here possessed, when they took him under their wing and placed him in the position he now occupies, was that he was the most successful thief in his time. If the Secretary of the Interior wants to make an example of any mill company on the Pacific coast, we don't know of any one which can be as strongly recommended to his notice, as this concern known as the Washington Mill Co., located at Seabeck, W. T.; has any other mill company on the whole coast enjoyed the same facilities for stealing? Look at their geographical position centrally located on Hood's Canal, where the forests run to the water's edge, where the water may be crossed almost any time in a small canoe, consequently it is not necessary for them to keep anything but an old flat bottomed tug to bring their stolen logs into Seabeck. The other mill companies on the Sound have worked to great disadvantage in this respect. They have been obliged to keep up expensive steamers for years, in order to get their logs to the mills, and we often hear of them losing boom after boom, consequently sustaining great losses, which the Washington Mill Co. have never experienced. Is it any wonder, or credit either, for them to take precedence of almost every other mill company on Puget Sound, taking everything into consideration? We don't see how the other mill companies on the Sound manage to compete with them either in the San Francisco market, or in the foreign markets, that look to Puget Sound for lumber. Some people who are ignorant of their practices will say that they are enterprising; so was Boss Tweed; they will also state that they employ a large number of people; so did Boss Tweed; they will also say that they spend considerable money in making improvements; Boss Tweed did the same thing; he spent a large amount of his dishonest gains in building, etc., etc., giving employment to a large number of laborers and mechanics, and there was a time when no man in New York city, dared publish a word against him, consequently he felt just as safe and defied the law just as much as the Washington Mill Co. are doing to day. This concern known as the W. M. Co., has, during the last seven years, settled up three estates of its former members amounting to several hundreds of thousands of dollars; have built large ships and steamers and an additional sawmill, besides spending tens of thousand of dollars in this town, and have acquired several thousand acres of valuable timber land, probably not less than $75,000 worth. We ask, is there any other mill company on Puget Sound that can make the same showing in the same length of time? We believe not; and why not? Not because their members and agents are not as smart as those of the Washington Mill Co., but because they have not employed the same facilities for stealing lumber.

The yoke which the whole inhabitants of Hood's Canal are expected to be under. Who(o)p.

27

THE REBEL BATTERY.

SEABECK. W. T., ... OCTOBER, 1878.

☞ All communications to the Battery must be addressed to R. Clayson, Seabeck, Kitsap county, W. T.

That Twenty-four Thousand Dollars

WHICH CLAYSON MAD AGAINST THE WASHINGTON MILL CO., AND HOW IT CAME ABOUT, SHOWING THE INCAPACITY AND TYRANNY OF KING RICHARD AND HOW HE WAS BEATEN WITH HIS OWN WEAPONS.

On a certain date, Mr. Clayson gave the Washington Mill Co. a written notice to remove their logs from off his premises, or the ground rent would be $20 per day; they at once recognized his claim by taking a number of men and a steamer and removing the logs; at the same time they nailed his notice up on the outside of their store, the object of which was to subject Mr. Clayson to the ridicule and criticism of their dirt-eaters. Some of the poor miserable creatures (the king's loyal subjects) felt greatly elated — the circumstance, and showed their loyalty to their king by various gestures and remarks, which they thought would please their master the most on this occasion. But little did the king think that it would be possible for Clayson to humble him in the presence of those same subjects through the very same instrument he was now making use of for holding him up to public scorn. After a few weeks, when the excitement was all over and everything had cooled down, Richard, without further ceremony, took possession of Mr. Clayson's premises. At the expiration of three and a half years, Mr. Clayson presented his bill for rent, which now amounted to about $24,000, and the very fact of that notice having been nailed up on the outside of the W. M. Co.'s store three years and a half before, for the sole purpose of subjecting Mr. Clayson to the public scorn, was now evidence against his majesty, and would be used to substantiate a claim for $24,000; that's paying rather dear for a day or two's sport! It was really surprising to see how courteously Mr. Clayson was received on this occasion; he was invited into the king's private sanctum, and treated with the greatest respect. After a long consultation with his majesty, a settlement was made for about $1,000, and Mr. Clayson left the office with the gratification of having humbled a tyrannical despot, which was more satisfaction to him than to have prosecuted the case and collected $24,000.

Dirt-Eaters Classified.

"Servants, obey your masters."

No. 1—Is a natural dirt-eater, constituted as such by nature; he cannot help himself if he would. As a general rule, he will work for any wages his master chooses to pay him; and will spend the same wherever he thinks it will please his master the most. His master, (or his owner, which is more appropriate) can rely on him on all occasions to do his bidding, no matter what the task may be, and after all this, he feels flattered if he should be so favored as to receive a grin or an insignificant glance from his master!

No. 2—This class of persons are those who have no particular object in life—are not self-reliant. They go in for a steady job, "wages no object" whatever; they assume no responsibility, but plod along in a state of subserviancy, all their greatest aspirations being to please their master.

No. 3—Are those characters who eat dirt for money and not from principle — generally to be found in positions where the highest wages are paid.

No. 4—This class of the fraternity may very properly be called "the Chief dirt-eaters;" they enjoy especial privileges under their masters, and are calculated to control the actions of their kind, from time to time, according to circumstances; they are generally aspirants for office and are calculated to run the whole machine, both judicially and politically—in the best interests of their masters.

Reading the Declaration of American Independence to such characters as above described, is the greatest mockery and indignity which that justly celebrated document can possibly be subjected to.

Whom the cap fits let him wear it.

We were greatly amused the other day, at seeing a number of the Washington Mill Co.'s hogs sticking up their backs and forming an hostile attitude towards some of Clayson's hogs as they passed quietly by; they (the hostile hogs, we mean,) are evidently dirt-eaters of the 5th class and are anxious to fraternize with their two-legged brethren, as they appear to fully realize the situation.

One of the Chief dirt-eaters remarked to a farmer of Hood's Canal, that he (the farmer) would not have any place to sell his produce if the mill company was not here; forcible argument in support of his master; just as well say that the mill crew would have nothing to eat if the farmer was not here.

County Commissioner! what a farce! We doubt very much if the Commissioner under his oath of office dare advocate anything at the county seat which would conflict with the wishes of his august majesty; as to how he shall serve his master's special interest, he is calculated to anticipate the same and act accordingly.

That celebrated writer, Lord Macaulay, remarks that tyranny and oppression may exist for ages and ages, where there is no free press. Surely, the people of Hood's Canal fully realize the truth of his remarks.

28

The Whiskymill Owner Contrasted With the Sawmill Owner.

The man who sells liquor and is generally treated with the greatest indifference by the sawmill owner as something beneath his notice, is an exemplary character in comparison to the lumber thief; in the first place he pays a license to the general government for the privilege of selling liquor; secondly, he pays the city, town or county another license, thereby swelling the revenue of the general government, also the particular county in which he does his business; the law also requires him to give bonds to conduct his business in an orderly and respectable manner; he also has to satisfy the officials granting the license that he is a man of good moral character.

What a contrast when considered in its true light! Which man of the two has the most demoralizing influence on society, the sawmill man or the whiskymill man! A boy is born and brought up in a sawmill town; he learns year after year, as he grows older, to look up to the mill owner; that he (the mill owner), is an exemplary character; that he is worth so many thousands of dollars. He sees one crop out with his hundreds of thousands, and still another, and another, with their tens of thousands of dollars; he also learns how these large fortunes have been made. Why should he not when he grows old enough, use every exertion he is capable of both mentally and physically, to grasp at any dishonorable project which presents itself! He is taught from his infancy to admire, respect and pay homage, to those who have done the same thing and made themselves makers of the situation by dishonorable and tyrannical means.

THE PRIVILEGE WHICH DOES TWEED'S SEAMEN ENJOYED, WHICH KING RICHARD'S DON'T—They could spend their money in what store they pleased, travel on what steamer they pleased, and were never questioned about what hotel they patronized, and last, but not least, they could always get the money which they worked hard for, when it was due and demanded.

ANOTHER.—Another Chinaman arrived by ————'s boat for the Palace. This makes nearly five all told, during the past year. A Chinaman will stand wind and tide, but that ———— is too bad for them.

SLAVERY IN SEABECK—FIFTEEN HOURS CONSTITUTES A DAY'S WORK.—Yea, we repeat, it is slavery of the worst kind, when men are forced to do it against their will. Show us the man who works willingly after supper three hours for the miserable pittance he receives for his services! Two men were discharged for not putting in an appearance after supper. This, we presume is an example to the balance of the crew to let them see what they may expect for insubordination. These same two men worked faithfully for the company for two years 12 1-2 hours per day, and when they tried to compel them to work three hours after supper they would not stand it. Twelve and one-half hours per day is long enough for any man to work all the year round; if this company's business has increased so much, why not put on a night crew as is done in all other mills on the Sound under similar circumstances! If all the men were to quit, who are actually working against their will after supper, there would be none left but the dirt-eater. This article will furnish material for the dirt-eaters to talk about; they will be found backing up their masters on the subject.

Hood's Canal.

Hood's Canal is a large sheet of water, some sixty miles in length, and from one to three miles wide, with small rivers and bays on either side, where is to be found quantities of good farming land. Quilcine bay, some fourteen miles N. W. from Seabeck, offers good inducements for settlers, as there is a large quantity of good farming land in that section of country open for settlement; it is impossible for such lands to remain vacant long, with the facilities which Hood's Canal now offers for travel. Seabeck is a large sawmill town located on the east side of the canal about nineteen miles from Port Gamble; the mill cuts not less than 70,000 feet of lumber per day, besides laths and pickets, the greater portion of which finds its way into the San Francisco market, although quite a number of large ships load here every year for foreign ports. It has only one store, at present, belonging to the mill company, although there is business enough for two. There are two hotels, one belonging to, and under the immediate patronage of the mill company, located on the sawdust; the other belonging to an outsider by the name of Clayson, and supported by respectable people, who paddle their own canoe regardless of local influence. Seabeck has also a good meat market, shoemaker shop, good school, brass band, base ball club, fruit stand, shaving saloon, &c., &c. In fact, everything necessary for a small community except, FREEDOM OF ACTION, the town unfortunately being governed by a king. The next town of any consequence is Union City, 28 miles south from Seabeck, supported principally by the lumbering done in that part of country. There are also quite a number of settlers at the head of Hood's Canal, about fourteen miles from Union City. The Skokomish is the largest river on Hood's Canal, its entrance being in the immediate neighborhood of Union City, the Indian reservation being on one side and a large farm belonging to Mr. Webb on the other; there are also several other settlers on the river. The farming lands on this river are very rich offering inducements to settlers. The fishing business on Hood's Canal will be of some importance before many years.

APPROACHING KING RICHARD UNDER DIFFICULTIES.—We had the pleasure, when a resident of the United States, and a large part of this precinct, to approach King Richard, and call his attention to the dilapidated condition of a certain bridge in this neighborhood, to which he replied heartily, and with a manner so grave of the road, that he did but want a bridge above, to which we ventured the assertion that it was very necessary to such conveniences and that we should strive to keep one there. Our presumption so incensed the king that he actually forgot his position in a moment of anger, and shook his fist vehemently in our face and threatened to "boot" us right then, to which we replied that he had estimated the abuse of his mental faculties in trying to "boot" us and was now running to brute force.

SAWDUST.—Seabeck is the first seaport town we were ever in, where it is considered popular, or even respectable to reside in the immediate locality of the wharf, blacksmith shops, warehouses, etc. It is certainly a bright prospect for the young bloods to become sawdust aristocrats.

WASHINGTON MILL CO., OR WHAT'S IN A NAME.—Was it the object of the few ambitious men who formed themselves into an organization and adopted the above honored name (which is reverenced by every patriotic American), to carry out the principles which that great and good man advocated, or is it their purpose to seize upon every available —— of land in the Territory and thereby —— control both socially and politically a —— of people of their own. Possibly ——— but indignity to the name of ——— could possibly be ——————.

THE REBEL BATTERY.

SEABECK, W. T. . . . . . . OCTOBER, 1878.

SEABECK ITEMS.

Whol(e)yoke being such a noted rustler, we intend offering him the agency of this paper.

The Rebel Battery will be read all over the Pacific coast, therefore it will be a good advertising medium.

In addition to other things, we shall devote ourself to exposing the system as practiced by the Washington Mill Co. for land grabbing.

We charge fifty cents a copy for the first issue of our paper, but after this, we shall publish a regular monthly; subscription, $1.00 per year.

We do not expect to set Puget Sound on fire with The Rebel Battery; but we think that all the guns King Richard has in his Kingdom will never silence it.

This paper will be sold at a great discount to Rebels; the qualifications necessary to constitute a Rebel, being rebellious to all tyrannical despots (and thieves), under all circumstances.

Clayson says that he thinks he shall locate at Port Townsend and spend considerable time in learning to talk Spanish fluently, as he thinks this is about the only qualification necessary at present to make a good storekeeper.

It is rumored that the king is about to abdicate the Throne, and that Hood's Canal is to become part and parcel of the Great American Republic, in which case The Rebel Battery will hoist the stars and stripes; fire a national salute; dismount its guns, and take part in the great celebration which must necessarily follow so grand an event.

Fishing in Seabeck Bay. — The Chinese fishing schooner having taken not less than twenty tons of fish of different kinds from the bay during the past year, their actions have attracted the attention of a number of white men, who are calculating to build a fish weir, and establish a fishing business at Seabeck. Look out for king Richard! don't knock that fish weir down!

The Seabeck Road Fund, and How They are Used. — Who dare question for a moment the actions of King Richard in such a trifling matter as this? Shall he not do as he pleases with his perquisites? If he chooses to use the public funds for the purpose of cutting a telegraph road from a portion of his Kingdom into the borders of civilization, who dare for a moment to question his prerogative? So sure is he of the fidelity of his subjects, that such a trifling matter as this is unworthy of his consideration.

Look out for the Next Issue — In which will appear a minute description of the different locations where the Washington Mill Co. had teams of their own employed for a number of years stealing lumber. We also have a list of names before us, of men who sacrificed their birth-right to the Washington Mill Co. upon about the same terms as Esau did to Jacob, the company taking about the same advantage of the poor devils as Jacob did of Esau. We intend, also, to publish a black list, the names being taken from the books of the Bay View Hotel, with a biographical of the individuals.

A Parable.

And it came to pass in the days of King Holyonshus the I., that a certain Claysonite did rebel against the king; and, behold! the king waxed wroth, and assembled his Chief dirt-eaters, and the king spake unto them, saying: Lo! for these many years have I ruled my Kingdom in peace from my stronghold in Seabeck to the utmost corners of Hood's Canal, and behold! I will smite the Claysonite and with my large feet will I stamp him out of existence. Thus sayeth King Holyonshus, and it came to pass on a certain day that the king did appear on the borders of his frontier, even to the *headwaters* thereof, and he arose in great majesty to his full height and beheld with amusement, the preparations being made upon rebel territory *for a long seige* outside the borders of his Kingdom, and so the king retired in silence, with a troubled spirit, into the heart of his stronghold.

Notice to Teamsters. — The most powerful yoke on Hood's Canal is Whol(e)yoke. Yes, gentlemen, he is a whole team. Just in the one capacity of yarding out for the W. M. Co., he is equal to five yokes; he is also postmaster, road supervisor, school clerk, treasurer and band master, which is equal to about four yokes more. So eager is he to snatch every dollar, that he will seize upon everything in sight except ring-shakes and bad butts.

A lady arrived in Seabeck the other day, and sent out her posters, announcing that she would lecture on certain interesting subjects at the hall, charging the very small sum of twenty-five cents admission. After being in town a few hours, she must have ascertained the deplorable financial condition of affairs, as we noticed she scratched out the twenty-five cents, and sympathized with the poor, money-less community by giving them a free treat.

It is rumored on the street that the little joker and his big brother-in-law calculate to buy out the Washington Mill Co. shortly, if everything goes favorably to their individual interests. Later — Since the above was put in type it appears that it is a false rumor, as we learn that it is only a half interest which they anticipate buying.

BAY VIEW HOTEL.

SEABECK, W. T.

The Clayson Family, - - Proprietors.

This Hotel is located just outside of the borders of the Kingdom, and the stone wall is not yet built for the purpose of keeping King Richard's subjects from trespassing on it, although we expect it the next. Clayson meeting it being made up principally of dirt-eaters, that it will be considered absolutely necessary for the best interests of the Kingdom, that the bridge leading towards the Bay View Hotel, and the Rebel Battery should be destroyed at once. This Bay View House is just five minutes walk from the steamboat landing. It is the first respectable hotel ever built in Seabeck. The charges have been brought down to the lowest figure of any public place on the Pacific coast.

Three reasons why the public should patronize the Bay View Hotel: First, because it is the cheapest; second, because you get better food for the small charges than can be had at any other place; third, because the money you spend in this house does not help, either directly or indirectly, to swell the funds of the already overgrown and powerful monopoly. It is should by all means patronize the Bay View House.

Three reasons why we can afford to give better entertainment at cheaper rates than elsewhere: First, because we have no rent to pay (to the king;) second, because we raise about all we want to eat; third, because we hire no help, the Clayson family being numerous enough to run the whole concern — from the concert room in the hotel buildings to digging out stumps on the farm.

The Bay View Hotel not only furnishes good hotel accommodations, but the amusement which it affords, which is just as necessary to our being so the food we eat. It has the best double ten-pin Alley on Puget Sound; it has a Concert room with musical instruments (the Clayson family can play them too), of several different kinds; it has a splendid Ball Ground (which the Kingdom does not afford, the whole empire being made up of billiards and bateau forks). Come and see us, and we will entertain you or "bust" in the attempt.

The best element of society either in, or visiting Seabeck, naturally find their way to the Bay View House and grounds, where the amusements are to be found which necessarily follow and assist in the advancement of civilization. Every civilized people take as much pride in their amusements as they do in their commercial business.

W. H. WHITE,

Attorney at Law,

Prosecuting Attorney Third Judicial District,

Seattle, W. T.

30

Jacob Hauptly
Journals Tell History of Seabeck

Diaries recording life at Seabeck and the Skokomish River Valley as seen through the eyes of one of The Canal's leading citizens, Jacob Hauptly, are securely protected in the vault at the Kitsap County Historical Society's museum. The diaries cover a period between 1872 and 1899.[43] One of the few men not directly associated with lumbering, his very livelihood depended on the economics of the Washington Mill Company and the appetites of loggers and millmen, seamen and shipbuilders.

Born in Aarou (pronounced Ah-roo)[44] Switzerland June 2, 1830, the son of John Henry and Frances (or Ferre)[45] Hauptli, he was the eldest of five children who embarked from LeHavre, arriving at New Orleans in 1840. A sixth child was born during the crossing. The family traversed the Mississippi to St. Louis, arriving there on Jake's tenth birthday.

They settled in Madison County, Illinois on 80 acres of land. Three more children were born in Madison County. Jake became head of household at age 13 when his father died (Aug. 2, 1843), supporting his mother and eight siblings.

Probate records give insight into the family's life. There was the property, half improved, the other half timber, one yoke oxen, ten head cattle, 18 hogs, a mare and colt, plow, three boxes, harness, cart, two acres of corn, six bushels of wheat, seven bushels beans, one suit, household furniture, two axes, a scythe, log chain, hay and corn and one barrel of tools. An auction

Jacob Hauptly
(Victoria Rowe, artist.)

was held Nov. 11, 1843 which brought in $153. The widow still had her property but all the livestock, the corn, many tools and a chair were sold.

Jake stayed with the family for ten years and at age 24 left St. Joseph, Missouri driving ox teams across the Plains. He reached Nevada City, California in 100 days and found work in the mines at Alpha. He tried his hand at the hotel business and was a tollgate keeper on the road between Nevada City and Grass Valley.

A family history says he tried to join Grant's army but was rejected because he didn't have a horse nor money enough to buy one.[46] Another family history states that he tried to join the Army of Dragoons

[43]Kitsap County Historical Society.

[44]Barbara Lindell Watts and Jean Webb Lindell, 1979-80 correspondence and 1993 interviews.

[45]Probate records held by Illinois Regional Archives Depository.

[46]Emma B. Richert. *Long, Long Ago in Skokomish Valley.* No date.

to fight Mexico in 1847 but was rejected because he was too light.[47]

Another attempt at gold mining proved futile. He owned the Yellow Jacket Gold Mine *"which made Clarence Mackey of the Postal Telegraph rich. He also owned a saloon and hotel. He paid George Hearst's board bill one winter and when Hearst finally struck it rich, Hauptly wasn't reimbursed."* [48] so he headed north to Portland where his first job was driving 100 head of cattle overland to the Caribou mines in British Columbia. He said he had to swim the Columbia River three times on the northward journey.[49]

There were 5,000 men in the mining camps and work for about 300. From the mines he walked 400 miles to New Westminster and crossed the Strait from Victoria to Port Townsend. He and his companion headed for Port Gamble. Each brought a blanket and hiked the trail to Port Ludlow, then took the beach and headed for Gamble.

He was later to say: *"When we got to Whisky Spit, we could see the Gamble mills but there was a mile and a half of water between us and them. Now what could we do but walk around Hood's Canal? We thought it was a small bay and we could walk around before night."*

When they realized that the *bay* stretched far to the south, they found an old ship's hatch and two large oars among the driftwood and started to sail across to Gamble. They used a blanket as rigging. Tides and wind made the crossing treacherous and they feared for their lives but a fleet of Indian canoes "hove" in sight and after some bartering about the cost of crossing, they arrived at Port Gamble, Dec. 15, 1862.

While waiting for a job, Hauptly's "wealth" was reduced to 25 cents. Even though he wasn't from Maine, he was given work as a steward in the mill. Later he was hired by Amos Brown, a logger, for $30 a month at his camp on the "Duquaboos" or, as we call it, Duckabush.

Jake and two others sailed a square scow over to the camp, a tough trip in the middle of the winter. *"We slept on the beach at Oak Head one night and about two inches of snow fell on our blankets. I looked out at daylight and here came a skunk and walked right over us. I didn't say anything for the darn thing might explode."* [50]

They spent two days at Oak Head and all they had to eat were apples and raw clams. They didn't have a match and were 15 miles from their destination and three miles from Seabeck.

Hauptly did everything at the camp and when the cook got sick, took over that job for $50 a month. A few games of poker strengthened his finances so that when paid for his first three months' work, he had enough money to go into business. He sold overalls and socks to loggers.

His logging adventures were cut short when he was caught cutting on Federal land, according to newspaper stories later in his life.

He went to Seabeck for a year and boarded with the Ninemire family, then bought out a claim of *Dutch Frank* at Dosewallips (Brinnon) and took the Ninemires across The Canal with him. For most of the year he made improvements on the property: fences, logging, hauling manure. He was selling potatoes, sausage, turkey and beef to the residents of Seabeck. John Ninemire farmed and Mrs. Ninemire made butter which Jake sold in Seabeck at $1 a pound.

Hauptly sold the Dosewallips property in 1872 to Ewell Brinnon (Mrs. Ninemire's brother) and moved with the Ninemires back to Seabeck. He put up a slaughterhouse (on the present Sprout property) and lived with the Ninemires near the head of the Bay, next to Ed Clayson's home and hotel. There was also a small cabin on the slaughterhouse property.

He built a scow to make his frequent crossings of The Canal, hiring a tow from the steamer *St. Patrick* or *Colfax*.

There are unusual purchases entered in the diaries, especially for a bachelor. In his

[47]Watts and Lindell.

[48]Richert.

[49]Edmond S. Meany. *Seattle Post Intelligencer, Jan. 27, 1916.*

[50]*Hood Canal Courier.* June 23, 1933.

diaries for 1871-72: *doll, ribbons, yarn, building blocks, red silk thread, dress yardage, Alpaca yardage, plaid dress goods.* The ledger also shows that he may have had some bad habits: *10 gallons whiskey, 22 lb. tobacco.* Perhaps he purchased for others.

Many entries up until December 1879 refer to *the old woman.* The entries end: *I moved my bed this forenoon. The old lady cried.* Since there are no divorce records and no clues to the identity of the woman in his diaries, she remains nameless.

He was important to Seabeck between 1872 and 1886 but his contribution to this present history is inestimable. He recorded births, deaths, marriages, "elopements", the town gossip, shipping records and his own ledger accounts, including details of his cattle buying trips and notations concerning what he supplied logging camps and ships. It wasn't uncommon for him to sell dozens of chickens and eggs, live milk-producing goats, vegetables and sides of beef to outbound ships.

He purchased a sausage machine in 1882, was salting down hams and smoking meat. He rendered lard and made head cheese. In 1882 he bought three large halibut totaling 322 lbs. from a Port Townsend supplier and sold it to the cookhouse and Denny Howard at the hotel. He also sold to Clayson's hotel and the *mad houses.*

These were good years, financially, for Jake. In 1882 he rented Thomas Dagnin's property at Colseed (Quilcene) for three years and bought Dagnin's 23 head cattle, two hogs and 30 chickens. He hired a man to work this ranch (at $35 per month and room and board) and sowed oats, plowed, built a bridge and fences. He lived at Colseed much of the summer and wrote: *Laid in house last night until 12 o'clock when nats, fleas & mosquitoes drove me out. Went to barn."*

He began building a house near Camp Union in late 1879 and chronicled part of the endeavor. Shakes were made on site and nailed down by a new workman who *"can neither make shakes, nail on shakes or do anything on the building. Slover and I done all the nailing and straightening of the shakes."*

In one day he and another man built the kitchen. He furnished the house with part of Robert Airey's furnishings including an old stove, writing desk and chair (for which he paid $13.) A load of 2,000 brick were taken to the house (which he purchased at Seattle for $18), and he wallpapered, built a smokehouse, barn and chicken house. He paid Enoch Young to build a chimney and paid him $1 a day for traveling and $20 for the work. After completion of the house, he moved his family from town.

During 1879-84 he proved up his land on his *Beaver Ranch*, provided papers of naturalization and filed his pre-emption claim after paying $222.51.

Hauptly served as Justice of the Peace for many years. Besides performing weddings, he was judge and jury in town.

"A little fight on board the Oregon. Had the Second Mate (Dougherty) hauled up. I fined him $5 and costs, $1 without any trial. He confessed that he struck the complainant.[51]

Squabbles among the local people were often settled by Hauptly: *Had to settle John Lantz and O. Petersons fish affair.*[52] Days later: *Lantz & Peterson finally settled. Loaned Lantz $6.*

He made out arrest warrants, tried cases of assault and battery, issued fines, delivered complaints. *(Frank Rounds swore out complaint against Dave Patterson for drawing and striking him with a knife.)* The following day he examined Patterson. A jury was summoned but they couldn't agree so he called another jury and the jury found Patterson guilty as charged.[53] Patterson was fined, ordered to pay the costs and was sentenced to 25 days hard labor.

A couple weeks later, Biddy DeCarty swore out a complaint against George Bray for murder. She said that he stabbed his partner, Fred. Hauptly's deputy found both men and although Fred had been stabbed in the neck, it wasn't serious. Bray paid expenses of $30 and was sent home.

There were cases of mutiny and often the offenders were sent to Port Madison and

---

[51]Hauptly diary. Dec. 14, 1878.

[52]Ibid. Nov. 15, 1883.

[53]Ibid. Nov. 17-21, 1885.

Seattle to serve their time in jail while the ships sailed out.

Hauptly began his cattle buying trips in 1873 and they took him to Grays Harbor, Lewis, Thurston and Cowlitz counties. The trips usually lasted a couple of weeks. Rain, snow and bad roads were commonplace. Nights were spent with farm families. He'd travel up to 20 miles on foot in a day. Sometimes he rode his horse. Rarely did he drive the cattle back to Seabeck without losing a few. Days were often spent searching for the lost cattle.

Only on rare occasions did he buy in other areas. In December 1881 he went to Waterman's camp on Port Orchard Bay and then to the Wach Shang's (Wa Chong) place. He bought ten head of cattle from *Wach Shang*, driving them to present-day Silverdale where he stayed with *"old man Littlewood."*

"Rain, mud and water. Hard days work. All wet.

He left Littlewood's at 10:30 a.m., crossed the trail (nearly present-day Anderson Hill Road), swam Beef Harbor and arrived at Seabeck by 4 p.m.

During the big snowstorm in January 1880, Hauptly took salt hides, deer and beaver skins, boarded the bark *Dublin* and sailed for San Francisco. Since Hauptly walked to the Northwest and came overland to California, he hadn't developed an appetite for the sea and suffered from sea-sickness. He complained about ham and eggs for breakfast daily.

In San Francisco, he stayed with a sister, attended the theater, drank a little, sold his hides for $448, bought a coat and watch. On the return trip, he came overland from Astoria. He beat the *Dublin* back to Seabeck by one day.

When he returned, he started courting an 18 year-old, Louise Reid (B. Nov. 28, 1861; D. June 13, 1898) of Montesano and they were married in May. He was 50 three days later. Four children were born of the marriage.

Their marriage was stormy. After building her a new home, he hired various women to help her with the chores and children. They either didn't like Lou or she didn't like them. On May 9, 1881 Ella Green "commenced work". She left May 23.

Sarah Ferguson arrived Sept. 24. One month later, Sarah was paid off. On Dec. 9 he "sent Miss M. Corns down to sew for my wife." On Jan. 21, he paid her off. In 1882 the hired women included Mary Green, Mrs. Burgess, Siwash Ellen, Hattie Warin, Ninemire, Belle Ninemire, Miss Griffen, Miss Hawks.

She disdained his drinking even though it was infrequent.

At least he doesn't often write about it.

He leased the Webb ranch at Skokomish in 1886 for $2,000 per year, moving there shortly before the Seabeck fire. Louise had an affair and Jake's suspicions were confirmed: she had been pregnant at the time of her death and the child was not his.

Even after leaving Seabeck, he continued providing meat for the Washington Mill Company camps up and down The Canal.

After Lou's death in 1898, he farmed at Clifton (Belfair) for the Puget Mill Company. He was married a second time to Lena Mickelson, a spinster and crippled lady who was 27: he was 74. He outlived her. After Lena's death, in 1916, he spent most of his time at his daughter's home in Seattle where he died in 1928.

His son, Cleveland C. Hauptly, (B. Oct. 6, 1884 Seabeck; D. Sept. 13, 1934 Union) worked with his father on the farm and in the store at Union with the exception of a few years spent in Port Angeles. He died as the result of a fire in the store at Union, [54] perhaps while trying to save his father's diaries.

His other children were Mary (B. April 16, 1881 Seabeck) who married Thomas Albert Hester; Ethel (B. March 5, 1883 Seabeck) who married Oscar Crosby; and Harry (B. Jan. 16, 1891 Skokomish).

Hauptly had a wonderful sense of humor:

Dreamed of pretty women. Waked up and the two goats were at the door.

I was alone last night. Still I had company: Plenty of fleas.

Fighting fleas last night and goats.

On April Fools Day 1882 he gave mother-in-law can. *Said it was peaches but was really tomatoes.*

---

[54]*Mason County Journal.* Sept. 13, 1934.

Best friends John Ninemire (B. circa 1832) and his wife, Mary (B. circa 1838), came overland from their birthplaces in Ohio. Because Jacob Hauptly lived with them for many years, much of their day-to-day activities are recorded in his diaries. John worked for Hauptly in the cattle business during the early 1870s but by 1880 worked as a filer in the mill. The diaries record the children's bouts with measles, family entertainments (*walked out to the spit with the children*). Occasionally some of the family would go to Seattle with Jake.

Maggie was married Sept. 20, 1873 at Seabeck to S. H. Davis and Hauptly wrote: *"John was going to stop it at noon. Davis had never asked him for the girl."* After the wedding, everyone went to a dance where there was *"plenty wine and whiskey. There was also a fight last night after the dance. Half drunk all day."*

The second eldest daughter, Ellen, was married to Eric August Sanders aboard the company-owned steamer *Colfax* Dec. 5, 1874 by Rev. John Damon. In June 1875 their first child was born at Seabeck. The couple is closely associated with the history of Restoration Point, Bainbridge Island, where they owned a farm. Hauptly and Sanders considered a partnership at one time but it did not materialize.

Ninemire sons, George (B. circa 1861 Missouri) and Pressley (B. circa 1867 Washington) worked for Jake. In early 1881 George took a job at the mill, but had one of his fingers badly torn by the trimmers' saw, so he went back to work for Jake.

Belle (B. circa 1864 Washington) was a favorite of Jake's. On March 29, 1878, he wrote: *Belle has a bow now days - 14 years old*. Two months later, she had a piano. *Cost $425.* Two days after Christmas, Jake took Belle on steamer *Patrick* for Port Gamble and then on the *Alida* to Port Madison, then to Seattle. After a night in Seattle (Belle stayed with Miss McNott) and Jake spent *considerable money*, they were off for Port Blakely to visit Gus and Ella. On July 25, 1883 Jake wrote: *Belle Ninemire was to marry today. No go.* Two years later, at age 24, she was still living at home and single. She was married, eventually, to

William Deverol, one of the owners of the Port Hadlock barber shop and said to be a *remittance man* from a wealthy English family. They later lived in Everett.

Mary and John Ninemire appear in the Port Hadlock census in 1889 [55] as do Margaret and Simon H. Davis and their children. Belle may be living with the Baker children during this census.

---

[55] Jefferson County Historical Society.

Book Two

Summer

A person was pounding again a cedar tree and Dokibatt asked him what he wished to do.

The reply was, "To break or split the tree."

Dokibatt said, "You may stop and go away and I will help you."

As the person went, wings came to him, also a long bill and a strong head and he became the woodpecker.

Rev. Myron Eells,
T he Twana, Chemakum and Klallam Indians of Washington Territory.

The Mill

Of course they'd seen white men and their great ships before, but somehow this was different. They'd anchored just off the spit and men were coming ashore . . . pointing, and shouting . . . and looking around as if perhaps other humans might be watching them.

What did these new men know of the natives other than what the newspapers in the East and San Francisco had printed. An 1852 account said that the Indians were not troublesome[1] but, the reporter claimed the Indians "*still, and rightfully too, consider themselves as the bonafide owners of the soil. They look with jealous eye upon the daily encroachments of the whites and regard with increasing and ominous distrust, the oft repeated and oft broken promises held out to them that their lands would be purchased under treaties by our government. It is a deplorable fact that up to this moment no step has been taken towards the accomplishment of this most desirable and necessary object.*"

Marshall Blinn believed that these were aboriginal to be reckoned with. Hadn't he seen first-hand the wrath brought by these natives while the bark *Brontes* was loading piles at Seattle on Jan. 26, 1856. The Indians made a savage attack on the village and he was obliged to suspend operations for two weeks to give shelter to the terror-stricken people.[2]

All of these millmen carried guns even though they'd been assured by the men at Port Gamble that these were peaceful people. In fact three of the seven partners in this new mill had been at Port Gamble during the Indian uprisings. The problems there were created by Northern Indians on a killing spree in Puget Sound waters. The first man of the United States Navy to die in action in the Pacific, Gustavus Engle-

brecht, had peered over a log to look at the results of his last shot. He was the only non-native casualty at the *battle* of Port Gamble, Nov. 20, 1856. The death toll was higher for the Indians: 27 killed, 21 injured.[3]

Glowing reports had been furnished newspapers from coast to coast about the virgin wilderness of the Puget Sound area. The editor of *The Pacific*, published in San Francisco, said in 1852: *"The vast forest encircling the shores of The Sound will long afford employment for the lumbermen while the wants of the present population are such as to render more attention to agriculture, a prime necessity in this part of the Territory."*

Construction of the mill probably started in April 1857 with the arrival of lumber and structural timbers from Port Ludlow.[4] Now as the workers listened to Marshall Blinn, delegating his unending authority and clout, some wondered if this isolated area could bring them the prosperity promised by newspaper ads in San Francisco. Their ship was laden with the most common necessities of life: flour, butter, cornmeal, lard, dried fruit, and medicines, all furnishings necessary for every day living, as well as used mill equipment was aboard. Many of the early Northwest mill workers were '49ers who now didn't have *"enough to buy a humming bird."*[5]

Many had lost their money among the sin houses of San Francisco where the ladies wore more in rich accouterments than the down and out who were heading North.

Marshall Blinn held his head a little higher and was much stuffier than the others in the group. Born in Dresden Mills on Maine's rocky coast, he was achieving some

---

[1]*Columbian.* Sept. 11, 1852.

[2]E. W. Wright (editor), *Lewis & Dryden's Marine History of the Pacific Northwest.* Superior Publishing Co., Seattle, 1967. P. 61.

[3]CMDR Samuel Swartout report to Secretary of the Navy, Nov. 22, 1856.

[4]Washington Mill Company Daybook. Feb. 8, 1857-July 23, 1858, P. 22. Washington Mill Company Papers, University of Washington, Seattle.

[5]*Puget Sound Courier.* May 19, 1855.

financial prosperity and success in San Francisco.

Adams, Blinn and Company was founded in San Francisco during 1856 as a lumber marketing firm. Major stockholders in that firm were Blinn, his brother, Samuel P. Blinn, William J. Adams and James N. Prescott.

Washington Mill Company was founded to produce lumber for the parent firm. It was comprised of the four Adams, Blinn and Company partners plus three other experienced mill men who each held a 1/8 share in the mill company.[6]

Hill Harmon, Minority Mill Owner and Prominent Pioneer

Of the three new partners in the Washington Mill Company, the man most experienced in the forests and waters of the Pacific Northwest was Hill Harmon. Harmon had come to the area at least by 1851 marking him as the most experienced man in the hardships of life here. With a group of other childhood and family friends from East Machias, he assisted in constructing the mill at Port Gamble in 1853.

Lying in the muck of Seabeck's harbor are the remains of the old Pacific Mail Line's sidewheel steamer, *Oregon,* converted to a bark by Washington Mill Company. At least we know her last resting place, but not that of one of its earliest passengers, Hill Harmon (B. Aug.12, 1823, Hadley Lake, East Machias, Maine; D. Oct. 26, 1899 Steilacoom). Harmon contributed to the history of the Pacific Northwest as much as anyone, yet history books ignore this multi-faceted man. He died a pauper and the Steilacoom Masonic Lodge paid $2 for transporting his body to its final resting place.

He came to the west coast on one of two voyages. Perhaps he left East Machias with friends Frederic Talbot, Andrew Pope and J. P. Keller, leaving New York Oct. 16, 1849 on the steamship *Ohio.* After crossing the Isthmus of Panama on foot, they

boarded *Oregon* and sailed into San Francisco Dec. 1[7] with a salvo of guns.

The three men were accompanied by four house carpenters and the intent of the long voyage was to help construct San Francisco buildings. By January Pope and Talbot had gone into the lumber business, leasing a beach lot, receiving lumber on commission.

If Harmon didn't arrive in San Francisco with Pope, Talbot and Keller, he did arrive on the brig *Oriental,* March 3, 1850 with passengers and the crew of Capt. William Chaloner Talbot.

In the census of 1850, Hill was keeping a hotel in Oregon City, Oregon. The following year he "fell in" with Luther Collins, Henry Van Asselt, and Jacob and

*(Photo Courtesy
Phyllis Howard Jones)*

Samuel Maples, early Tacoma and Seattle pioneers, and came to Puget Sound country.[8] After looking around, he returned to San Francisco on board Capt. Lafayette Balch's vessel, *Demaris Cove* during October 1851[9]. Balch was related to the Talbots by marriage and had often stopped

[6]Thomas Frederick Gedosch. *Seabeck, 1857-1886: The History of a Company Town,* Master's Thesis, University of Washington, 1967.

[7]*Machias Valley News Observer.* Dec. 18, 1991.

[8]Clinton Snowden. *A History of Washington. Century History Company, New York, 1909. Vol. III, P. 104.*

[9]Gedosch.

at East Machias to pick up lumber.[10] Balch also owned the store at Steilacoom and it was he who sold the first cargo of lumber to Pope and Talbot in February 1850. By 1851, 10 or 12 vessels were plying between The Sound and San Francisco bringing piling and hand-made shakes. For economic purposes, Pope and Talbot decided to set up a mill, which they did, at Port Gamble, then known as Teekalet. Before making this move, Pope and Talbot decided to return to Machias for their families. The stay lasted 18 months.[11]   It was at this time, that Harmon returned to East Machias, bringing out his wife, Bathalina (Clendennin) (B. Jan. 5, 1828 St. Stephen, NB; D. Dec. 11, 1876 Steilacoom) and children, Edward G, and Olive.

Harmon helped his East Machias friends set up the mill at Port Gamble and moved to Whidbey Island where he worked getting out logs for the company. It was Harmon who found Col. Isaac Ebey's headless body Aug. 12, 1857 and it was his home where the Ebey neighbors took refuge. Bathalina, pregnant with Emma, sought safety at Port Gamble with friends and family there. Emma was born Sept. 23, 1857 and was recognized as the first born non-Indian child at Port Gamble.

It was perhaps because of his knowledge of the area and the skills needed to set up a milling operation that he was invited to join the new firm, establishing the new mill on Scabock bay.

Later Harmon moved to Steilacoom where he was assigned 160 acres as a pre-emption claim. He continued logging and was proprietor of the Pacific Hotel, Olympia. When the Territory purchased land from the Federal Government at the abandoned Fort Steilacoom, Hill became the first superintendent of the Insane Asylum of Washington Territory for a five year contract to "clothe and keep" the Territory's mental patients.

He was permitted to occupy the Fort Steilacoom property, rent-free, and to use the labor of patients able to work. Reports of

brutality and ill treatment became so prevalent under Harmon that an investigation was ordered. Harmon's contract was terminated.[12]

Harmon's first wife, Olive, died in East Machias April 22, 1845, ten months after their marriage. A year later on April 21, 1846 at Calais, Maine he was married to Bathalina.   Their children were: Edward (B. circa 1847 East Machias); Olive C. (B. circa 1849 East Machias); Ella Amanda (B. Oct. 19, 1855 Whidbey Island; D. Nov. 30, 1931 Spokane); Emma Keller (B. Sept. 23, 1857 Port Gamble; D. July 22, 1928 Spokane); Ida F. (B. circa 1859 Whidbey); Nanina (B. circa 1860 Seabeck); Lincoln L. (B. July 19, 1870 Olympia; Died July 16, 1871 Steilacoom.)

Harmon married a third time.

William Sinclair

Another of the three minority owners was William B. Sinclair who came to Washington via California. After leaving Seabeck, he worked at Port Madison (Bainbridge Island) where he married Mary Low, that town's teacher, she a member of the Denny party which landed at Alki Point, Seattle's first settlement, in 1851. The Sinclairs are closely associated with the history of Snohomish County.

These two minority partners were later active in politics. Sinclair was elected to the Legislature representing Kitsap and King counties at a special election in 1863 while Hill Harmon also served in that same body.

John R. Williamson

The third outsider invited into the Washington Mill Company was John R. Williamson (B. Feb. 16, 1827 Schenectady, New York; D. Jan. 22, 1892 Seattle), another of the true pioneers of Northwest lumbering. Unlike the vast majority of early Kitsap settlers, he came overland, arriving in San Francisco in 1851 where he worked a couple of years in blacksmith shops, engine rooms and mechanical shops. A machinist, Williamson had assisted in the establishment of other area mills including Port Madison and Port Gamble. In 1864 he

[10] Edwin T. Coman and Helen M. Gibbs. *Time, Tide and Timber: A Century of Pope & Talbot.* Stanford University Press, 1949. P. 6.

[11]*Machias Valley News Obsterver. Dec. 25, 1991.*

[12]*Seattle Times. Aug. 29, 1965.*

established the mill at Freeport (West Seattle). He could operate mills, foundries, machine shops, steamboats and other boats: in fact, everything connected with a sawmill and its accompanying town.

Was Williamson's *invitation* prompted by the *fact* that he owned the land upon which the mill was built?

Williamson purchased 159 acres of Daniel T. Pierpont's "Soldier's claim", land comprising the mill site and land in Section 29. The patent granted to Williamson by the government says: *Whereas, in pursuance of the Act of Congress approved March 3, 1856 entitled 'An Act in Addition to Certain Acts granting Bounty Land to Certain Officers and Soldiers who have been engaged in the Military Service of the United States' there has been deposited in the General Land Office, Warrant No. 81986 for 160 acres in favor of Daniel T. Pierpont, Private, Captain Boling's Company, California Volunteers, California Indian Wars, with evidence that same has been duly located . . . said warrant having been assigned by said Daniel L. Pierpont to John R. Williamson in whose favor said tract has been located. Now Know Ye: That there is therefore granted by the United States unto said John R. Williamson, as assignee, as aforesaid and to his heirs and assigns forever the tract of land described.* [13]

Edward Clayson refers to "Grizzly Williams" in his book.[14] Clayson wrote that Marshall Blinn and Williams (sic) had a mutual understanding where their respective lines should be whenever the government survey should be made. Blinn was to have all the north part of the town site, containing all the improvements, consisting of the mill, wharves, warehouses, etc., and Williams was to take the south part which took in the head of the bay, but no improvements except his own house. *"As soon as the government survey was finished and placed on file at Olympia, Williams (sic) slipped into a canoe, bolted off to Olympia without consulting Blinn and as he was the first settler, he exercised his right by filing his claim as he saw fit, regardless of the protests of anyone else. This gave Williams every particle of improvement in Seabeck; Blinn did not have a single thing but the ship that came to Seabeck in those days, the old Brontes, which Marshall Blinn owned. So Marshall Blinn chartered 'his ship' to Port Gamble and left old Grizzly Williams all alone in his glory with an idle mill."*

Clayson is mistaken and some of his information can be questioned because he wasn't yet living in Seabeck when this incident supposedly occurred.

Williamson was married to Julia Flynn at Steilacoom in 1857. Their son, William (Feb. 4, 1859; D. March 16, 1930 Seattle) was the second born at Seabeck. Johanna Galvin was the first born on Sept. 4, 1858. (Her widowed mother, Catherine, married John Condon of Port Gamble.)

Scaboc Bay was not the best of harbors that might have been selected. Certainly Port Blakely was the overlooked gem of Puget Sound. It was finally settled in 1864 by Captain William Renton who after getting out of earlier ventures at Alki Point and Port Orchard (now Enetai Beach near Bremerton) established what was to become the largest lumber mill in the world.

The advantage of the Scaboc site was that ships could load at dock-side and the lagoon behind the spit was a natural millpond where logs were towed and easily hoisted to the giant saws. Scaboc was also the most southerly potential mill site on Hood's Canal giving easy access to most of the 60 miles of timber standing close to the shoreline on both sides.

Marshall Blinn, Owner in Residence

Marshall Blinn (B. March 19, 1827 Dresden Mills, Maine; D. May 19, 1885 San Francisco) married Julia Baker (B. circa 1830 Pittston, Maine; D. December 1916, Portland, Oregon) and they had one child, Ida May (B. Oct. 29, 1865). He was a shipwright in Pittston and Damariscotta, Maine before going to California.

---

[13] Abstract owned by H. W. Sprout.

[14] Edward Clayson, Sr. *Historical Narratives of Puget Sound: Hood's Canal.* R. L. Davis Printing Co., Seattle. 1911. Pp. 6-7.

Marshall Blinn
(Photo courtesy Olanie family)

At a meeting of the Pioneer Society in Seattle in 1888, Mrs. Blinn said that she first came to Washington Territory in 1854. Marshall and his brother, Samuel, were the sons of Gilmore and Hannah (Young) Blinn and were descended from the first Blinn in this country, Peter Blinn, who lived in Wethersfield, Connecticut. Marshall went to California in 1850 on the brig *Crosus* of Gardner going around Cape Horn in 198 days. Blinn escorted William Henry Seward, returning from an inspection trip to Alaska, from Victoria to Port Townsend aboard the steamer *Wilson G. Hunt* in 1868.[15] Blinn was unsuccessful in investments outside of the lumber business. He lost money in establishment of two ice houses on Puget Sound, in cattle in Eastern Washington, and also lost as Republican

candidate for Congress in 1871. When he died he was said to have been worth $500,000. He served in the Territorial Legislature in 1867 and 1869 representing Kitsap and King counties and in 1875 representing Thurston and King Counties.

Blinn was living on Puget Sound at the time of his death and had traveled to San Francisco for graduation exercises of his daughter, Ida. Note was made in a Seattle newspaper that he died of *"swollen intestines"*.

He was also a member of the Olympia City Council on more than one occasion. After selling the mill, he engaged in speculating and mining.

Blinn may have first visited the Northwest as master of the *Brontes* as early as 1852.[16] That voyage proved to be an unexpected loss of revenue for its intended purpose, but profitable for the balance of Blinn's lifetime. Need for ice in San Francisco impelled the owners of *Brontes* to send it, along with Blinn, to Puget Sound in the winter of 1852-53 for a cargo of ice. To their astonishment, no ice was to be found but he took on a cargo of squared timber, piles and returned home in triumph with a cargo many times more profitable than the ice would have been.

He came again in April and June 1853 *"16 days from San Francisco."* [17] and took on piling at Alki Point, now West Seattle. In 1855 he had some form of residency in Kitsap County as he was one of three Kitsap men (H. C. Wilson of Port Gamble and William Renton of Port Orchard were the other two) who were ordered to enroll all persons liable to militia duty during the Indian uprisings of 1855-56. Where he was living at that time is unknown although it could have been near Seabeck where he supervised loading logs and piling from the decks of the company-owned ship *Brontes*.

Establishment of this, Kitsap County's fourth mill, was a move by the parent firm to save expense of transporting the huge logs to San Francisco for milling or buying

[15]Jefferson County Historical Society. *With Pride in Our Heritage, 1966. P. 357.*

[16]*The Columbian.* Nov. 25, 1852.

[17]*The Columbian. June 26, 1853.*

lumber from the established mills on The Sound.

As well, food was plentiful from the waters and forests. As today, although more plentiful in 1857, were salmon, clams, the giant geoduck, sole, berries, venison, crab, ducks ... even bear although the flavor and texture left a lot to be desired.

As Joe Emel said: *Tide's Out. Table's Set.*[18]

Samuel Blinn, San Francisco Partner

Samuel Preble Blinn
(Photo courtesy Olanie family)

Samuel Preble Blinn (B. Jan. 7, 1825 Dresden Mills, Maine; D. Jan. 31, 1872) was married in Sacramento in 1854 to Helen Goodwin (B. March 22, 1832 Dresden Mills; D. Jan. 16, 1908). They had three children: Fred, Faustina and Frank Lincoln. Flags on the Merchants' Exchange in San Francisco were flown at half mast at the time of his death. Samuel and his wife were buried in Laurel Hill Cemetery, San Francisco, on Lone Mountain and later interred at Mountain View Cemetery, Oakland. When he died he had an estate estimated at $250,000. Samuel purchased property at the northwest corner of Second and Brannon Street, San Francisco, in 1862 and it was held by the family until 1937.

William James Adams, Eventual Sole Owner of Mill

William James Adams came to California in 1850 after working as a pilot on a Mississippi riverboat. When gold was discovered in California, he came west where he was engaged in the wholesale grocery business in Sacramento and San Francisco. He sold out and returned to his home in Thomaston, Maine where he married Cassandra Hills, daughter of Dr. Cyrus Hills. They returned to California.

After fire destroyed his San Francisco warehouse, Adams went into the lumber business. He built a home in Menlo Park on 50 acres of land in the 1870s. The Adams' had five children: William, Cassandra, Sarah, Olive and Charles. Charles' only son was Ansel Adams, the well known photographer born in San Francisco in 1903 and trained as a musician. According to Ansel Adams' office, there are no photographs catalogued of Seabeck.

William James Adams
(Photo courtesy Olanie family.)

---

[18] Joe Emel interview. May 1993.

When the census taker came through Seabeck, Slaughter County, Washington Territory (Slaughter was the original name of Kitsap County) in 1857 there were less than 50 men working here. Seven were aliens, one was a Negro and the others came (mostly) from the New England states. (See appendix.)

Most were listed as lumbermen, although there were three blacksmiths, a mason, one cook, a ship in port, and several neighboring farmers including H. J. Van-Winkle, George Abraham and Charles Bayley. Ewell Brennen (sic) who later lived across the Canal in the community which bears his name, Brinnon, worked here as the fireman. The average age of these men was 32.5, a slightly older crowd than at the other County milltowns. It doesn't appear as if the mill was yet operating as there are only occupations listed necessary for starting up a milling operation.

The used mill equipment had been purchased in San Francisco for an amount less than $20,000. [19] It was a rough, ramshackle conglomeration of structures. Crude bunkhouses were built to house the workers although the owners probably had small cabins on the hillside overlooking mill activities.

By June 1857, the bulk of construction was completed and this included mill, wharf, blacksmith shop, company store, cookhouse and hay barn, all located on the spit.[20]

"It is difficult to determine when the whir of the 60-inch head saws was first heard for much of the early production was required to complete company buildings. Market production was also delayed by faulty castings which forestalled operation of the edger until August; only low-grade lumber could be manufactured without it. By mid-September, the plant was in full operation and market production began." [21]

The edger (needed to perfect the lumber or square it) wasn't in operation until about this time but it can be assumed that the saws provided enough crude lumber to build the necessary buildings giving the harbor and surrounding land a look of habitation.

The first boom of logs bought by the mill company and sawed was hauled here by O.S.Young who later lived on the Snohomish River.[22]

Loggers were key to the success of the mill. Everyone got into the act. Jacob Hauptly, known more for his work as a butcher, began his career on The Canal as a logger, as did Edward Clayson who was known more as a hotelkeeper and newspaper editor.

All it took to get into the logging business at this early date was an ax, handspikes and a boat. Typically a logging outfit would pull up to a likely stand of trees growing at water's edge and start sawing without permission from the government or owner. This landed many men in hot water with government authorities. They'd tow the logs to the mill or put together a boom of logs and wait for a steamer to pull it into the millpond.

In February 1862 Robert Wenborn settled his $2,400 debt with the Washington Mill Company by forfeiting his logging camp located at Fish Harbor, Jefferson County. The deal included five yoke oxen, barn, cookhouse and quarters for men plus all equipment for rafting logs, saws, pike poles, boat and oars and all provisions.[23]

Marshall Blinn had a dozen men heading up logging camps along The Canal in 1864-65: [24] Hale, Whitney, Fulton, H. C. Temple (Fish Harbor) Jackson, Lockwood, Atkins, "Dutchman" from Fish Harbor, Folsom, J. A. King, Granger, Albee, Cottle, Balch and Norton. Jackson, Lockwood, Granger and Norton specialized in cedar

---

[19] *Washington Territorial Auditor's Office, Assessments and Statistics of the Counties of the Territory of Washington, Vol. II (1859). The value of the entire mill was set at $20,000 and this included additional machinery as well as buildings.*

[20] Thomas Frederick Gedosch. *Seabeck, 1857-1886: The History of a Company Town.* Masters' Thesis, University of Washington, 1967. P. 4.

[21] Ibid.

[22] *Seattle Intelligencer.* June 1, 1880.

[23] Paul B. Raymond correspondence. June 2, 1992.

[24] Marshall Blinn diary 1864 owned by Jefferson County Historical Society and 1865 diary owned by Kitsap County Historical Society.

shingles which were shipped directly to San Francisco.

During this early period, Blinn would measure the logs and then put their credit on the company books at the store.

Logging camps became more sophisticated and employed more men. In 1885 Richard Brown sold his logging outfit to the Washington Mill Company. The purchase consisted of [25] nine head oxen (grey, "Dick"; great "Jersey"; red "Bill"; red "Darby"; white steer "Bally"; white steer "Swan"; white steer "Duke"; roan steer "Buck"; red steer "Bright"), seven mules, one logging car, five ox yokes, three pair double harnesses, two grindstones, one jackscrew, one boat, four oars, two iron snatch blocks, one cook stove, furniture, one falling rope, one falling chain, one barrel flour, one sack coffee, 1/2 barrel sugar, one lot dishes, knives, forks, spoons and other utensils, camp equipment, axes, saws, chains, logs and 50 bales hay.

Logs from Hood's Canal supplied not only the mill at Seabeck but those at Port Ludlow and Port Gamble. It seemed that there was a near endless supply of timber growing close to the water, but after it was exhausted, men and beasts moved a little inland, building skid roads, hauling the logs to the water with oxen or dropping them off a cliff into the water.

The principal loggers (worth from $1,000-2,000) during Edward Clayson's residency at Seabeck were:[26] Billy Balch, John Sweat, Clement & McDonald, Bill Fulton, Angus Frasier, John Walker, Hank Whitney, Cam Whitney, Tom Pierce, Ben Turner, Amos Brown, Amasa Miller, D. B. Jackson, Charley Wiggins, ? Kellogg, McReavey and Purdy, Charley Stowell, E. Clayson.

There were several smaller outfits, according to Clayson that worked but a "very few men with one or two yoke of cattle".

By the end of the 1850s, there were nine houses and nearly 20 acres of cultivated land and orchards and several hundred fruit trees in the residential area immediately east of the mill. Water was supplied from the springs on the hillside. When the census taker took count a few months later, there were 278 people in the area, but not necessarily the town.

Adams and Blinn were in charge of the daily operation of the firms although Adams (with a new company partner Prescott) remained in San Francisco where Adams managed both firms, hiring laborers and selling lumber. Blinn lived on-site until 1869. A diary for 1864-65 kept by Blinn[27] records the day-to-day life of the milltown and construction of the company's first vessel, *Colfax,* which was used for towing log booms to the mill pond and towing ships in from the Strait of Juan de Fuca.

Prior to the establishment of the Seabeck operation, Henry Yesler's Seattle mill and others supplied lumber to Adams, Blinn & Company. Lumber produced at Seabeck during this early period was sold in San Francisco through the parent company although there were other limited markets. Because of the structuring of the two firms, most of the profits went to Adams, Blinn & Company.

Millworkers Arrive

A typical story of those early years of milltown life was told by Edwin Sanford Bucklin.[28] Born in Warren, Maine he was one of the few Down 'easters who returned to his home state. Two brothers, Nathan and Eben, remained in the Northwest raising large families.

"He decided to go west. The fare from New York to San Francisco was $350 first cabin; $275 second cabin and $135 steerage. The boy chose the cheapest but he says: 'To think how that food was prepared and served to the steerage passengers makes me squeamish now.' The voyage to Aspinwall on the steamer Moses Taylor *was uneventful.*

"They crossed the Isthmus and were lighted off to the steamer Golden Gate *half*

[25]Kitsap County records. Abstracted 1980.

[26]Edward Clayson. *Historical Narratives of Puget Sound: Hood's Canal, 1865-1885. 1911.*

[27]Blinn diary 1864, Jefferson County Historical Society. Diary 1865, Kitsap County Historical Society.

[28]Edmond S. Meany. *Seattle Post-Intelligencer.* Oct. 31, 1914.

mile from shore. The boy had noticed Donato's comet while in Maine and out on the Pacific he saw the comet's head in mid-ocean while the brilliant tail reached to the horizon.

"He had as traveling companion Isaac Spear, ten years his senior. When they reached San Francisco they went to the What Cheer House. *They had letters to W. J. Adams formerly of Thomaston, Maine and then a member of the firm of Adams, Blinn & Co. who hired them to go to work in the mill at Seabeck. The boy was to get $30 a month and Mr. Spear, $50.*

"Again they took steerage fare on the steamer Northerner *for Puget Sound by way of the Columbia River. Portland had about 2,700 population but was so attractive that Mr. Spear declared he would stay right there if he had not contracted to work for Mr. Adams.*

"The steamer anchored at Port Townsend at 9 o'clock on Oct. 9, 1858. The boy and the man were put ashore in a boat. They had not eaten supper on board, expecting to get a good meal on shore but they found the cook had gone to bed and their hunger had to be endured.

"That was the time of the Fraser River gold excitement. The next morning five disappointed prospectors joined the passengers at breakfast. A man stood at the dining room door and collected four bits from each. Hot cakes, rolls, coffee, venison steak, potatoes all disappeared and when they called for more a man shouted: 'Sorry gentlemen, but we can't do anything more for you until we see the grocer. If you will come back at noon we will fill you up at $1 a head.' Then turning to his partner, he said, 'It's no use; these beachcombers will bury us.'

"They engaged passage for Seabeck with the well known and trusted Robert Larry but with unpropitious winds and tides, they spent one night near Port Gamble and another at Hazel Point before reaching Seabeck on Oct. 12.

"J. R. Williamson, the working boss, jerked his thumb over his shoulder. The two men followed him and were soon at breakfast in the cookhouse. Young Bucklin went to work at once and continued at it constantly until December 1862 when he came to Seattle to improve his education, hoping to fit himself for a bookkeeper. His teacher in arithmetic was Dillis R. Ward, a Seattle pioneer.

"When school closed, Bucklin worked on a farm on Black River for Capt. John Hill. He then returned to Seabeck and was employed cruising timber from Thorndyke Bay to the head of Hood Canal. His cruising mate was Nat Harmon, a veteran with 20 years experience in Maine and ten years on Hood Canal.

"Mr. Bucklin's most precious memory of Seabeck was when his brother, the late Nathan Bucklin, joined him there in 1859.

"In April 1864 Edwin Bucklin with Henry McQuillian of Seabeck, James Pulk and Capt. Sam Jackson went to the Boise Basin, Idaho, seeking gold. Bucklin returned to Puget Sound in November 1868 and spent the winter with his brother, Nathan, at Port Madison. In March he returned to Seabeck as filer in the mill."

University Land Grants

Reserving lands in western territories for educational purposes was a standard practice and Congress adopted a memorial July 17, 1854 setting aside two townships of 36 sections of land each for university purposes. The 1855 Territorial Legislature sanctioned a proposed university at Seattle. A Seattle Methodist minister, Daniel Bagley, and two others were named University commissioners and were authorized to select a site in Seattle for the University and were empowered to sell any and all lands after entering them at the land office at a price of not less than $1.50 per acre. The sales were to provide funding for necessary building. Bagley was accused of selling land to his friends.

One wonders whether Bagley and Blinn were friends and if the charge was true. A letter from Bagley to Marshall Blinn acknowledges Blinn's bill for $418.76 for lumber and also *"Thanks Mrs. Blinn for the gift of a canary to Mrs. Bagley."* [29]

All Kitsap milltowns contributed supplies and in return they were rewarded with the right to select and purchase land at $2.50 an acre, taking an actual credit in

---

[29] Washington Mill Company papers. June 2, 1862.

land for materials needed for construction. Seabeck was credited with $680.34 for 37,869 board feet lumber and six doors and other materials worth an additional $1,397 while Puget Mill Company at Port Gamble had a paltry $62.24 and G. A. Meigs at Port Madison, $6,961.32. [30]

Roads Connect Seabeck

Nearly all transportation around the Puget Sound country was by water. In 1858, County Commissioners passed on a petition signed by citizens of Seabeck and Port Orchard precincts for a road connecting Seabeck with Port Orchard.[31]

The Seabeck petitioners were Marshall Blinn, Theodore Burr, J. R. Williamson, S. B. Hinds, Julius Heneke, C. W. Kingsley, C. A. Mable, S. T. Montgomery, Martin Campbell, George Smith, Hill Harmon and C. M. Marshall. The delegated road viewers reported back to the Commissioners in June 1858.[32] They pronounced the proposed road as quite practicable *"and as a general thing of easy construction and with the exception of a deep gulch about one and one half miles from Seabeck, the road can be opened with light expense. The route recommended is to commence at or near the steam sawmill at Seabeck and to run as near a direct line as possible to the head of Port Washington, thence in a direct line to Port Orchard Mill at Port Orchard."* The report was signed by Marshall Blinn and William H. Brown.

In 1860 a petition was signed for a road from Fort Kitsap (Suquamish) to Seabeck and signed by Blinn, James Clark, Robert Wenham, Williamson, J. F. Mathews, L. S. Harrison, A. B. Young, G. A. Meigs, Peter Primrose, Henry Spaulding, P. Brown, William Severence and Joe Francisco. This was proposed to connect Seabeck with the county seat at Port Madison on Bainbridge Island. The county was redistricted in 1862[33] with District No. 3 being that road from Fort Kitsap and the road between Seabeck and Port Washington. Blinn was appointed supervisor. In January 1863 an act locating the Territorial road from Oakland (Shelton) to Seabeck passed.[34] This would later serve as Jacob Hauptly's overland cattle trail.

In November 1874[35] another petition was signed by Seabeck citizens for a change of the County road *"commencing at the Eagle Hotel and running south nearer the water than the present county road west of the school house and intersect the old road near the burying ground."* The commissioners accepted the petition and appointed Thomas Mulhern, H. C. McQuillian and Richard Holyoke as viewers, those men who were empowered to make sure that the road work had been done properly.

Financial Problems

The firm was in financial difficulty from the early days and a big bridge contract forced them to the edge of bankruptcy. Seabeck could not fill the bridge contract and meet needs of the retail market and Adams began purchasing lumber in San Francisco to sustain the bridge construction.[36] As a result of shortage of capital, the flow of supplies to Seabeck stopped and the millmen had to purchase food at Port Gamble.

The first three quarters of 1858 were an even more difficult time for the company. In January, Adams had to pay freight bills in cash. This was a serious threat to the company as they owned only two vessels, Brontes *and* Blunt. [37]

The Fraser River Gold Rush (1858) drained all milltowns of those men who came to the West Coast originally because of the lure of gold. There was even concern, rightfully so, of ships' crews jumping when they reached a Puget Sound port.

---

[30]*Washington Standard.* Jan. 4, 1862 and Charles M. Gates. *The First Century at the University of Washington. University of Washington Press, Seattle. 1961.*

[31]Kitsap County Commissioners, Jan. 12, 1858.

[32]Ibid. March 15, 1858.

[33]Ibid. May 5-6, 1862.

[34] *Washington Standard.* Nov. 29, 1862.

[35]*Seattle Intelligencer.* Nov. 12, 1874.

[36]Gedosch. P. 7.

[37]Gedosch. P. 8.

Seabeck was providing lumber for another bridge and Mare Island and business picked up in late 1858. Other retail markets also drained the lumber yard in San Francisco and a high volume of sales continued through the next year. Then a lack of oxen made it impossible for loggers to move enough logs to Seabeck to keep up with mill needs. [38]

A number of changes were made in the company's ownership in these early years. Sinclair and Harmon took less interest in the operation of the mill in 1858 and established independent logging operations: Sinclair near Port Madison and Harmon on Whidbey Island. Harmon sold his interest in the mill in 1860 to John R. Williamson for $2,000 and Williamson became the largest single holder of shares. The following year, Sinclair sold his share to Granville O. Haller getting twice as much as Harmon had. Williamson severed his relations with the company in 1862 selling to Joseph H. Newell. Marshall Blinn bought Haller's interests in 1865. [39]

The result was the loss of three original partners and the addition of one. Newell was running the bark *Ella Francis* out of Seabeck in 1860 and later that year on the *Brontes* so was familiar with the economics of such an investment.

Thomas Pierce

Dozens of small logging camps were operating on The Canal and one of the earliest was that of Thomas Pierce who may have had the longest residency at Seabeck and adjacent lands.

Thomas Pierce (B. 1832 Jacksonville, Maine); was one of the early Canal settlers who supplied logs to the Seabeck mill from his headquarters on the west side of The Canal on the Duckabush River which he purchased from Ewell Brinnon. He left East Machias, Maine in 1859 on *Toander* with James Thompson who became prominent in the history of Port Gamble where he was a filer in the mill. There was

much contact with the Seabeck area, primarily because of the economic necessity.

In 1860 Thomas was joined by his wife and eldest son. A family history says that Mary Ellen (McCabe) (1842-July 15, 1898 Duckabush) was the sixth non-native woman at Seabeck[40] although they do not appear in the 1860 Seabeck census. When Mary Ellen arrived, Indians wore blankets and feathers. They'd walk into her home without knocking and sit and watch her work letting her know they were hungry. She'd graciously allow them to help themselves as she didn't want to get on their bad side.

Thomas Pierce
(Photo Courtesy Ida Bailey)

In 1862 their youngest son drowned off a boom of logs and was buried at Seabeck. This lends credence to Ella Olanie's comments that there were 14 graves at the original cemetery location and they were moved to the present location in 1872.

The Pierce family lived at Lilliwaup and Seabeck, but took up a 200-acre homestead on the Duckabush and it was here that he logged until the early 1900s. Pierce made yokes for oxen and also shod them.

---

[38]Correspondence Adams, Blinn & Company to Washington Mill Company, March 18, 1859.

[39]Marshall Blinn diary.

[40]Daisy Cotter Hirschi on file at KCHS.

The Pierce couple had eight children (including Clinton, a stepson). The Pierce home at Duckabush was turned into a summer resort which operated between 1910 and 1930. It had a dance pavilion, tents, restaurant, laundry, dairy and vegetable garden caretaker.

Daughter Josie, who may have been the eldest daughter, enjoyed the social life at Seabeck and Hauptly talks of her *"running"* with various of the young men. *"Mr. Pierce is over after Josie, but could not go."*[41] The following day Pierce was still in town, his boat grounded by strong winds. Hauptly always referred to Thomas' area as *Duckaboos* rather than Duckabush.

A sad day in the Pierce family when Mary Ellen arrived at Seabeck with *"two twin babes to bury them. They died yesterday. Were buried at 3 p.m."*[42]

Daughter Annie was married to Asahel R. Burtt in Seattle Dec. 20, 1887. Asahel was a logger on The Canal. They were married at the residence of Gorham P. McFaddin who was identified as having spent years at Seabeck.

Simeon C. Bowker, Bull Puncher

Another man associated with logging on The Canal was Simeon C. Bowker (B. circa 1825 Maine; D. June 8, 1883 Seabeck) who arrived on Puget Sound around 1869. He was a bull puncher, driving oxen and hauling logs to the tidewater via skid road.

He made several trips back to Maine before bringing his family to Puget Sound. On his last trip, after telling many friends of the wonderful opportunities in Puget Sound country, several married couples decided to accompany him. Unfortunately some of them came down with smallpox before reaching their destination. When they ship entered Puget Sound, it was quarantined on Discovery Bay and many of Simeon's "friends" were buried there.[43]

The wives blamed him for their husbands' deaths. It was at this time that he sent for his wife and children: Martha, Joseph and Samuel. A son, Frank, was born in Seabeck in 1878.

In the 1880 Seabeck census, Sam and his wife, Francis, were living with their daughter and son-in-law, Ensley and Martha Doncaster.

Mrs. Bowker died Oct. 15, 1881 *"at 11 a.m."*[44] She was buried two days later. *"Large turnout,"* Hauptly wrote. She left three children who presumably were cared for by their sister, Martha. Two years later "Sam" Bowker was killed in a mill accident.[45] Sam had worked as a watchman at the shipyard but was working as a "millman". In the 1883 census, he was married to "Francis" although no marriage records were found in Kitsap, Jefferson or King counties.

Thomas Butcher, Blacksmith

Another man long associated with Seabeck's history was Thomas Butcher, a blacksmith who came to Seabeck by 1868. He died here April 21, 1883. On the following day, Hauptly writes: *I went around with subscription paper and raised about $150 for the Butcher family. Funeral of Butcher this eve at 5:30 o'clock. Craig read a prayer. Large turnout. A little sprinkle while at grave."* The following day Hauptly totaled the donations: $184.25.

His Scottish-born widow, Christiana (Veitch) was the daughter of an early Hudson Bay Company employee at Victoria. Three of the Veitch sisters lived in Seattle during the early part of the 20th century. The Butcher children were Isabella, Frederick, Amie, Mary (B. Seabeck May 4, 1873) and Bessie. A child, Thomas, was buried at Seabeck in 1879. Isabella(e) was teaching school in the County in 1880 at age 16.

Civil War Period - The 1860s

Events of the Civil War and Reconstruction were followed through newspaper

---

[41] Hauptly. March 25, 1879.

[42] Hauptly. March 21, 1882.

[43] Ensley James Doncaster. *Stories of the Early Days as Told to Me by My Family.* Undated manuscript.

[44] Hauptly. Oct. 15, 1881.

[45] Ibid. June 8, 1883.

accounts but great patriotism grabbed at Seabeck pocketbooks when in November 1862 Marshall Blinn collected $704 from the following residents for the Civil War effort:[46]

J. A. Newell, $100	Oscar Newell, $20
Hill Harmon, $20	Jas. P. Minor, $35
M. Fredson, $10	E. S. Willey, $10
Wm. S. Stone, $5	B. W. Clench, $5
D. Llewellyn, $2	R. Madison, $1
Solomon Hopkins, $1	B. E. Wheeler, $10
George Smith, $3	John Milborn, $3
Edmund Lindsay, $5	Joseph Leonard, $15
Eason B. Ebey, $5	H.A.Troutman, $2.50
J. B. Wallace, $10	S. L. H, $3
Robert Wenborn, $10	Harrison Hall, $5
Isaac Strickland, $2.50	Marshall Blinn, $250
John Gordon, $5	W. K. Temple, $2.50
William Warin, $10	Mrs. E. Newell,$100
J. K. Doane, $5	G. B. Wilson, $5
H. R. Hatch, $10	H. W. Harmon, $5
John Stevenson, $2	E.F.Bunker, $10
John Reagan, $5	Jeff Smith, $10
	W. Carrick, $2.50

~ ~ ~

Late 1860s

During 1869 the first major change in management occurred when Marshall Blinn retired from active participation in company affairs although he retained his share of ownership. His responsibilities at Seabeck were assumed by his brother, Samuel. Sam didn't appreciate the isolation of Seabeck and less than a year later, he returned to San Francisco.

Later that year Samuel Blinn *"bought a double team [to] go out riding to pay for being cooped up in Seabeck."*[47]

During the 1860s, the mill company continued a respectable output of lumber although they were never the leader in Kitsap mill company production. The primary market continued to be San Francisco although there were a number of cargoes delivered to foreign ports. After construction of the company steamer *Colfax in 1865,* several cargoes were sent to Victoria and Port Townsend.

Additional steam engines were installed in the mill twice during the decade with

daily capacity increased to 40,000 b.f. in 1863 and 47,000 b.f. in 1867. R. H. Calligan was operating a lath mill between 1865 and 1868. [48]

Company earnings were good throughout the decade. Marshall Blinn's 1864 income tax return showed taxable income of $31,300.[49] This included income from his shares in Adams, Blinn and Company as well as income from his supervisory roll at Seabeck.

Growth in the 1870s

The 1870s were difficult times for Washington Mill Company and other Puget Sound mill companies as they struggled through a series of depressions.

The 1870 assessment of Kitsap County mills including steamers, sailing craft, mills, merchandise, land, improvements, cash and stock on hand: Puget Mill Company, Port Gamble, $282,387; Port Madison Mill Company, $173,191; Washington Mill Company, Seabeck, $128,186; Port Blakely Mill Company, $91,705.[50]

From 1870 to 1873 shipping volume to San Francisco decreased, falling to its lowest point in 1873 when only 21 ships left Seabeck for the Bay Area. Efforts were made to sell in foreign ports and during 1872 lumber was sent to Valparaiso, Chile and Callao, Peru but no major and permanent markets were established.[51]

---

[46]*Washington Standard.* Nov. 22, 1862.

[47]Samuel Blinn to Richard Holyoke. Dec. 5, 1870. WMCP.

[48]Gedosch. P. 18.

[49]Philip D. Moore to Marshal Blinn. Aug. 25, 1864. Washington Mill Company papers, University of Washington.

[50]*The Intelligencer.* Aug. 22, 1870.

[51]Gedosch. P. 19.

The Seabeck Mill - Summer 1877
Photographer Charles Huntington
(Photo courtesy Kitsap County Historical Society.)

Shipments increased to California in 1874 and 1875 but then began another decline. *"During this depression, the company sought foreign sales to increase total volume. Trade with Australia, largely neglected since 1866, was revived between 1874 and 1878. Trade with South America which had ceased during the recovery year 1875, was reinstated in 1876. These new markets were able to sustain shipping volume during 1877 but in 1878 and 1879 they took less lumber and the full effects of the San Francisco depression fell on the company. Only two shipments leaving Seabeck in 1879 did not pass through the Golden Gate: one destined for South America and one for China.*"[52]

Oversupply was said to be the cause of lumber market depressions. By 1877 Kitsap's mills (at Ports Blakely, Madison, Gamble and Seabeck) and possibly Hanson & Ackerman of Tacoma formed the Pacific Pine Manufacturers' Association. The organization was empowered to impose production restrictions on member mills by limiting operating hours. In 1878 when it became apparent that the association could

not improve prices, the agreement was canceled.[53]

In 1871 a gang saw was installed and daily capacity increased to 50,000 b.f. and in 1879 a special machine to cut ship timbers began operating.

Another ownership change was created by the death of Captain Joseph A. Newell in June 1871. His 1/4 interest in the mill company for which he paid $5,000 and an undetermined interest in more than 6,500 acres of timber land, was purchased by the remaining partners for $53,750. The "remaining" partners at this time were William J. Adams, Marshall and Samuel Blinn and Peter Taylor comprising the firm of Adams, Blinn and Company.[54] Less than a year later, in February 1872, Samuel Blinn died. His interest in the two firms was purchased by the surviving partners.

In 1875 Peter Taylor purchased interest in Adams, Blinn & Company and from then until July 1879, when he sold his share to William J. Adams, the parent firm operated under the name of Adams & Taylor. In August 1879 the company resumed its original name. Just two months before

---

[52]Gedosch. Pp 19-20.

[53]Gedosch. P. 21.

[54]Kitsap County Probate Records.

Taylor left, Marshall Blinn sold his interest in the mill company to Adams. Included in the sale were *"the Seabeck property and all timber lands."* [55]

Blinn did not relinquish his interest in the parent firm nor *Colfax.*

At the close of the decade, the mill company was owned by Adams, Richard Holyoke, the resident manager, and possibly James Prescott. The parent firm was owned by Adams, Marshall Blinn and possibly James Prescott. [56]

Richard Holyoke, Clayson's King Hollyhawke

Richard Holyoke (B. Sept. 1, 1832 New Brunswick; D. March 11, 1906 Bellingham) spent his boyhood in New Brunswick and a short time in Wisconsin and California. He probably came to Seabeck in 1860 and worked on The Canal as a logger. When he was employed as mill manager, the Washington Mill Company purchased his logging outfit. He and Annie Hammond (B. October 1833 New Brunswick; D. Sept. 24, 1918 Seattle) were married in 1870 in Thurston County. Holyoke worked at Seabeck 14 years. After leaving Seabeck, he moved to Skagit City and was president of the Samish Logging Company and sold his interest to Blanchard and Company in late 1886.

He then became prominent in Seattle business, assisting in establishment of the National Bank of Commerce and was elected its first president. He built the Holyoke Block in Seattle in 1889 and it still stands at the corner of 1st and Marion. They had two children, Richard, Jr. (B. June 1873 Seabeck) and Marion. [57] Marion died when she was 13. The family moved to Seattle April 11, 1883. [58]

Years later a relative talked about Richard, Jr.: *"When Holyoke (Sr.) died, he left his money in trust for his son as the kid*

was feeble-minded. In 1928-29, the Raymonds began to wonder about the only survivor of the family and decided to visit him. When they found him, he was living in a run-down apartment room, eating only corn flakes. All his money was gone and he'd never worked. He died shortly after that." [59]

Prosperous 1880s

Despite low prices, dull trade and a restricted market base, the two companies were prosperous earning income from the company store, lumber sales at the dock and operations of *Colfax.*

During the 1880s, shipments continued, primarily to California although foreign trade was sought during the early years of the decade.

Fire struck the California plant of Adams, Blinn & Company and the planing mill there was destroyed at a loss of *"several hundred thousand dollars."* This combined with the loss of two company vessels were serious financial blows. All the mill people were talking about it and the *Seattle Daily Intelligencer* reported: *"Seabeck running but eight hours. Things are dull there. No ships in town. Ten or twelve men are employed on a ship being built there."* [60]

The following month, *The Intelligencer's* "stringer" (signed SMT) reported that the mill was running 2/3 time. "Stringers" would send news to the local newspapers about their communities. *Oregon* and *Dublin* were in port and the *Dublin* was up on the beach for cleaning. *Colfax* was being repaired.

Valentine's Day had been a huge success: *"Young ladies and gentlemen gay as ever. On Saturday they had a kissing bee. Girls objected to mustaches and promised to exclude them from next parties. Thus far, 13 mustaches have been sacrificed."* [61]

In March, news was received that the bark *Oregon*, lumber laden from Seabeck, collided with *Germania. Only her cargo kept*

[55]Marshall Blinn to Richard Holyoke. May 20, 1876. WMCP.

[56]Gedosch. P. 24.

[57]Bagley, Clarence. *History of Seattle.* Vol. 3, Pg. 21.

[58]Hauptly diaries. April 11, 1883.

[59]Paul B. Raymond interview, June 1992.

[60]*Seattle Intelligencer.* Jan. 31, 1880.

[61] *Seattle Intelligencer.* Feb. 25, 1880.

her afloat.[62] She was towed back to Seabeck for repairs, but damage was too extensive. The last vestige of *Oregon* lies in the mud north of the Seabeck dock.

There was a shipbuilding boon in the spring of 1880 and a jig saw adapted for cutting ship frames was installed, the only one north of San Francisco. Fifty extra ship's carpenters arrived from San Francisco to work on three ships under construction.

That same summer, *The Intelligencer* called Seabeck *"The liveliest milling town on the Sound."* [63] The article must have been written by the president of the local Chamber of Commerce or Ed Clayson. It was lively though on Aug. 21, 1880 when occurred the double launching of *Eva* and *Olympus.* (See shipbuilding chapter.) Excursionists from all over The Sound came to town, 80 alone from Port Gamble. There were four ships loading for lumber at the time.

Many of the excursionists stayed the night for the free dance given by the mill company in a pavilion erected for the occasion. The description of Seabeck from that day:

"The sawmill, store, cookhouse, wharves and warehouses are on a spit or beach island, between which and the mainland is a long, narrow channel which the logs are floated up to the mill. Across this channel, the town is built which consists of the shipyard, Howard's Hotel, 20 or 30 family cottages with gardens and as many cabins for the unmarried men. It is laid out uniformly and is quite a pretty town.

"The mill cuts about 75,000 (board feet) of lumber every working day of 12 hours. The mill has recently been added to and is now L shaped, the added arm being intended principally for the getting out of ship timbers for which purpose it has been provided with machinery of a character superior to anything of the kind elsewhere to be found on The Sound. Of the mill, Mr. Hewitt is foreman, while Mr. Raymond is bookkeeper of the whole establishment, Mr.

Holyoke superintendent and Mr. W. J. Adams of San Francisco its sole owner."

George Raymond, Holyokes' Brother-in-Law, Arrives

George F. Raymond, according to his grandson, was *"an outgoing man, a trait probably inherited from his father. In 1881 at age 33 he was elected to one term in the Territorial legislature meeting in Olympia as a Republican representative for King and Kitsap counties. Details of what he may have accomplished as a lawmaker are not known except for one bill which passed the Territorial House with his help: HB70 'an act to confer the right of suffrage on women citizens of the Territory'. The bill failed when the Upper House failed to pass the bill. He had a keen wit, lively sense of humor, traits passed on to his children."* [64]

George (B. Sept. 27, 1848 Woodstock, New Brunswick; D. Jan. 21, 1916 Bellingham), his wife, Celia Hammond (B. circa 1852; D. March 6, 1929 Bellingham) and daughter, Annie, left New Brunswick and came across the country by Railroad in 1875, arriving in San Francisco. What few household goods they had came around Cape Horn.

He came to Seabeck on *Cassandra Adams* at the request of his brother-in-law to work as manager of the Washington Mill Company store. Mrs. Raymond arrived on *Oregon* Feb. 25. 1877.[65] With Holyoke as superintendent of the mill, Raymond received valuable business experience as an accountant and manager of the Washington Mill Company office. Celia Raymond and Annie Holyoke were sisters.

Two sons were born to the couple while in Seabeck: Frederick R. (B.1877) and Charles (B. 1880). Another son, Willie, died in 1880 and Charles died young. It is believed they are buried in Seattle. Three more sons were born in Seattle: Harrison (1883), Chester (1886) and Laurence (1893).

When the Raymonds tired of the rugged life in the milltown in 1880, they packed their belongings and took a steamer

---

[62]*Seattle Intelligencer.* April 8, 1880.

[63]*Seattle Intelligencer.* July 27, 1880.

[64]Raymond interview.

[65]Hauptly diaries. Feb. 26, 1877.

to Seattle where he began his career as a merchant in the boot and shoe business located at 705 Front Street in one of Seattle's first masonry buildings. He was a partner in Treen & Raymond[66], Boots and Shoes. When Treen sold his shares to George, the business became known as Raymond Shoe Company.

C. T. Conover writing in his column "Just Cogitating" said that "as long as they were in business, that was where I bought my shoes."[67]

The couple were strong Baptists, teetotalers, non smokers and active supporters of YMCA. Raymond was elected mayor of Bellingham and began his term Jan. 4, 1916. He died 17 days later.

Their great grandson said that the Raymonds tried to preserve moral spirit of Seabeck. He thought that they really hated it at Seabeck.[68]

In July 1881 it was estimated that Seabeck could produce 80,000 b.f. of lumber daily while Port Gamble handled 200,000', Port Madison, 100,000' and Port Blakely, the same.

On September 14, 1881 the town lost its pride, *Olympus,* built on the beach in 1880. It burned at sea. Three passengers were aboard: Mr. and Mrs. Thomas Lewis and Guy Phinney of Port Ludlow. Phinney saved his valise with the celebrated recipe of *"Swamp Angel's Rheumatic Cure",* the only sure cure for rheumatism in all its forms. Phinney guaranteed the cure and would forfeit $100 to any one taking *"Swamp Angel's Rheumatic Cure",* according to directions, who was not cured. He sold the recipe to the SARC Management Company, Seattle, by 1885.[69]

Newspaper men called on the town annually. In an 1882 story[70] note was taken of an orchard blight, common elsewhere on Puget Sound which was destroying the leaves of apple trees and smaller boughs as

if scorched by fire. It was believe that it was caused by a small green fly.

An increasing demand for more lumber production was announced and the need for three or four additional employees. This was the first mention of erecting a new mill and then Seabeck would have a total daily capacity of 120,000 b.f. per day. The new mill was begun in February 1883 and completed in March 1884. The new facility had a daily capacity of nearly 100,000 board feet. The head saw of the mill was a gang saw of 50 blades, 50 inches long.[71].

Even San Francisco newspapermen took advantage of their jobs to travel to this place off-the-beaten track. In the fall of 1882, one from *San Francisco Alta* wrote a lengthy story, obviously influenced by mill owner Adams:

Mr. Adams, during his proprietorship, has always dealt fairly with all his employees by whom he is much esteemed and everything about the mill is conducted in a straightforward and business-like manner and the result is that all the work if first class about the mill and the magnificent vessels that have been built here speak well for the timber and finished workmanship.

William L. Adams, son of William J. Adams, came to Seabeck as bookkeeper in October 1882. When Richard Holyoke left Seabeck in April 1883, Charles Craig took his place as manager, followed by Rodney Kendrick.

Louise, a 92-foot sternwheel steamer was launched in 1883 and it looked like the end of shipbuilding when Hiram Doncaster moved to Port Ludlow to continue his success at building great ships in the Northwest.

Hiram Doncaster, Departs Seabeck to Build at Ludlow

Hiram Doncaster (B. 1838 Nova Scotia) came to the Pacific Coast in 1856 and two years later was heading north to the Fraser River gold mines. He remained there a short time before beginning his trade at shipyards along the Pacific Coast.

[66]1888 Polk's Puget Sound Directory.

[67]*Seattle Times.* Jan. 25, 1951.

[68]Raymond interview.

[69]*Seattle Post-Intelligencer.* May 3, 1885.

[70]*Seattle Post-Intelligencer.* Sept. 20, 1882.

[71]Washington Mill Company Letterpress Book: March 6, 1883-December 22, 1883.

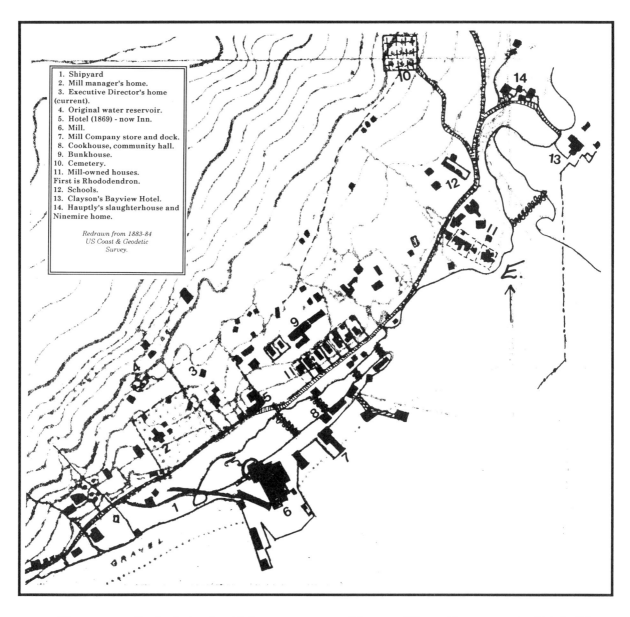

1. Shipyard
2. Mill manager's home.
3. Executive Director's home (current).
4. Original water reservoir.
5. Hotel (1869) - now Inn.
6. Mill.
7. Mill Company store and dock.
8. Cookhouse, community hall.
9. Bunkhouse.
10. Cemetery.
11. Mill-owned houses. First is Rhododendron.
12. Schools.
13. Clayson's Bayview Hotel.
14. Hauptly's slaughterhouse and Ninemire home.

Redrawn from 1883-84 US Coast & Geodetic Survey.

He came to Seabeck in the 1870s to superintend the shipyard. Hiram isn't mentioned again until March 24, 1879 when Hauptly writes: *"Hiram Doncaster arrived last night with a bran new wife!"*

Hiram moved to Port Ludlow May 30, 1883. Tragedy struck Hiram and Jennie Doncaster on Feb. 22 and 23, 1888 when their two sons died.

More on Hiram Doncaster in Shipbuilding chapter.

US Coast & Geodetic Survey

In the summer of 1883, Capt. J. J. Gilbert was surveying the harbor for the United States Coast and Geodetic Survey. According to notes attached to the survey, the southeast shore had been surveyed in 1878 but found slightly in error "perhaps owing to uneven shrinking" and they were rubbed out and the entire shore run in

---

[72]Original topography. Structures redrawn from original microfilm copy.

again.[73] The crew was "giving Seabeck a nautical appearance by its United States flag and ten tents." The following summer, the surveying schooner *Earnest* was ensconced in town "*while her crew leisurely engaged in taking soundings of the surrounding shores.*"

The new mill was not yet running regularly but *when it is practicable to run both the new and old one, full time an average of about 150,000 b.f. marketable lumber (produced) daily.*"[74]

There was a general depression at all The Sound milltowns in the summer of 1884. At Seabeck "*A lazy appearance. Six steamers in the harbor: Louise, Phantom, St. Patrick, Colfax, James McNaught. Three deep water vessels are taking cargoes bound for California.*"[75] Most mills were running half time.

Chinese Laborers Arrive

There had always been a few Chinese working in the washhouse and cookhouse and as servants in area homes. There were a few Chinese farmers scattered up and down The Canal and some were employed in fisheries, supplying dogfish oil to logging camps.

Washington Mill Company had not previously employed Chinese although other Kitsap milltowns were taking advantage of cheap labor offered by the displaced railroad workers. Wa Chong, the Seattle Chinese labor broker, was advertising in 1877 that he had 9,000 men available for any type employment.[76]

It was that same year that Washington Mill Company announced that they were proposing to use Chinese to a certain extent in the mill.[77]

In 1877 a shingle was hung out on the spit announcing "*Ah Sin. Washing and Ironing.*" Hauptly referred to him in October 1878 as *China Wash.*

Up until this time Biddy DeCarty was the town's washerwoman. She was furious. Clayson described her as "a very strong, very coarse, very ignorant, very honest washerwoman." Fred DeCarty worked in the mill and they were parents of two children. Mrs. DeCarty made as much money as any man in the mill.

Biddy did everything to annoy her competition. She even cut down his clothes line and more than once. The mill company was much annoyed and, according to Clayson, fired Fred. Clayson advised Fred to seek employment at Port Gamble, which he did, and when the mill company needed summer help, he'd be hired back. According to Clayson, that's exactly what happened. What Clayson didn't expect was to have the DeCarty's turn on him. From his book:[78]

"Now I had everything to lose and nothing to gain in standing by these poor people, but when the 'miserable ingrates' became thoroughly re-instated (in the slavery where they belonged) they became my worst enemies. You have heard the story of a sympathetic man who picked up a frozen snake in the hedge row, took it into his house and warmed it into life; then the reptile turned upon him and stung him? That was my experience with these miserable degenerates."

Chinese had been imported in large numbers but when the railroads were completed, they migrated to the cities, including Seattle. Through Wa Chong, they offered cheap labor and organized labor rallied against them. Seattle was no exception. Newspapers during the mid-1880s helped spread the hate and riots ensued. Chinese were willing to take any job and accepted any wage. They wanted to stay in the United States and others who didn't want to stay, couldn't afford to get home.

The Chinese millworkers at Seabeck were paid between $30 and $32.50 monthly, competing with the lowest paid workers. R.H.Calligan who ran the lath mill hired

---

[73]The map was copied at NOAA, Seattle, then enlarged, touched up by the author before reducing to its present size. The original copy was badly damaged and was nearly completely covered with symbols for trees. It has been "clear-cut" for purposes of delineation of structures.

[74]*Seattle Post Intelligencer.* July 30, 1884.

[75]Ibid.

[76]Gedosch. P. 58.

[77]*The Weekly Intelligencer.* March 10, 1877.

[78]Clayson. P. 77.

five additional Chinese in 1884, paying them 30 cents per thousand feet. The mill company paid Calligan 62.5 cents per thousand. Their salary was their only benefit.[79]

A grand jury was called in Seattle, headed by J. M. Colman who by this time was known as a railroad engineer rather than a mill manager as he had been known for the previous two decades. The Grand Jury indicted 17 Seattle men for conspiring to deprive the Chinese of their rights. The men were found not guilty. Chinese were also deprived of owning property and the Territorial Legislature considered restricting immigration. In February 1886, 25 Port Gamble Chinese were "expelled", but no mention is made of the Seabeck residents.

Rather than relying on dogfish oil lamps for light, the new facility used electricity. The carbon arc lamps offered better light and promised less fire danger. Carbon arc lighting was comparatively new in the area although Port Blakely Mill had been utilizing it since the previous year.[80] Both mills operated simultaneously for a week when the old mill shut down. It remained intact, apparently, according to Gedosch, as a supplement should demand for lumber exceed the capabilities of the new mill.

Construction of the new mill represented a gamble by the mill company. To finance the construction, it was necessary to *stove off* payments due loggers and in every way curtail outlays of money.[81] The new mill cost an estimated $75,000 and had a daily output of 100,000 b.f. per day, ranking it still fourth out of four in the production. Richard Holyoke left as the mill was opening and Charles Craig took over management. Holyoke resigned in September 1884 and moved his family to Seattle.

Seabeck's library had increased to 750 "choice volumes" supported by a voluntary subscription. *"A fine organ is in the hall with the library which is over the cook house, the bell rings in a good congregation*

and we feel that this is a model of wilderness civilization. The families are intelligent, neat and very tasty. The boys are quiet and the saloon is the only quarter from which we hear a noise. An old man gets too full of spirits and attends church, but is ejected by a volunteer and departs on the next steamer to be known no more here."[82]

Both mills were running by November 1885 producing in excess of 200,000 b.f. per day. Eight logging camps were supplying the mill employing from 150 to 200 men.[83] In April, 1886 the mill was idle, and the company decided to reduce the price of meals to 12-1/2 cents.

Seabeck weathered the first six and a half years of the decade although Washington Mill was in serious financial difficulty because of poor markets and construction of the new mill.

Times were slow. The mill shut down periodically during the summer. But it started up full-time on Aug. 11, 1886.

Fire!!! Fire!!!

August 12, 1886

Fire. While Retriever was discharging freight she set the old hay barn on fire about 2:25 p.m. [and] with strong south wind and in less than two hours, the whole, both mills, were burned down. All hands worked as hard as we could but without success. All burned. When all hopes were gone, we saved a few ropes and belts. Wind changed to north. Made store in danger. Retriever caught and her whole stern on fire.[84]

Alice (Nickels) Walton described the events slightly differently:[85]

"A vessel was unloading freight with a donkey engine and a spark from the engine ignited a lumber pile. A heavy south wind was blowing and swept the flames to the two mills and shops. The men worked hard all day, but by night nothing but ruins were left. The heat was so great that it cooked

---

[79]Gedosch.

[80]Gedosch. P. 31.

[81]Gedosch. Pp. 31-32.

[82]*Seattle Post-Intelligencer.* Sept. 15, 1883.

[83]*San Francisco Chronicle.* November 1885.

[84]Hauptly. Aug. 12, 1886.

[85]Alice (Nickels) Walton memoirs. 1938.

the apples on the trees in the orchard near the road. It was a terrible day, but none of the men were hurt."

All that was left standing were the three chimneys and a large engine which was almost ruined but repaired and put in at Port Hadlock in March of 1887.

In the days and weeks following the fire, everyone was wondering if the mill would be rebuilt. Hauptly knew that the fire would affect everyone in the community. He had already moved his main operation to the Webb ranch on the Skokomish River, but he still had his home near what is now Camp Union and the slaughterhouse operation near the head of the bay.

Four days after the fire, the Knights of Labor struck for ten hours. Hauptly left town to attend the County Democratic convention. On his return, he stopped at Seabeck for an hour, then went on to Union City and home.

On Aug. 19 millowner W. J. Adams arrived and put some of the men to work cleaning debris. He said that another mill would be built immediately and the workers and families began to feel better. He and mill manager, Rodney Kendrick, went to Seattle and purchased wheelbarrows for clearing debris and contracted for new mill machinery. After the fire, 1,000 tons of salvageable materials had been taken to Hadlock.[86]

A month later, the rumor had spread that the mill would not be rebuilt and that Adams had negotiated for the purchase of the mill at Port Hadlock from Western Mill and Lumber Company. On September 17 Kendrick and other mechanics left for Hadlock to take charge of the property. Adams said that they would have more time to rebuild Seabeck, saving $10,000 and *"The Washington Mill Company can't have too many mills."* [87] Three days later most of the mill employees were taken to Hadlock on steamer *Louise.*

In October, Kendrick announced that the mill would not be rebuilt during the winter, but that they would continue the store at Seabeck. There was a building boon at Hadlock where a new cookhouse with second floor hall for dancing and meetings was going up as well as cabins for the single men. Construction for family houses would begin when the cabins were finished.

In January 1888, *Colfax* made one last journey out of Seabeck taking 30 tons broken iron from Seabeck to the foundry in Seattle.

The Port Hadlock mill was founded in 1885 and continued, after the fire and move, under the ownership of W. J. Adams. The mill was closed due to financial depression in 1907. The mill was leased to Charles Nelson Company of San Francisco in 1910, closing after a year's operation. The machinery was sold to the Miller Machinery Company of Seattle by the Adams estate in 1913, the same year that it burned.

During its heyday, the Hadlock mill produced a daily average of 150,000 b.f. lumber daily. It supplied lumber for construction of Forts Worden, Flagler and Casey. The work roster lists 125 men and the docks accommodated seven ships at one time. Employed were 30 stevedores for loading ships.

Those mill company papers are held by the Jefferson County Historical Society and are comprised of journals and correspondence files.[88]

Families known to have resided at Seabeck prior to the fire who were living at Port Hadlock in time for the 1889 Territorial census included:

Robert and Jane Airey, the children of Jasper Baker, William and Nellie Chillman and family, Simon H. and Margaret (Ninemire) Davis, Robert Hirsch, Rodney and Iva Kendrick, Con Kennedy, Frank and Mary Little, William and Martha (Walton) Little, David and Hannah Maloney and children, John and Mary Ninemire and an adult son.

Rodney Kendrick was manager at both Seabeck and Port Hadlock. No biographical data has been found except from California death records which indicate that he died

[86]*Seattle Post-Intelligencer.* Jan. 31, 1888.

[87]*Seattle Post-Intelligencer.* Sept. 18, 1886.

[88]*Jefferson County Leader.* July 22, 1971.

March 19, 1922 in San Joaquin County. His wife, Iva (Jones) Kendrick died in San Francisco County May 4, 1935. A physician living at Seabeck for the 1880 census was transcribed as F. P. Kendrick and, like Rodney, was born in Canada. Their ages are within two years, comparing this census and the 1889 Hadlock census. There is a possibility that Rodney was Seabeck's first, and only, practicing physician.

Ensley D. Doncaster (B. either Aug. 21, 1850 or 1846 Amherst, Nova Scotia; D. Dec. 19, 1917, Seattle) left home at age 14, taking passage from Boston for the Isthmus of Panama. He, like thousands of others, rode a mule across the Isthmus and boarded another vessel for San Francisco where his brother, Hiram, was living.

In San Francisco he was an apprentice at Middlemas and Boole for three years. He left their employ after throwing a topmall at one of the owners. He was then hired to build a steamer under construction at Lake Tahoe.

After completion of the only boat built on Lake Tahoe, he bought a horse and headed for Oregon where his brother had a ranch on the Umpqua River. Along the way he ran into poison ivy and when he stopped at a farm house that evening and asked for lodging, the family, thinking he had small-pox, made him sleep in the barn and placed his food on a nearby stump. They then ordered him to leave at dawn.

Hiram didn't like farming and moved to Port Ludlow. Ensley later took a steamer to Victoria , then hired Indians to take him to Point Roberts and another group of Indians to take him to West Point (Seattle), finally arriving at Port Ludlow where his brother was working. The two started a shipyard at Port Ludlow, then moved to Seabeck continuing to add vessels to the Pacific Coast fleet.

After his brother left Seabeck in 1883, Ensley continued living at Seabeck. Hauptly mentions Ensley only once after his departure: *"E. Doncaster brought his cow down either to let or sell. Do not want to buy at present. Will feed and milk her for what she gives."*[89]

After the fire, the family moved to Iron-dale where Ensley had a repair shop at Hadlock.

Ensley was married to Martha Grace Bowker Oct. 19, 1878 receiving the permission of her parents. Martha was probably 17 years old at the time. She is referred to as Mattie in the license application, signed by Nelson McCallum, Kitsap County auditor. They were married at her parents' with the Rev. Eells performing the ceremony. She was the daughter of Simeon, who had arrived in Seabeck in the 1860s. The Doncasters were the parents of Ensley James (B. July 17, 1885 Seabeck); Lloyd (B. May 3, 1888 Irondale) and Ruth (Meenach) (B. June 19, 1916 Hadlock.)[90]

Hauptly's diaries contain many references to the Doncasters. On Nov. 7, 1877 he mentions that Doctor Calhoun, from Port Gamble, came to see the Sic (sic) man, Mr. Doncaster. *"Dr. Kendrick is about played out"*, he wrote.

Ensley Doncaster and family moved to Irondale where he established a ship repair shop and "ways" for beaching small vessels and barges. It was located a quarter mile from the new Washington Mill Company sawmill.

Those established families yet residing in Seabeck in 1889 who had been there during the mill period were:

John and Alice (Nickels) Walton, Samuel and Lucinda Green and children including married daughters, Tom and Agatha Lewis, Sam and Clara Nickels and family, Robert Airey and family (he also appears in Hadlock census). Suffrage and Prohibition were on the Washington ballot in November 1889 and indicative of the decreased population, there were only 48 voters in the Seabeck precinct, 35 voting against women's suffrage and 33 voting against prohibition.

There were four Chinese living in Seabeck working as cooks and washman. In Hadlock there were 63 Chinese, all working as laborers.

[89]Hauptly. Jan. 24, 1886.

[90]KCHS. Manuscript.

Those who stayed at Seabeck took up farming and those new settlers were also farming or logging. There were some steamboat men living in town, the storekeeper (H. W. Clarke), a dressmaker, teacher (Agnes Heath), bartender, hotel keeper and blacksmith.

Families Move to Port Hadlock

The Seabeck fire affected, as Jake Hauptly predicted, just about every family in town. There was no way many of the families could stay at Seabeck and when the mill company offered jobs at Port Hadlock, it seemed logical to leave. Many thought they'd return when the mill was rebuilt. But that day never came.

Frank E. Libby (B. May 5, 1855 Whitneyville, Maine) came to Seabeck as a 21 year old logger on August 15, 1876. There was a demand for strong, young men then and Seabeck was a metropolis among Hood Canal towns with two sawmills, several logging camps and about 300 inhabitants, he was later to write.[91] *"Full-rigged sailing ships on Hood Canal were a common sight when I first arrived. There were no traffic ways overland then. Lumber schooners warped their way into port and left with loads of fir planking and cedar shingles for the East Cost or foreign ports, daring the fates on the dangerous passage around The Horn.*

"Haste was the order of the day and machinery soon came in to displace the animals who were unable to cope with timber the size of that."

Once he rowed his boat 15 miles to Port Gamble to join the Odd Fellows lodge.

He was married to Mary E. Green, the daughter of Samuel Green, in Seattle Oct. 21, 1888. They were both in their 30s at the time, unusual for a woman of the Northwest to be single that long.

After the fire, he moved to Port Hadlock where he appears in the 1889 census with his wife.

At the time of an undated *Bremerton Searchlight* story he said that he was prob-

ably the third oldest resident of the county still living. The other two were Joe Pitt of Manette, and John Walton of Seabeck.

He worked in the Navy Yard as a coal handler and was made a leading man. For 20 years he directed the handling of fuel for ships of the type that sailed in Roosevelt's *White Navy.*

Gilbert Little (B. May 21, 1830, Scotland; D. Dec. 26, 1910, Hadlock) came to Washington Territory in 1856,[92] settling at Coveland, Whidbey Island, then moved to Seabeck in the 1860s where he worked at the mill until it burned in 1886. He and his wife, Helen (Walker) (B. Oct. 1827 Scotland; D. Oct. 26, 1901) had four children: Archibald (B. Jan. 7, 1856 Chili; D. May 1, 1942 Seattle); Isabelle (B. Dec. 20, 1857 Coveland; D. April 8, 1920 Seattle) married Jasper Baker; William (B. February 1862 Seabeck); Clara (B. 1868 Seabeck; D. May 9, 1885 Seabeck).

Helen Walker Little
(Photo courtesy Theresa Baker)

Jacob Hauptly mentions the Littles throughout his diaries and spelled their name as "Lyttle". To quote Hauptly: *Sold a*

[91]Kitsap County DAR Pioneer Project, 1937.

[92]Theresa Baker correspondence, 1987-1993.

cow to Lyttle for $40 cash (June 28, 1874). *Mrs. Lyttle very sick last night. They sent to Patrick for Doctor.* (June 9, 1878). *I hauled . . . 7 loads* (wood) *for Mrs. Lyttle.* (Oct. 8, 1878). *George Ninemire and Will Lyttle quit school today.* (Feb. 28, 1879). *Surprise party at Littles tonight.* (Feb. 16, 1881). Two days later Will Ninemire arrived to play in honor of Archie Little who is "going away." On Feb. 19 Archie Little, Erick, George Ninemire and Willie Little all went off on *St. Patrick* and Archie went on to San Francisco. *A good many shed tears this morning.* He returned to Seabeck 11 months later with a wife.

William Little married Martha E. Walton Dec. 20, 1883, probably a sister of John. He moved to Port Hadlock after the fire where he worked in the mill and was an overseer in the company-owned cookhouse. He and Martha had four children (Nellie, Edward, Anna, Albert H.)

Isabelle married Jasper Baker Jan. 12, 1873 at Port Townsend. (See Baker bio).

David Maloney and his wife, Hannah, immigrated from Ireland with their eldest daughter, Mary (Minnie) and came to Seabeck at least by 1878. He was employed by the company on several of their vessels, including the *Dublin,* and when the mill burned, he moved to Port Hadlock. It was here that his daughters, Nora, Margaret and Hannah, and son, Michael David, spent much of their youth. David was captain of the *Toby,* a tug built for the Washington Mill Company after operations were switched to Hadlock.

Maloney piled the *Dublin* up on the rocks in San Francisco Sept. 7, 1882. When the subject came up, he'd always say, *"She's on the rocks and I wish my head was under her keel."*

Cornelius Kennedy, Mrs. Maloney's brother, lived with them at Seabeck and Port Hadlock. He was head tallyman at the Hadlock mill, a job requiring the worker to keep track of the lumber.

Some Families Chose to Stay

Samuel A. Rounds and his wife, Sarah, arrived in Seabeck in 1871 from Fort Ross,

Samuel Rounds
(Photo courtesy Olanie family.)

California, another sawmill town, according to Ella Olanie, granddaughter-in-law. They had four children, all born in San Francisco, when they arrived: Frank,(B. Jan. 18, 1865); Fanny (Laursen) (B. July 25, 1867), Eliza (Francis) (B. Dec. 6, 1868) and Marcella (Luke) (B. April 14, 1871). Two more sons were born in Seabeck George (June 14, 1873) and Howard (B. July 10, 1879).

Sarah was from Boston and he from Nantucket, but they met and married in San Francisco. Family legend says that Rounds was picked up at sea and adopted by the Rounds family.

Jake Hauptly writes often of the family. The first mention was in July 1873 when he moved them into their new home.

Samuel worked in the mill as a sawyer *"but because of his wife's devotion to a medical line of work which was carried on without special training, he also read medicine and was useful to his wife when things were going badly in her line of work."* [93]

"The Rounds did for Seabeck what a great many pioneers have done for other communities throughout this nation," [94] wrote Dr. Esther (Clayson) Lovejoy. And her words were not empty as she went on to

---

[93] Esther Clayson Lovejoy letter to Ella Olanie, April 1, 1959.

[94] Ibid. Oct. 26, 1959.

distinguish herself internationally in medicine.

Both Sam and his wife assisted in delivering many Seabeck babies. She was present for the birth of at least one of Hauptly's children and stayed with Mrs. Hauptly while Jake went off on a cattle buying trip after the child was born.

Rounds was the resident town preacher at least as early as 1877, holding services in his home. He also conducted funeral services and, according to Mrs. Olanie, held funeral services in his home *"especially for single men and the settlers from across The Canal. The deceased would be towed over in a rowboat or canoe and then be buried in the Seabeck cemetery."*

On a Sunday in April 1882, Hauptly watched from afar as the Rounds were baptized in the saltwater in front of the Ninemires house by the Rev. Mr. Wirth of Seattle. *"Large assemblage,"* he wrote.

Mrs. Dagnin went to Hauptly to swear out a complaint against Rounds[95] for striking her son, Johnny. The following day, Hauptly "tried" S. A. Rounds for assault and fined him $5 and the cost of the suit. His son, Frank, was also in an altercation and swore out a complaint against Dave Patterson for drawing and striking him with a knife.[96]

They lived at Seabeck until the spring of 1886 when they moved to Seattle, hoping to break up the romance of their daughter, Eliza, and Henry Olanie. It didn't work and shortly after Eliza turned 18 they were married.

Daughter Fannie was married to Robert C. Blythe on July 21, 1885 at Seabeck by Rev. A. T. Wirth.

Samuel Starr Green and his family caused quite a stir when they showed up at Seabeck, a rather unexpected sight! The family left California in July 1876 stopping at Springfield, Oregon for five weeks, then they were off for Olympia where they stayed for a few days.

When the old sidewheel steamer *Colfax* pulled up to the dock in September, there

Samuel Starr Green
(Photo courtesy Marcel Colp.)

was a covered wagon, parents, five kids horses and all their wordly belongings. No one had ever come to Seabeck in a covered wagon before.

They had waited at Union City for the boat for a week. Another son, probably Franklin, had arrived earlier and had written his parents glowing accounts of the area. Another son, Adelbert, stayed in California but joined the family later.

Sam (B. April 24, 1826 New York; D. Feb. 6, 1901 Seattle) had gone to California in 1859 from Michigan with his wife, Lucinda Melvern Lee (B. Sept. 9, 1828 Lockport, New York; D. Feb. 9, 1900 Seattle).[97] They were married Dec. 3, 1849 (Lyndon

[95]Hauptly. Feb. 9-10, 1881.

[96]Ibid. Nov.17, 1885.

[97]Marcel Colp correspondence, 1989-1993.

Township, Michigan). In California he worked in a vineyard and, after coming to Seabeck, worked for a time at the store but was primarily a farmer. A brother of Samuel's, John Willis Green, walked from Joliett, Illinois to Sacramento in 1850. It took him five months. After an unsuccessful try at gold mining, he returned to his home, then headed for California again in 1852 where he mined at Nevada City, making $6,500. Perhaps Samuel accompanied him on at least one of these trips.

Due to an epidemic in Marysville, California, where they lived, the Greens and two other families left town, slowly flowing northward, all with covered wagons. Along the way they encountered Indians who held Ella and Mayme hostage, exchanging them for horses. No harm was done to the girls.

Samuel would tell his daughters *"A lady is a woman who always thinks of others but never forgets herself."*

The family name was spelled Greene in New York, but when they moved to Michigan, the E was dropped. They were constant entries in Hauptly's diaries, perhaps recorded more often than any of the other inhabitants of Seabeck. Sam relied on his sons for income and supplemented that by working his own land.

Hauptly has many entries, using just the name "Green". It is believed that these references are to Frank Green. Hauptly writes: *Green sawed his hand so bad, had two fingers taken off.*

Frank learned the butchering trade from Jake and earning $30 a month. In July 1877 Hauptly writes: *Green had a breakdown. The pony throwed him while after sheep.* A few days later, he wrote: *Green played himself out. He is getting "cultus". Want him no more.*

The Greens built a home *"up the hollow"* in 1878 and then for a week or so employees of Hauptly moved them. When the big snow of 1880 hit, town people were worried about the family and some of the men opened a trail to their home. That land, 100 acres, was sold, after Samuel's death, to the Green's daughter-in-law's bachelor brother, Veborg Peterson.

Two of the Green daughters, Mary and Ella, worked for Mrs. Hauptly, caring for the children, sewing and doing housework. Most of the Green family worked at one time or another for Hauptly. Even Ella Green's first husband, Frank Doyea, fixed wheelbarrows, split stove wood, hauled hay and worked for Hauptly. Ella's other husbands were the well known Seattle photographer, Theodore E. Peiser, and Alphonse Muller.

The Green children: Franklin (B. circa 1853 MI): Adelbert (B. circa 1854, MI); Winfrey (B. Sept. 17, 1860 Marysville; CA; D. Oct. 12, 1935 Port Blakely); Ella (B. Feb. 3-4, 1862 Marysville; D. Oct. 14, 1929, Seattle); Mary or Mayme (B. September 1865 Marysville); Lilla or Lillie (B. Dec. 19, 1868 Marysville) and Stephen Rupert (B. June 26, 1869 Marysville; D. February 26, 1928 Snohomish.)

Samuel and "Lucy" are buried in Lakeview Cemetery, Seattle as are Winfrey and his wife, Christina, and Ella and her last husband, Alphonse Muller.

Peiser was the one who photographed Princess Angeline in 1885 in the pose that was reprinted on thousands of post cards that visitors to the Northwest sent home to friends and relatives. His health failed in

Lucinda Green
(Photo courtesy Marcel Colp.)

1907 and, it was reported, he was "broken in health, bronchitis and asthma having left him in the wake of a severe grip attack.

"Theo. E. Peiser, a pioneer photographer of Seattle and the city's leader in that business previous to the great fire, when he lost everything, has been brought down to actual want.

"There is left to him only the memories of what fortune was once his and what he might have been. Just now, the only possible move, his physician tells him, that will save his life, is a change of climate and Lake County, California has been designated as the place where he should go. This will be made possible only through the sale of his photograph gallery outfit, including many valuable plates, views and portraits. Among the plates are many of pioneer scenes of Seattle, Peiser having come here in 1883. He is at the present time the oldest photographer in point of local service in the city." [98]

The change benefited him as he lived for another 15 years, dying in San Francisco County on Feb. 11, 1922, according to California death records.

Peiser took the cover photo and is the man on the left.

Samuel T. Nickels and his family were at Seabeck in time for the 1870 census with two children, Alice and Augusta aged 5 and 1. Sam (B. July 22, 1840 Maine; D. March 16, 1924) and his wife Clara (B. April 13, 1845 Maine; D. April 30, 1923) had four more children at Seabeck. In the 1880 census there were Nellie, 8, Frank, 4, and Arthur, 2. In the 1889 Territorial census a son, Samuel, 8, is listed.

Augusta and Frank never married. Nellie married Fred Chadwick while Sam married Bessie Henderson. Art married a woman from Tacoma in his later years. Alice was the wife of John Walton.

In Jacob Hauptly's diaries: April 12, 1874: he says that Sam Nickels is crazy. The following day: *"Put Sam Nickles [sic] on board the Colfax for Steilacoom. I come off on her with Samuel Rounds up Sound and took Mulhern on board at Three Spits and all off for Madison."*

Alice (B. 1865 Pitchden,(probably Pittston) Maine; D. 1948) married John A. Walton. That union has produced several hundred descendants. They were the parents of eight children.

A couple of versions of Alice Walton's memories of early Seabeck have been found and although they differ only slightly, they have been combined for the following: [99]

I came to Seabeck with my parents in the fall of 1870 when I was five years old. We came from San Francisco on a barkentine, a small sailing vessel. It was loaded with freight for Seabeck. As we landed, there were several Indians on the wharf, but no white men. I asked Mother if they were the only kind of people who lived there. Never having seen Indians, they looked terrible to me and I was afraid of them.

Our vessel reloaded with lumber for San Francisco. Other sailing vessels plied between Seabeck and San Francisco with cargoes of lumber.

At the end of the dock there was a general merchandise store; also a two story building. The first floor was a cookhouse and dining room where the men boarded; the second story was used for a community hall. We had Sunday School every Sunday afternoon, church service once a month and a dance every Saturday night for the young folks.

There was a small red schoolhouse, also a hotel which was later named The Eagle Hotel, and, of course, several saloons.

Transportation was very poor. There were no roads, only Indian trails. We had to depend upon sailing vessels. The *Kate Alexander*, a one-masted sailboat or sloop, brought the mail from Port Gamble once a week usually, but we could not always depend on the wind. Later a small steamer, the *St. Patrick*, brought the mail three or four times a week. She carried passengers also.

As the demand for lumber increased, a shipyard was built. This brought large numbers of ship carpenters, machinist helpers, blacksmiths and other workmen. Business boomed. A new school house was needed.

In 1879 a new one was built next to the old building. It was fixed up in first class shape, plastered, fine blackboards, a new library and a second hand piano. We were very proud of this new building.

There were seventy pupils but only one teacher. The older pupils helped the younger ones. Our books were bought by our parents, but some of the children had none, for their par-

[98] *Seattle Times.* March 10, 1907.

[99] Alice Nickels Walton memoirs. 1938.

ents couldn't afford to buy them. So they had to borrow books from the others.

In 1881 (sic), six feet of snow fell one night. The roof of the schoolhouse was too flat and it collapsed, destroying everything. We had to move back to the little red schoolhouse which was a great disappointment.

The teacher used to take us all into the grove back of the school to hear our lessons rather than keep us shut in the stuffy little one-room of the old schoolhouse. There was a beautiful grove there where we used to have Sunday school picnics. This little red schoolhouse was in use until the present building was erected, about 25 years later.

The first vessel launched was a barkentine, christened the *Olympus*[100]. The largest sailing vessel ever built in Puget Sound was the *Cassandra Adams*, named for Mr. Adams' wife. It was built and launched at Seabeck. Then some steamers were built for Mexico. One was named *American Boy*. I was 15 years of age then and Mr. H Doncaster, the builder of the *American Boy* asked me to christen the boat as I reminded him of his daughter who was dead. Mother made me a white swiss with many ruffles.

Sailing vessels came from South America, Australia, and other countries for lumber. These sailing vessels had to be towed in from Cape Flattery. As these boats rounded Hazel Point, the whistle at the mill blew one long blast and we all knew what that meant: a ship was coming. The crews on the vessels talked a strange language. Some of them looked like Indians but were very tall. We were used to our Indians who were different. Our Indians lived in shacks built of odd pieces of lumber, down on the beach. Some of the Indian children went to our school.

We had many good times. The weekly dance with an organ and a violin for music, consisted usually of square dances and the waltz. Occasionally supper was served in the cook-house on the first floor. Christmas trees, where everyone received presents, was a part of the community fun. I remember we had two large trees one Christmas. The Sunday School gave entertainments and also the little red school house pupils.

Fresh meat was scarce. The company bought a lot of hogs and turned them out in the town. There were troughs back of the cookhouse where the hogs used to be fed a barrel of refuse a meal. Every Saturday there was a fresh dressed hog hanging at the cookhouse and any of the families could buy pork there.

I was always a kind of scardy cat. I hadn't been married very long and wasn't use to keep-

Alice Nickels Walton
(Photo courtesy Joe and Pat Emel.)

ing house and being alone all day. We lived on the other side of town away from everybody and I always stayed in the house with the door locked. The day of the fire, I didn't know anything had happened and I saw a crowd of women in the road, coming toward my house. Well I thought, what kind of women are they, flinging their arms around like that? They came and knocked on the door, but I hid. But they called and told me what had happened so I unlocked the door. Lots of the women knelt right down in the road and prayed that day.

The fire left many men out of work and most of the families moved away. Seabeck was deserted. The town lay dormant for many years.

---

[100] See shipbuilding history.

Some of the houses were sold and moved away. Others were torn down and the remainder were fast crumbling.

Sam Nickels had a brother, Edward A., (B. 1838 Maine; D. Sept. 25, 1907 Bremerton) who was one of the last of the old-time shipmasters and began sailing on the Pacific Coast in 1860. He began steamboating on Puget Sound in 1867, his first vessel the tug *Katie*. He was master of several tugs including *Tacoma* and retired from the Navy Yard tug *Pawtucket*.

Henry J. F. X. Olanie (B. May 1865 Oakland; D. Jan. 2, 1902 Port Gamble) followed his sister, Agatha Marie (Olanie) Lewis, wife of T. J. Lewis, to Seabeck. He had worked for his father for a year in the pattern making business in San Francisco. His father continued in the business until the 1906 earthquake and fire.

Henry married Eliza Rounds, against her parents' wishes, and they moved back to Seabeck, living in one of the cottages after the fire hoping the mill would be rebuilt. When that didn't materialize, they took up a homestead at Crosby and Henry commuted to the Port Gamble mill while Eliza and the children stayed on the land. He completed the required clearing and improvements on the property.

Mr. Olanie was killed in a log boom accident at Port Gamble and was buried there.

The couple had six children, the first, Agnes, who was born at Seabeck in 1887 died at Crosby two years later. The other children were Francis X. (1889-1976); Samuel A. (1892 - 1958) and Irene Eliza (1895 - 1935) all born Crosby and Henry (1897 -?) and Howard (B. 1901), both born at Port Gamble.

**Henry J. F. X. Olanie
and his bride
Eliza Rounds**
(Photo courtesy Olanie family.)

J. M. Griffith
(Photo courtesy Michael Jay Mjelde.)

Shipbuilding at Seabeck, Washington Territory

By Michael Jay Mjelde

In the summer of 1865, the principals of the Washington Mill Company made a decision to build their own sidewheel towboat. Prior to this time non-company-owned Puget Sound steamers had regularly provided essential services to the mill from various locations on Hood's Canal: towing log booms to Seabeck, passenger and freight service and towing of sailing vessels.

For instance, head winds or absence of wind, coupled with treacherous tidal currents were always affecting the movements of a ship powered by sail alone. Coupled with this, the constricting limits of Hood's Canal with its average width of one-half mile and length of 21 miles from Seabeck to its entrance to the north necessitated the services of a tug for incoming and outgoing square-rigged lumber vessels of this era.

The 75-foot sidewheel steamer *Ranger* had been hired by the mill proprietors as early as 1859,[1] and similar type jobbing vessels provided towboat services for the following six years but by 1865 their role had been taken by the new Pope and Talbot steamer, *Cyrus Walker*,[2] a 128-foot wooden sidewheeler built at San Francisco in 1864 for towboat and passenger service on Puget Sound.

On Aug. 31, 1865, Marshall Blinn purchased the old Canadian sidewheel steamer *Caledonia* for $7,000 with the intent of removing her machinery and placing it in a new hull, ultimately to be named the *Colfax*. On Sept. 9th, Blinn took delivery of

Caledonia[3] and thereafter began preparing for the construction of the new wooden-hulled steamer at Seabeck. Shortly piles were driven about 200 yards northeasterly of the mill complex to provide a foundation for the construction ways for the *Colfax*.

Colfax was to have registered dimensions of 121.6 foot length; 18.7 foot breadth; and 6.8 foot depth of hold. Moreover she was to have a round stern and a straight, "sharp" stem. Her registered tonnage was, however, only 83.30 tons (100 cubic feet equaling one ton) which indicated that she was not to be a very large craft.[4]

On Oct. 4, 1865, *Colfax'* keel was laid. It consisted of one fir timber approximately 12 x 15 inches and had a total length of 120 feet, and it was specially cut at the Seabeck mill for this purpose. The main construction work on *Colfax* was to be accomplished by about ten to fifteen workmen, five of them shipwrights who arrived the day before construction began.[5]

Marshall Blinn was an ardent Republican and was influenced in his decision to name the steamer after Schuyler Colfax who was visiting the Puget Sound area at the time.[6] Colfax was Speaker of the United States House of Representatives representing the new Republican party. He served as

---

[1]Gedosch, *op cit.* P. 143.

[2]Marshall Blinn's 1865 diary. Transcribed by Fredi Perry, 1992, Kitsap County Historical Society, Accession No. GA61-18-1. Pp. 3-18, incl.

[3]Ibid. P. 15.
Also Roland Carey. *The Sound and the Mountain.* Alderbrook Publishing Co., Seattle. 1970. P. 45.

[4]First document issued to *Colfax* Dec. 15, 1865, at Port Angeles does not list her builder, nor does the application for her official No. 5121. Carey op. cit. P. 46.

[5]Ibid. P. 16.

[6]Samuel Bowles. *Across the Continent: A Summer's Journey to the Rocky Mountains, the Mormons, and the Pacific States.* New York. 1866. Pp. 198-201.

Colfax - wooden-hulled steamer built at Seabeck 1865.
Only known photo of *Colfax* and taken from Seabeck panorama, 1883.
(Fredi Perry collection.)

Vice President of the United States from 1869 to 1873 during the first term of President Ulysses S. Grant.

Once actual construction on *Colfax* commenced, the work proceeded rapidly. By October 20th her hull was fully planked, ready to receive upper decking and deck houses. In the meantime, *Caledonia* had not been stripped of her steam engine because, as late as October 21, she towed the company bark *Brontes* up The Canal to Seabeck.[7]

Colfax was launched at high tide, 9:20 a.m. on Nov. 5, 1865, and was then brought alongside the mill dock for installation of her machinery. By the first week of November, *Caledonia's* machinery was fully removed and installation was underway in putting her 85 nominal horsepower engine into *Colfax*. Meanwhile, *Colfax'* deck houses were constructed, paddle boxes built, and her paddle units installed which was finalized by installation of a tall, narrow smokestack sufficient in height to provide draft for her single steam boiler.

After several dockside tests, *Colfax* was loaded with cord wood (called "wooding")

and on Dec. 5, 1865[8], she made her first trip under command of Marshall Blinn. Thereafter she became a combination towboat and passenger vessel for the mill and was operated with a regular crew consisting of captain, engineer, two mates, two deck hands and a cook[9]

No new shipbuilding took place at Seabeck until John T. Connick built the 68-foot screw steamer *Georgie* in 1872. This little 39-ton vessel was specially constructed to provide passenger and freight service between Seabeck and Port Gamble.[10] The glory days of shipbuilding at Seabeck, however, didn't begin until 1876. Up until this time, William J. Adams and his partners in the Washington Mill had been content to utilize second-hand craft to haul their lumber products between Seabeck and San Francisco. Early in that year, Adams decided to build a new vessel, a medium clipper bark, especially designed to, not only haul lumber on the Pacific Coast between

[7]Ibid. P. 17.

[8]Ibid. P. 20.

[9]Gedosch, *op.cit.*, P. 110.
Cary, op.cit., P. 46.

[10]Gordon R. Newell. *Ships of the Inland Sea*. Binfords and Mort, Portland, 1951. P. 208.

Washington Territory and California, but also well suited to enter the offshore trades. This vessel was ultimately named *Cassandra Adams* in honor of his wife and daughter who were both named Cassandra.[11] The *Cassandra Adams* would eventually have the distinction of being classified as a "Cape Horner," a special breed of sailing ship engaged in the "clipper trade" between New York and San Francisco via Cape Horn.

The hull design for *Cassandra Adams* originated in the mind of George Middlemas, senior partner in the shipbuilding firm of Middlemas and Boole of San Francisco.[12] In comparison with other ships of the Washington Mill fleet, she was to be unusually large for a West coast-built vessel with a total hull length of 210 feet and beam of 40.3 feet. She was also to be two-decked and would spread double-topsails, double topgallants and single royals. Middlemas, however, oversparred her by placing a 90-foot fore and mainyard on her.[13]

William J. Adams hired the services of one of George Middlemas' master shipwrights, Hiram Doncaster, to oversee construction of the *Cassandra Adams* at Seabeck. Doncaster had previously built the 511-ton bark *Forest Queen* (designed by Middlemas) in 1868 at Port Ludlow so was not a stranger to Hood's Canal. A 38 year-old native of Nova Scotia, Doncaster had learned his trade in the Middlemas and Boole shipyard at San Francisco [14] and was well qualified to oversee construction of the *Cassandra Adams* which at 1,127 tons

Hiram Doncaster
(Photo courtesy William Doncaster.)

would be more than double the registered tonnage of *Forest Queen*.

Once Doncaster arrived at Seabeck in the spring of 1876, he proceeded to oversee the expansion of the construction site of the *Colfax* to accommodate the new bark. Moreover, workmen connected it to the mill by an elevated tramway which would soon be utilized for transportation of large timbers from the mill to the shipbuilding site. Building a vessel the size of the *Cassandra Adams* necessitated setting up a sufficiently strong foundation to support the new hull. A pile-driver was soon brought on site to drive an additional series of piles on which the enlarged shipbuilding ways were to be installed.

By April 1876, construction on *Cassandra Adams* was ready to begin. Initially the after section of her 184-foot fir keel was laid by Doncaster's workmen, on which fir frames, each sized 24 x 18 inches over the keel, were set up. As the summer months of 1876 passed, the large mass of wood fastened with locust treenails and long wrought iron bolts continued to grow. Accompanying lower deck beams, sized 15 x 18 inches, and decks and planking slowly came together in one large mass as day in, day

[11]There is an apparent difference of opinion in various works as to who *Cassandra Adams* was named after as well as who served as the model for her figurehead. Frederick C. Matthews, *American Merchant Ships, 1850-1900, Series Two*, Marine Research Society, Salem, MA. 1931. P. 56 states: *"She was named after the wife of Mr. Adams and a life-sized image of the lady served as the vessel's figurehead."* Whereas, the photograph caption of an image of the first figurehead of *Cassandra Adams* situated at Peabody and Essex Museum, Salem, states that *"The finished figurehead* [and it is assumed also the name of the ship] *represents his daughter, Cassandra."*

[12]Matthews, *op.cit.*, P. 56.

[13]Hall, *op.cit.*, P. 135. Also *Post-Intelligencer*, Oct. 21, 1876.

[14]Wright, *op.cit.*, P. 185.

Mrs. William J. (Cassandra) Adams
(Photo courtesy Olanie family.)

following brief note appeared:

"To be launched -- The new bark being built at Seabeck will be launched on the 10th prox. [sic]. We are informed that she is a model of beauty and excellent workmanship, great pains and care having been taken in her construction. As soon as she is off the ways, the construction of a new tugboat will be commenced at that place."

Launching date was actually high tide, Tuesday, Oct. 17, 1876. Thereafter, the *Cassandra Adams* was towed alongside the mill dock by the *Colfax*. There the remainder of her spars were installed and she was equipped for sea and loaded with lumber in a matter of two weeks. She had cost $72,000 to build.[16]

The following May (1877), Hiram Doncaster began construction of a new screw tug of wooden construction more than double the tonnage of *Colfax*. She was to be named *Richard Holyoke* in honor of the superintendent of the Washington Mill. Although Doncaster was in charge of construction, among his work crew were two master shipwrights, his brother, Ensley,

out, Hiram Doncaster and his crew of about 30 men worked on the *Cassandra Adams*.[15] Less than six months after construction began, the *Cassandra Adams* was ready to launch. Unlike many square-rigged vessels of this period, all of her masts were stepped before launching and wire standing rigging was installed, as well as her lower yards. Unlike the launch of the *Olympus* four years in the future, news about the *Cassandra Adams* didn't merit much space in the Puget Sound newspapers other than describing size of her timbers and some of her equipment. In the Sept. 30, 1876 issue of the *Seattle Intelligencer*, the

Richard Holyoke
(Painting by Steve Mayo, courtesy Kirsten Gallery, Inc.)

---

[15]Hall, *op.cit.*, P. 135.

[16]Ibid. P. 135.

and William McCurdy. McCurdy was already known as a skilled shipwright and joiner on The Sound, having done extensive work on the old tug *Goliah* in 1872; but in the years to come, Ensley Doncaster would acquire a similar reputation in the Hadlock area as well as Tacoma.

The *Richard Holyoke* was designed with the capability of going out beyond Cape Flattery to pick up sailing ships inbound for Puget Sound ports. George Middlemas had designed her to be a slightly smaller version of the 136-foot steam tug *Tacoma*, built for the Tacoma Mill at San Francisco in 1876. *Richard Holyoke* was to be 115.6 feet in length with a beam of 24.3 feet. In September 1877 she was launched and equipped for sea.

The *Holyoke* was launched without engines or boiler and was initially classified by the Puget Sound District Customs' office as a two-mast "schooner", not a steamer.[17] Shortly thereafter, she sailed for San Francisco. On Oct. 13, 1877, brief mention was made of her in the *Alta California*:

"The new tug Richard Holyoke *arrived on Tuesday* [October 9th] *from Seabeck . . . and has come to this port for the purpose of getting her boilers and engines for which the Pacific Foundry has the contract. Everything is to be first-class and the tug will be used on The Sound in the business of the owners."*

The reporter's statements were true with the exception of her initial service area as a tug. The *Holyoke* wouldn't be returning to Puget Sound for another six years. In the meantime Adams, Taylor & Company would be utilizing her as a San Francisco bar and harbor tug.

The following year, 1878, saw the most ambitious shipbuilding project at Seabeck begin, construction of a full-rigged ship, the second ever built on Puget Sound; also a vessel which would have the distinction of being the largest vessel ever built at Seabeck, the magnificent three skysail-yarder *Olympus*.

This was to be the most important shipbuilding project that Hiram Doncaster ever oversaw, construction of a single decked, wooden-hulled vessel with a length on deck of 237 feet, a beam of 43.5 feet and a loaded draft of 23 feet. In comparison to the *Cassandra Adams*, all timbers going into her construction would be proportionally larger, necessitating 65 tons of wrought iron fastenings as well as locust treenails to hold the immense mass together.[18] A contemporary writer, Henry Hall, wrote about *Olympus'* construction:

"The long keelson bolts were over 11 feet long, and were of 1 1/2-inch iron, a 250-pound hammer being used to drive them pile-driver fashion."[19]

Olympus' keel consisted of several seasoned fir timbers from the Seabeck mill sized 20 x 48 inches and scarphed together to a total length of 210 feet; also her frames over the keel were 24 x 19 inches. On top of the frames were situated keelsons measuring 20 x 81 inches with sister keelsons 20 x 40 inches; thus the new ship was to have an immensely strong backbone nearly 14 feet in height and five feet in width.[20]

Most of *Olympus'* spars and much of her rigging and miscellaneous gear had been salvaged from the wrecked full-rigged American ship *Frank Jones* which went aground on the south shore of the Golden Gate in 1877.[21] In spite of William J. Adams being able to acquire items from the *Frank Jones*, it still took two years for Hiram Doncaster and his workmen to complete *Olympus'* construction. It ultimately cost $80,000 to build her.[22]

About mid-June 1880, Charles Murray, a West coast master shipwright, commenced construction on the three-mast schooner *Eva* at Seabeck. This latter vessel was built near *Olympus* and looked quite diminutive in comparison. *Eva* was almost half her

---

[17]Certificate of Tonnage and Measurement. Vol. 1, Puget Sound Customs District National Archives, RG36, Seattle, WA.

[18]Ibid. P. 135.

[19]Ibid. P. 135.

[20]Ibid. P. 135.

[21]Matthews, *op.cit.*, P. 253.

[22]Ibid. Sept. 12, 1882.

total length.[23]   Shortly thereafter, construction began on a 170-foot steamer, the *State of Sonora (Estados de Sonora),* under the supervision of Martin Bulger, former engineer with Pacific Mail, and William Bell, master shipwright.[24]   This was unheard of on Puget Sound to have three vessels under construction at the same time by three different boss shipwrights.

One of the reasons for this increased construction of vessels at Seabeck was that William J. Adams had recently installed a large band (jig) saw in his mill for the express purpose of cutting out ship frames. It had the distinction of being the only one situated in Washington Territory at that time and it immeasurably sped up the time necessary to frame a wooden vessel.[25]

Meanwhile, in August 1880, the time neared for the *Eva* and *Olympus* to be launched, although the *State of Sonora* was only about two-thirds complete. Hiram Doncaster and Charles Murray mutually decided to launch their two charges on the same day, something unheard of on Puget Sound and extremely newsworthy at all the shipping ports.

Saturday, Aug. 21, 1880, at high tide was the time chosen and in conjunction with their festivity, Adams and the owners of *Eva* publicized the launch on Puget Sound in all the major newspapers. The *Seattle Post-Intelligencer,* for instance, not only announced in detail the impending double launching, but also subsequently reported the event on Aug. 24 as follows under the heading of "Double Launching at Seabeck":

"Saturday, Aug. 21, 1880 was a great day at Seabeck. For the first time in the history of the town, two new ocean-going vessels were to be launched from the place of their building into the sea. Such an event is of rare occurrence anywhere and its announcement was received with interest in all parts of The Sound.

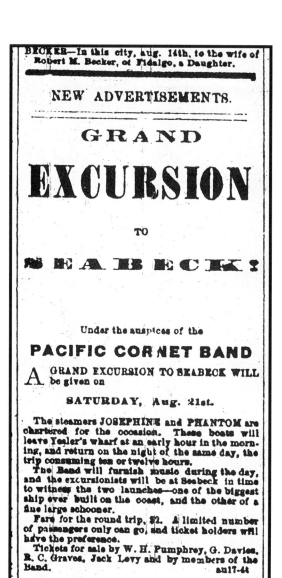

NEW ADVERTISEMENTS.

GRAND

EXCURSION

TO

SEABECK!

Under the auspices of the

PACIFIC CORNET BAND

A GRAND EXCURSION TO SEABECK WILL be given on

SATURDAY, Aug. 21st.

The steamers JOSEPHINE and PHANTOM are chartered for the occasion. These boats will leave Yesler's wharf at an early hour in the morning, and return on the night of the same day, the trip consuming ten or twelve hours.

The Band will furnish music during the day, and the excursionists will be at Seabeck in time to witness the two launches—one of the biggest ship ever built on the coast, and the other of a fine large schooner.

Fare for the round trip, $2. A limited number of passengers only can go, and ticket holders will have the preference.

Tickets for sale by W. H. Pumphrey, G. Davies, R. C. Graves, Jack Levy and by members of the Band.   au17-4t

"Excursions were got up at various points and happy parties taken thither by five boats. Seventy-five persons by the Josephine *and 15 by the* Phantom *from Seattle; about 80 from Port Gamble on the* Nellie *and a score or more each on the* Virginia *from Port Townsend and* St. Patrick *from Union City. These five boats added to the mill company's boat* Colfax *made a larger steam fleet in port than Seabeck had ever before enjoyed. The people on board these steamers joined to the operatives of the hill, the women and children of the town, the seamen on the vessels in port and the ship carpenters filled Seabeck as it never was filled before; the day seemed much like a Fourth of July; the mill shut down, flags flying, the band playing and everybody out in their best rig and looking happy.*

"The first of the two vessels launched was a three-master schooner [the Eva built by Charles Murray] for John Kentfield and

[23]*Post-Intelligencer, op.cit.,* Aug. 24, 1880.

[24]Ibid., Aug. 24, 1880.

[25]Ibid., April 8, 1880.

Company. . . . Her length on deck 141 feet . . . She will measure 350 tons and is expected to be a good carrier . . .

"The other vessel launched was a full-rigged ship that has been building the past two years by Hiram Doncaster for W. J. Adams . . . She enjoys the distinction of being the largest [full-rigged] ship built on the Pacific Coast . . . She is very sharp and has beautiful lines. The Dashing Wave, Forest Queen and other fast sailers will certainly have to exert themselves to keep up with her while we doubt the ability of any sail vessel on the ocean to get away from her.

"Preparations for the launch had been under active way all day and at half past four [p.m.] the men began to get ready to introduce the vessels to the water. Both vessels had their masts in and the ship was about half sparred. They were appropriately decked in bunting. The schooner was launched first. Everything connecting her with the shore was knocked loose and a few minutes before five she shot down the incline and into the water amid the delighted shouts of hundreds on shore.

"Miss Minnie Dagnin breaking over her bow the bottle of champagne and naming her Eva. The schooner was barely in the water before the men began the final blows necessary to make the ship follow her.

"These were quickly driven and a few minutes after five this proud vessel started. No vessel ever left the land more beautifully than she. She didn't list an inch but straight as an arrow stood up, gracefully taking her place in the bosom of the element for which she was made. Miss May Edwards, daughter of the Captain, christened the ship Olympus after the lofty mountain under the shadow of which she was built."

In October 1880, Martin Bulger and William Bell completed the State of Sonora with the exception of installation of engines and machinery. She was expressly built for a firm of Mexican nationals for service in the Gulf of California. However, like the Richard Holyoke, she was to receive her engines at San Francisco, so after loading a timber cargo, she would be temporarily

Ensley Doncaster
(Photo courtesy William Doncaster)

rigged as a three-masted schooner and sail to the Bay port.[26]

Many years later, a former Seabeck resident, Edward Clayson, Sr., reminisced about the launch of the State of Sonora and provided some background in how his daughter, Etty, came to be chosen as official launching sponsor. He wrote:

"A ship launch[ing] in a small town like this . . . was always an event of uncommon interest . . . it was quite a social ambition and distinction amongst the young girls and their friends, particularly their mothers, as to who should receive the honor of christening the new ship.

"Mr. Bulger, the superintendent . . . was to select the one for this desirable distinction . . . At length, as a compliment to her father [Etty Clayson] who was but a little over eleven years of age, but was a pert little miss . . . [was chosen].

[26]Ibid., Oct. 17, 1880. Also *Post-Intelligencer*, Oct. 30, 1884 reported the loss of *Estados de Sonora [State of Sonora]* on Sept. 19, 1884 during a storm near the mouth of the Gulf of California. She *"rolled over and went down with 57 souls aboard"*. All that was found was wreckage including her pilot house.

"On the day of the ship launch[ing] it was one of those very fine days in October. The town was full of people from the adjoining lumber camps and ranches. The ships in the harbor had their flags flying, the two hotels also had their flags flying, and the W.M.Co. had hoisted their bunting at the company's headquarters. It was high water about 11:30 a.m. when the 'proudest man in town [the author] walked down from the Bay View Hotel to the shipyard, a distance of about three-quarters of a mile, with his little daughter as the central figure of the day. State of Sonora went off the ways very gracefully amidst the applause of the crowd.

"There was a champagne supper at the Bay View that night, about fifty guests participating. The champagne came up from San Francisco, the beer came from Mehlhorn's Brewery at Seattle, whilst the chickens, sucking pigs, choice fruits, and vegetables were raised upon the Clayson ranch."[27]

The following spring of 1881 Hiram Doncaster began construction on another vessel. He completed the 155-foot barkentine *Mary Winkleman* in July followed by the 162-foot barkentine *Retriever* in December 1881. Then in 1882 Doncaster oversaw construction of the 106-foot two-masted schooner *American Boy*, completing her in May followed by the 163-foot barkentine *J.M.Griffith* which he completed in October of that year.

The launch of *American Boy* was recounted many years later by Alice (Nickels) Walton who was specially asked by Hiram Doncaster to act as sponsor. Hiram Doncaster told Alice that she reminded him of his deceased daughter, so on that special day in May 1882, 17 year-old Alice acted as guest of honor at *American Boy's* launching. She wrote: *"When the important day arrived, I didn't want any one to see my dress until the last moment, so I put on a cape and went to the launching grounds and was taken up the plank to the bow. Then my cape was slipped off and Mr. Doncaster gave me a bottle of champagne tied with red, white and blue ribbons. At the right time, a signal was given and with the help of a man who had hold of my arm,*

I broke the bottle and the American Boy slid into The Canal. There were no people on board.

The ship rested on its keel with planks on each side to support it upright. When it was ready to be launched, the men knocked the scaffolds away and the ship began to move down to the water and into the water, and gathered speed and went almost to the other side before it stopped. When you heard the men knocking the planks away, it sounded dangerous, but no one was ever hurt at a launching.

Shipbuilding at pre-Statehood Seabeck was to end with the construction of the sternwheel steamer *Louise* in May 1883. Of 91.6 foot length and a registered tonnage of 167.75, she was built for William J. Adams. Hiram Doncaster oversaw construction of her hull; however his brother, Ensley, was boss carpenter for con-struction of *Louise's* upper works which included pilot house, captain's quarters, two dining rooms and four staterooms containing two berths each.[28] After the completion of *Louise,* Hiram Doncaster permanently left Adams' employ and moved to Port Ludlow where he was soon superintending construction of vessels for Pope and Talbot.

All told, in a span of 18 years, the town of Seabeck had seen the construction of five steamers, two schooners, three barkentines, one bark, and one ship. Hiram Doncaster's crowning achievement, however, construction of the full-rigged, first-class ship *Olympus,* had especially brought honor to the little community of Seabeck. It was remarkable indeed that she was built so far away from a major commercial center.

Although a newspaper reporter for the *Seattle Post-Intelligencer* described Seabeck on Oct. 24, 1880, as being *"off the usual routes of travel and but few persons have an idea of its location and appearance,"* the careers of these 12 vessels and their having been built at Seabeck perpetuated the significance in Washington Territorial history of Seabeck as an important Puget Sound shipbuilding community.

---

[27]Clayson. Pp. 93-94.

[28]*Seattle Post-Intelligencer.* April 1, 1884.

Oregon
(Photo courtesy Puget Sound Maritime Historical Society.)

The Washington Mill Fleet at Seabeck

By Michael Jay Mjelde

In September 1857 exportation of lumber began at Seabeck. The ocean-going craft utilized in this service were small in comparison to the four and five-mast, wooden-hulled schooners in use on the West coast of the United States at the beginning of the 20th Century.

Typical of these early craft sailing out of Seabeck was the bark (ex-ship) *Brontes*, the pioneer vessel in the Washington Mill fleet (which at San Francisco was more commonly known as Adams, Blinn & Company fleet.) Built in 1836 at Plymouth, Massachusetts, she had a registered length of 106.5 feet, beam of 26.5 feet and depth of hold of 19.2 feet. The registered tonnage of her wooden hull was 398 tons (100 cubic feet equals one ton) and she had a lumber capacity of about 310,000 board feet.

Five cargoes[29] were shipped to San Francisco from Seabeck on vessels similar

---

[29]Thomas Frederick Gedosch. *Seabeck, 1857-1886: The History of a Company Town,* Master's Thesis, University of Washington, 1967. P. 9. The first indication in the *San Francsico Alta California* that Adams, Blinn & Co., were shipping lumber from Puget Sound on their account other than at Seattle appears in the Nov. 3, 1857 issue of the *Alta. Brontes* arrived at

to *Brontes* in 1857. The following year the fleet was expanded by addition of another vessel, the *Blunt*.[30] Then between 1860 and 1864, an average of 33 cargoes per year were exported, two-thirds of which were hauled to San Francisco.

In April 1865 the American Civil War ended. Shipping from the Pacific Northwest could again be centered around development of the West Coast rather than a war economy. That year of 1865, 34 cargoes were loaded at Seabeck, 33 of which went to the Golden Gate.[31] This was the year that the principals of Washington Mill decided to build their own towboat, ultimately named *Colfax,* instead of relying on such vessels as Pope and Talbot's *Cyrus Walker* to tow incoming ships, log booms, etc. After the *Colfax* went into service in December 1865, she would oftentimes pick up incoming ships at Dungeness Spit or Port Townsend and then tow them up The Canal to Seabeck. *Colfax* customarily received a fee of $100 to tow a ship from the Strait of Juan de Fuca to Seabeck.[32]

The bark *Fremont* was typical of the medium-sized vessels owned by the mill in the mid-1860s. In January 1866 this vessel went ashore during a heavy storm on Dungeness Spit about a mile from the lighthouse.[33] Fortunately she was successfully hauled off the beach by the *Colfax* and the passenger steam *Eliza Anderson*. Several months later, *Fremont* arrived at Seabeck from San Francisco with one of the types of cargoes carried on incoming sailing ships of this period. On May 3, 1866, a customs' officer for Puget Sound made a record of her having on board *"90 cows and 40 calves"*.[34]

By 1869 the Washington Mill Company fleet had increased to eight wooden-hulled vessels including *Colfax*.[35] The largest vessel in the fleet was the *Isaac Jeans,* a 157-foot, full-bodied vessel built at Philadelphia in 1854. The following fleet list was as of November 1869 and did not include the ex-steamship *Oregon* which was being rebuilt at San Francisco as a lumber bark for the mill company.

Rig	Name	Tonnage
Ship	*Isaac Jeans*	814
Bark	*Carlotta*	484
Bark	*Fremont*	477
Bark	*Florence*	430
Bark	*Brontes*	398
Bark	*Jenny Pitts*	552
Brig	*Tanner*	255

All of the above vessels had been built on the East Coast prior to the Civil War and were well past their prime. In the next several years, all would be replaced with the exception of the *Jenny Pitts* which was a two-decked vessel of medium clipper design. The *Pitts* was built at Rockland, Maine in 1852 and had the distinction of being the fastest vessel in the Washington Mill fleet up until the arrival of *Cassandra Adams* in 1876.

For instance, between October 25, 1872 and November 15, 1873, *Jenny Pitts* made nine consecutive voyages between San Francisco and Puget Sound. Her round voyages were 22, 21, 29, 44, 28, 27, 30, 37 and 29 days respectively. This amount to a 29.7 day average per voyage, remarkable time for a sailing vessel.[36] However the *Jenny Pitts* was not just a lumber carrier. This is illustrated in her service in 1872 on

San Francisco on Nov. 22, 22 days from Puget Sound without mention of the cargo being from Seabeck. Neither is it recorded in Entrance and Clearance Records, Vol. 1, Puget Sound Customs District, RG 36, National Archives, Seattle, that *Brontes* was officially cleared from any port on Puget Sound around Oct. 11, 1857. It is apparent, however, that the first Adams, Blinn & Co. cargo went from Seabeck to San Francisco on the *Brontes*.

[30]Gedosch, *op.cit.*, P. 8 and 35.

[31]Ibid. P. 9.

[32]Ibid. P. 18.

[33]*Seattle Weekly Gazette*. Feb. 2, 1866.

[34]Series 17, Vol. 10, Feb. 1864- Feb. 1866, Puget Sound Customs District, RG 36, National Archives, Seattle.

[35]Gedosch, *op cit.*, P. 8 and 35.

[36]E. W. Wright (editor), *Lewis & Dryden's Marine History of the Pacific Northwest.* Superior Publishing Co., Seattle, 1967. P. 210.

two trips. She discharged a general cargo of merchandise at Seattle and returned to the Golden Gate with 800 tons of coal. Moreover, showing that she also served as a passenger vessel, the *Jenny Pitts* arrived at Seattle on September 15, 1872, three weeks up the coast from San Francisco, with two adults and four children as passengers.

By 1873 the Washington Mill fleet consisted of *Jenny Pitts,* the bark (ex-ship) *Dublin,* bark *General Cobb* and the bark (ex-steamer) *Oregon.* Most of the lumber cargoes were still going to San Francisco but an occasional cargo went to Vallejo, San Pedro or San Diego.

These were the days before longshoremen's unions had been established on Puget Sound. The day laborer at Seabeck was paid about $2 for 11.5 hours work, 6 a.m. to 6 p.m. with a half hour off for lunch. The loading procedure of a typical sailing vessel was described in an 1870 issue of the *Overland Monthly,* a contemporary periodical: "[A lumber ship] *is hauled head-on to the wharf, and her bow-ports knocked out; a stage is rigged; the men are divided into gangs; the mates take their stations in the hold --- the Chief on the port, and the Second on the starboard side --- when the work of loading commences. The men on the wharf run the lumber down the stage into the ports, stick by stick, each time singing out* 'starboard' *or* 'port', *according to the side that at the moment is receiving it.*

"The Mate stows the cargo on the one side, and the Second Mate on the other (if a coaster). After the hold is full, the deck load is put on, or rather piled on; for some of the finest vessels, built expressly for the trade, carry deck-loads 10-11 feet high . . . "[37]

In 1876, the Washington Mill fleet became very well known in shipping circles with the addition of the *Cassandra Adams* as a regular lumber vessel on the Pacific coast. On December 9, 1876, Captain John L. Delany with a crew of 16 men brought the new queen of the Washington Mill fleet into San Francisco Bay on her maiden trip six days from Seabeck. Although she had

1,000,000 board feet of lumber on board, including deck load, the *Cassandra Adams* beat every other vessel which arrived at San Francisco from Puget Sound On that day. For example, the bark *Oregon,* Captain William Edwards, (320 M lbr, 200 M laths, 16 M piles) made the voyage in nine days; and Hiram Doncaster's earlier creation, the *Forest Queen,* made a 14-day passage from Port Ludlow.[38]

Following the entrance of *Cassandra Adams* into Adams' fleet, he and his partners decided to dispose of the *Jenny Pitts,* retaining *Oregon, General Cobb* and *Dublin* as regular carriers between Seabeck and California ports. It was strange that Adams chose to keep *Dublin* instead of *Jenny Pitts.* Apparently the *Pitts'* high market value was a factor. *Dublin* was the oldest vessel in the fleet and probably the most decrepit, having been built at Brunswick, Maine , in 1839. *Dublin* had been showing her age for some time as indicated by a comment made by a newspaper reporter in 1873: *"The lumber bark* Dublin *was yesterday hove down until her keelson* [sic] *was out of water, when ship carpenters and caulkers went to work to stop some leaks that had become a source of annoyance.* "[39]

Holyoke, newly built at Seabeck for William J. Adams, was engined with a 125 indicated horsepower steam engine at San Francisco and soon became a unit of the "Merchant's Tow-Boat Line" which regularly towed sailing ships, not only in the harbor, but also out beyond the San Francisco Bar.[40] She would be used in this capacity until 1883.

In 1880 several disasters struck the Washington Mill Company fleet along with a downturn of lumber shipments from Seabeck. The fleet total was only 23 cargoes for the year, the fewest since the mill's first year of operation.

On January 14, 1880, while en route from San Francisco to Seabeck, the *General*

---

[37]Charles Marvin Gates. *Readings in Pacific Northwest History: Washington, 1790-1895.* University Book Store, Seattle. 1941. P. 217.

[38]*San Francisco Evening Bulletin.* Dec. 11, 1876.

[39]*Alta, op.cit.,* Jan. 15, 1873.

[40]*San Francisco Daily Commercial News.* Dec. 24, 1878.

Cobb, Capt. J. L. Oliver, went aground near Portland Point, Vancouver, Island, during a heavy gale and was a total loss. Capt. Oliver described the mishap as follows:

"About 7:30 p.m. the main topgallant sail was carried away and two men were sent aloft to repair the damage. Land was sighted, but before we could get the ship around, she struck. The second sea lifted her over and off the reef and the wheel was put hard up again, but she immediately brought up on a large rock. The masts were cut away and the anchors dropped."[41]

Six weeks later, the second disaster to the Washington Mill fleet occurred. On the night of March 1, the bark *Oregon* was in a collision with the bark (ex-ship) *Germania* in Juan de Fuca Strait. *Oregon,* Captain Sloan, was bound from Seabeck to San Francisco with a full cargo of lumber. *Germania* struck her on the port bow, cutting *Oregon* down to her between deck beams and carrying away her bowsprit and all her headgear. She also damaged her anchor windlass. *Oregon* began filling with water and the only thing which kept her from sinking like a stone was her lumber cargo. Subsequently *Oregon* was towed to Seabeck where her cargo was discharged and transferred to another vessel.[42] Unfortunately the damage to her hull was considered too extreme to merit repair; so the old *Oregon* was ultimately run up on the beach north of the mill and left to the elements. In two short years a newspaper reporter for the *Seattle Post-Intelligencer* wrote:

"A short distance below the shipyard lies the dismantled hulk of the Oregon, *said to have been the first sidewheel steamer which came around The Horn after the discovery of gold in California . . . [she] lies rotting, her sides covered with barnacles and mussels, her hold filled with slime and bilge water, her upper works blackened and shattered by storm and tempest, her frayed ropes and rusted chains and ropes and rusted chains flapping idly in the wind . . .*

A few more years and the last vestige of the wreck of the Oregon *will have vanished."*[43]

Following completion of the *Olympus* in the fall of 1880, William J. Adams felt that the *Cassandra Adams* was now surplus to the Washington Mill Company needs and could be disposed of at a profit. Again Adams displayed prudent business skills in deciding to retain *Dublin* in his fleet and sell the *Cassandra Adams.* In October 1880, Adams sold *Cassandra Adams* to Dunsmuir, Diggle and Company for $55,000 for use as a British Columbia/San Francisco coal carrier. Six months later, however, she was resold for service as a Cape Horner, and in this capacity made her special niche' in American maritime history as a unit of John Rosenfeld's "Dispatch Line" joining such notable vessels as *Sovereign of the Seas, Young America* and *David Crockett.*[44] In 1882 the *Cassandra Adams* made a 115-day voyage from Liverpool, to San Francisco, beating the medium clipper *Glory of the Seas;* and the following year she sailed from San Francisco to New York in 94 days, a record for a West coast-built vessel.

In 1880, Washington Mill's *Olympus* was the largest single-decked, full-rigged ship in the world. She carried an average of 1,250,000 feet of lumber and on one trip *Olympus* loaded 1,450,000 board feet, 700,000 of which was on her main deck. In her first eleven months, she earned $40,000 in freights in seven voyages, paying half her cost.[45]

Olympus' career, however, was disastrously cut short on September 14, 1881, when she burned at sea about 300 miles southwest of Cape Flattery. The *Seattle Post-Intelligencer* reported:

BURNED AT SEA. Port Townsend, September 18. The ship Olympus, *Capt. Edwards, bound from San Francisco to Seabeck with a partial cargo of hay, oakum and oil on the morning of the 14th when in latitude north 47.19, longitude west 132.25,*

[41]Wright, *op.cit.,* P. 279.

[42]*Seattle Post-Intelligencer.* March 11 and April 8, 1880.

[43]*P.I., op.cit.,* Sept. 20, 1882.

[44]*Alta, op.cit.,* June 18, 1883.

[45]Henry Hall. *Report on the Shipbuilding Industry of the United States.* Government Printing Office, Washington, DC, 1882. P. 135.

11 days out, took fire and was burned to the water's edge, despite the efforts of the officers and crew to extinguish the flames. All on board, numbering 26 souls, passengers and crew, took to the boats and were picked up the same day by the ship War Hawk, Capt. Hinds, and taken to Port Discovery. The following is an account of the disaster as given by Guy C. Phinney of Cariboo, BC who was a passenger on board:

"About half past six on the morning of the 14th, I was standing near the aft hatch when I heard the cry of fire. The Captain appeared immediately on deck and gave the order to close the fore hatch, get buckets ready and the pumps to work. The order was promptly obeyed. A portion of the aft hatch was then taken off and water pumped into the hold. The fire ran over the hay and oakum like a brush heap and in a moment was coming out of the hold ten feet high. The hatch was then closed with difficulty, the first and second mates getting their eyebrows singed in doing it. When the fire burst through the main and after hatches, the captain gave the order to clear away the boats, and all on board safely embarked, taking their most valuable effects. Together with the master and crew, there were three ladies, the captain's wife and daughter, and Mrs. Lewis. Fortunately we fell in with the ship War Hawk a few hours after bound for Port Discovery which came to our assistance and took us on board after which we were well cared for by Capt. Hinds and his estimable wife. Too much praise cannot be given to Capt. Edwards for his coolness and bravery under the trying circumstances. He was the last to leave the ship and his orders throughout were carefully obeyed by the crew, thereby saving the lives and a good part of the property of those on board. Before night fell, nothing was seen of the ship Olympus but a black, charred hulk. All unite in praising the conduct of Capt. Hinds and his wife who did everything they could for the unfortunate party and landed them today at Port Discovery."[46]

In August 1882, the old bark *Dublin* made one final voyage to San Francisco with lumber from Seabeck, a voyage she was not to complete. During a dense fog, the captain mistakenly drifted too close to shore and was caught in a strong incoming tide. *Dublin* went ashore with all sail set on August 30 just below the Cliff House. The *Richard Holyoke* was sent to her assistance and even with her steam engine running under full power, she was unable to pull the old *Dublin* off the beach. The following day, the *Holyoke* and three other tugs attempted to pull her loose but were unsuccessful and with the onset of bad weather, *Dublin's* 43 year-old wooden hull and spars began to

Retriever
(National Maritime Museum, San Francisco.)

[46]*P.I., op.cit.,* Sept. 20, 1881.

81

break up. This brought to an end the career of the oldest ship in the Washington Mill Company fleet.[47]

In the meantime, the barkentines *Mary Winkelman* and the *Retriever* had been added to Adam's fleet in 1881 and in October 1882 the barkentine *J. M. Griffith* was also added.

In May 1883 it was decided to return the tug *Richard Holyoke* to Puget Sound as a regular unit of the Washington Mill Company fleet.[48] She was far more suitable for deep-water towage purposes on The Sound than *Colfax,* especially with the advent of larger foreign-built sailing vessels loading cargoes on Puget Sound.

Lumber shipping from the Washington Mill at Seabeck effectively ended August 12, 1886 with the burning of the mill complex.

In the following months, William J. Adams decided not to rebuild the mill and thus commercial shipping died at Seabeck. During a 29-year period (1857-1886), the residents of workers at Seabeck had seen, not only some old sailing ships like the old *Dublin* and *Brontes* "on their last legs", but had also viewed magnificent vessels like *Cassandra Adams* and *Olympus* majestically sail from the bay laden with lumber products from the Seabeck mill.

These memories are what make Seabeck retain a modestly important place in Pacific Northwest maritime history.

---

[47]Ibid. Sept. 12, 1882.

[48]*Alta, op.cit.,* May 12, 1883.

Mosquito Fleet
By Water and Land They Came

Several small sloops or plungers operated on The Canal during the early years' of settlement, ferrying freight and passengers from Port Gamble to Seabeck and logging camps on both sides of The Canal.

The largest, according to Clayson, was *Bushwacker*, owned by Captain Johnson. *Kidder* belonged to loggers Purdy and McReavy of Union City who made four or five trips annually to Port Gamble for merchandise. No other information has been located on it.

William Gardner operated a plunger *Wild Irish Rose* and while crossing between Seabeck and Oak Head in 1870, he was hit by a sudden northwest gale and the plunger was sunk, Gardner drowned.[1]

Other small craft running on The Canal between 1857 and 1872 included *Kate Alexander* (Sam Alexander), *Phinney* (George Carpenter), *Carswell* (Harry Taylor), *Shark* (Edward Clayson), *Restless* (Higgins), *Maria* (Coupe), *Midnight Cry* (Charles Janes), *Industry* (Johnsen), *Wanderer* (Apple Miller), *Abraham Lincoln* and *The Bee*.[2]

Clayson while running his mailboat recalled a six week period in 1868 when the entire Canal was shrouded in fog. Fog settled in late August and extended into October. Each morning it was almost as thick as mush and while the wind blew it back and forth, it never cleared. There were no maritime accidents during this period as the navigators were careful and knew their routes well.[3]

Alice (Nickels) Walton writes that *Kate Alexander* was a one-masted sailboat or sloop bringing weekly mail from Port Gamble *"but we could not always depend on the wind."*[4]

From Jake Hauptly's diaries, the following passenger boats are mentioned: *Georgie* (1873), *St. Patrick* (1874-1887), *Shoo Fly* (1878), *James Mortie* (1878), *Rip Van Winkle* (1882), *Phantom* (1882-84), *Gem* (1882-83), *Hope* (1883), *James McNaught* (1883-84) *Louise* (1884-86), *Josephine* (1885-86).

These small vessels carried merchandise, excursionists, regular passengers, furniture, wagons, horses and cows. Often they towed scows loaded to the gills with everything needed for day-to-day living. Some vessels availed passengers with food and sleeping accommodations. Groups would charter the boats to go from Seabeck to Port Gamble or Seattle to play baseball or attend entertainments.

Colfax

Colfax, built 1865 Seabeck, a 121-foot sidewheeler, lists Marshall Blinn as master when it was registered at Port Angeles Dec. 15, 1865 although Capt. George Miller took over for a couple of months before John Connick took command and ran her for several years. Hauptly mentions going to Seattle on her several times. She was used primarily for mill company business, towing logs and hauling lumber carrying vessels in and out of Seabeck harbor.[5]

Robert Airey (B. 1847 Scotland; D. 1926 Seattle) worked as engineer on *Colfax* and it was at Seabeck that he met Mrs. Thomas Butcher's younger sister, Isabelle Veitch, visiting from Victoria. They were married in Victoria at her parents' home in 1872, turning to Seabeck to make their home. He followed the Washington Mill Company to Port Hadlock after the fire, although retaining Seabeck residency. It was during this period that he purchased a steamer which he called *Isabella* and used it for towing purposes.

[1] *Weekly Intelligencer.* Oct. 31, 1870.

[2] Edward Clayson, Sr., *Historical Narratives of Puget Sound: Hood's Canal.* R. L. Davis Printing Co., Seattle. 1911.

[3] *Seattle Post-Intelligencer.* Oct. 11, 1908.

[4] Alice (Nickels) Walton memoirs. 1938.

[5] Roland B. Carey. *The Sound and the Mountain.* P. 45.

Jasper Gage Baker (B. Machias, Maine about 1840; D. Seabeck March 7, 1885) served as captain of *Colfax* nearly 20 years.. He earned more than twice as much as the average millworker between 1868-1870, his monthly wage being $95.

"When Colfax went into operation in 1865, her crew members took advantage of the opportunity her travels offered them to buy in other communities. Indebtedness of Jasper Baker between 1868 and 1870 (at the company store) was only $43.24."[6]

Once when Edward Clayson and his family boarded *Colfax*, Richard Holyoke, archenemy, came aboard and *hissed* in Clayson's ear that no passengers would be going that day to Seattle. Clayson ordered his son to get a gun. But before a confrontation took place, Jasper Baker came down from the company's office and very quietly informed Clayson that no passengers could take passage on *Colfax* that day. So Clayson with all the others went ashore. *"It was very proper to comply with the orders of the captain of the Colfax."*[7]

Baker sought medical treatment at Victoria and Hauptly wrote: *"He is bad off."* His death was attributed to consumption (tuberculosis). He left a wife, Isabelle, and five small children. There were two children deceased prior to this time. Jasper had been connected with steamboats of the inland waters for 20 years.

In the 1871 census Jasper is listed as a farmer, born in Maine, age 28 living in the Little household. Isabelle Little was 11 at the time. They were married Jan. 12, 1873 at Port Townsend by P. E. Hyland. Isabelle (B. Dec. 20, 1860 Coveland, Washington Territory; D. April 8, 1920 Seattle) was 13 years old at the time and "3 months pregnant."[8]. If her birth date is correct, she was 12.

The children of Jasper and Isabelle were Isabelle May Baker (B. June 1873, married Peter Shibler); William West Baker (B. March 12, 1876, Seabeck; D. June 4, 1907 Spokane, married Maude A. Welch);

Isabelle Baker - Child Bride
(Photo courtesy Theresa Baker)

Gilbert Little Baker (B. February 1879 Seabeck); Clara E. Baker (B. April 1881 Seabeck, married John Phillips); Henry A. Baker (B. May 1883 Seabeck); Arthur J. Baker (B. 1886).[9]

By 1889 Isabelle's children were living at Port Hadlock but she is not in the census. She next is found in Jefferson County (1900) living at Hadlock with sons Gilbert and Henry, and again (1910) at Hadlock with her father, Gilbert Little, and son Henry. Her obituary which appeared in the *Port Townsend Ledger* says that she was survived by four children: Isabelle, Clara, Arthur of Seattle and Henry of Everett.

Georgie

Captain John T. Connick built the small propeller *Georgie*[10] at Seabeck in 1872 and ran her as a passenger and towing steamer between Seabeck and Port Gamble.[11] (She was often called *Georgia* and many maritime accounts refer to her as that.) The ad-

[6]Gedosch.

[7]Clayson. Pg. 82-4.

[8]Theresa Baker correspondence. July 14, 1993.

[9]Theresa S. Baker correspondence, 1987-1993.

[10]Certificate of Enrollment (P.E. No.1) issued at Port Townsend July 2, 1872 specifically spells it *Georgie,* National Archives. RG36. Washington, D.C.

[11]Seventh Annual Report, 1875, *List of American Merchant Vessels* refers to it as *Georgie.*

vent of the locally operated steamer just about ended the small sloops and plungers that made a modest living transporting passengers in and out of town. She would connect with *North Pacific* at Port Gamble for the run to Seattle.

Sold in 1873, she was used in British Columbia as tender for a dredge in Victoria harbor, ending her days under the British flag.[12]

Connick returned to the Northwest in the summer of 1881 after living in San Francisco three years, working as master of the Washington Mill Company tug *Richard Holyoke*. He died Dec. 6, 1881.

Saint Patrick

St. Patrick, a small 50-foot propeller, was built at Waterford, Washington in 1874 by James Williams. She made her trial trip April 14, 1875. It was sold to Dennis K. Howard of Seabeck who navigated *St. Patrick* from Portland to Puget Sound in 1876.[13] It carried passengers and mail between Seabeck and Port Gamble until 1887.

William Warin was captain in early 1882 when an anonymous Canal poet submitted a poem to *The Port Townsend Argus* about Warin's adventure with a whale:[14]

The Adventures of Capt. Warin
The little steamer Saint Patrick
Was running on Hood's Canal
Captain steered his course south
Started up the mid channel.

Oh the wind that blew a hurricane
Rode thick the icy mist
And a little vessel groaned again
As she veered on the starboard list.

The skipper stood at the helm
Looking sharply into the gloom
When suddenly out of the darkness ahead
Down the wind with out a boom.

Russing down on its pitiless course
Throwing high spray as it flew
With the speed of the Flying Dutchman
To cleave the Saint Patrick in two.

Russing the down on its course
Came a long and low deck craft
No look out stood on its forward deck
No skipper stood abaft.

St. Patrick's noble craft
To his little vessel true
Put the helm over hard a starboard
And two land whistles blew.

No answer made the stranger craft
Right on the St. Patrick now.
Pish sh and a great bull whale went down
Within 20 feet of his bow.

By September 1882 Julius Macomber was captain of *St. Patrick.*

After the fire in August 1886, Hauptly loaded his scow with two horses, cow, calf, wagon and his family and *"The Paddy"* towed them to Union City where he was taking up residency at the Webb ranch.

Howard's steamer *St. Patrick* was laid up in Seattle during the winter of 1886-87 receiving much needed repairs to her boilers and machinery.

In July 1887, Julius Macomber was running *St. Patrick* on The Canal again.
> Monday: Seabeck to Union City
> Tuesday: Union City to Port Gamble.
> Wednesday: Port Gamble to Seabeck.
> Thursday: Port Gamble.
> Friday: Port Gamble to Seabeck.
> Saturday: Seabeck Port Gamble.
> Sunday: Port Gamble to Seabeck.

It was laid up in October and towed to Seattle, disabled. Howard decided in November to quit the Canal and leave *St. Patrick* in Seattle to be used in jobbing.[15] But it returned when the shaft on *Josephine* broke at Port Gamble in November but was back on the Canal within weeks, then withdrawn because of rough weather in early

---

[12]*E. W. Wright (editor), Lewis & Dryden's Marine History of the Pacific Northwest.* Superior Publishing Co., Seattle, 1967. P. 199.

[13]*Seattle Times.* Jan. 26, 1916.

[14]*Puget Sound Argus.* Jan. 13, 1882. The author was probably Edward Clayson.

[15]*Seattle Post-Intelligencer.* Nov. 3, 1887.

December. *St. Patrick* was sold by Howard for $2,000 to a Tacoma man.

Phantom

Phantom, built at Port Madison in 1869, was operated as a passenger and freight boat operating between Madison and Seattle until 1871 when she was taken to Lake Washington and used in towing. By 1876 it was operating on The Canal. Howard purchased it from Jacob Scoland in July 1882. He intended using it for mail, passengers and freight on The Canal. William Warin skippered the steamer and on a trip to Seattle announced that Howard had bought the runs between Seabeck and Port Gamble in connection with *St. Patrick.* The hull had been painted a deep sea green and a new house was put on.[16]

In December 1884 Howard announced the schedule of *Phantom* which would leave Seabeck for Seattle every Friday at 7a.m., touching at Port Gamble and returning from Seattle Saturday morning, touching at Port Gamble and Seabeck and continuing on to Union City. It would carry the mail.[17] *James McNaught* was to be "temporarily" withdrawn from the route.

"Denny" Howard, operator of Seabeck's hotels, sued the steamer *Messenger "her boilers, engine, tackle, apparel and furniture and all persons, lawfully intervening for their interest in the same in a cause of collision, civil and maritime."*

Howard alleged, and because judgment was in his favor alleged correctly, that *Messenger* had on Dec. 26, 1884 run into the *Phantom* while she was lying at Yesler's Wharf "at the foot of Mill Street in the City of Seattle". Howard sued for $250 in damages and an additional amount for costs. He settled for $77.05 on Nov. 24, 1885.[18]

She was 65 feet long, 11 feet beam and six feet hold. *Phantom* assumed British colors in 1885.

James McNaught

The 87-foot *James McNaught* first appeared on The Sound in 1882.[19] Hauptly hired the *McNaught* to go across the Canal with horses, oxen, wagon and harrow. *"Run aground and stopped. You bet,"* Hauptly wrote in his diary.[20] The steamer was running up and down the Canal and into Port Madison in 1883, the County seat.

In the summer of 1884 there were three steamers running on The Canal, besides those belonging to the mill companies. Two, *Phantom* and *St. Patrick,* were owned by Denny Howard and the third was the *James McNaught* under command of Capt. Fred Dyer. It made two trips each week from Seattle to the head of The Canal carrying excursionists, land hunters, campers, loggers and all other passengers besides large quantities of freight. *"On a recent trip, she carried ten tons of freight for McReavy Brothers to their logging camp on Union River."*[21]

Gem

The steamer *Gem* was launched in Seattle in 1878, built for Captain George W. Gove who used her mostly for towing. The sternwheel steamer was destroyed by fire off Appletree Cove on Feb. 7, 1883 and five people lost their lives. By this time it was owned by McReavy and Latham, loggers, and was primarily employed as a tender for their camps.

It was en route from Seattle to Union City in command of Captain William Williamson with P. L. Plaskett, chief engineer. The steamer was loaded with a considerable quantity of hay, stowed aft of the boiler. This is where the fire started, burning the tiller ropes and rendering the steamer unmanageable. Four passengers were on board: F. C. Vickery and wife, Miss Vickery and F. G. Buffum. The two former were drowned in attempting to get away from the steamer as also were E. Raisback and George Gowan, deckhands, and the Chinese

---

[16]*Seattle Post Intelligencer.* Aug. 23, 1882.

[17]*Seattle Post Intelligencer.* Dec. 10, 1884.

[18]Third District Court, Washington Territory. Case No. 4414.

[19]Lewis & Dryden. Pg. 297.

[20]Hauptly diaries. March 23, 1883.

[21]*Seattle Post-Intelligencer.* July 26, 1884.

cook, who left in a small boat which capsized. The others stayed with the burning craft until they were rescued by some loggers living in the vicinity and afterward picked up by the steamer *Addie* which started to tow the wreck, but the *Evangel* came along and threw such a swell that it was swamped and went to the bottom. The steamer had 500 barrels of flour for Port Gamble, five tons hay and potatoes.

Williamson was born at Seabeck, son of John R. Williamson, one of the minority partners of the original Washington Mill Company group.

Josephine

"The Hood's Canal Country is filling up rapidly. Two steamers are making regular trips to the headwaters of Hood's Canal, the Josephine and steamer Enterprise from Port Townsend."

Josephine was under the command of Capt. H. Gillespie in December 1889. It left Seattle Wednesday and Saturdays at 6:30 a.m. to Port Gamble and all way-points on The Canal.

An advertisement announced that the fast sternwheeler *Josephine*, D. K. Howard, sole owner, would be carrying the United States mail on Hood's Canal, making a weekly trip to Seattle. It would leave Seabeck every Friday morning, touching at Port Gamble for passengers and freight and would arrive in Seattle in the afternoon. The return trip would leave Yesler's wharf at 7:30 a.m. every Saturday, taking the mail to Port Gamble, Seabeck and Union City, stopping at Lilliwaup Falls and other places of pleasure or business at the demand of any passenger. *"Persons visiting Hood's Canal will find the best of attention with good table and rooms at D. K. Howard's Hotel in Seabeck,"* at the Cliff House. The steamer also traveled between Seabeck and Port Gamble daily, except Saturday, with passengers and freight and *"receive orders for any point on Hood's Canal."*[22] Captain James Hennessey was in charge. In July, the schedule was modified with two trips weekly into Seattle.

While Denny Howard was touting his *Josephine*, the opposition boat, *Lone Fisherman*, announced: *"Steamer* Lone Fisherman *will leave Harrington & Smith's wharf, Seattle, every Wednesday at 7 a.m. for Port Gamble, Seabeck, Union City and way ports, arriving same day and connecting with stage for Oakland and Olympia. Return will leave Union City for Seattle every Friday at 6 a.m., touching at Seabeck and Port Gamble and arriving Seattle the same day."*[23]

The Seabeck mill burned Aug. 12, 1886 and in December Denny Howard announced that he had withdrawn his steamer, *Josephine*, from the Seattle/Seabeck run but continued in the jobbing and freighting business on The Canal. He planned to lay her up for a couple of months and bring her out fresh and bright for the spring and summer trade, 1887.

Denny Howard wrote a letter to the *Post-Intelligencer*[24] responding to a story in the newspaper: *"I noticed an item in the PI that the steamer Lone Fisherman has been bonded to carry the mail on Hood's Canal. You can just say that there are two steamers on Hood's Canal which are not bonded, but which will run steadily between Hood's Canal and Seattle and I'll give you the schedule for publication in a few days."*

A month later the overhauled steamer *Josephine* made her initial Hood's Canal trip of the season. He had decided to make a specialty of carrying excursion parties to and from The Canal.

Josephine was back on the run between The Canal and Seattle in August 1887. It was the same month that the *Josephine's* owner, D. K. Howard, announced that he was moving to Seattle. Macomber went back to *Josephine*.

The Seattle newspapers were generous giving space to the history of the Mosquito Fleet. In December 1887 it was reported that *Josephine* had taken 17 immigrants up Canal where they would become residents of Kitsap County.

[22]*Seattle Post-Intelligencer.* June 26, 1885.

[23]Ibid.

[24]*Seattle Post-Intelligencer.* April 27, 1887.

Josephine was pulled off The Canal in January 1889 to replace the burned *Leif Erickson* which had run between Seattle and Sidney (now Port Orchard). The master of the ill-fated boat, Capt. John Nibbe, purchased *Josephine* for $5,000.

An unusual run was started when Washington Mill Company's steamer, *Louise,* began a weekly run between Port Townsend and Union City in April 1889. *"The establishment of this steamer route fills an urgently felt want and will be a great convenience to many persons at Port Townsend and to logging camps on Hood's Canal."*[25]

Other Small Vessels

The Shoo Fly was running to Union City with the mail in 1878 [26] but its origins are unknown. She was an open, scow built, schooner rigged craft *"the most unprepossessing vessel on The Sound."*[27] In April 1879 *Shoo Fly* and *St. Patrick* consolidated their two runs and *"The Paddy"* was running alone.[28]

The little steamer *James Mortie* was purchased from the Western Union Telegraph Company and ran on Lake Washington from Yesler Avenue to Newcastle beginning in 1870. Its original name was *Lizzie Horner* and when she had her name changed, she was fitted up as a passenger boat. Afterwards it was taken to Port Gamble and plied between there and Seabeck. In 1878 it was running between Port Townsend and Union with Al Wissell.

In February 1882, *Rip Van Winkle* was sold at Astoria to Jensen & Smith of Seattle who put her on the Hood's canal route.

The steamer *Louise* was constructed at Seabeck in 1883. She was a sternwheeler 92 feet long, 22 feet beam and was handled by Captain Parker and Engineer Robert Airey.[29] Hauptly first mentions that

Louise went out with hay from Webb's ranch in March 1886.

In 1885 *Lone Fisherman,* Captain S.H.Willey, began The Canal run, leaving Seattle every Tuesday at 10 a.m. and calling at Port Gamble, Seabeck and Union City.[30] Within a month, Denny Howard sold *Phantom* and bought steamer *Josephine,* putting it on the run, and sold *Phantom* to the *Josephine's* owners.

It was also in 1885 that a 65-foot steamer, *Rosalie,* was built at Dewatto by Captain Bain for use in trading with Indians, loggers and farmers along The Canal.[31] To add to the competition, Capt. Ellis was advertising the steamer *Ellis,* a convenience, he espoused, for Seabeck people going overland from Port Washington. The distance between what is now Silverdale and Seattle was much shorter and the cost less expensive.

The propeller, *Gold Dust,* was brought to The Canal by Smith Brothers in the spring of 1886. They put it on the Port Gamble/Union City run and announced that if it didn't make money, it would be sold. No more was heard of her, so it is assumed that it was taken off the run.

Delta

Delta started on The Canal in 1889 and continued (probably) until 1898 carrying the mail and passengers to Canal towns. A Holly youth, Cyprian Wyatt, once rowed the 12 miles to Seabeck for mail, but joined up with Dan Troutman on *Delta* in 1893 to avoid the long haul. He said that he delivered mail and made stops at 42 places along Hood's Canal. [32]

Wyatt described a typical Canal delivery: *"When logging camps didn't have a dock, a gangplank was balanced over the water from freight deck and the animal led on it until its weight tilted the board and it sat down on its haunches, slid into the water to be guided ashore."*

[25]*Seattle Post Intelligencer.* April 14, 1889.

[26]Hauptly diary. June 30, 1878.

[27]*Seattle Post-Intelligencer.* May 7, 1884.

[28]Ibid. April 1, 1879.

[29]Lewis & Dryden. Pg. 322.

[30]*Seattle Post-Intelligencer.* May 21, 1885.

[31]*Seattle Post-Intelligencer.* Sept. 1, 1885.

[32]*Seattle Times.* Dec. 30, 1951.

Perdita
Asahel Curtis photograph
(Photo courtesy Washington State Historical Society.)

Delta was a 50-footer, owned and skippered by Captain Daniel Troutman and worked The Canal until 1898 when he purchased *Dode,* replacing *Delta. Dode* was on the Seattle - Hood Canal route and stopped at Kingston, Port Gamble, Seabeck, Brinnon, Holly, Dewatto, Lilliwaup Falls, Hoodsport and Union City. It had been rebuilt in 1898 from a Gold Rush schooner (*William J. Bryant,* built 1895) and was a wooden-hulled 99-footer. It would leave Pier 3 in Seattle after loading with freight and head for The Canal. Troutman bought her and his wife sold it in 1903.

Troutman mysteriously disappeared in 1899 and his wife, one of the best known of the early day women working on the inland waters of the Pacific Northwest, took over the operation. Dora (Wells) Troutman filled all the needs of the steamers. She was captain, purser and cook. Wyatt worked for Capt. Troutman on the *Delta* as mate and then went on Troutman's *Dode.*

Perdita

Perdita was built in Seattle in 1902. She was 103' (although later enlarged to 143') and was advertised as having electric lights, fine staterooms and first class cuisine.

A promotional brochure for the *Perdita* discussed various towns and sights along the Canal. The Cliff House was described as *"boasts a hotel capable of accommodating*

100 guests." The *Perdita* stopped on its daily (except Monday) run leaving Port Ludlow and stopping at a number of stops including the Cliff House *and* Seabeck. On the return, the boat did not stop at the Cliff House.

The brochure continued: *"The steamer ride along Hood Canal is, we might say, an abbreviated trip to Alaska. The Olympic Mountains lying to the westward along The Canal, are almost equal to the mountains along both sides of the Inside Passage to Skagway."*

She was operated by W. W. McKenzie until 1905 when she came into the ownership of Puget Sound Navigation. She left the run, temporarily, replaced by her competition boat, *Garland,* which was said to be faster and lower priced. The *Perdita* returned to Hood Canal to run in competition with *Garland* and a rate war ensued: *Garland* lowered her freight rates from the standard $2 a ton to 50 cents while passengers were carried from Seattle to all Hood Canal points for 25 cents. Within a year, the *Perdita* was sold to Puget Sound Navigation Company in 1905 and left The Canal. She ended her career in 1911 in a spectacular disaster.[33]

The *Perdita* was *"jogging along"* on her regular route and was nearing Port Ludlow at 7:30 on the morning of Oct. 10, 1911. In the engine room a sudden, muffled explosion startled the engineer on watch and, seconds later, fire erupted on deck. An oil heater had exploded and the engine room was a seething pit of fire.

Nobody had stopped to shut off steam so the *Perdita* kept right on full speed. Boats were lowered, but the ship's speed capsized them as soon as they hit the water. Captain

[33]Lucile McDonald. *The Sea Chest.* Puget Sound Maritime Historical Society Quarterly. December 1976. Pp. 60-63.

Potlatch
(Photo courtesy
Puget Sound Maritime Historical Society.)

State of Washington succeeded the *Perdita* on the Hood Canal route. Built in Tacoma in 1889 and originally ran on the Bellingham Bay Route out of Seattle. In the spring of 1907 she was transferred to The Canal route under the flag of the Thompson Steamship Company. Later it ran under the Puget Sound Navigation banner to Hood's Canal and was transferred out in 1912, replaced by *Potlatch*. It then operated in Portland as a towboat until 1920 when its boilers exploded.[35]

Potlatch

Potlatch is the Mosquito Fleet boat most remembered by those old-timers still living in Seabeck. Many families and all their possessions were brought to the Seabeck dock by *Potlatch*. She was built by Puget Sound Navigation Company in 1912 and replaced the old *State* and its wooden hull. *Potlatch* was a steel construction and was running by the summer of 1912. She was 150 feet in length, 575 tons with a triple expansion engine of 750 horsepower with steam from two water tube boilers at 200 pounds pressure. Year-round Passenger service on The Canal ended in 1917 when Puget Sound Navigation withdrew her from the run.[36]

McAlpine, who had faced emergencies before, ordered the crew to tear off the stateroom doors and chuck them overboard. The crew and passengers (there were just two aboard that trip) followed the doors over the side and used them as improvised life rafts. They watched the sea-going bon-fire that had been their steamer continue her wild dash and pile up on the beach. There the *Perdita* proceeded to burn herself completely out of existence. Saved, however, were the stateroom doors and all the passengers and crew."[34]

A baby boy was born aboard *Potlatch* in January 1912 and, appropriately, named Potlatch Holbrook Lynch. R. B. Holbrook was master

State of Washington

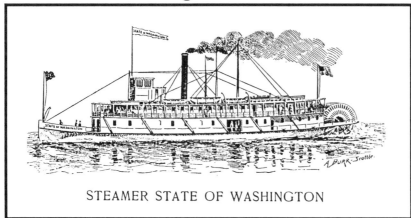

STEAMER STATE OF WASHINGTON

---

[34]Gordon Newell. *Ships of the Inland Sea..* Binfords & Mort, Portland. 1951.

[35]Gordon Newell. *The H. W. McCurdy Marine History of the Pacific Northwest.* Superior Publishing Company. 1966.

[36]Ibid.

The Nickels' Brothers
three-car scow.
(Photo courtesy Seabeck Christian Conference Center.)

of the vessel at the time.[37]

City of Angeles or *Kingston* ran the summers of 1918-20. It was the freighter *Aloha* that carried on after than until 1926.[38] Robert Leithead, a noted Northwest maritime historian, added additional information about passenger and freight boats which operated at various times on The Canal including: *Sarah M. Renton* (1891), *Buckeye* (1893), *Rainier* (1894), *Albion* (1897), *Chehalis* (1896), *Alaskan* (1901), *Olympic* (1901), *Georgia* (1905), *Inland Flyer* (1905). And there was, of course, *Discover*, Capt. Al Walton.

Nickels Brothers and Bess

By 1911, a network of roads had been established on the Olympic Peninsula. It was at this time that service was established for cross-Canal auto and wagon traffic. A scow towed by an old fishing boat left the dock at the Cliff House, making its way to Quilcene.[39]

Few at this early date could afford the luxury of an automobile yet brothers, Art and Sam Nickels, kept their scow running beginning in 1917, but not on a regular schedule. When they operated out of The Cliff House dock, they used an old fishing boat to pull the scow, then shoved the scow up on the beach. Planks were laid on the beach if the tide was out. If a car couldn't

make it up the embankment, everyone but the driver would push it up to the road.[40]

Part of the character of the Nickels brothers' operation was their chief assistant, Bess (or Bessie) Henderson. She rarely missed a trip. Sam was the pilot and Art the deckhand. C. A. Spriggs, an early resident of Maple Beach, who has allowed "thousands" of Seattle people to camp on his property, announced a proposed change in the schedule.

"The Nickels brothers have begun building a ferry slip on Mr. Spriggs waterfront property at Capitol Point. The ferry, capable of carrying six automobiles, will run from Capitol Point, two miles southwest of Seabeck. The ferry will go to Pleasant Harbor. The new ferry location will shorten the route across to Brinnon by seven miles which measured in the matter of time means cutting The Canal crossing from two and one half hours to less than an hour."[41]

It is unknown if a dock between Scenic Beach and Maple Beach was built but if it was, it didn't last long. Sharon Barney notes that a road had been built directly to the beach, a necessity for a ferry landing.

The Nickels brothers and Bess, continued the back and forth trip for many years,

[37]Robert Leithead interview.

[38]Ibid.

[39]*Bremerton News.* July 8, 1911.

[40]Floyd Lowe interview. 1992.

[41]*Bremerton News.* March 17, 1919.

The Pioneer
(Photo courtesy Floyd Lowe.)

but out of the Cliff House property. That dock was torn down in the early 1940s by Boyer Halvorsen. It was not the original dock that served passenger and freight boats at the turn of the century, according to Floyd Lowe.

In 1921 *Pioneer* was built at Seattle as a replacement for the scow. Art, Sam and Bess decided that crossing time was far too slow for their 3-car scow. The new vessel could carry three or four times this number and do it in half the time. She was the first self-powered ferry to cross Hood Canal. Launched in Seattle May 8, 1921 it was Bess who broke the champagne over the bow.

She is often mistaken for *Pioneer* which ran between Bremerton and Manette.

She was a single-ended wooden craft equipped with a 50 horsepower Fairbanks-Morse "CO" semi-diesel engine and had a small passenger cabin on the upper deck, aft of a raised pilothouse. A short engine exhaust stack emerged from her texas. Two trips per day were made originally, but these were doubled soon after.

Business increased and by late 1923, both the route and the ferry were bought out by Puget Sound Navigation Company and a larger ferry, *Airline,* soon replaced the 61-foot *Pioneer.*

Pioneer was chartered out to the Oak Harbor-Utsalady route in 1928, serving as standby to the *Acorn.* It was sold in 1930 and taken to the Columbia River.[42].

Sam, Art and Bess were the true characters of Canal waters. Bess lived alone until she married Art, then lived with both brothers. Sam left the area and moved to Olympia where he worked for Weyerhaeuser and retired when he was 70. He married (Sarah) and died in April 1968 and was buried in Seattle, Holyrod Cemetery.

Bess was always on the ferry, dressed in men's clothes many times.

Art and Sam were native sons. Their father, Samuel, Sr., a former millworker, stayed on after the fire and farmed. The boys had fish traps at Misery Point, Big Beef, Miami Beach and operated a herring fishery in the bay. They also logged piling on Nickels Hill, now known as Sea View. Their old skid road is still visible going up Sea View road as it turns left.

Bess smoked cigarettes continually in a day and age when women didn't smoke. Joe Emel thinks that she probably smoked hemp: it was a common crop in many back-yard gardens around Seabeck.

Billie (Halvorsen) Barner remembers that she'd always have a pack of cigarettes stuffed down the front of her blouse and she'd pull them out and say *"Have a pill?"*

Art and Bess built a large house with ten bedrooms: seven upstairs and three down. They catered to loggers, fishermen and the men working the log boom at the head of the bay. (When West Fork Logging at Camp Union was operating, the bay was filled with logs. Four big engines hauled rail cars loaded with logs down to the dump.) They called their place *"Bessamart".*

Bess cooked in her filthy kitchen, usually barefoot. One local woman, now many times a great-grandmother, visited Bessamart Inn when she was a teenager and Bess introduced her to "the girls" who were very well dressed and wore fine jewelry. It

---

[42]Robert C. Leithead. *The Sea Chest.* Puget Sound Maritime Historical Society Quarterly, June 1984. Pp. 135-6.

Fish Traps operated by Nickels Brothers around the bays of Seabeck.

was rumored, but no one would confirm, that the girls were permanent fixtures.

Bess rode back and forth across The Canal, entertaining passengers with her stories and foul language. Everyone who lived at Seabeck during Bess' lifetime remembers one story or another about her.

Bertha (Brumm) Sibon wrote a story which showed another side of Bess as she grew old:

"Everyone called her "old Bess". She was the first woman I ever saw smoke. She worked with the Nickels brothers on the Seabeck to Brinnon ferry --- worked like a man and wore men's overalls. She married one of the Nickels brothers, Art, and lived with both.

"They built Bessamart Inn near Seabeck and rented rooms. When the ferry stopped running, they sold the inn and moved into a small house at what is now Sea View road corner.

"Time passed and they did what they could to earn a living --- growing older and one year, while getting cedar for Christmas wreaths which they sold, Bess fell and fractured her hip.

"There was no insurance and she was sent to what was then called The Poor Farm in Port Orchard. She was very frightened, thought she was going to be killed in her sleep and made such a fuss she was finally sent home with Art.

"Our Sunday School (Lone Rock) heard of their plight and a group went to see how we could help.

"Bess was in bed, unable to get up. The house was very unkempt. Ashes had fallen through the draft in the front of the wood heater creating a fire hazard. One of the men cleaned the stove and took the ashes

out in a washtub. Art was shelling oysters on the kitchen table and filling pint jars to sell. Oysters, shells and spilled water littered the kitchen --- windows, walls and floor.

"Other women cleaned. I was given Bess to bathe and change. She was very dirty, her hair was matted, long and tangled. But saddest of all were her feet: Bunions and toe nails like rooster feet.

"I soaked her feet, cut the toe nails and washed her poor, bony body with several changes of water, found a clean gown and with help, sat her up in a chair while I changed the bed. She was talking all the while and finally showed me where there was a piece of ribbon on a corner shelf and wanted it tied in her hair.

"The work finished, Bess back in her clean bed and Art thanking us for our work, we all went back to our own lives.

"Bess died not too long after. She lived in her own world, still thinking the Germans were in the attic and that their German Shepherd dog kept them from getting her.

"One day several weeks after her funeral, at which Mr. Hart from our Sunday School sang what she'd told me was her favorite hymn "Life is Like a Mountain Railway" (said her Mother used to sing it). I opened the door to a knock and there stood Art. He had a patchwork quilt in his arms and through his tears he told me "Bess said when she died she wanted you to have this. Her Mother made it for her."

"The quilt was hand made and quilted, a treasure Bess had cherished over a lifetime. I unfolded it. The mice had chewed holes in it and it was musty with

age. But never had I received a more treasured gift."

Capt. William P. Thornton

Captain William P. Thornton (B. October 1878 Iowa; D. January 1963 Bremerton) began his steam boating career on *Lydia Thompson* at age 12. His family had moved to Friday Harbor from the midwest. He also served on U. S. Revenue cutters and was working on *Garland* as mate when it was purchased by Puget Sound Navigation in 1902.

After obtaining his master's papers, he was transferred to *Rosalie* and *Whatcom*. He ran for a short time on the *State of Washington* while it was running on The Canal. While serving on *Lydia Thompson*, it is said that he and his crew transported the first automobile in the Northwest when they took a Stanley Steamer from Hoodsport to Seattle.

Thornton formed a tugboat company after working as harbormaster in Seattle. For ten years he had exclusive contracts with large lumbering firms, towing logs and he hung on through The Depression until the Longshoreman's strike. Then he went to Captain Charles Peabody who offered him three runs, but Thornton only wanted one: Seabeck. He purchased the ferryboats in 1935 from Puget Sound Navigation. His biography said that he worked on all of the larger vessels of Black Ball Line. In 1929 Puget Sound Navigation operated 17 routes including Seabeck/Brinnon.

His four children, Frank, Bill, Phil and

Phyllis spent summers at the Seabeck dock, never forgetting the fun of life in the hustle and bustle of a summer resort.

Thornton ran *Clatawa* and *City of Kingston* across The Canal. *Kingston* caught fire at the Seabeck dock about 1938 and Thornton and his eldest son, Bill, fought it from *Clatawa*. Only the upper works was destroyed. The insurance company was so pleased at their feat that they authorized a complete rebuilding from the deck up (the diesel was undamaged). Because of nautical superstition, the boat's name was changed to *Lake Constance*.[43]

At the outbreak World War II, he left the ferry to enter the Army Transportation Corps as master of the *Frederick Funsten*, 18,000 tons, and her sister ship, *James O'Hara*. He later was on the Alaska run and spent seven months shuttling from Juneau to the Aleutians. Then he served as Associate Marine Superintendent of the Seattle Port of Embarkation. He was transferred as master of the Training Ship *Teapa*. After leaving the training ship, he took over the "Welcome Home" ship as mas-

Kingston burned at Seabeck dock and rebuilt as Lake Constance. *(Linkletter photo.)*

[43]Frank Thornton correspondence. 1993.

ter. He retired from that service in March 1947.

Frank Thornton remembers his father as a man who was practically self-educated but was articulate, a math wizard and one who was never down even though the Depression took his lovely Seattle home and all his tugs. *"Dad owed a fortune but paid it all back and this before Social Security, the Small Business Administration and all the rest of the agencies. Beside that, he was a great father and I treasure his memory!"*[44]

In 1939 Thornton sold the route, including boats, for $12,000 to Bertie Olson.

Andy Olsen, Last of Ferryboat Operators

Andy Olsen thinks his captain's hat must have worn out. As well it should have. He worked for an indefatigable boss, his sister, the oft referred to *"Tugboat Annie"* of Hood's Canal (if not Puget Sound), Berte Olson.

Olsen is an *old salt*. Born within sight of Puget Sound at Clinton on Whidbey Island, he lives within a few feet of Hood's Canal. Howling winter winds slam down The Canal and spray his comfortable retirement home with saltwater. Andy, his wife and their sons built the cozy home at Maple Beach near Seabeck.

It was at Seabeck in the Fall of 1941 that he hung up that old Captain's hat, a sad day when he and his sister gave in to government regulations concerning tonnage on the old dock. The run to Brinnon could not be profitable without the beer and gas trucks. And there weren't enough passenger vehicles to support continuation of the route.

Andy's Dad jumped an English ship in 1886 with a couple other sailors (including Stan Boreson's grandfather) and took up a 160-acre Whidbey Island homestead. Then he sent to Stavanger, Norway for his wife and three daughters.

The Clinton land was covered with cedar and fir and the family lived off profits from selling shingle bolts to mainland mills and wood to steamers passing *down Sound*. His father might have been one of the first

men, in 1910, to traverse the length of Whidbey in an old buggy, dodging gullies and stumps. By the time he reached his destination, the cream he was transporting had turned to butter.

The immigrant wife died shortly after arriving and the three daughters, including Berte, were sent to Poulsbo's orphanage, a stroke of good fortune for the widower as a young Norwegian immigrant girl who was working there agreed to marry him.

After their marriage in Poulsbo in 1893, they moved back to the homestead. Six more daughters were born and finally on June 27, 1902 a son, Andrew, arrived. Two more sons and another daughter completed the family. In 1911 the family moved to San de Fuca, also on Whidbey.

There was that day in 1908 when Andy saw his first auto. His younger brother thought that with its big eyes it must be some sort of monster. Only secondarily to Andy, it was the day he heard Billy Sunday preach.

Berte married Agaton Olson and beginning in 1921 they ran a scow towed by Agaton's fishing boat, *The Rainbow*, from Whidbey on the Deception Pass route. In 1924 the couple had two boats built, the *Deception Pass* and *Acorn*, then establishing a monopoly, of sorts, on the Deception Pass route. Andy was skipper of *Deception Pass* from 1924-35 and Agaton and his two brothers ran the Utsalady run beginning in 1925.

Berte has gone down in ferryboat annals as the first female automobile ferryboat operator on Puget Sound.

Berte and Agaton bought the *Central II* in 1930 as a spare boat on the Deception Pass/Utsalady route. Andy warned the engineer not to stoke up the fire as they returned to port each night. His warnings went unheeded and the *Central II* burned in the summer of 1931. It was later sold and rebuilt. They then bought *Pioneer*.

Completion of the Deception Pass Bridge in July 1935 meant a breakup of not only the ferry run but Berte's marriage. In 1936 Agaton took *Pioneer* and *Deception Pass* to operate on a South Sound route. Berte, with Andy as her key employee, bought the Port Gamble/Shine route from Capt. Alexander Peabody and took *Acorn*

---

[44]Ibid.

(which had been on the Utsalady run) with them. That ferry route saved motorists 120 miles by crossing Hood Canal directly rather than driving around the south end of Hood Canal.

Berte and Andy tore out the Whidbey/Camano docks (Oak Harbor-Utsalady)and rebuilt one at Port Gamble. Utsalady). Their first day of operation brought in $32.50.

In 1939 the Canal ferry operation expanded when Berte purchased the Seabeck/Brinnon crossing from Captain Thornton. The deal included the *Clatawa* and *Lake Constance (ex-City of Kingston)* and cost $12,000, according to Frank Thornton, son of Captain Bill Thornton. Berte sold the *Clatawa* to the Government for $10,000 for the run between Hadlock and Indian Island during W.W.II. It later burned.

Lake Constance was used as a spare boat for the Seabeck run. Andy was in charge of the Seabeck operation while Berte continued operating at Port Gamble.

Captain Peabody approached Berte with an offer to buy the Port Gamble franchise. Berte's little ferry would not, could not, handle the increased number of motorists expected with the completion of the Agate Pass Bridge. In 1950 she sold the Port Gamble franchise back to the Puget Sound Navigation Company.

Desirous of a shorter run, Peabody dedicated the Lofall/Southpoint crossing on June 10, 1950. And on December 30, the State of Washington purchased Peabody's system. The State ran the Lofall run until the Hood Canal Bridge opened on Aug. 12, 1961.

Andy would ease *Clatawa* into the Seabeck dock and unload cars over the bow. She carried 14 cars and the charge was 50 cents one way or 75 cents round trip. Passengers paid 25 cents or 45 cents for a round-trip.

When the Seabeck service was discontinued in 1941 because of dock weight restrictions, Andy received permits to build a dock at Miami Beach. Berte and Andy had secured piles from Port Ludlow and a pile driver and were ready to begin work. Only because of the War, steel was unavailable and their dock plans were scrapped.

An earlier attempt at a ferry crossing didn't work out. In the late 1930s, Stan Reeve obtained his captain's license and put a down payment on a ferry to run out of the

Clatawa
(Photo courtesy Frank Thornton)

Cliff House dock. Puget Sound Navigation disallowed clearance for Reeve's boat to land at Brinnon.[45] The Reeve family were owners of the Washington Route, operating around Dye's Inlet, Bremerton and to Seattle. Because of the fierce competition between the two lines and Peabody's stronger hand, the project was scrapped.[46]

Corduroy Road to Seabeck and Back

The very geography of Kitsap gives a vivid picture of early travel in the area: it was by water. The earliest land route out of Seabeck was a trail along the shoreline north. Near Anderson Landing (Sunset Farm), an overland trail followed much the same route as today's Anderson Hill Road. It has been said that it was an Indian trail which makes some sense since it's only three miles from Anderson Landing to Dye's Inlet at Silverdale. (More logical for Indians and their followers to go overland rather than 60 miles around the Kitsap Peninsula. In 1896 the Little Beef Bridge was completed, followed by Big Beef Bridge and then a rough, rutted one lane road was

---

[45]Helen Reeve. Interview 1993.

[46]Bob Leithead interview.

established from Seabeck along the beach front, across the bridges and up Anderson Hill.

In 1914, A. B. Newell, the Seattle Realtor who had purchased the mill property from Rodney Kendrick, announced that a stage would be coming eventually, especially with the advent of the summer resort planned at his town.[47]

The Conference center opened in the summer of 1915 and although some of the guests came by charter and regularly scheduled boats, others preferred an option made available by the Hall Brothers, a stage which ran between Bremerton and Seabeck. The fare was $1 each way. This was the same time that the Crosby road was finished and telephone poles were set from Silverdale to Seabeck..

In early 1917 the Halls had competition when J. B. Rice and J. A. Prenatt of Seattle put two big Packards on the run for fishing season.[48]

Seabeck Stage - 1923
1917 Pierce Arrow
(Photo courtesy Dennis Dibley)

The Halls ran the stage line for two years, selling to Arthur Kellum in 1917. Kellum moved his family to Seabeck the following year. With the purchase, Kellum received an old Chevrolet Touring car that didn't run, according to his son, Floyd Lowe, and consequently they never used it in the service. Kellum purchased a Pierce Arrow and Packard, later enlarging the

---

[47]*Bremerton News. April 8, 1914.*

[48]*The Bremerton News.* March 27, 1917.

fleet. *"They had five or six at one time,"* Lowe remembered. There were two Pierce Arrows, a Packard and a six-passenger Page. Most of the vehicles transported 7-8 passengers. One Pierce Arrow transported 12 passengers although sometimes when loggers were transporting their gear, passengers sat on each other's laps. Others rode in jump seats. Kellum lengthened the vehicle and then he could easily haul 14. Primary travelers were the loggers, conference attendees and fishermen.

The largest vehicle had been owned by Mary Pickford, using it like a motor home. When Kellum got that one, he had it gutted and it could carry 40 passengers. This Pierce Arrow was painted orange and was called "The Apple Bus" because of its color.

Kellum (also known as Arthur Lowe B. Dec. 23, 1882; D. May 24, 1960) and his wife Louise Bailey (B. Jan. 20, 1885; D. June 11, 1955) were the parents of eight children who were given the Lowe name. There were Mae (Raymer) (1908-1970); Anna (Lee)(1910-1981); Floyd (1913); Lucille (Peck) (1915-1993); Archie (1917); Chauncey (1920); Bernard (1921); Myrtle (Davis) (1923). The Kellum/Lowe family lived near the Cliff House and the Halvorsen store. The end of the stage line was at the Cliff House dock.

Kellum also ran a stage around The Canal to Port Townsend. Passengers most likely were those who wanted to take the scenic all-day journey along the narrow and unpaved roads. Reservations were required.

While Kellum's kids were growing up, they were responsible for washing and sweeping the fleet of vehicles and for pay, they were allowed to keep any loose change they found.

For a time the firm was known as Kellum-Benbennick as Clarence Benbennick ran a stage from Bremerton to Poulsbo, Suquamish and Kingston and the lines were complimentary.

For Floyd, big money was earned in the summer of 1924 when, as an 11 year-old, he was hired by a gypo logger to peel piling lying in the bay. He earned two cents a foot. At night, he and a friend, Melvin

Hagen, donned swimming suits and went under water, driving holes through 50-foot piles, then pulled a chain through. For that, they earned five cents a hole. For five-inch holes, they received 45 cents.

At age 15, after the stage line was sold, Floyd worked at Camp Union, following the five locomotives with a shovel to put out any fires that might start.

Art Kellum's brother, Archie, earned a fairly decent living by raising skunks imported from Michigan. He'd de-scent them and sell the fur. He also ran the garage and blacksmith shop and serviced the stages, selling gas and repairing the new *fangdangled* autos. When the road near the head of the bay was altered, Kellum moved his shop, in pieces, up to the road, hauling the various parts with horses.

By the time Art Kellum sold the business in 1928, there were several other vehicles in the fleet. The buyer was R. G. Purves who renamed the stage line, The Olympic Motor Transit Company. Their offices were at 52 Front Street on the First Street dock. Purves made two round trips daily between Bremerton and Seabeck. Lowe has one of the schedules.

The boat schedule didn't correspond well with the school schedule and Minnie Winsor, the teacher at Seabeck 1922-23, took the stage with her husband and daughter to Bremerton to catch the ferry to Seattle. *"The road was called a 'corduroy road' as many parts of it went through boggy areas and the stage driver would lay down logs, then we'd drive over them and it felt like driving on corduroy."*[49]

Stage Schedule

	Lv.	Lv.
Ferry Landing	8:45	3:30
Seabeck	8:50	3:35
Crosby	9:00	3:50
West Fork Logging Co	9:05	4:00
Wildcat Lake	9:20	4:20
Mountaineers	9:35	4:25
Kitsap Lake	9:40	4:30
Bremerton arrive	11:45	6:30

At the bottom of the schedule, it was suggested that Seattle people take the 10:30 a.m. or 5:15 p.m. boat from Colman dock. Arrangements for special stage trips could be made with the owners. Anyone standing along the road would be picked up.

Blacksmith shop and later the area's first station to service autos.

(Photo courtesy Dennis Dibley.)

---

[49]Bernice Morton interview.

Hotels, Saloons and Entertainment
Antithesis of Conference Center

Dozens of small logging camps dotted the shoreline of Hood's Canal and a couple hundred men worked for these outfits. Isolation and boredom brought them to Seabeck on payday. Some checked into one of the four local hostelries but more likely than not they'd throw their sleeping roll on the ground and belly up to the bar of at least one of many saloons where began some serious drinking.

Marshall Blinn preached abstinence. He was a man whose family was steeped in a tradition of sobriety and morality. Liquor was a problem not only in Blinn's heart, but in the eyes of families and lawmen.

Another booming business was to sell liquor to Indians, a practice found reprehensible not only to Marshall Blinn, but for all who would fear for their personal safety.

Despite the vigilance of the District Tax Collector, Col. Simpson C. Moses, vast quantities of liquor were often smuggled ashore, brought across the Strait of Juan de Fuca from Victoria. Indians who had previously led tranquil lives were suddenly addicted to liquor.

One of the most illustrious liquor peddlers was Samuel Howard. Howard was arrested in Victoria in 1860 along with his Indian wife, Lucy, on a charge of selling whiskey to Indians of that region. He was bound over to authorities and his wife was fined 10 pounds in Victoria's courts. When the bonds were furnished and the fine paid, the two were set at liberty.

About a week after they were set free, Howard filled a small canoe with 300 gallons of whiskey, cleared customs (claiming it was camphene) and retailed to Indians on Vancouver Island. After selling as much as he could there (to lighten his load) he crossed the Strait and sold between Port Townsend, Port Gamble and Seabeck. He got into a little difficulty, actually big difficulty, with the Indians near Seabeck and was killed and his wife made prisoner.

The authorities in Victoria thought it retributive justice and didn't regret his loss, they saying that it should prove as a warning to others engaged in his trade.[1]

The availability of liquor up and down The Canal was responsible for at least two more murders.

Tom Pierce, who maintained a logging camp across the Canal at the Duckabush River, got in a fight over a bottle of whiskey hid behind a stump in the woods by Jim Allen. Allen hid it again for private consumption. But a *"lag"* from Australia, *Gassey Charley*, watched Jim hide the bottle, then stole it.

This theft brought on an altercation between them and Jim Allen was killed on the spot. The principal witness, Pierce, testified in court against the murderer and "Gassy Charley" (or Charles Young as the locals knew him or John N. Young according to court papers)[2] was sent to prison, but at the end of his term came back and hung around Seabeck for a few days, according to Edward Clayson.

The witness, Bill Blair, had moved to Victoria before "Charley's" release, knowing that here he would be safe as the escaped convict from Australia didn't dare set foot on British soil or he'd be sent back to his homeland in chains.

Eagle Hotel and United States Hotel

Two hotels occupied land which is now the Conference Center Inn. The first, The United States, operated until late 1869 when it was torn down and the present Inn was built and named The Eagle Hotel. The first mention of the hotel is in land records. From these: *"Alexander Preston died Feb.*

---

[1] *Victoria Colonist.* Sept. 1, 1860.

[2] *Seattle Intelligencer.* Aug. 16, 1869.

21, 1863 and his widow, Margaret, sold the U.S.Hotel to William Warin for $401 on Feb. 6, 1864. "3

On Jan. 26, 1869, a couple of local drunks were whooping it up at Seabeck's US Hotel, run by Warin.[4] George Bryant ordered a drink and threw down a 50 cent piece. Sitting next to him was Hiram Bryant, no relation, who picked up the coin and put it in his pocket. Words passed between them and Hiram choked and struck George. George seized a tumbler and flung it at Hiram. As it broke, a shard struck Hiram's jugular vein and he bled to death on the spot.[5]

George Bryant was charged with manslaughter and a grand jury, Arthur Denny, foreman, was called and found Bryant not guilty of assault, let alone murder.

That *was* pioneer justice.

Hiram's wooden grave marker hangs in the Inn lobby.

The seven witnesses called to testify received six nights' free lodging in a Seattle hotel and payment of $26 each for attending court. They were William Fulton, Samuel Evans, Charles Baker (who signed with an *x*), John Walker, William Warin, Thomas Stark and Charles Brown.

William Warin ran the U.S. Hotel from 1864-69. His customers were a wild bunch and it must have been difficult for families to sleep at night when some of these loggers hit town.[6]

Ned Smith, a logging camp cook, weighed over 200 lbs. Edward Clayson saw him in September 1868 push his dugout under the wharf alongside the old store at Seabeck. He'd been working steady three months. This would make his *"time check"* something over $200. He went to the hotel where he threw his blankets into a corner, took off his coat and hat and threw them into a corner with his blankets, unbuttoned his shirt collar and rolled up his sleeves.

He walked up to the bar and threw down his check and said: *"Bill. I'm a going to have a time. Let me know when I get down to $10. Let's all take a drink."*

He'd stand on his feet and keep talking and walking around the floor continually for three days and three nights.

Another Warin customer was Teddy Durgin, a logging camp cook who came to town for no other purpose than to get drunk.[7]

His spree would not last over two days and then he'd go lie down and have a snore. Said he to Bill Warin: *"Put that down to me, Bill"* as he walked away from the bar. *"Ho hell,"* said Bill, *"I'm not going to be fooling about with slate and pencil. I'll charge you $15 a day."*

This was quite reasonable to Teddy considering the extensive wine list behind the bar which consisted of two bottles of Jersey Lightnight, two bottles California port, two bottles grape brandy bitters, one Hostetter's, one empty cider keg and a dozen boxes of Wah Chongs "Chinese stinkers".

In December 1870 at one of the undetermined saloons, a rough and tumble fight broke out around 3 a.m. between Dennis, the engineer on the *Shoo Fly* and William Brown, a logger. Dennis had his nose bit off.[8] It wasn't the last time in the county that a nose was lost in a fight.

A couple similar incidents were reported in the press including an altercation in Port Gamble when Daniel Manchester tried to intervene in a fight and Tom Coleman struck him, knocked him to the ground and nearly bit his nose off. Manchester went to Seattle where he was treated by Dr. Maynard who was successful in replacing the detached portion to its proper position. Coleman was given 18 months in the penitentiary for biting Manchester's nose.

Warin and Bill Brownlee played the fiddle pretty well. When you heard fiddle playing, it was pretty sure evidence that the spree was over or was subsiding, according to Clayson, *"for listening to the fiddler*

---

[3] Kitsap County land records.

[4] Territory vs. George Bryant. Third Judicial District, Case No. 894.

[5] *Seattle Intelligencer.* Feb. 1, 1869.

[6] Clayson. P. 33.

[7] Ibid. P. 34.

[8] *Seattle Intelligencer.* Jan. 2, 1871.

whilst the more important entertainment of getting drunk was going on would have been breech of loggers' etiquette and would not be tolerated."

The motto for the Seabeck imbibers was:[9] *The man who treats has the floor* and they all competed with each other for this prestige.

When Marshall Blinn decided to run for Congress in 1869, he campaigned on the principles of sobriety and morality. In an effort to clean up the town, Blinn took away management from Warin, tore down the hotel and built the present Inn offering it rent free to anyone who would run it on prohibition principles. And, he promised, if anyone dared open a saloon in competition to his hotel, he'd offer free booze and smokes.

Loggers' and sailors' mouths began to water at the prospect of free whisky and cigars. Several tried to run it but couldn't make money and then Blinn lost the election and left town. Dennis K. Howard, known as Denny, took it over and ran it for many years. He ran an advertisement announcing his ownership:[10]

Eagle Hotel, Seabeck
Only best brands
of liquors and cigars kept.
Open on the 12th.

Hauptly's diaries record frequent financial transactions with Howard for the next several years. The Hotel was serving food as well as cigars and liquor.

Whether it's fact or fiction is not certain, but among the old papers at the Kitsap County Historical Society is a story about a young logger's wife with two children who came up from San Francisco on July 3, 1879. (According to Jacob Hauptly's diary, *Oregon* arrived on July 2.)

She stayed at the hotel until her husband could be notified that she had arrived with the children.

"The lady took a room at the hotel and on the night of July 3 the locals had started celebrating at the bar, directly below her room. As the night wore on, the noise became unbearable. The bartender attempted to quiet things down by refusing to sell any more liquor.

"Then shots rang out and every window in the building was shattered. The woman dragged her mattress off the bed and placed it against the window frame in an attempt to protect her children, and herself, from the gun fire. The celebrants demanded and got more liquor.

"She heard a peculiar bumping and dragging sound as if bodies were being hauled down the steps. All of the 22 drunken men had passed out and were laid in a row on the lawn to sober up. The terrified woman, daring to glance out of her broken window, saw what she thought were 22 dead men."

The hotel prospered during the mill period and guests stayed, albeit infrequently, after the fire. In September 1887 Canal logger Robert Frazier fell off the hotel porch and "struck upon the chime of a beer key". He broke his collarbone and was taken to Seattle's Providence Hospital. A month later,[11] a logger, John Jacobs, came to Seabeck, got drunk, raised the window during the night, fell out and broke his neck. He died, of course. Room Six.

The Bay View

The fourth (or fifth) hotel at Seabeck was that of Edward Clayson. As it was near Hauptly's "town house" and next door to Ninemires where Hauptly lived for many years, it was only natural that that's where Jake Hauptly, town butcher, spent a lot of his time.

Clayson purchased 133 acres with 450 yards waterfront in July 1868 from Herod Wells. He cleared land, cultivated a large garden of fruits and vegetables and raised pigs, cows, chickens. He ran a logging camp, then built his hotel and saloon which he called The Bay View. It was located at the head of the bay.[12]

---

[9]Ibid. P. 35.

[10]*Seattle Intelligencer.* April 5, 1873.

[11]*Seattle Post-Intelligencer.* Oct. 25, 1887.

[12]Clayson. P. 25.

Shipwrights were boarding at the Bay View while building the ship *Olympus*. This, according to Clayson, irritated mill manager Richard Holyoke. *Holly Hawke,* as Clayson called him, took a desperate move to shut off all communication with the Bay View so he chopped down one section of the bridge at the north end. This was not a private bridge, according to Clayson, but property of Kitsap County.

But shipwrights the next morning, instead of going to work, began to pack up their tools. Hiram Doncaster knew that they couldn't be replaced short of San Francisco and the ship was to be launched in the next few weeks. Holyoke was forced to submit temporary repair of the bridge in order to appease these men until the ship was launched.

Clayson said that the Grand Jury assembled in Seattle and Clayson went over but Grand Jury would not indict Washington Mill Company for their crime.

In May 1874 liquor licenses were granted to Clayson and Howard and a billiards license granted to Howard. Clayson received a bowling alley license beginning Nov. 12, 1874 for six months at a fee of $12.50.

Saloon altercations were common at Clayson's *family hotel.* Once Jacob Hauptly, as Justice of the Peace, was called on to arrest *"Clifton, alias Mike, for shooting of Joseph Edwards through the arm on the 22nd at Claysons."* [13] Hauptly appointed James Tart as special constable to arrest John Clifton. Captain Howe and Hauptly fixed up a wanted poster with picture. He discharged his special constable a couple days later when the wanted man could not be found.

When Clayson and family quickly moved from Seabeck in February 1883, they left Jake Hauptly with about $450 in old liquor bills plus his last month's beef bill. The property was rented to Denny Howard for five years. The hotel then became known as "Hotel Howards".

The Bay View Hotel business was sold by Robert and James Fraser to John Pike in March 1886. The sale included:[14]

Two dozen chairs
10 lamps
One pigeon hole desk
3 round tables
One lantern
Two kitchen tables
Three stoves
12 table knives and forks
12 heavy teaspoons
12 pictures
Two coffee pots
Two teapots
Nine Window blinds
One mirror
One clock
All wines, liquor and cigars
Bar fixtures
Restaurant outfit
Two dozen plates
Two axes
One hatchet
One hammer
50 decks cards
One hand saw
Four pair blankets
12 bar towels
Two tablecloths
5 lbs. nails
Two 5-gallon demijohns
Ten gallons coal oil

The total selling price was $878 which did not include building or land.

Cliff House

William Warin, unemployed in 1869, secured a liquor license for himself, selling liquor for a little while at his shanty upon the side hill just back of the hotel. The location was not suitable for his purpose but he found a location north of town which was ideal.

Knowing that the Puget Mill Company at Port Gamble, arch enemy of Blinn, was determined to beat Marshall Blinn for delegate to Congress, Warin conceived a plot.

---

[13]Hauptly diaries. April 28, 1877.

[14]Kitsap County records.

He was broke but there were about a dozen logging camps within 15 miles of Seabeck and they all voted at Seabeck and every last one of them were friends of Warin. He went to Port Gamble and asked that they accept his services at Seabeck for the campaign. A compact was made and credit placed at the Port Gamble store subject to the order of Bill Warin for $1,700 worth of provisions and lumber.

Blinn was furious. He coerced the majority of Seabeck voters to sign a petition protesting the issuance of a liquor license to John Collins and William Jameson, Port Gamble hotel/saloon operators who were fronting for Warin. Despite Blinn's efforts, the license was granted anyway.

The *Bushwacker* made several trips loaded with lumber and provisions and in four weeks the Cliff House was built and stocked with liquors and cigars.[15] *"The squaws came along in their canoes and their tents and a hilarious old time soon ensued."*

William Warin was an Englishman, son of a doctor. He married an Indian girl, Sally Klanbish, who was granddaughter of Chief Chilewatched of the Twana and Skokomish tribes. They had four children: Jessie, Harriet, Katherine and William, Jr.[16]

Warin's Cliff House was far enough from town that the loggers and farmers felt more comfortable there than in town where women and children could monitor their antics.

The Gedosch thesis says: *"A third saloon, The Cliff House, opened in 1870. Being located about a mile and a half from Seabeck,* (immediately across the road on the beach from the south end of Pioneer Road) *it did not have to conform to the standards of family entertainment and consequently was able to offer the added attraction of 'hostess service.'*

There are two abstracts describing the general Cliff House property and they differ in several ways. The one describing the hotel and saloon refers to Government Lot 2, while the second one deals with Gov-

This small shack on the beach
may have been the first
Cliff House saloon. The dock was built
by Peter Emel.
(Photo courtesy Dennis Dibley.)

ernment Lot 3, both located in Section 21, Township 25 North, Range 1 West.

A patent was recorded to Josephine Wells, wife of Herod Wells for Government Lot 2 in 1869. Her fee was $20 for the 16 acres. She and her husband deeded property to (William) Warin, (John) Collins and (W. S.) Jameson in 1868, selling it for $60. No legal description was included although it was in Lot 2. The following year, she sold Warin eight acres, also in Lot 2, followed by an additional 16 acres. Again no dollar amount was included. William Warin deeded eight acres of Lot 2 to Ewell Brinnon in 1870 for $100 and at the same time, on June 13, 1870, deeded Brinnon one half interest in *"my house known and advertised by name of the Cliff House, together with one half of all the furniture, stock, etc., etc."*

Less than a year later, Warin deeded the property to Brinnon for $1,000. Brinnon sold the 16 acres of the property, although structures are not mentioned, to Dennis Howard and William Watson in 1872.

That portion of the Cliff House property (Government Lot 3) was sold by the original patent holder D. B. Jackson to Samuel

[15]Clayson. P. 20.

[16]Ida Bailey letter. June 12, 1993.

Alexander for $350 in 1875.[17] Jackson was the great, great grandfather of former Governor and United States Senator, Daniel Jackson Evans. (This was later the Cliff House store.)   Alexander fed on the weaknesses of loggers and millmen, owning several other *mad houses*, shacks built in the woods and at least one on the spit. These *mad houses* supplied women.

Alexander wasn't popular with Seabeck folk, or at least those who didn't frequent his establishments.   In the end, Seabeck folk rejoiced when he was murdered.

Before purchasing the property, he presented a petition for a liquor license to County Commissioners. It was accompanied by a protest signed by Seabeck citizens. Some residents signed both.

The citizens' petition was presented to the County Commissioners praying that *"your Honorable body not to grant a license to Saml. Alexander for the purpose of keeping a Squaw Dance House in this place."*[18]

Alexander's request was approved but was to be reconsidered in two months and he was required to give $500 bond,[19] a bond not required by other retail liquor dealers.

In November 1873 Alexander's liquor license was revoked, there being another petition signed by the inhabitants of Seabeck, but he was granted an application to sell lager and beer and that license was renewed in May 1874 and again in November.

Alexander sold the property to D. K. Howard in 1879 for $200.

There weren't tears shed at Seabeck when the *Intelligencer* arrived, announcing the death of Alexander:[20]

"Sam Alexander, an old well known resident of the lower Sound whose occupation was boating but who sometimes lives ashore at Whiskey Spit between Port Ludlow and Port Gamble, was shot and instantly killed on Wednesday afternoon at Squamish Harbor while in an altercation with Charles O'Green.

"A coroner's jury was summoned and repaired to. the place yesterday and an inquest held. O'Green testified that Alexander and his klootchman (Indian wife) came to O'Green's cabin Wednesday afternoon bringing with them some alcohol and burnt sugar, with which liquor was made.

"After about three bottles of the liquor had been drunk toward evening, he ordered Alexander to leave but he made no attempt to do so. O'Green then took a double barreled shotgun and fired, hitting Alexander in the head.

"Several of the Coroner's jury state that the entire upper part of the head was shot off and that Alexander was probably sitting down smoking at the time, a pipe being found in his right hand.

"O'Green is under arrest and was taken to Port Townsend by the sheriff (of Kitsap County). Justice Dwelly of Port Gamble who arrested and held the prisoner was held on bail as a witness."

Dennis K. Howard purchased the saloon and property but it doesn't appear that Howard ran the saloon there until 1881 and he was then running both the Eagle Hotel and The Cliff House as Hauptly writes: *"Made out liquor license bonds for D. K. Howard for both houses."*[21]

Once, when Jacob Hauptly was living at Brinnon, he picked a bucket of strawberries and rowed to the Cliff House. The saloon was crowded. Hauptly got a table from Dennis Howard and sold the berries at 50 cents a saucerful. He made $20 before he got in his boat and rowed back across The Canal.[22]

Howard was farming at the Cliff House property in April 1881. *"Mr. Howard is the fortunate owner of a tract of land about half a mile from town upon which he has erected a wayside inn. About eight acres are cleared and these eight acres are capable of being wrought into fine effects by a competent landscape gardener."*[23] Beginning in 1885, Hauptly talked of walking to Howard's wharf, buggy rides to the Cliff

[17]Abstract owned by Billie (Halvorsen) Barner.

[18]Ibid. Sept. 16, 1873.

[19]Ibid. July 13, 1873.

[20]*Seattle Intelligencer.* Nov. 29, 1884.

[21]Hauptly. Nov. 6, 1881.

[22]*Hood Canal Courier.* June 23, 1933.

[23]*Seattle Post-Intelligencer.* Sept. 20, 1882.

Original Cliff House Hotel built 1886 by Dennis Howard.
(From the photo collection, Washington State Historical Society.)
Photographer Asahel Curtis, circa 1905.

House and *"Howard has commenced to grade for to build a house on the lot that use to belong to Warin, Brinnon & Company."* [24] In July 1886 Howard was advertising for plasterers and painters to complete the hall he had just built at Seabeck. That hall was The Cliff House hotel.

In May 1886, Hauptly wrote *"The Cliff House is running. Frank Libby bartender"*.

William B. Seymore wrote about pioneer "innkeepers" on Puget Sound and presented his *paper* to Kitsap's Pioneer Association.[25] It was later published in the *Washington*

State Historical Quarterly. No date is given for Seymore's visit to Howard's.

"Going up Hood's Canal some 18 or 20 miles brings us to Seabeck and the hotel there conducted by D. K. Howard, familiarly known as "Denny" Howard. A most genial host in deed was this same "Denny" but Seabeck being off the ordinary line of travel, not as well known as some of the others. When the mill burned and the Company decided not to rebuild, "Denny" was forced to leave, but among the Hood's Canal people, D. K. Howard has never been forgotten."

He was married to Miss Nellie Lyons of Victoria at the residence of S. F. Putman in Port Madison June 6, 1875 by John F. Damon. At least two sons were born at Seabeck on Dec. 10, 1876 and Aug. 4, 1878.

---

[24] June 3, 1886.

[25] Frank Wetzel, Bellevue, owner of original manuscript.

Howard had a colorful career while at Seabeck. He arrived in 1868 and engaged in logging on The Canal, purchased the *St. Patrick* eight years later, operated all three hotels at Seabeck at one time or another and during all of this opened the first brewery in the Puget Sound area at Steilacoom with Governor Solomon's son-in-law, a Mr. Shafer. The famous old Russian gunboat, *Politkofsky,* was purchased by a company composed of Howard, John James, William Campbell, Capt. Primrose, Captain Chilcott and Robert Turner. It was dismantled at Port Blakely and loaded with gold seekers, started North. Her engines quit but good fortune favored the vessel and it drifted before wind and tide into the very harbor to which she was destined and died on the beach.[26]

Howard (B. circa 1846 Jerome, near Montreal, Canada; D. Jan 23, 1916 in Seattle) was operating the First Avenue Hotel in Seattle at the time of his death. He was survived by sons William C. and Dennis K., Jr. and a daughter, Catherine (Mootz).[27] At one time Howard owned Government Lot 2 and 3 plus the nearby 80 acres that had had a hotel and saloon on it.

The County Commissioners appear not to have set a standard for fees for liquor licenses.

Clayson presented the commissioners with a petition for a license for his liquor saloon and it was granted, but with the fee fixed at $150 per annum. [28] *The Auditor was ordered to inform Mr. Clayson to file a bond of $500. Others seeking liquor permits were not required to post bond.*

At the next Commissioners meeting, a petition were presented to grant a liquor saloon license to Miles Brennan and (Denny) Howard and they were charged $75 for six months although others in the County were being charged $200 a year.[29] *This was for the Cliff House saloon and for many years*

afterwards, the license was renewed for six month periods. In 1872 Howard had a new partner, only known as Watson in County records.

Business slackened after the Fire in 1886 and the Howards moved to Seattle.

The property eventually came into the hands of John and Alice Walton and they deeded lot 2 to Peter Emel in 1901. He at once began repairs and changes and *"a substantial wharf has been run out to deep water for ship building and reports say that the recent owner is to conduct various lines of business there."* [30] The following month, Emel announced that he was opening a saloon and variety joint at The Cliff House. *"But the worthy citizens do not intend to allow such an innovation."* [31] The hotel was leased to a Mr. Arronson at that time. It was announced in January 1902 that Emel was demolishing the Cliff House and selling the lumber[32] although this was never done. By March, Emel was at the Cliff House *"making extensive preparations for the introduction of dairy stock and a creamery and constructing suitable buildings for this enterprise."*[33]

Emel leased a *"one story frame store house located just west of the Cliff House, three rooms in the Cliff House and use of the wharf"* to H. P. Frazier in July 1902. In 1909 Hutoka Hufnagle assigned her lease (from Emel) for the store dated May 4, 1908 to Barton and Gooding while leasing the Cliff House to Ben Kaiser.

The lease was reassigned in 1911 to W. W. Barton for the "Cliff House property" at $150 annually. Barton was to make all necessary improvements and keep fruit trees in good condition. In 1912 Barton leased the store to Albert and Marie Halvorsen at $5 monthly and Mrs. Barton leased the dock to the Halvorsens at $2 monthly.

Asahel Curtis photographed the hotel in 1905 while on an excursion with The Mountaineers. In the summer of 1906 Bremerton

[26]*Seattle Post-Intelligencer.* Jan. 27, 1916.

[27]*Seattle Times.* Jan. 24, 1916.

[28]Ibid. March 6, 1871.

[29]Ibid. May 8, 1871.

[30]*The Bremerton News.* Nov. 2, 1901.

[31]Ibid. Dec. 14, 1901.

[32]*Ibid.* Jan. 25, 1902.

[33]Ibid. March 1, 1902.

The Cliff House shortly before fire destroyed it.
(Photo courtesy Olanie family.)

The rebuilt Cliff House on water side of old road. Ferry *Pioneer* leaving dock.
(Photo courtesy Olanie family.)

was moved just north and remodeled by the Halvorsens who rented it out.

Maud Emel Halffman sought the court's relief to validate a sale she made of the property to C. F. (Fred) Miller on March 25, 1922. The court agreed and in 1923 Miller recorded his plat of Cliff House View Tracts.

Pennell and Newland's

In 1870 an interesting fellow was a partner in ownership of a government patent adjacent to the Cliff House property. J. W. Pennel(l) and Alexander Newland were granted the SE quarter of the NW quarter and the SW quarter of the SW quarter of Section 21.

Pennell was a former operator of brothels on San Francisco's Barbary Coast. He built a cedar log shack on Seattle's sawdust pile near Yesler's mill, nailed down a dance floor, improvised a bar of planed boards riding sawhorses and on the other side a series of small rooms with opaque curtains. He then negotiated for the most promising Indian girls he could discover and personally saw to their scrubbing down in a large wooden tub. He decked the girls out in calico and opened the doors to Seattle's loggers, millmen and seamen.

The tract consisted of 80 acres and A. A. Newland deeded his 40 acre share to William Y. Newland(s). The property was said

publisher E. L. Gale and his wife were spending a few days at the Cliff House.

Not long after the arrival of the Halvorsens who ran the store (they were there in 1912), the Cliff House leasor stoked up the fireplace and left for the weekend. As the ashes of the Cliff House cooled, wood still blazed in the fireplace. A photo postcard of the Cliff House, owned by the Olanie family, is dated 1915 so it may have been about this time that it burned. Another structure was built on the water side of the old road, later moved across the road and eventually fell to ruin. A small one-room cabin adjacent to the Cliff House

to consist of :[34] *"40 acres, one half mile more or less from the Washington Mill at Seabeck, Washington Territory, being one half that tract of 80 acres described in the Receiver's office at Olympia, WT as purchased by A. A. Newlands and J. W. Pennell . . . together with buildings, tenements and improvements, and known as Newlands Dance House, said buildings comprising the hotel, barroom, restaurant and dwelling and all other property real or personal belonging to (them).*

This may mean that Pennell and Newlands had competition with Warin's facility. And it also seems to indicate that there was a fourth hotel in the Seabeck area.

The first note in County records of a liquor license being granted to this "hotel/saloon" was in 1870 and County Commissioners charged $75 for Newland and Matthew to keep a saloon for the ensuing six months.[35] Six months later, Newland was seeking a reduction in the amount of his liquor license and the amount was reduced to $125 per annum. There was another reduction, then a credit applied. It seemed that the Commissioners took what they could get.

Other Entertainments

Isolation created a need for entertainment and improvisation. Of course for the loggers, bachelor millworkers and shipbuilders, there were the saloons, floating hurdy-gurdy houses and the *madhouses.*

Another form of entertainment for the loggers and bachelor millworkers and shipbuilders was visiting Maloney and Dixon's house. But in April 1877 the Maloney-Dixon house burned and all the millworkers were woken up and fought it. It was totally destroyed. [36] Jacob Hauptly had been out of town when the conflagration occurred but he recorded in his diary on May 22, 1877: *"The Mad House burned while I was away."* A *"mad house"* was known to all on Puget Sound as a dance hall furnished with girls of the night.

Jesters, magicians, and the circus came to town every couple of years and there were lectures and panoramas. Rev. Mr. Wirth brought his Magic Lantern in 1882 to entice the locals to listen to his sermon.

The Brass Band was formed in January 1877 and from Jacob Hauptly's diaries it appears that members had to "buy in". They ordered new instruments. Performances aren't mentioned in Hauptly's diaries even though he was a member for awhile. In 1882 residents were enticed into attending the circus performance and word-of-mouth publicity brought a big crowd when a man performed a "slight of hand" act on the spit. The circus performance even had another man walking a tight rope.

Of Kitsap's five milltowns, only Port Gamble had an actual church building. The other milltowns had visiting ministers, at least twice a month. They included Rev. Eells of the Skokomish Reservation, Dr. Lane who combined medicine and religion on a regular basis at Port Gamble, Rev. Mr. Wirth, Rev. Nickerson and Mr. Wisker, who Hauptly said *"was the shortest and homlyest* (sic) *white man in Washington Territory."*

Rev. David Sires ran a Port Townsend saloon before realizing how lucrative the traveling pulpit circuit might be. He retired in Seattle where he became a policeman and was murdered in the line of duty.

Even one of the local teachers, Miss Winser, read from the bible, both on Wednesdays and Sundays.

On one occasion[37], Jacob Hauptly and his wife went to Seattle and attended a Baptist church meeting where Mrs. Butcher, Mrs. Airey, Mrs. McQuillian and Mrs. Holyoke were baptized. Rev. Mr. Wirth came to Seabeck and baptized a millworker, a young woman, Mrs. Ensley Doncaster and *old* Mrs. Green. *"They were all soused under in front of Ninemires about 3 p.m. and it (was) raining. Wirth preached*

---

[34]Abstract to property owned by Joe and Pat Emel.

[35]Kitsap County Commissioners. Nov. 15, 1870.

[36]*The Intelligencer.* April 28, 1877.

[37]Hauptly diary. Sept. 11, 1881.

both morning and night. We attended baptism but not preaching." [38]

Hauptly was not a man without sinful ways but he seldom broke his self imposed Sabbath rule.

Traveling troupes came through in the 1870s including the Wilton troupe which visited all Puget Sound ports and minstrels, The Chicagoans. Hauptly took the school marm and Belle Ninemire to that show. [39]

The *"celebrated Scotch piper and vocalist",* Professor Ferguson gave a concert on Feb. 12, 1876, giving a humorous account of Scottish life.

Itinerant shows, quack MDs, peddlers and quaint elocutionists of theological matters roamed all over the Northwest and although off the-beaten track, hit Seabeck. One such fellow was described as *"the demon Wyman with brass jewelry and coonskins"* who entertained a full house.

Hauptly celebrated every new year's eve by eating oysters and drinking eggnog and dancing out the old year at the hall.

Seabeck had its own baseball team as early as 1882. Two steamers, *City of Quincy* and *Fanny Lake* brought 80 Port Gamble residents and their baseball club, known as *The Unknown Club.* The game lasted 2-1/2 hours. Port Gamble won 31 to 10. Hauptly thought that all the excitement looked like *"an old fashioned 4th of July."* [40]

Richard Holyoke, as manager of the mill, made an artificial baseball ground and for nearly three years ran a sawdust cart from the mill to the sloping hillside. The site was nearly 3/4 mile from the mill and the sawdust filled up a small swamp. [41] Clayson was a bit miffed, thinking he had the ideal location on his property at the head of the bay. The mill company baseball diamond was not large enough and it failed and *"every other ball landed amongst the logs,"* according to Clayson.

Holyoke then found another site, just below the long row of white cottages and sent several men out grubbing stumps and removing boulders from the site but Clayson wrote: *"About every third ball found its way down the hill into Biddy DeCarty's backyard."*

When the Port Gamble and Snohomish teams came to play, they came to Clayson's property. *"This was a harvest for The Bay View. Jolly crowd. No local influences could restrain them."* [42]

The Fourth of July was always a big occasion. Guns were fired at daybreak and often the town was full of baseball players and excursionists.

In 1877 preparations were underway for several weeks. Jacob Hauptly wrote: *"Hauled five loads of blocks and 'cultus' lumber on the picnic grounds and two loads scantling and two of flooring delivered to the same place."* The pavilion that he built was covered with sailings. On the morning of the Fourth, there was "heavy" firing of the cannon with a procession at 11 a.m. and dinner at two. The Declaration was read and races held in the afternoon with a dance at night in pavilion. The following day he tore down the structure.

The following year, he wrote: *"All kinds of amusements. Mill race, hundred yard race, jumping, greased pole, pig & etc. Dance at the new school house at night.*

In 1879 there was a depression in the lumber market and the event was toned down. Hauptly wrote: *"Any amount of drunken men on the spit. Greased pole over the wharf was all the amusement. A dance in the hall. 18 ladies there. Had supper at D. K. Howards at 12 o'clock and run the dance till four. Mr. Clayson did not do much last night as I understand."*

On July 4, 1882 he wrote: *"Played bugles at 9 a.m. Sports commenced at 2:30. Jumping. Trenholm jumped 17 feet, 10 inches. Hops, skip & jump. Three yard race. 100 yard. Greased pole. Sack race. Wheelbarrow.*

In 1883 a "public feast" was held in the grove behind the school for which Hauptly paid D. K. Howard $300. A pavilion was

---

[38] Ibid. Dec. 10, 1882.

[39] Ibid. Jan. 31, 1878.

[40] Ibid. June 25, 1882.

[41] Clayson, Edward. *Historical Narratives of Puget Sound: Hood's Canal.* P. 36.

[42] Clayson. P. 37.

built for dining and dancing. Three horses entered a race and Jake Hauptly's sorrel mare won the purse. A pavilion was erected for dancing.

Hauptly wrote on July 4, 1884: *"Firing of the cannon waked me up at 4 o'clock. Marching school children at 10 and reading Declaration. Had shooting match at 9 a.m., base ball at 2 p.m. Races and greased pole."*

In 1886 it was determined to celebrate the Fourth on Monday, the fifth. Of that day Hauptly wrote: *"Raining, raining. Salute at 5 a.m. 13 guns. By 11 a.m. we went to the new hall of Howards where school children sang. Kendrick read Declaration of Independence. Noland orator. Recess of two hours and sports commenced but it rained so hard that there were but few out to take any part. I paid out for prizes $85. Subscription and entrance fees were $90."*

Patriotic Volunteers At Seabeck Are Alive to Their Duties
(Seattle Times, Dec. 26, 1895)
(tongue-in-cheek)

"Residents of the Hood's Canal town who will defend their smokestack even to the last gasp, are fully prepared for a six month siege. The little town of Seabeck (toward the head of Hood's Canal) is preparing for a state of siege. About 30 people live there and the community commands fully seven or eight Great Britain men (when they are all at home) all of whom are patriotic and more or less worked up over the report of war between this country and Great Britain.

"As most old-timers know, Seabeck was far larger 100 years ago than it is today, having been an outpost and garrison for the Hudson Bay Company's[43] fur hunters in the Olympics. It is also interesting to note that at that time Great Britain occupied the soil and the English flag floated over the garrison and cabins.

"But the Seabeck of today is intensely American. A few days ago someone found in the sand an old cannon with the cipher of George III cast in its rusty neck. This piece, which is made of cast iron and is a 16-pounder, has been cleaned with kerosene and the

volunteers, commanded by Capt. S. Green, an old time rancher, have gathered a large supply of ammunition in the shape of rocks that are of sufficient size to fit the muzzle. While there is nothing at Seabeck anymore but the lone smokestack of the Seabeck Mill Company's plant, the ranchers are proud of the relic and they are prepared to defend it at the peril of their lives to their last gasp.

"The Indians of the locality have been pressed into service and for the past two weeks, scouting parties have been out endeavoring to trace down an alarming rumor to the effect that an English warship had entered the channel and was approaching the fortifications. The rumor also had the effect of making the volunteers look forward to the state of siege and they now have six months supply of clams collected and are therefore ready for almost any emergency.

"But the sturdy volunteers who are proud of the distinction of having the first fortification on The Sound, have been looking about for suitable uniforms. One or two have secured some lot of stage costumes which had at one time been the property of a barnstorming company. The costumes had been left at Sidney after having been attached by the Sheriff and writs sworn out by creditors. The costumes are not mates but the volunteers at Seabeck, when arrayed in all their new glory, will no doubt present such a grizzly appearance that no foreign man-o-war will ever venture near that cannon."

(Probably written by Frederick Prosch.)

~

So what if this little village was on the edge of civilization, where men, women and children were satisfied with home-grown entertainments. There were some who came to hide their pasts and others to find their futures. This is a spot like no other on earth. The beauty and serenity should have made up for what it was lacking in communication with the outside world. Seabeck's economy and that of every individual in the area was controlled by the whims of the mill owners, the market economy the weather and those characters who found their utopia on the shores of Hood's Canal.

---

[43]No ducmentation supports this statement.

Newspaper reporters called frequently. Much of what we know of the day-to-day activities can be recreated through their writings.

The cottages were described in 1875 as *"neatly furnished and surrounded with cultivated gardens that indicate taste and refinement. There are 36 families with as many ladies the head of them as men. There are 60 men, 63 children and 20 of a floating population making 176 residents. There is a good school here and a superior teacher for the children. The Mill Company provides an excellent dining room and meals for the millhands and a large hall for public meetings for instruction or amusement."*[44]

(Interestingly the same edition of the newspaper stated: *"Mr. J. M. Colman who runs the Seattle sawmill has invented a board machine to take the place of the edger table that is a vast improvement in speed in cutting lumber to perfection, thereby saving in his mill $25 daily by avoiding imperfect lumber. If all that Mr. Coleman (sic) claims for it is correct, the invention is deserving the early attention of all the mill owners on The Sound. He will have it patented in a short time. Mr. Coleman (sic) has the reputation of being one of the best mechanics on the Sound, a man of superior inventive genius."*

It was this same Colman whose sons envisioned a deserted town site some 40 years later as an idyllic Chatauqua grounds. Colman had worked at both the Port Madison and Port Orchard mills during the 1860s.

Another reporter from Seattle wrote in 1883: [45] *"A fine school with a spacious grove around it shows the enterprise of the people. The library has 750 choice volumes, free to all and supported by a voluntary subscription revealing a high literary taste.*

"Above the cookhouse, a fine school has an organ and the library. The bell rings in a good congregation and "we feel that this is a model of wilderness civilization. The families are intelligent, neat and very tasty. The boys are quiet and the saloon is the only

quarter from which we heard a noise during our four days' sojourn.

"An old man gets too full of the spirits and attends church, but is ejected by a volunteer and departs on the next steamer to be known no more here."

A newspaper story [46] panned one of the lecturers:

"Last week a lady selling a book entitled 'The North Star and the Southern Cross' of which she claims to be the author. We are very sorry to learn that our village produced a very unfavorable impression on her mind. However we would advise her in her future travels to talk less and think more."

A grand masquerade ball was held to celebrate Washington's birthday in 1874 and the ladies who attended included Blair, Rounds, Bowker, Phelps. The men were Clark, Thompson, Rounds, Winters, Slorah, Little and Chillman. *"At 10:30 all unmasked to great surprises!"*[47]

Dancing school was initiated in 1879. The first time Charles Ried attended the lesson was the *mesyouvian*.[48] Either dancing school or dances were held at least weekly during 1879. Dance lessons, according to his ledger, cost $2.50 but the number of classes included for that fee is not mentioned.

Seabeck had its own hairdresser and he benefited the community by giving a dance at the hall with music furnished by Clayson and Chillman and paid for by F. Green.

Gedosch says that the only fraternal organization in Seabeck was the Knights of the Good Templar, a temperance organization, with branches in each of the milltowns. At least at Port Madison, membership of women was encouraged. Many Seabeck men belonged to fraternal organizations but traveled outside the community for meetings.

In 1877 Hauptly wrote that there was a *"Lodge of the Champion of the Red Cross"* started although he wasn't sure of the encampment number.[49]

---

[44] *Victoria Colonist.* June 25, 1875.

[45] *Seattle Daily Post-Intelligencer.* Sept. 15, 1883.

[46] *Seattle Post-Intelligencer.* Dec. 1, 1884.

[47] *The Intelligencer.* Feb. 28, 1874.

[48] Ried, Charles diary. Jan. 4, 1879.

[49] Hauptly. Feb. 10, 1877.

There were few times when something wasn't happening, socially, at Seabeck. But the Northwest's worst snowfall in January 1880 when up to five feet of snow fell in a few days was the exception. The weight of the snow collapsed the roof structures of many of the buildings. Everyone stayed home. The weather is described in detail in Hauptly's journal:

Jan. 7, 1880: Cold. And the snow about 3 1/2 feet deep. Hard work to get to the barn. Snow up to my arms wherever I went. A Hard chance to get to slaughterhouse. Companies barn and slab shed down.

Jan. 8: My slaughtrhouse came near going under heavy weight of snow. Hired five men to shovel snow off slaughterhouse and barns.

Jan. 9: Snow four feet deep. This is the stormiest day I ever witnessed in any country.

Jan. 12: Another 11 inches of snow fell. Raining & snowing. By 10 a.m. had to carry hay on our backs to feed with. Damages done everywhere in the Territory.

Jan. 15: Still two feet on the ground.

Most of the snow had melted when it started again January 24 and it remained cold. The mill was shut down during most of this period. On Valentine's day it started snowing and continued with cold winds. Snow stopped briefly on March 1, only to begin again, snowing off and on for a week.

If nothing was going on, gossip kept things interesting at Seabeck. One of the more interesting Clayson stories concerned Charles Craig and his "wife":

(About 1868) *a couple from New Zealand landed in Seabeck and stayed for years. They came up from San Francisco on the old* Isaac Jeans. *They were passed off for man and wife for years but "cat got out of bag" and they were discovered. They were both criminal absconders from New Zealand. The man was not a convict but he was a criminal just the same as he skipped New Zealand with another man's wife.*

At length they both showed their criminality. The man was a young, good looking, educated Scotchman, younger than the Eng-lish hag he had with him. She was as smart and criminal as she was illiterate and ignorant.

Useful as a midwife, a business she learned with the surgeons on board a convict ship on the way out from England to New Zealand. She soon accumulated considerable money. She hungered to go back for a visit to England. She became too demonstrative so the English authorities arrested her and she had to serve out her time in an English convict prison.

When she returned to Seabeck after eight years, she was received with open arms and heralded as a martyr to sickness who had been in a hospital not as a patient but as a nurse to sick convicts.

The Craigs left Seabeck in October 1884 to live in Seattle. *"He has many friends here whose best wishes will follow him to his new home."*[50]

Arrival of a ship sometimes meant a lot of fun for the local boys. When the bark *Columbia* was in port on March 26, 1877, Hauptly corned beef for Captain Johnson and delivered two barrels. He wrote: *"Shangtied last night on board the* Columbia. *The* Columbia *sailed this morning at 5 o'clock shouting and firing of guns. She left the beef on wharf.* Columbia *bill $95.62."*

---

[50]*Seattle Post-Intelligencer.* Oct. 12, 1884.

Store and Post Office History Aligned

The original store and cookhouse were just a few feet apart until about 1918 when store moved to mill site.
(Author's collection.)

Company Store to Country Store

Candy to cartridges, hats to Turkish towels, nutmegs and venison: the Seabeck store has not lacked for imaginative commodities. The staples of life were carried in the beginning . . . and the staples are carried now. Like now, the store has always been the gathering place, a place to share ideas, to argue politics, to spread gossip or at least share gossip.

The beginning of the store history preceded even mill production.[1] The nearest stores before establishment of the company store were at Port Townsend, Port Gamble and Port Madison. The first store sold foodstuffs, clothing, tools, personal items and virtually everything, save liquor.[2]

In 1859, the following prices prevailed:

Flour	*6 cents per lb.*
Venison	*8 cents per lb.*
Potatoes	*2 cents per lb.*
Beans	*5 cents per lb.*
Coffee	*23 cents per lb.*
Butter	*40 cents per lb.*
Beef	*18 cents per lb.*
Nutmegs	*$1.50 per dozen*

The original store was most likely located on the spit. A second store, the one visible in old photos, was built in 1865 and the construction is documented in Marshall Blinn's diaries:[3] Beginning in April 1865

---

[1]Washington Mill Company Daybook. Feb. 8, 1857-July 23, 1858.

[2]Gedosch. P. 157.

---

[3]Marshall Blinn diary. 1865. Owned by Kitsap County Historical Society.

piles were driven for the foundation of the "new store". By May 4, the crew had finished driving the piles and were putting on floor timbers. Five days later, the crew was raising the frame, then the sheathing and on May 19 they "commenced building a new chimney for the store." Area loggers were making shingles at the camp and a load was brought in for the store. No actual notation was made for a date that the store was opened for business.

In 1864-65 the cookhouse/hall was built and in 1865 new wharves were built and sheds for hay and lumber added, according to Blinn's 1865 diary. A second Blinn diary was discovered late in production of this book at the Jefferson County Historical Society for 1864. Blinn's diaries record arrival of ships, discharging ballast, loading lumber and dates of departure with names of passengers. He spent more time talking about the weather and mill breakdowns than the social history of the town. Unfortunate.

The company, if not the store, wrote to Jacob Brothers & Company of Portland on Sept. 10, 1879 requesting prices and terms for items which they were bidding on to supply to the Skokomish reservation.

6 Gross buttons (for girls' dresses)
Rubber.
1 dozen belts for girls dresses
100 yards cottonade Hard Times
1 dozen hats for girls, winter
100 yards muslin, unbleached,
"Cabot H"
100 yards Oregon Hard Times
Cassimores, all wool
3 pairs ribbon, 1/2 inch wide,
assorted colors.

The bid request was signed by Charles F. Holton.[4]

The value of merchandise in the company store in December 1870 was $13,362.49, or 19 per cent of the total value of all mill property.

When Jacob Hauptly started his butcher shop in 1872, the store had its first competition but eventually he was dealing directly with the store and the company-owned cookhouse as well as supplying meat to the logging camps up and down The Canal.

Gedosch points out in his thesis that *The Colfax* crew members were purchasing outside Seabeck. This is reflected in the relatively small amount of merchandise debated to their accounts and the disproportionately large amounts of cash withdrawn. It was the policy of the store to credit each mill employee on company books, debiting their purchases.

To support this:

	Total Credit	Purchases at store
Thos. Stark	$ 879.59	41.36
Robt. Airey	910.69	143.82
Jasper Baker	1,253.30	288.41
Bill Hayter	1,633.30	112.76
John Connick	2,548.27	42.46

The balance of their accounts were taken as cash withdrawals or drafts.

After 1876, residents purchased from stores in other towns and had their goods delivered by the steamer *St. Patrick*.

Hauptly purchased a new black suit at the company store to celebrate his 47th birthday on June 2, 1877 for $41.

Most company-owned towns paid workers in script worth face value only when exchanged for goods at the company store. If disposed of elsewhere, it was common to discount the script from 10 to 30%.[5] This practice appears not to have been used at Seabeck although the extension of easy credit was the primary media of trade at Seabeck.

The store continued operation after the fire. In November 1889 Nat Sargent paid his account at the store, amounting to $9.65 and purchased one can corned beef (25 cents), one package tea (50 cents), one lantern ($1).[6] Later that month[7] he purchased a pair of boots ($4.25), sugar ($1), yeast cakes (10 cents) and canned milk (25 cents).

---

[4]Undated manuscript at Kitsap County Historical Society by Patricia Granger.

[5]Gedosch. P. 159.

[6]Nat Sargent diary. Nov. 1, 1889.

[7]Ibid. Nov. 30, 1889.

Sargent, during this period, was cutting wood and stacking it on the dock, probably for sale to passing Canal steamers. Other times he'd deliver the wood to neighbors at Crosby and Seabeck. At the end of December he *"made a sale of 36-1/2 cords of wood at $1.25 per cord."* He made $45.60 and paid his store bill of $13.95. He filled in at the store as clerk and after working three days was paid $4.50.

Rodney Kendrick, who worked at the mill as manager and later was to own all the original mill company property, invited his sister, Sarah Edith Macfarlane (B. Sept. 13, 1845 Ontario; D. 1932), and her son, Walter Rodney Macfarlane, (B. May 6, 1869 Brandon, Mississippi; D. May 5, 1935 Seattle) to visit him. The two arrived at Seabeck in 1885. She wrote a letter to Rev. Peter Macfarlane, her husband, telling of her train trip to Seattle and subsequent arrival at Seabeck:[8] The letter is dated Dec. 28, 1885.

Mrs. Macfarlane's train arrived late at St. Louis and she was *obliged*, she wrote, to remain in St. Louis until evening. The passenger agent took care of their *baskets* and introduced them to one of the officials of the Missouri Pacific, then went to his home where *"we were cordially received by his charming little wife and served with the daintiest lunch and most refreshing cup of tea imaginable."*

Some ladies of St. James church presented her with a basket for her continuing journey. It consisted of quail, biscuits, turkey, chicken, cheese, bread and cake and, in Kansas City, she purchased a bucket of coffee. The food lasted until she arrived in Huntington, Oregon. *"We had grown fat on the way. I was thoroughly smoked and I imagine that my general appearance was that of a female tramp. Walter was quite presentable as he never failed to do his laundry work when the dust of travel had made perceptible hieroglyphics on his immaculate celluloid."*

The two traveled north to Portland where they transferred to the Northern Pacific station and started on the final leg of their journey. *"The weather had been ex-*

[8]Sue Bush manuscript.

ceptionally fine from the time of our leaving home until Sunday night when it began to rain and it has rained ever since until today. I entered Seattle in a rainstorm. Rodney was there to meet us, but expected to see in Walter a boy just half his size. We remained in Seattle all night and left next morning for Seabeck, reaching here after dark.

"We are keeping house with a John Chinaman to do the work. My paper is done, so is my time and will therefore postpone a description of this place until I write again."

Rodney Macfarlane
(Photo courtesy Sue Bush.)

Blanche Hotchkin Macfarlane
(Photo courtesy Sue Bush.)

Although neither mother nor 16 year-old son appear in the 1889 Seabeck or Hadlock census, Rodney Kendrick and his wife, Iva, were living at Hadlock. Sarah and Walter may have been out of town when the census taker came through but at least Walter came back and was named postmaster at Seabeck on Sept. 5, 1891. One year to the day later, he was married to the town's teacher, Blanche Hotchkin, (B. June 22, 1870 Troy, New York; D. Aug. 26, 1947 Seattle) daughter of Albert L. Hotchkin, Sr. who was to succeed Macfarlane as postmaster in 1894. The newlyweds lived in Orchard House or Holyoke House or Cedars. The Postmaster's job carried the added responsibility of running the store. Macfarlane did move to Hadlock later. He and Blanche were the parents of four children born between 1894 and 1907 in Hadlock, Cosmopolis and Aberdeen: all milltowns.

Albert L. Hotchkin, Sr. (B. March 8, 1833 Chatham, New York; D. Oct. 16, 1899 Seabeck) left home at age 12 with only a sixpence in his pocket to make his way in the world. He first stopped in Troy, New York where he worked in a drugstore for two years, then returned to the family farm. He was a haberdasher in Troy until fire destroyed the city and his business. He was in the furniture business, politics (he was sheriff and county treasurer). He came to Washington in 1890, living first at Seattle, then moving to Seabeck. Hotchkin was hired to serve as caretaker for the Washington Mill Company property interests at Seabeck.

He died at Seabeck from heart disease. His remains were buried "temporarily" at Seabeck and were removed to Seattle's Mt. Pleasant cemetery on Queen Anne Hill.

Albert, Sr. was described in his Post Intelligencer obituary: *"There was certainly not a finer looking or more athletic man in the surrounding country. Dressed in the uniform of the famous old Troy volunteer, he attracted attention wherever he went." He was survived by his wife, Delia, three daughters and a son.*

Within months of the mill fire (Aug. 12, 1886), the workers had moved to Hadlock. Rodney Kendrick, mill manager at Seabeck, announced that the company store would remain open as there was $30,000 worth of merchandise there for loggers and residents.[9]

He served *officially* as postmaster from April 30, 1894 to Jan. 15, 1900, a full three months *after* his death when George C. Johnson took over that position and presumably that of the store. Perhaps Hotchkin's wife took over postal duties without officially changing the government's records in the interim.

A child of the Hotchkins, Harry, died at age 14 at Seabeck on June 20, 1895 of *croupous pneumonia*.[10]

Albert L. Hotchkin, Sr.
(From Seattle Times obituary.)

George C. Johnson taught throughout the County during the early part of the Century. He was postmaster less than a year (1900) giving up groceries, gossip and stamps for education. He may have taught at Seabeck during this period but was active in other schools in the Central Kitsap region.

Frederick Prosch, son of one of the Northwest's earliest publishers, and his wife, were running the store and serving at the post office beginning November 5, 1900 through May 1905. Mrs. Prosch took over the postmistress duties again in May 1906 with two men running the intervening years. The store underwent major improvements in 1902 when new shelving and counters were installed. [11]

Prosch was the son of Charles and Susan Prosch[12] who came to the Pacific Northwest in 1855 from Brooklyn, New York. The father was a printer and in 1858 founded *The Puget Sound Herald* at Steilacoom. In 1869 father and sons, Frederick and Thomas, acquired the *Pacific Tribune* in Olympia. The family name is

[9]*Seattle Post-Intelligencer.* Oct. 3, 1886.

[10]Kitsap County death records.

[11]*Bremerton News.* March 1, 1902.

[12]Kathy Merz research 1993.

116

synonymous with newspapering in the Northwest. Frederick (B. Aug. 6, 1848; Brooklyn; D. August 24, 1901, Seabeck) entered the printing business as a boy and during the following 35 years worked almost continuously at his trade, employed at the *Victoria Colonist, Portland Oregonian, San Francisco Call* and *Seattle Post Intelligencer.* By 1889 he had taken up a quarter section near Seabeck (Pioneer Road) and at the time of his death he was wharfinger, postmaster and the merchant at Seabeck as well as Justice of the Peace. The spent the summer of 1889 at the farm.

The store as it appeared when the Halvorsen family bought.
(Photo courtesy Olanie family.)

He was married on New Years' Day 1869 in Olympia to Helen Elder and they had two children, W. C. and Mabel. Cause of death was tuberculosis.[13]

Prosch was buried at Seabeck.

Albert Hotchkin, Jr. and/or his wife served at the post office and store from April 1, 1907 to May 17, 1919 when the Halvorsen family bought the store and Marie Halvorsen became postmistress.

As the community gathering spot, Postmaster Hotchkin solicited donations for Mrs. Sarah B. Brown, a widow, whose house burned. Her child died in the fire and all of the family's possessions were lost.[14]

It was during the period of the Hotchkins' ownership that the store was moved from its original location during the mill period to its present position, atop the old mill foundation and utilizing what remained of the old mill dock. Many old-timers still remember the original mill boilers rusting on the beach by the store.
Billie (Halvorsen) Barner[15] was twelve when her parents, Marie and Albert Halvorsen, leased a 30 'x 14' structure adjacent to The Cliff House a mile north of the town

site for $5 monthly from William Barton (Government Lot 2, Section 21). The old relic Cliff House saloon and appurtenances had been built in 1869 by William Warin as a place where loggers and seamen could flop, drink lager or whiskey and rent girls. But by 1912 few stayed at the rooming house and the girls had long since moved to more prosperous areas. A second lease was granted to the Halvorsens by Mrs. Euphemia Barton for $24 annually for use of the dock. Freight boats would stop and unload supplies for the store that ran competition to the old company-owned store. across from the town site.

Not far from the store, on the road to Seabeck a tree grew, dividing the road like a Jersey barrier. The road in those days ran closer to the beach and fragments can still be seen in some yards.

The Halvorsen's had an opportunity to lease the old company store and moved their operation in 1918 to the Seabeck dock.

Water Trough - on road
between Cliff House store and Seabeck.
(Author's Collection.)

[13]*Seattle Post Intelligencer.* Aug. 26, 1901.

[14]*Bremerton News.* May 20, 1911.

[15]Interview with Billie Halvorsen Barner Feb. 7, 1993.

**Marie Halvorsen
Storekeeper and Postmistress**
(Photo courtesy Billie Halvorsen Barner.)

Marie became postmistress running between the store and the post office located in an annex on the south side of the building. It was, according to Billie, a beautiful room with paneling and a fireplace, the only heat in the entire building. Later the post office was housed in the back of the store, partitioned off from the main store. The family's quarters upstairs consisted of living room, kitchen and three bedrooms.

The store didn't deal in foodstuff as much as items of survival for loggers, fishermen and farmers. Loggers boots and "tin pants", hay and feed , coal oil and sacks of spuds. There were two warehouses, one at the end of the dock for the hay and another attached to the backside of the store for other items. A barrel of *scorpa* as the Norwegian store owners called it was a popular commodity with patrons. *Scorpa* was a loaf cut lengthwise, then toasted.

Marie would dig down into a big barrel of hard candies and give customers a sample. Loggers would buy "tin pants" and cut them off at the top of their boots. They were such a popular commodity that while the store was burning in 1933, one logger, going through a stack of tin pants, refused to leave the building until he found the correct size.

All the Halvorsen children (Billie, Hazel Margaret, Boyer, Sig, and Dotty) had jobs around the store and dock. When Billie was home in the summers, one of her jobs was standing at the end of the dock when the freight boat came in, checking off the bill of lading. A winch would lift freight out of the boat and onto the dock. She also learned the difference between a two penny nail and a ten penny nail. *"The store had little do with groceries."*

Boyer and his Dad would talk sea stuff. Boyer would move logs around the bay with his father's boat, *Hazel.* It was not a tug, so Boyer built a tug to do the job more efficiently naming it *Billie.* It was the beginning of a business that continues with offices in Seattle and Ketchikan. Dozens of Boyer's tugs work the inland waters of the Northwest and Alaska. Every member of the family now has had at least one boat named for them. In 1993 Billie (Halvorsen) Barner christened a barge for her brother's firm, naming it *Seabeck.* Boyer died earlier in the year.

Customers were primarily fishermen and loggers from up and down The Canal. Farmers came in with their horse and wagons to get feed and exchange gossip. The store closed late during the summer, but early in the winter.

The Colmans came to the Conference grounds in the summer, usually on their yacht. Billie met only the mother and her son, Ken. Marie Halvorsen knew the family well.

Mrs. Halvorsen was too generous with credit. Behind the counter, each customer had a ledger book where she carefully entered their purchases and payments. Purchases far outweighed payments. If a logging camp went bust, Mrs. Halvorsen was left with unpaid bills. Often creditors would

Store during the 1940s.
(Author's collection.)

give her land in exchange for bills owed. She was one of the most extensive land owners in the Seabeck area at one time.

When Billie needed to return to school in Seattle, she'd board the *Potlatch* at 11 p.m., settle into one of the staterooms and wake in the morning as the boat arrived in Seattle at 7 a.m.

Billie, then in her final month of pregnancy, and her husband, Dr. H. A. Barner, attended a party in Bremerton in February 1933. "Barnie" as everyone called him, didn't want to tell Billie before the party that her mother's beloved store had burned that day because of a defective flue. Marie moved store and post office to a boat house and that too later burned. Mrs. Halvorsen rebuilt the store six months after the fire and the store was operated for two years by J. R. Ragsdale.

Harold Althoff purchased the store in January 1936 from the Halvorsen family and was appointed. postmaster a year later. The store was sold in 1949 to William Hewitt while Althoff remained postmaster until his retirement in 1968.

Althoff was born in Wisconsin and moved to Seattle as a child where he met his wife, Vivian (Cramer). They had visited the Kitsap peninsula many times and when the opportunity arose to buy the store, they gave up Seattle life for Seabeck. Their only child, Vivian (Brodigan) was born in Bremerton while they owned the store and she grew up in the upstairs' apartment. Her fondest memory was the soda fountain inside the front door of the store which dispensed hamburgers, malts, and shakes.

The 1949 earthquake shook the building, knocking cans and bottles to the floor. Upstairs Mrs. Althoff had the pressure cooker stewing beans and it blew up, spewing beans all over the ceiling and floor. During their residency, many winter storms knocked out power for up to two weeks creating an atmosphere much like that of the original store.

Mrs. Althoff was the part-time bookkeeper and clerk at the post office and was fully qualified to run the post office when Harold was off hunting.

Tom and Nondis Burkell purchased the store May 1, 1961, selling it 15 years later to Wanda and Robert Coffey of Snoqualmie. During the Burkell's ownership, they remodeled the upstairs and worked hard in improving the store and dock. Emil Naygard and Wally Martin rebuilt the dock during this period, tearing out the old piling and putting on new decking. It was then that the old ferry building was cut in two and piling was driven to anchor the floats.

The Coffeys sold to Jerry Zaspel and it's been sold three times since.

The store history follows that of the post office. More often than not, the person in charge of the store was also responsible for postal duties.

Postal Service - 135 years

Woodbury B. Sinclair was appointed first postmaster on July 1, 1858. He was one of the original millowners and moved to Port Madison, probably at the time that he ended his tenure on June 8, 1860.

Some notable personages have been associated with the Seabeck post office. Sinclair and Blinn were part owners in the mill; Richard Holyoke managed the mill for many years; Mrs. Nellie Howard lived in the town for more than 20 years and her husband was long associated with three of the town's hotels.

Frederick Prosch was the son of a well-known Northwest author and newspaper publisher. He was a newspaper editor as well.

There were two Hotchkins, father and son. George Johnson was a teacher and is known throughout Kitsap County as that rather than as a postmaster.

Marie Halvorsen was a much loved member of the community and ran the store at both the Cliff House and present location. While on the Seabeck dock, the post office was located in an annex attached to the south side of the building. Billie Halvorsen Barner enjoyed posting the month-end books because the room was so inviting with its fireplace and lovely paneling, overlooking The Canal and mountains. The original store, a full two-stories, had an attic full of old things left over from the mill period, but Billie never got up there.

* * *

Marshall Blinn had some difficulty communicating with the San Francisco headquarters because of the inadequacy of mail delivery. Although a postmaster was selected on July 1, 1858 and a name given to it (Seabeck), it wasn't until late 1859 that regular mail service was established between Seabeck and Port Gamble and then Washington Mill Company subsidized the bi-weekly delivery. Deliveries by government courier or contract began in 1868.

Marshall Blinn only makes two mentions of his postal duties during 1865.[16] On Oct. 30, 1865 he ordered post office blanks, paper and a pen, 104 one-cent stamps, 100 five cent stamps and 100 ten- cent stamps. The end of his tenure coincides with his departure from Seabeck.

Edward Clayson tells of the advent of the mailman:[17]

In May-June 1868, the U.S. Postal authorities at Washington, D.C., appointed Marshal (sic) Blinn of Seabeck postmaster and authorized him to advertise for a U.S. mail service to be carried twice a week, in boats, between Seabeck and Port Gamble. The P. O. Department furnished Marshil (sic) Blinn with the regular forms for advertising; these advertisements were nailed up at the company stores in Port Gamble, Seabeck and Port Madison for several weeks.

There was no paper published in Kitsap county at that period although (now don't faint at what I am going to tell you) Kitsap county at that period was the richest county

in the United States in PROPORTION TO POPULATION. The five large sawmill towns of Port Gamble, Port Madison, Port Orchard, Port Blakely and Seabeck were all in Kitsap county, running night and day at times, loading fleets of ships with lumber for California, Mexico, Chile, Peru, New Zealand, Australia, Honolulu and China and this great industrial activity went on and on, in Kitsap county, for nearly a quarter of a century without a publication or a lawyer within her borders.

This U. S. mail service was to begin on the first Monday morning of July 1868 at Seabeck, leaving at 8 a.m., due at Port Gamble the same day at 4 p.m., leave Port Gamble at 8 a.m. Tuesday morning, due at Seabeck 4 p.m. same day, leave Seabeck at 6 p.m. Wednesday evening, due at Port Gamble Thursday morning at 6 a.m., leave Port Gamble Thursday at 4 p.m., due in Seabeck Friday morning at 6 a.m.

This finished the week's service. The bids for this mail service were open till June the 20th 1868. When the bids were opened it was shown that there were three bidders, John Connick, Jasper Baker and E. Clayson, the bid of the latter being $25 a year lower than the other two.

The contract was awarded to E. Clayson for two years with John Condon and old Joe Kinnear as bondsmen in the presence of Steve Hovey, postmaster at Port Gamble, who acted as agent for the U. S. Department in this instance.

The successful bidder for this "strenuous" service, E. Clayson, had lived in Port Gamble for three years previous to this date, having a wife and two children at the time. As this service began in Seabeck and ended in Seabeck every week, I was living at the wrong end of the route, so I sold my little dwelling house to Billy Llewellyn and went up to Seabeck, the "metropolis of Hood's Canal," where I was an utter stranger.

So I was known for several weeks or months as "the mail man." Well, they discovered eventually that I was not a "fe-male man."

---

[16]Marshall Blinn diary 1865. Owned by Kitsap County Historical Society.

[17]Clayson. P. 9.

The Discoverer - Mailboat on The Canal
(Photo courtesy Joe and Pat Emel.)

Clayson owned a sloop *The Biddy* for the US mail boat. Once Clayson carried a man he called "Union City Wilson" on the run from Port Gamble to Seabeck. They left Port Gamble about 8 a.m. with a light wind but when they got seven or eight miles up The Canal, the wind died. When the wind died, Clayson started rowing with his 16-foot oars and "swept" along at about two miles an hour. Wilson was impatient to get to Seabeck to catch the steamer *Colfax* for Union City and when he saw a canoe paddled by two Indians, Wilson shouted to the Indians that he would give them money if they'd take him to Seabeck.

Wilson bargained and agreed on a two dollar fare. Within an hour the wind picked up and *Biddy* with Clayson at the helm flew about ten knots an hour and overtook the canoe about a mile from the wharf.

When Wilson realized that Clayson was going to beat the canoe, he offered the Indians an additional two dollars if he beat *Biddy*.

Clayson landed the passengers and got the mail into the office when the canoe came in and Wilson, according to Clayson, *"had the mortification of seeing the* Colfax *steam off around Point Misery without being able to catch her."*

Clayson's mail contract ended June 30, 1870. Amasa Miller of Port Gamble then secured the mail contract and the little steamer *James Mortie* or the *Shoo Fly,* as it was more commonly known, became the first steamer to carry the mail on The Canal.

The captain (and owner according to *Seattle Intelligencer)* was John M. Brisbane, the engineer Tom Hoy. In September 1871 while making his usual run from Seabeck to Port Gamble, the wind shifted and that necessitated Brisbane to haul in the jib. The halyards parted and Brisbane fell overboard and although the engineer stopped the vessel, he could not be found.[18]

Another of the early carriers on The Canal was Thomas Hood, born in Wareham, England who settled on Puget Sound in 1863. He held the contract for several years, ending his service in 1875.[19]

Various vessels were used on The Canal after this for carrying the mail and when passenger service was scheduled later, mail was brought in by them. In 1886 the mail contract was awarded to William Warin. He was required to take the mail from Port Gamble to Seabeck and Skokomish and back, 50 miles each way, three times per week. He was awarded an annual contract of $1,394.

When Fred Miller moved to Little Beef and bought the Clark property, he wanted a yacht. John Walton set up his mill while the Johnson brothers, Seattle, came and in 1912 built the 60-foot vessel and named it *The Discoverer.*

---

[18]*Weekly Intelligencer.* Sept. 18, 1871.

[19]Clarence Bagley. *History of Seattle. S. J. Clarke Publishing Company, 1916. Vol. 3, P. 251.*

Al and Marie Walton bought *The Discoverer* from Miller around 1917. They replaced the gas engine with a diesel to save excessive fuel costs and purchased an additional propeller for towing jobs. The towing propeller had a shallower pitch and more towing force for large loads. Al Walton said that with two or three log booms in tow, he could pull an additional log boom off the beach.

The Discoverer was used primarily for passenger, mail and light freight service on Hood's Canal from 1917-28. The route included Dewatto, Holly, Nellita, Brinnon, Seabeck, Coyle, Lone Rock and Vinland. The Waltons ran this boat and *Ladonna* year-round, even in bad weather, using the whistle and echo time during fog to determine their location from shore.

Billie (Halvorsen) Barner, whose mother ran the Seabeck store, attended high school in Seattle. Before Walton started the mailboat, Billy would leave Seabeck at 11 p.m., arriving in Seattle at 7 a.m. When Walton started the mailboat, she'd take the boat from Seattle to Silverdale, the stage to Anderson Landing, then catch the mailboat to Seabeck.

The only accident they had was when Marie hit a dock hard and tore off the railing and bent a davit on *The Discoverer*. Al never let Marie forget that mishap. He kept the bent parts for 20 years, even after they sold the boats to remind Marie that she was not the best pilot on Puget Sound even though she was the *first* licensed woman pilot in the State.

After the advent of good roads along The Canal, the mailboat was no longer needed. *The Discoverer* wasn't idle. It towed logs and for one season and was a fish tender in southeast Alaska at a cannery owned by John Emel.

The Waltons hauled dynamite and caps from Dupont (near Steilacoom) to Seattle and Hood Canal. It was so dangerous that they asked to be released from the contract. Their request was denied. The Waltons then threatened to report to Seattle authorities this illegal activity of delivering explosives to the inner harbor of the city. The contract was quickly terminated.

The Discoverer and *Ladonna* were sold when larger, competitive boat companies were able to offer the same service for less money. Once the small companies were out of business, the large firms would raise their rates.

The Discoverer was sold in 1928 and it was taken to Alaska where it hit an iceberg and sunk.

The starting pay of Betty Witwer, who served Seabeck from 1968 to 1985, was 65 cents an hour. There were 192 post office boxes then. In 1993 there were 550 with 383 rural route stops.[20]

In 1946 Bob Josephsen was hired by the postal department to deliver mail for Bremerton, Star Route 1. Josephsen delivered between Chico, Silverdale, Lone Rock, Seabeck and Holly and there were 150 boxes to fill, 100 of those between Chico and Silverdale. His route has changed in the intervening 48 years and now he begins at the junction of the Miami Beach and Seabeck/Holly roads and he drives the 50 miles to Dewatto.

At one time he kept a map with the names of all his patrons and a description of the cars they drove. He knew the comings and goings of the subscribers and often the hours they kept. He heard the gossip and for awhile would pick up passengers, for a $1, hauling them from Seabeck to Holly. He'd make the passenger stuff the boxes. Complaints were lodged against him and he eventually discontinued the *taxi service*. He wore out 27 Volkswagen "bugs:", putting more than 200,000 miles on each.

Before his three sons (Danny, Dick and Bob) were old enough to drive, they were helping their parents fulfill a contract with the government in transporting mail from Bremerton to Seattle. As soon as they turned 16, they were legally driving the trucks. Mail service out of Bremerton was several times daily with a two hour delivery time. Once one of the Central Kitsap teachers called the Josephsens and alerted the parents to the *fact* that the boys were falling asleep in class. Josephsen told her that should be expected: they'd worked half the night.

---

[20]*Bremerton Sun.* July 2, 1993.

Seabeck Postmasters

- Woodbury Sinclair: July 1, 1858-June 8, 1860
- Marshall Blinn: June 8, 1860-Dec. 14, 1869
- Charles Cass: Dec. 14, 1869-June 30, 1870
- Edgar Vrooman: June 30, 1870-Jan. 17, 1872
- Richard Holyoke: Jan. 17, 1872-Jan. 24, 1884
- Arnot G. Dickins: Jan. 24, 1884-April 1, 1887
- Mrs. Nellie Howard April 1, 1887-March 31, 1888
- Harry Clarke: March 31, 1888-Sept. 5, 1891
- Walter Macfarlane Sept. 5, 1891-April 30, 1894
- Albert L. Hotchkin, Sr. April 30, 1894-Jan. 15, 1900
- George C. Johnson: Jan. 15, 1900-Nov. 5, 1900
- Frederick Prosch: Nov. 5, 1900-Sept. 13, 1901
- Helen Prosch: Sept. 13, 1901-May 8, 1905
- Jacob Krom: May 8, 1905-March 10, 1906
- Frank Blakefield March 10, 1906-May 25, 1906-
- Albert Hotchkin, Jr. April 1, 1907-Feb. 26, 1915
- Irene N. Hotchkin: Feb. 26, 1915-May 17, 1919
- Marie Halvorsen: May 17, 1919-Oct. 1, 1937
- Harold A. Althof: Oct. 1, 1937-Jan. 12, 1968
- Betty J. Witwer Jan. 12, 1968-Feb. 28, 1985
- Donna McMillan July 1, 1985-present

The post office was operated near the Cliff House when the Seabeck store burned in 1933 by Marie Halvorsen.

Great Storm of 1990

The pre-Christmas storm of 1990 will long be remembered for as winds whipped the harbor from the north, the dock broke up, pitching boat against boat, float against float.

Although the National Weather Service said wind gusts of up to 50 knots were recorded on the Hood Canal Bridge, those hitting Seabeck were stronger. When winds subsided, there were 65 sailboats, fishing and ski boats and yachts littering the shoreline.

Winds started picking up in the morning of December 20, 1990 and continued stronger by the hour. At 4 p.m. the wind started crumpling boats and the floats. For a time there was fear that the entire dock would be lost.

The losses were staggering and amounted to several million dollars. Repairs were made and new or repaired boats began filling up the floats. No one will ever forget.

123

Schools

The First School

Education continues today as a prime concern of Seabeck residents as it was when the first children arrived, probably in 1859. It was in the fall of that year that Mr. D. L. Pierpont begin teaching. The first students were probably:[1]

The children of Hill Harmon
Edwin, 12
Olive, 11
The children of James Clark
James, Jr., 11
Ellen, 6
The children of A. B. Young
Frederick A., 9
Horace H., 6

There were probably other children from across The Canal who boarded at Seabeck to attend school.

The first school directors were J. R. Williamson, Hill Harmon, James Clark and L. S. Harmon with Marshall Blinn as clerk. Others who served on the board in early years were E. C. Lindsey (1864), Nathaniel Harmon and E. L. Miller (1866), Michael Fredson and Nathan Bucklin (1867) and Richard Holyoke (1877).

Pierpont had no supplies, texts or school when the first students registered. Classes were either held in a home or perhaps in the cookhouse. During the spring of 1860, a lot was cleared on the site of the present fire station and the first school completed[2] at a cost of $367.98.[3] The room was 20' x 28' with an apartment for the teacher and the children who might board. It has been referred to as *"the little red schoolhouse."* Peder Hagen bought that building in about 1916 and constructed a tool shed out of the lumber and probably used the windows. It still stands on Ingvald Hagen's property, immediately adjacent to the Hagen home.

In 1860, the Washington Mill Company presented the community with a library consisting of nearly 550 volumes with a value of about $700.[4] These books supplemented classroom texts and included: Two volumes *Demosthenes, Liddles' and Scott's Greek Lexicon, Cicero Translated,* Two sets of eight volumes each of *Shakespeare's Works,* two sets of eight volumes each of *Byron's Works, Hughes' Guide to Chaucer,* 12 volumes of poetry, two sets, eight volumes each *Burns' Works, Boswell's Johnson,* four volumes *Goldsmith's Works, Homer's Iliad,* Four volumes *Dickens.* Also works by Chitty, Franklin, Story, Benton, Calhoun, Bancroft and *Cook's Voyages, Fremont's Expedition, Two Years Before the Mast* and *Tale of Two Cities.*

Other works were included on medicine, religion, history, travel, other cultures, sports, geography, homemaking, humor, recreation and an assortment of popular novels.

The library was located in the school and was open several nights a week and on Sundays.

The classroom was supplied with English and Latin grammar, arithmetic, algebra, geography and biology textbooks and McGuffey's Readers plus a set of world maps.

By 1870 there were ten school age children enumerated by the census taker in Seabeck but this is again not indicative of the number of students. Many of the loggers had alliances with Indian women and these children were often not included in census figures.

The Second School

The original structure served until October 1878 when a two-room school was completed and the furnishings moved from the original building to the other.[5] The cost of the new building was $1,267. The

---

[1]Kitsap census, 1860.

[2]Washington Mill Company Journal.

[3]Washington Mill Company Papers.

[4]Gedosch. P. 162.

[5]Hauptly diaries. Oct. 8, 1878.

buildings stood side by side. The new school, paid for by the mill company, had plastered walls and blackboards and a second- hand piano.

Needing two classrooms required hiring a second teacher and Mrs. Walker and Miss Merwin were hired. Seabeck, District No. 3, had the lowest enrollment of the five districts in 1879 The County's allocation to schools that year was $3,145. Seabeck received $371.18.

On June 2, 1879 County Superintendent of Schools Charles McDermoth visited Seabeck and reported:[6]

Visited school at Seabeck, Mrs. Jennie Walker, teacher. School in good condition. Found school furniture as follows: maps of the world, Africa, N. America, Washington Territory and McGuffy's charts. Miss Isabella J. Butcher, one of the larger scholars, assisting in the primary department. Schoolhouse large, nice accommodations.

Teachers between 1869 and 1876 were Mary Shelton (1869-70), Frank Hanford (1871), Mary Theobalds (1872-73), Miss Winser (1874), Miss King (1875), Mrs. Thomas Mulhern before her marriage (1876).[7]

In Clayson's chapter about schools he writes: *Sam Blinn was a man about 50 years of age in 1870, and a very gallant gentleman, too; so to relieve the monotony of the place, he got the two mules saddled up one Sunday and invited Mary Shelton out for a ride (nothing wrong about that, but an 'infamous scandal' was started by the lying tongue of the ugliest looking women in town concerning the gallantry of Sam Blinn towards Mary Shelton, the handsome young school teacher.) This infamous scandal even reached San Francisco when up came Mrs. Blinn, all unawares, bringing her two children with her, for the purpose of watching the pranks (?) of her innocent husband. This was a surprise to Sam Blinn as his wife landed in Seabeck when he thought she was in San Francisco.*

But this scandal was met with fierceness by the brothers of Mary Shelton. They silenced it in their neighborhood with

loaded rifles in their hands. The only way to silence a scandal is to kill it upon the spot and this the Shelton boys did.

But it stuck to innocent Mary in a secret manner for a long time and was the means, no doubt, of her not getting married until late in life. There came very near being a big lawsuit concerning this malicious matter and the mischief-making woman who started it is now upon her last legs and still exists in Seattle"

Clayson describes other teachers:[8]

Frank Hanford was appointed school teacher at Seabeck soon after graduating at the old Territorial University in 1871-72. (He was) 20-21 years of age and was for a young man at that period of life of very steady habits and gave close attention to his duties as school teacher. There are now (1911) several gray-haired men and women in the Northwest that Frank Hanford taught their alphabets. This efficient teacher was a steady boarder at Clayson's for his term of six months. Frank Hanford served only one term as teacher.

Mary Theobalds (taught at) the next term. This young monitor was lithesome, strong, tall, muscular, intellectual and good looking. She could row a boat, paddle a canoe, sail a sloop, jump a six-rail fence and could "Dance all night till the broad daylight, And go home with the boys in the morning."

She was one of those young "woman suffrage jades" who mistook insolence for dignity. She was very deficient in those graces that are such a charm to men and women of refinement but she had a whole lot of the boys on a string. In this respect she had Mother Craig beat.

Why, even old Bill Thorn began to dress up and show, at a distance, his gallantry for this rude bounder, and Martin O'Toole, too, with that cock eye of his, he too, had an eye upon Mary. Why, even old Knight, with his sawdust cart, would pause to cast that north eye of his upon rampant Mary. But gallant Tom seemed to take prestige of them all. Old Poetry Mills of Chimacum was building that big smokestack at this time and he wrote some verses about "Gallant

---

[6]Kitsap County Superintendents' Minute Book, Jan. 1, 1879- Nov. 12, 1889.

[7]Clayson. Pg. 38.

[8]Clayson. Pg. 39-42

Tom and Mary Theobalds" and Tom Mulhern got mad. That which Tom got mad about, at 24 years of age, he would laugh about at 64. Mary Theobalds aspired to teach the school children to sing, a very worthy ambition, indeed, but as she could not sing herself she could not impart to children that which she herself did not possess.

Miss Winser *(was in) marked contrast to the rollicking Mary Theobalds (in that she was) of the gentle, refined, culture, whose age must have been about 24 and not pretty by any means. Her term as school teacher, in her spare time, was devoted to religious exercises. Being a good musician, in both vocal and instrumental music, she made the Sunday school a great success. Seabeck had never heard the "Moody and Sankey Gospel Hymns" until Miss Winser brought them there and she could sing them, too, with great feeling.*

She started the first Sunday with a very small attendance, which Mrs. Holyoke had brought together, possibly a dozen altogether. Mrs. Holyoke's little Sunday school had been in vogue two or three years before the advent of Miss Winser.

The second Sunday, school had doubled in number; the third Sunday it was still larger; the fourth Sunday the hall was crowded. Miss Winser, with her playing and singing, was the center of attraction. Mrs. Holyoke was jealous! She quit, leaving Miss Winser in full charge of the Sunday school, which she had started and had jogged along with for two or three years in the most monotonous and uninteresting manner.

You must remember, my readers, that Mrs. Holyoke was the "Hyas Tyhee Clootchman" in Seabeck, as her husband was the "King of Hoods Canal," and Miss Winser was not one of his subjects as she was in the employ of the Washington Mill Company and another distasteful habit too frequently at the Bay View Hotel. Being very fond of music, it was quite natural for her to be attracted to Clayson's where there was always abundance of it, both instrumental and vocal.

This gifted young woman was earnest and sincere in her religious views. She was

Original Seabeck School
Later dismantled and rebuilt on
Peder Hagen's property.
(Photo courtesy Olanie family.)

no hypocrite and though an ardent prohibitionist herself, she loved cheerful company and would sit in Clayson's parlor and play the organ and sing beautiful songs amidst convivial company who were drinking wine and beer. And being a good conversationalist as well as a good musician, she would, between the singing, give the company a little earnest talk upon the great virtues of prohibition.

One of her favorite songs was "The Beautiful Gates Ajar" and she could sing it with great pathos. Miss Winser although a good school teacher never got a second term of teaching at Seabeck. She was inconvenient to that bird of prey, the Holly-Hawke.

By 1880 there were 36 children between the ages of 6 and 17, according to census records, although the Superintendent's book states that there were 63 students in 1879 and support for the year set at $11.34 per student or $717.44. The difference is accounted for because students from across The Canal attended here and children of Canal loggers probably boarded in area homes but were not counted in the census but rather at their homes in Jefferson County.

The quality of education must have been good as the teacher's assistant, Isabelle Butcher, took her teacher's examination in 1880, passed and was teaching at District No. 4, Port Orchard which had been described the previous year as consisting of

Indians and half breeds. While Miss Butcher taught at Port Orchard, McDermoth noted :"School well provided but poorly attended." (The Port Orchard school was located near what is now the east end of the Manette bridge.)

Because of the large number of students and the inability to afford two teachers. the older students assisted in classroom teaching. Emma Wheeler took charge of the school in the fall of 1880.

In 1881 Elizabeth M. Ordway became Superintendent of Schools for the second time. She was one of the original "Mercer girls", nine young women recruited by Asa Mercer in New England ostensibly to teach school. Her ledgers are far more colorful than McDermoth, who was also a minister at Port Madison. While on one of her visits to Port Madison, Ella Olanie says that "She came to town, rowing a boat and smoking a cigar." Ordway, it might be remembered, was the only one of the nine original Mercer girls who didn't marry. From the superintendent's journal:

March 25, 1881: Visited school in District No. 3, Seabeck, Miss C(lara) E. Lombard in charge. Found pupils undergoing a written examination, rather an unfavorable time to judge of efficiency of teacher or progress of pupils. Miss Lombard was also a new teacher, taking the school at Seabeck sometime in January. Has had the advantage of teaching in the Normal Course at the Territorial University and with experience will undoubtedly prove a valuable teacher.

Miss Lombard had been teaching under a special permit and passed her County examination on May 5, 1881.

By 1882 there were 90 students at Seabeck marking attendance at second highest of the five districts. Only Port Gamble had more students.

A reporter late in the year stated:[9] "A commodious school house was built a few years ago, the old building becoming too small for the increased attendance. Between 40 and 50 pupils are daily instructed in the ordinary studies by a competent teacher."

Superintendent Ordway did not visit Seabeck in 1882 "Owing to the sickness of the Superintendent." Mr. Newton McCoy is the teacher. This sickness was long and tedious and thereby hangs a late statement of the results.

In February 1883, she wrote a note of explanation about her illness and the treatment received at Port Gamble where she had been teaching. A note from the physician who had attended the County Superintendent, teacher of the school in Port Gamble as well during her sickness and who had been elected Director for the District the November preceding, notified her that the school would be closed that week. In other words that her services were not needed any longer. The term of three months was half out! No charges were made, the simple fact being that the school was needed by the physician's wife, hence the conspiracy. An appeal was made as directed by a taxpayer of the place to the County Superintendent for the Directors to show cause for this summary dismissal, etc. As might have been expected, the case went by default and it was afterwards ascertained that the Directors had not been legally elected, the voting being done by acclamation and not by ballot as the law requires. Three Directors and a clerk were therefore appointed by the Superintendent and behold the case settled and the school continued.

Miss Ordway got her job back by appealing to the Superintendent . . . herself.

In May 1883 she visited Seabeck again and found the school in charge of Mr. R. E. Ryan. "This gentleman had been a successful teacher in Jefferson County and was the holder of a teaching certificate. The only drawback to his success anywhere was a perceptible deafness which did not always enable him to detect the correctness of an answer given by a pupil."

Six months later she again visited the school and wrote: To atone for the lack of a visit to the school in Seabeck in the fall of 1882, I have made two this year and can see the improvement made under Mr. Ryan's tuition.

---

[9]San Francisco Alta. November 1882.

The school was described in 1883[10] as being located with a spacious grove around it.

By January 1884, Seabeck had more students than any other district in Kitsap County. There were 96 students and $907.04 was allocated for school operation or $9.44 per student.

In October 1884 the school was in charge of S. A. Dickey, later a Superintendent of County Schools and prominent in the early history of Silverdale. *"Here he seemed to be at home in his work and I was pleased to see the progress made. The only objectionable thing I saw was the memorizing and repeating by rote a history lesson with apparently but little comprehension of its meaning or bearing upon other portions of the history. This may be a mistake of mine. I had been trained so differently to memorizing ideas and furnish the language myself.*

The arrival of "Professor" Dickey was noted in the Seattle newspapers[11] with another interesting comment: *"Professor Noland of Seabeck will conduct a class in French during the coming winter so that any person desiring this accomplishment will now have the opportunity to acquire it."*

Dickey knew the importance of honoring students. He submitted a list of students with perfect attendance records during the month of December 1884 to a Seattle newspaper.[12] They were Addie Brown, Hattie Brown, Frank Bowker, Harry Brown, Gertrude Chillman, Annie Geddes, Willis Geddes, Willie Howard, Denny Howard, Martha Jones, Minnie Maloney, Maggie Maloney, Laura Moore, Frank Mulhern and Marcella Rounds. The average attendance during the month was 30 while the cost of attendance was 90 cents.

In 1885 there were 102 students at Seabeck but Port Madison by then had 127 students. The per capita contribution to the schools was $8.51, down nearly 10% from the previous year on a per capita basis. The teacher in October was Miss Louise Cotes.

---

[10]*Seattle Post-Intelligencer.* Sept. 15, 1883.

[11]*Seattle Post-Intelligencer.* Oct. 23, 1884.

[12]*Seattle Post-Intelligencer.* Dec. 28, 1884.

"This young lady had recently come from the East where she had some four years experience in teaching. This was very evident in her manner and method with which I was quite pleased."

In March 1886, school enrollment had dropped to 86. Both Port Madison and Port Blakely had more. In December, four months after the fire, Miss Ordway visited Seabeck and wrote: *"Mr. _____. This was after the fire which destroyed the mill at Seabeck and I found a great change. Many of the people had removed to Port Hadlock and of course the school had decreased in numbers very materially. This seemed a pity as Seabeck has the finest school building in the County."*

In March 1887, the school census showed 650 students in the County with a per capita tax of $6.16. Seabeck was down to 66 students and payment per student had drastically dropped.

On March 4, 1889 Miss Ordway ended her entries: *Thus ends my eight years of service as Superintendent of School in Kitsap County. L. M. Ordway.* Sylvanus A. Dickey, the teacher of history by rote, took over her position.

His first census of District schools on March 18, 1889 shows only 32 students at Seabeck marking it as one of the smallest schools, in attendance, in the County. Dickey never visited Seabeck during the Territorial period, perhaps because he served on the State Constitution committee, revising the Territorial constitution to be more in line with one needed for impending Statehood.

School officers elected in November 1889 found Clerk H. W. Clark, Directors A. R. Burtt and Thomas Mulhern.

During the terrible winter of 1891, the roof collapsed on the *"new"* school, the one built in 1877 and students transferred back to the original 1866 structure.

The Seabeck area began to be filled with farmers and settlers. Crosby school district was founded in 1891 with Harry Zeek as the teacher. The Crosby folk demolished the Seabeck school (the one with the collapsed roof) and rebuilt it in that community. After a new school was built in Crosby, this two-room school became the teacher's cottage.

The Lone Rock school was founded in 1895 and the original structure, with additions, is now the Lone Rock Chapel.

Limited educational facilities at the turn of the century posed a real problem for many families. The district operated for as much of the year as the parents could afford to pay the teacher. The Veldee children of Stavis Bay attended four months a year and then it was difficult because they only spoke Norwegian but they were able to teach their parents English. That family moved to Bremerton for better educational opportunities.[13]

Teachers at the school after the fire included George Fairfield, A. J. Peake (1901), R. E. Ryan, W. B. Clough and George Cady Johnson.[14] Usually the teachers taught three months, then moved on to another school. *"Some of the older children, in order to get more schooling, would attend the school terms at the different places. They often walked many miles through the long forest trails. Sometimes they rode horseback."*[15]

Third School

In 1916 plans were drawn and bonds voted for erection of a new school at Seabeck, replacing the one built 50 years earlier.

School directors John Walton and E. O. Berg worked hard to convince voters of the need of a new structure. The district was financially impoverished and was *"obliged to issue bonds to pay for it, but a nice two room building was erected and again Seabeck had one of the nicest buildings in the area. Some years later a basement was added and the grounds improved with WPA labor."*[16]

Crosby and Holly were also in need of a new structure and they borrowed plans from Seabeck, creating identical structures in those two districts.

---

[13]*Kitsap County: A History.* Kitsap County Historical Society. 1977. Central Kitsap section, P. 60.

[14]Dedication address, Seabeck school, 1958.

[15]Ibid.

[16]Ibid.

Minnie Winsor
(Photo courtesy Bernice Morton.)

Minnie Winsor (B. Jan. 13, 1881 Metropolis, Illinois; D. March 1941 Tacoma) taught at Seabeck 1922-23. She and her daughter, Bernice (Morton) lived in one of the cottages, rented to them by Ken Colman who really didn't want to rent the cottages in winter. Rather than allowing them to use a 3-room cottage, they lived in eight rooms and used less than half of those.

Mrs. Winsor arrived in Seattle just after the June 1889 fire, coming by rail from the midwest to Tacoma, then steamer to Seattle. She attended Central School, T.T.Minor and was graduated from Seattle High School. Not yet 18, she waited to take her teaching exam and after having passed it, applied to several districts. She accepted a position at Brownsville but when let off the boat at the dock, no one met her. That night she slept in the woods. She also built a chimney at the Brownsville school as there was no way to heat the primitive building.

She taught in several districts prior to her marriage, then "retired to motherhood", but returned to teaching when her husband, a marine engineer, was injured in a Seattle streetcar accident. Although the Winsors didn't believe in their women working, she went back to teaching for the family's survival. After leaving Seabeck, she returned to the classroom, but as a student, attending what was then known as Bellingham Normal.

Her daughter, Bernice, remembers Seabeck well, especially her birthday in 1923 when a snowstorm hit the night of February 14. Mr. Berg walked ahead of mother and daughter, breaking a trail for them and his own children. Although few students could get to school that day, Bernice still had a birthday cake. Memories of childhood are wonderful: Bernice remembers sitting on the beach, trying to skip rocks and watching logs skid into the bay and the men who would roll them and move them around the bay.

A number of years ago, Bernice met Berge Berg, quite accidentally, and he reminded her of the day the ram (who had been turned loose with the ewes on the Conference Grounds) took after her. She'd skip down the hill to the Berg's house to walk to school with the children, but that day the ram took after her. She ran up against a house. Only Mr. Berg's prompt action with a large stick saved her from injury. Mr. Berg later told his sons that he was *scared green*, fearing that he might be attacked by the ram. There were only about 30 students when Mrs. Winsor taught there and although the school had two rooms, only one was used.

Andy Rogers remembers his teachers names, indelible in his mind: Emoreah Morlock, 1925, she from an old Charleston (West Bremerton) family; Lillian Probsfelt, 1926; Nora Salyer, 1927; Dorothy Peake, 1928-29; Dorothy Bye who taught for a year or two after Andy left the school. Andy's five children also attended the Seabeck school, but in the newer school building.

Dorothy (Bye) Higgins wrote her memories of teaching days at Lone Rock and Seabeck. While a teacher she boarded with area families and rented the Halvorsen's little cottage which had once been a saloon on the Cliff House property, according to her daughter, Bernice Morton.(There was) *a*

Andy Rogers' comments:
Arlene Keller Buchanan lives at Brewster. Lucille Lowe Peck lived at Erland's Point. The Lowe brothers live at Shelton and Holly. Walter Swanson moved to Brinnon in 1926 and won the World Championship log rolling competition in Seattle in 1936. (See Emel, Dahl and Hagen history elsewhere.)

Seabeck School, September 1925: (Front) Arlene Keller, Lucille Lowe, Roxanna Gilbert, Walter Swanson, Alben Berg, Archie Lowe, David Dahl, Betty Davis, Phyllis Davis. (2nd) Andy Rogers, Russel Emel, Elizabeth Hennicke, Martha Dahl, Klare Hagen, Margret Hennicke, Mabel Hagen, Melvin Hagen. (3rd) Lonnie Keller. (4th) Laura Hagen, Dina Dahl, Ramone Kelson, Miss Emoreah Morelock, Isaac Dahl, Halder Dahl, Lawrence Hagen, Floyd Lowe. (Photo courtesy Andy Rogers.)

lady who lived up the road from Pete Emel's and she would have us up for dinner. She said she was a spiritualist and she was always telling me about my deceased father. I heard later that she lost her mind and they found her running down the road.

While I lived at Emel's, we would walk down the road to the Comptons. They had a radio and we would listen to Amos 'n Andy.

Fred Miller used to pick me up if I was walking and give me a ride. They used to say he flew his own plane to Canada and pick up his liquor. The murder happened after I left Seabeck.

I have such wonderful memories of the Halvorsens. Mrs. Halvorsen would start a fire in our little (rental home next to theirs) Sunday nights and would also put hotwater bottles in our bed. I spent many weekends sleeping on their sleeping porch.

Mrs. Halvorsen would sit by the fireplace knitting while we played cards. She was very hard of hearing but managed to hear what they didn't want her to hear.

When I taught at Seabeck I would go to the store after school for my mail and Mrs. Halvorsen would say, "Go upstairs and have coffee with the girls."

One weekend when I returned from Tacoma, there was a lot of excitement over immigration officers intercepting a boatload of Orientals on the beach. Then during a storm, a pile driver near the ferry landing was sunk and men were trapped in the living quarters on the raft.

One experience I had while living at Smiths was being shot at. I had walked down to Point Misery and was sitting on a log. It was twilight. As I stood up, a shot went over my head. Someone from the house had walked down to meet me and also heard the short. I guess they mistook me for a deer.

Andy Rogers' comments:

The Hoppe family came to Seabeck in 1928 or 1929 and lived in Seabeck and Lone Rock until World War II. Jim Whittaker still lives at Seabeck and his sister, Jane, is deceased. Jack Wall left the area when Camp Union closed. Bob, Roy and Jean Brinker are deceased. Alf, Andres and Martha Dahl came from Norway in 1929 and left after Camp Union closed. Along with older brother and in laws started Tacoma Boat which grew into large business before they sold it.

Seabeck School 1929 - (Front) Leslie Hoppe, Jane Whittaker, Myrtle Lowe, Bernard Lowe, Chauncey Lowe. (2nd) Archie Lowe, Jack Wall, Jim Whittaker, Bob Brinker, Alben Berg, Francis ?, Miss Dorothy Peake. (3rd) Mabel Hagen, Lucille Lowe, Rosemary Rogers, Richard Hennicke, David Dahl, Ray Hoppe, Alf Dahl, Roy Brinker. (4th) Andrew Dahl, Roxanna Gilbert, Martha Dahl, Andy Rogers, Martha Dahl, John Hoppe, Jean Brinker, Melvin Hagen. *(Photo courtesy Andy Rogers.)*

131

Dorothy Peake had Andy Rogers in school and said he was a very intelligent boy. Mrs. Rogers had us for dinner and we had an enjoyable time. I was quite surprised to see an examining table in the front room. I knew Mr. Rogers had been a doctor.

Ethel Smith bought the Miami Beach property around 1928 or 1929 and she started a resort and called it Miami Beach. This was during the Depression and things were hard for her.

The Indians used to have their potlatches where Smith's house was. When she attempted a garden, there were layers and layers of clam shells.

I shall always remember the wonderful people of Seabeck and the many, many dinners I was invited to. I had a lovely dinner in Joe Emel's nice home overlooking the water. When I took my family to Scenic Beach, I saw the old home.

For some years after separation of Lone Rock and Crosby school Districts, the number of children at Seabeck decreased and the school became a one-teacher school.

When Lone Rock outgrew its one-room school, the two districts were consolidated and two teachers were again employed. Then Crosby consolidated with Seabeck, necessitating double shifting and a new building. After completion of the new school, the third school was barged to Brownsville where has since served as a church.

The Fourth School

A former employee of the Central Kitsap School District, Ray Darling, supervised preparation of the new school site. *"The land was purchased adjoining the existing school site and the grading and drainage work was turned over to the maintenance department. The site, a swampy, frog infested piece of property was a real challenge. A great deal of drainage tile and landfill was required and an almost worthless piece of property was reclaimed for the present Seabeck Elementary School site.*

Seabeck School 1932 - Dorothy (Bye) Higgins, teacher. Students autographed photo but names not in order. They include Roy Brinker, Mabel Hagen, Jack Wall, Alf Dahl, Joe Emel, Richard Hennicke, Jack Ungren, Bobby Brinker, Joyce Peterson, Chester Brinker, and four Lowes. *(Photo courtesy Dorothy (Bye) Higgins.)*

School Moving Day
(Photo courtesy Seabeck PTA.)

The new building was dedicated Nov. 1, 1956. Designed by Bremerton architects, Branch and Branch, it was built by Bremerton contractor Hal D. Burton. The six grade building was laid out with a main corridor down the center, offices, storeroom and three classrooms on the east side and a gym, kitchen, furnace and storage rooms, lavatories and three classrooms on the larger west side.

Five months later, on Jan. 18, 1959, the new school burned. As Seabeck then didn't have a fire department, Silverdale, Navy Yard City, Kitsap Lake, Bangor and Puget Sound Naval Shipyard firemen fought the blaze, laying hose 1,000 feet to the bay. They pumped saltwater on the fire, concentrating efforts on the furnace and boiler rooms.

First and second graders were transferred to Chico using the library and bookrooms as classrooms while third through six graders used four new classrooms just completed at Silverdale.

Schoolbooks and furniture were borrowed from other District schools and other Districts.

The State Legislature passed a resolution authorizing an investigation into the cause of the fire. Legislators determined, within 12 days of the fire, that lack of an ample water supply with adequate pressure was a factor in the $214,540 loss with an insurance recovery of $185,574. Not covered were the architects' fees, underground sewers, concrete paving and boiler room equipment.

The committee report concluded that school boards require automatic alarms, separate telephones, pressure water tanks and outside exits for each classroom in school buildings of non-fire resistant construction. State Representative Charles Savage said after visiting the ruins with the state investigating committee that no obvious neglect on anyone's part can be blamed for the cause of the fire.

The Fifth School

The new school was built with a concrete slab floor rather than wood and a fire-resistant material was used in the walls.

The new school opened Jan. 2, 1958, just 16 days short of the first anniversary of the fire. When the school opened, second and fourth grade classes were combined because of low attendance. The average attendance figures were 22 first graders, 12 second, 22 third, 16 fourth, 27 fifth and 19 sixth graders. Dedication of the replacement school was Feb. 20, 1958.

It is doubtful that there's been a year in the history of the school, since the arrival of Sam Nickels, when a descendant of his family (and allied lines) hasn't attended classes in Seabeck. Sam was progenitor of many Waltons, Emels and dozens of other families in the area.

Bertha (Brumm) Sibon wrote a history of the Seabeck Parent Teacher Association: It was organized in 1942 following consolidation of grade schools in the Central Kitsap District.

Mrs. Leigh Hume, a member of the Silverdale PTA met with Mrs. Shield and myself and plans were made to call a meeting of area parents and elect officials.

At his meeting Mrs. Shield was elected President, I vice president and Mrs. Ilene Ramsey, secretary. There was NO competition.

The Association's first project was a hot lunch program. F. C. (Hank) Whitacker and Al Kassoni volunteered to wire the old school basement for an electric stove. Their wives told them that if any money was paid it was to be donated to the Association.

Inga Cicelski was hired as the first cook and the PTA underwrote her salary. There were times when the treasury was empty and members contributed to meet the obligation. The project was a big success and Mrs. Cicelski a great cook.

The PTA also helped sponsor Boy Scout Troop No. 515. Funds raisers were the usual annual bazaar, carnival and bake sales.

Mrs. Shield remarried and became Mrs. Trowbridge and with her family left the area. I completed the term and served another year as president.

Attendance grew and parent interest increased as speakers from county government, library and law enforcement volunteered programs.

The Cemetery
Toppled Monuments of Community History

One of many wooden grave markers found at the Seabeck Cemetery up until the late 1950s.
(Photo courtesy Adele Ferguson.)

A one-way dirt road leads from the Seabeck-Holly Road to the small, historic cemetery that holds the remains of a hundred or so souls from Walter J. Williams (1860) to Andrew Just (1993), the first and last burials. The cemetery was closed officially in 1993.

There were several deaths and burials in the community before an order was issued by the mill company to prepare a burial ground. Jacob Hauptly was given the chore. Ella Olanie[1] said that the 15 or so graves previously interred nearer the town were moved to this new site. It might be assumed, it should be assumed, that as soon as there were residents and death that a community burying ground was established. A recent community disagreement arose over the size of the cemetery: was it one acre or five acres? Frankly nothing has been found, to date, that indicates that any land was *officially* reserved for burial. It just sort of happened.

The U.S. Coast and Geodetic survey drawing of the community (1883-84) shows what appears to be a parcel of about one acre. However a Trustees Deed and Bill of Sale from the J.M.Colman Company to Walter L. Wyckoff Company, dated Dec. 16, 1950 transfering certain land holdings specifically exempts *"five acres for cemetery"*. That document, according to Sharon Koch, would probably stand up in court. She will continue her search for documentation establishing authenticity of the size and any incorporation papers that might have been drawn.

A rumor (or legend, perhaps) says that cemetery records were lost in Puget Sound while being transported from Port Madison, the original County seat, to Sidney (now called Port Orchard). Incredulously the records were lost,

---

[1]Ella Olanie interview. 1977.

according to the "legend" when a canoe transporting the records upset. All County records were moved in 1893 in a day and age of modern steamers. Canoes were not used. And no maritime accidents occured during this process.

In a *Seattle Intelligencer* article May 26, 1877, the reporter noted as follows: *"Recently an acre of land was laid off for a burying ground and it was grubbed and graded and a neat picket fence put around it."*

In January 1877 Hauptly and and several other men worked on the graveyard but *"the committee on graveyard would not receive the work yet."* [2] They continued working through the balance of the month when Hauptly was paid $138 by the committee but they *"kept $50 back for not burning the logs on the ground. I took them all off the ground."* he later wrote.

The first death in the community after acceptance of the cemetery by the committee was that of Captain Louis Alexandre of the ship *Erminia Alvarez.*

Jacob Hauptly built a wagon road to the burying ground and took care of the burials from 1877 to 1886. Diary entries have been added to previously compiled lists. Other *assumed* burials will be added taken from deaths listed in the newspapers.

Among the earliest reported deaths were those of Walter J. Williams, master of the British bark *Sea Nymph* in November 1860. Solomon Hopkins, age 48, a native of Milford, Maine died from his injuries May 24, 1864. He was cut by a circular saw. He left a large family in the East.

Clara Little's tombstone shares forever the sorrow felt by her mother: *Hush Mother. I live still; A bright loving Angel. Earth was too cold for me. Here immortality. Safe. Weep not."*

Mrs. Dennis Bradley died Jan. 21, 1880 while there was still two feet of snow on the ground. That was a particularly bad winter with some estimates of 7 feet of snow at times. Richard Holyoke, with horse and sled, broke a road to the graveyard. On the day of the funeral, Hauptley fixed up the old sled and hauled the corpse of Mrs. Bradley to the Graveyard at 4 p.m. *"Quite a turnout. Snow about 15 inches on graveyard."* [3]

If there is a ghost in the Inn, perhaps it's Cam Whitney who died July 13, 1880 at the Eagle Hotel. Three people died that same week, according to Hauptly's dairies: Harry Shaffer (in Seattle), Cam Whitney and Mrs. John Clements.

In 1959 Adele Ferguson wrote a series of articles in the *Bremerton Sun* and devoted one column to the cemetery:

The history of the town can be read on the faded cedar slabs and discolored tombstones in the little cemetery almost hidden from view by the tangles of salal and the branches of the giant firs and pines that grew up to shelter the graves of the many who died in the building of the community.

Records were unknown in those days and many a man's obituary was chiseled into a slab of cedar:

"A native of Maine. He was struck on the head with a bottle of whiskey and killed."

"He drank too much strong liquor, tried to walk the boom, fell into the bay and drowned."

"Killed in a feud."

"Killed in a brawl."

"Murdered."

"Earth was too cold for me."

Nearly all the old markers are now preserved in the University of Washington historical department. But many old stone markers still lie covered with pine needles and hidden in the density of the undergrowth.

* * *

It is fortunate that the University preserved some of the old markers as vandalism over the years has taken its toll.

In 1971 one of the oldest markers was stolen, that of William Bell, 1831-1869, who drowned. It made its way all the way to Port Orchard where sheriff's deputies found it after an anonymous tip.

[2] Ibid. Aug. 22, 1878.

[3] Ibid. Jan. 22-23, 1880.

136

Other Hauptly diary entries concerning the cemetery:

July 18, 1882: Mrs. Thomas Moran died at 3 p.m. The corpse arrived from Three Spits in sloop. Hot day. (July 19) July 20: Funeral. She was enterred at 10:30 a.m.

April 21, 1883: Mr. Thos. Butcher died this morn. I went around with subscription paper and raised about $150 for the Butcher family. Funeral of butcher evening of 22nd at 5:30 o'clock. Craig read a prayer. Large turnout. A little sprinkle while at grave. Total subscription $184.25.

June 10, 1883: Sam Bowker was buried at 11 a.m. He got killed at the mill on Friday, the 8th.

Many of those listed as buried in the cemetery come from newspaper obituaries or family records. Several lists have been used to compile names and many names have been corrected from previous lists.

Allen, James: 1868.
Alexandre, Captain Louis. 1877.
Ames, Ellen: Aug. 8, 1898 - June 20, 1954.
Ames, Raleigh: 1970
Andersen, Emel: June 7, 1893 - June 12, 1893
Andersen, Emma: Nov. 9, 1894 - Nov. 30, 1894
Andersen, Hulda: Jan. 15, 1873 - Aug. 20, 1900.
Andersen, Oluf: 1860 - 1909.
Baker, J. G.: March 5, 1885
Baker, Millie: 1875 - 1876.
Baker, Nichols S.
Barrett, Jason: March 26, 1883.
Bassett, Ann
Bassett, Samuel J.: 1850 - June 23, 1940.
Beatty, James
Bell, William: Oct. 17, 1831 - Jan. 17, 1869.
Benson, Child: May 17, 1885.
Bern baby. Oct. 29, 1889.[4]
Bolan, Ida (Hintz): April 21, 1860 - Jan.1, 1937.
Bonney, James: June 8, 1883.
Bowker, Frances: Oct. 15, 1881.
Bradley, Marjorie: D. Jan. 22, 1880.

Branham, Helena C.: June 16, 1888 - April 29, 1932.
Brown, Larry: Dec. 22, 1952 - Jan. 23, 1953.
Brown, Amos
Brown, Sarah: Aug. 26, 1864 - Feb. 13, 1928.
Brown, William B.: Aug. 20, 1908 - Oct. 18, 1943.
Bryant, Hiram: 1823 - Jan. 26, 1869.
Burn, Leo: `1889 - 1889.
Butcher, Thomas: April 21, 1883.
Card, William: March 3, 1858 - April 1, 1926.
Cichey, Andrew: Nov. 17, 1865 - Feb. 27, 1936.
Clements, Ann: 1838 - July 19, 1880.
Clements, John
Clough, Caroline
Clough, Julia Anne: Sept. 29, 1856 - Nov. 7, 1938.
Clough, Lewis
Clough, Warren L.: 1847 - Oct. 7, 1923.
Cottle, Ham
Cottle, Ursula: 1830 - 1872.
Craft, Mary: 1859 - 1915.
Craft, Thomas H.: 1855 - 1918.
Dahl, Anna: 1894 - Jan. 25, 1919.
Dahl, Borghild. circa 1908-1916.
Emel, Peter F.: Dec. 25, 1853 - Feb. 21, 1924.
Emel, Ruby C.: 1909 - Apr. 17, 1911.
Fenwick, William: Nov. 23, 1854 - Mar. 16, 1947.
Fogg, Horace: 1848 - Jul. 23, 1878.
Foley, John: died July 23, 1878.
Francis, Frank:
Furger, Joe: Jul. 30, 1878 - Dec. 20, 1938.
Hafner, Karoline: Feb. 20, 1865 - Aug. 16, 1936.
Hagan, Jacob
Hallier, Sofie: 1885 - Sep. 16, 1888.
Hanby, Leslie C.: Jun. 27, 1926 - Dec. 20, 1933.
Hintz, Julius: Mar. 14, 1857 - Jan. 10, 1928.
Hite, Alice J.: Jan. 28, 1853 - Feb 28, 1931.
Hite, Asahel: Jun. 15, 1847 - Aug. 16, 1931.
Hite, Robert Bruce: Sep. 1, 1881 - Dec. 11, 1951.
Hoar, Evelyn: Jul. 12, 1905 - Jan. 2, 1971.
Hoar, John: Nov. 23, 1891 - Feb. 8, 1970.
Hopkins, Solomon. May 24, 1864.
Hunt, William
Johansen, Carl: Sep. 2, 1891 - Jul. 29, 1896.

---

[4]Nat Sargent diary. Oct. 20, 1889.

Johnson, Albin T. Jun. 11, 1882 - May 2, 1901.

Johnson, August: 1848 - 1926.

Johnson, Edward: Oct. 30, 1882 - Nov. 4, 1930.

Johnson, John A.: Jun. 26, 1846 - Dec. 26, 1926.

Johnson, John August: Sep. 4, 1848 - Jan. 2, 1926.

Johnson, Louisa: Sep. 20, 1848 - Apr. 21, 1904.

Johnson, Maggie: Apr. 12, 1847 - Oct. 5, 1925.

Johnson, William: Oct. 5, 1858 - Nov. 27, 1938.

Johnston, infant: Apr. 2, 1931 - Apr. 9, 1931.

Johnston, Norma L.: Apr. 18, 1931 - Dec. 6, 1932.

Johnston, Wayne: June 29, 1935 - Sep. 24, 1935.

Johnston, William: Aug. 12, 1867 - Apr. 25, 1939.

Just, Andrew: Oct. 8, 1859 - July 25, 1928.

Just, Andrew: 1966 - 1993.

Just. Frederick R.: Sep. 27, 1903 - Jul. 30, 1921.

Just, Richard Carlton: July 1, 1909 - Feb. 2, 1932.

Juvan, John: 1875 - Nov. 23, 1928.

Keegan, William: May 15, 1838 - Aug. 23, 1880.

King, George B.: 1826 - 1875

Langworthy, Harvey J.: 1895 - Apr. 28, 1923.

Lantz, Mrs.: died Apr. 4, 1880.

Lantz, Richard: April 1872 - Aug. 20, 1878.

Lewis, Elizabeth (Fenn): Jan 16, 1833 - Feb. 10, 1913.

Lewis, Henry King: Feb. 5, 1882 - Feb. 6, 1882.

Linde, Anna: 1845 - 1909.

Little, Clara E.: 1868 - May 9, 1885.

Little, Clara. April 5, 1868 - May 9, 1885.

Little, Helen (Walker): B. Oct. 1827; D. October 26, 1901.) (Also known as Ellen.)

Maher, Elizabeth Emel: Jun 16, 1875 - Apr. 29, 1909.

Alder leaves hid the last name of George B. King as second-growth timber and young alder trees steal back the graveyard which was cleared in 1877 behind Seabeck. Many of the old graves have carved fences surrounding the family plot, but only a few of these are still standing. The cedar grave markers were carved by the sawmill workers or a member of the bereaved family when a death occurred.

(Photo courtesy Adele Ferguson.
Cutline taken from her 1959 story about the Seabeck Cemetery.)

Matson, John M.: 1894 - Oct. 26, 1903.
McDonald, Angus: died June 17, 1873.
McDonough, William C. 1856 -
    Oct. 30, 1888.
Melenowski, Frank: B. Oct. 23, 1906 -
    D. Jan. 8, 1907.
Moran, Sarah: D. July 18, 1882
Myre, Brithe: 1830 - 1894.
Myre, Nils: 1829 - 1893.
Nelson, Andrew. Feb. 12, 1849 -
    March 19, 1917.
Nelson, Mr.: D. April 17, 1879.
Nelson, Anna: July 7, 1850 -
    Jan. 21, 1934.
Nelson, Johan Frederick: D. Apr. 12,
    1934.
Nelson, Malina: July 3, 1853 -
    Apr. 12, 1894.
Neyhart, Ralph Jacob: June 3, 1888 -
    May 19, 1969.
Neyhart, Robbin
Nickels, Clara (baby): D. July 16, 1874.
Nickels, Clara: Apr. 13, 1845 -
    Apr. 30, 1923.
Nickels, Frank: 1877 - Nov. 15, 1901.
Nickels, Augusta (Gussie): 1880 -
    Mar. 4, 1954.
Nickels, Samuel: July 22, 1840 -
    Mar. 16, 1924.
Noble, Joseph: died Apr. 4, 1874.
Olanie, Agnes: 1887 - 1889.
Olsen, Bessie.
Pierce, (twins): died Mar. 20, 1882.
Prosch, Frederick: Aug. 7, 1848 -
    Aug. 24, 1901.
Rensch, Frank B.: 1859 - Dec. 12, 1914.
Rensch, Paul: 1847 - 1911.
Rogers, Albert: Jan. 25, 1867 -
    Aug. 4, 1930.
Rogers , Frances: Jan. 2, 1892 -
    May 16, 1943.
Rostad, Edward: Feb. 14, 1917 -
    July 13, 1933.
Rostad, Christian: Oct. 7, 1862 -
    Dec. 12, 1945.
Rostad, Marie F.: Mar. 24, 1876 -
    Dec. 10, 1945.
Russell, Martha: Sept. 11, 1864 -
    May 31, 1940.
Russell, William J.: Nov. 27, 1862 -
    Sept. 17, 1938.
Sargent, Nathaniel J.: July 7, 1863 -
    Aug. 16, 1954.
Sayer or Sager, Jacob: died Aug. 25,
    1877
Selby, Joe S.: Apr. 3, 1889 -
    Apr. 26, 1958.
Selby, Margaret Wilson: Sept. 1, 1862 -
    Aug.3, 1935.
Selby, Mary I.: Jan. 16, 1893 - 1907.
Shaffer, Harry D.: 1840 -

Buried July 8, 1880.
Sheridan, William: 1844 - June 1881.
Spencer, Hanabel H. Nov. 5, 1862-
    June 1, 1945.
Stilwell,Sarah: June 16, 1858.
Stout, Margaret S.: Oct. 31, 1885 -
    June 28, 1932.
Taylor, Glen W.: June 27, 1888 -
    Jan. 11, 1960.
Thompson, Merle: 1856 - 1953
Uelan, Oscar: D. 1953
Veldee, Martha. 1893-1893.
Veldee, Pearl Irene. B. 1901 -
    D. Jan. 17, 1903.
Voegele, Barbra: Dec. 4, 1847 -
    Jan. 23, 1916.
Voegele, Edward: Nov. 20, 1849 -
    Feb. 15, 1930.
Wach (no first name): Jan. 21, 1883.
Wanderschied, Anna: Apr. 16, 1868 -
    Mar.   5, 1938.
Wanderschied, Frank: Dec. 6, 1861 -
    Apr.   9, 1936.
Wares, George. 1876[5]
White, George: 1844 - 1874
White, Jas. H.: died Oct. 19, 1883.
Whitney, Calmon: 1836 - Jul. 13, 1880.
Williams, Grizzley: 1865 - 1911.
Wilson, Dempsey: Feb. 2, 1823.
Wilson, Margaret: Jun. 4, 1829 -
    July 14, 1912.
Wilson, Minnie: Nov. 21, 1890 -
    April 27, 1962.
Wilson, Nellie A.: Mar. 19, 1859 -
    Nov. 3, 1916.
Wilson, Sydney J.: Feb. 7, 1866 -
    Apr. 16, 1934.
Wood, Elizabeth: Apr. 10, 1963 -
    Dec. 3, 1924.
Zuber, Jacob A.: Sep. 16, 1851 -
    Apr. 13, 1933.
Zuber, Sarah J.: Mar. 11, 1858 -
    May 14, 1933.

---

[5]Adele Ferguson notes taken 1949.

Book Three

Autumn

A boy who knew that Dokibatt was coming to make great changes was in mortal fear as he did not wish to be changed; he began to run away, carrying with him a water-fox with some water in it; but as he ran, wings came to him and he began to fly. The water shaking sounded something like *pu-pu-pu* repeated rapidly and the sound was changed into the present noise of the bird as it begins to fly.

So the dove then began its present mourning cry, *hum-o-hum-o*. And the Twanas to this day call the turtle dove *hum-o*.

Rev. Myron Eells,
*The Twana, Chemakum and Klallam
Indians of Washington Territory.*

Death, Transition and Rebirth

All that was left of Seabeck after the fire.
(Photo courtesy Seabeck Christian Conference.)

Seabeck was a ghost town. Most of the old families followed mill work and moved to Port Hadlock. Those who stayed eked out a living from the natural resources. With no work, Joe Emel's motto, *Tide's Out; Table's Set* was all too true. The Nickels, Rounds, Lewis, Walton, Olanie families stayed and new people wandered in like Frederick Prosch, son of an old, well-known publishing family, and Peter F. Emel, a Seattle saloonkeeper and hotel owner. What they found here is impossible to describe. One must watch black storm clouds rush through mountain valleys, smell the salt air, or stare at a summer sunset to know the feeling of Seabeck.

H. A. Stanley, a well-known author of the late Nineteenth Century, came here and we almost can see him scrawling his novel

in long-hand. His book[1] chronicles Rex Wayland's arrival in the Northwest, meeting with William DeShaw and Princess Angeline and the discovery of the location of a missing Spanish diary in the volcanic (sic) Olympic Mountains. He goes in search of the diary and spends some time at Seabeck before crossing The Canal to seek his treasure. He writes:

~

Seabeck is a typical "has been" town of Puget Sound. Years ago it was as large as, or larger than Seattle. It had its mills, and at its dock ships were loaded with lumber for the furthermost ports of the world. Yea, more --- ships were built there, as many as three large vessels building at a time, and the land-boomer had high hopes. Why should it not be a great city? It had timber lands all about it, a fine harbor and splendid mills. Here is the widest portion of Hood's Canal, it being twelve miles across to the

---

[1] H. A. Stanley. *Rex Wayland's Fortune or The Secret of the Thunderbird.* Laird & Lee, Chicago. 1898.

beach of Taraboo Bay. Directly across to the west were the towering Olympics, with their vast stores of mineral, lumber and game. The Olympics are there yet, but so rough and inaccessible that the timber and minerals as well as the game are quite likely to remain undisturbed. In fact, the Olympics have never been fully explored, and may not be for another fifty years.

And what of Seabeck? Its mills are burned, wiped out by one mammoth fire. Its ship building is a story of past days. Its stores, hotels and saloons are closed. Its wharves are rotted, torredo-eaten and very shaky. From the water it looks very attractive even yet, for it is beautifully situated, but seven-eighths of the pretty little houses that show up so well are vacant. The green lawns and spreading fruit trees are neglected. Its business is practically nothing, all its mail being taken up from the wharf in a small hand-bag every other day. It ships very little if any fish or oil. Its inhabitants have not even enterprise enough to go out and shoot the duck, which in season fairly cover the waters of its bay. In short, if natural decay is not soon arrested, beautiful Seabeck will be as Tyre and Sidon of old --- a place of barrenness and ruin on which fishermen spread their nets to dry.

As the *Delta* swung in toward the town that January day, it seemed to Rex he had never seen a more beautiful spot. The water all through the sheltered bight was of that pretty green so common to certain bottoms of the sound. The forest to the east, south and north was of softly rounded outline, and the entire prospect was in strange contrast with the rugged, broken mountains rising up so many thousand feet and so abruptly from the opposite shore.

~

Rex' fictional uncle, Festus, had come here to start a logging camp for a San Francisco firm and it created a considerable stir in this "sleepy little town. It meant business for the store-keeper, for the rancher who had butter or spuds to sell, for the small boy who caught fish for profit as well as pleasure, for the saloon man who retailed a very high-priced quality of *'moisture'*.

Uncle Festus sent Rex back to Seattle for supplies and to secure men to work in the logging camp. While in Seattle, his mother pleaded to go to the logging camp as cook, and Rex agreed. And then Rex was off for the mountains. Not a lot about Seabeck, but at least people were visiting.

Seabeck ~ The Deserted Village

By Claes Leonard Hultgren
Alaska-Yukon Magazine
October 1908

By a strange perversity of Fate, Seabeck, one of the most beautifully located of all the pretty little towns in the Northwest and once one of the most important industrial centers on Puget Sound, has become a deserted village.

Houses long since abandoned make up the greater part of this little hamlet which looks out over Hoods Canal. They dot the lower western slope of a wooden hillside and cluster at its foot amid orchards and gardens where the woodland growth has long since become firmly rooted and now mingles in riotous confusion with the domestic trees and shrubs.

It is a sight which gives one a peculiar and inexplicable sensation, yet is less striking than the tall brick chimney which rises in solitary grandeur from the sand near the water's edge -- the first object to meet the eye of the incoming traveler. On the wharf itself, where the steamer lands, are two large, dilapidated frame structures which are also worthy of notice, for with the exception of some reservoirs on the hillside in the edge of the village, this is all that remains to give the visitor a glimpse, as it were, of Seabeck's former greatness and the only indication of her early prosperity. Here the old structures stand, silent reminders of the days when Seabeck was a busy lumber town and the most important port and shipbuilding center of Puget Sound.

In those days half a dozen ships, flying the flags of various nations, could been seen at her wharves at the same time loading lumber for the markets of the world, and vessels ranging from a schooner to a full-rigged ship were built at her yards.

That was in the palmiest days of Seabeck's glory, and one or two gray-haired pioneer residents love to linger over those old memories and to talk of the events of former days. With pardonable pride they tell how their town, with its magnificent lumber industry, its sawmill, planing mill and shipyard, was larger and far more important than the Seattle of those days.

At that time Seabeck flourished. Well directed activity was the order of the day. Her busy workers turned the giant trees of the surrounding forests into boards and planks and spars in her mills; built them into ships to plow every sea in her spacious wharves to be carried down the coast to California, across the broad Pacific to the Orient and Australia, and even to Europe.

Then Seabeck flourished. The pay-roll was large and prosperity reigned in the little town. The homes were made more comfortable and their surroundings improved and beautified.

A water system was installed carrying the pure water of the hillside springs into the houses and storing it in large reservoirs for use in emergencies.

Of churches there were none, but occasional services were held in the town hall above the "company" dining-room, which was the general meeting place.

Saloons, dance-halls and gambling dens flourished much the same as in any new frontier community, and no expedient for separating the men from their dollars was left untried. But all this was merely incidental in the history of Seabeck. Her mission was work and activity, and her destiny, as her builders and workers fondly believed, was to become the most important city on the Pacific coast and to rival those of the Atlantic.

But all the air castles of her dreamers dissolved into a mist and all her busy activity was stopped one night, twenty-three years ago, by a fire supposed to have been started by sparks from one of the ships at the dock falling into a lumber pile. In a moment, it seemed, the entire plant was ablaze. All industrial Seabeck went up in smoke. Everything was consumed -- the vast lumber piles, the mills, the shipyard, the vessel under construction, the wharves, and

some of the vessels in the harbor even had great difficulty in avoiding a similar fate.

Of all the "company's" property there remained only the store and the cookhouse with

**Original Mill Cookhouse and Store
after they were separated.**
(Author's collection.)

the dining-room adjoining, and over that the town hall, as it is still called. The old brick chimney stands as solid as if it had been built a month ago, and around it are scattered the old and rusting boilers, looking as if they had been carelessly dropped there.

In the gravel and debris where once the shipyard was located may be seen the surfaces of immense blocks on which, in the long ago, was laid the keel of many a good ship that still furrows the foam.

Scattered about, silent reminders of this long past catastrophe, are rusting bolts, once half molten and nearly shapeless chains intended to hold the wanderers of the deep in the fiercest storm, and anchors, half buried in the sand.

Along the shore, running southward from the site of the old mill and shipyard is a plank sea-wall, a remnant of the old wharves, where the fishermen spread their nets to dry in the sun and fasten their boats when coming in with a catch.

Nearby on the one remaining wharf stands the old, dilapidated company store, and a few feet away the old cook-house and dining-room with the old town hall above. Occasionally this is still used as a meeting place, and in the other building is the post office and general merchandise store, patronized by the fishermen, who live in the otherwise deserted village, and the small farmers of the surrounding country.

145

The deserted houses of the little village still dot the hillside, looking out across the deep blue waters of Hoods Canal, which occasionally take on a tinge of emerald and sometimes glow like amethyst under the rays of the sinking sun.

Across the canal are seen the forest-clad foothills of the Olympics, rising precipitously out of the waters, and farther on the serrate tops of the hills rise higher and higher until their mantle of evergreens gives place to a coverlet of glistening, eternal snow and the summits are lost among fleecy clouds floating in the azure blue above.

On the other side, back of the village, rise forest-crowned hills, forming a background as well as a shelter for the little hamlet. Here rise the springs which formerly supplied the water system of the town, many of them forming rivulets which bubble and sing in the mad downward rush to the salt sea water. Here are hidden values and unfrequented hillsides where the nature lover may hear the unmistakable "call of the wild:" even on the very threshold of civilization.

In this spot of sylvan beauty Seabeck has nestled, warmed by the sunshine of more than fifty summers and veiled in the mists of as many winters.

Now, as formerly, it is an ideal place for a home, but so far only a few fishermen have taken advantage of the beautiful location. In fact, most of them are those who remained at the time of the general exodus which followed the fire and the certainty that the mill would not be rebuilt. This knowledge did not come for a long time after the fire. Indeed, rebuilding was begun immediately by the proprietors, the Washington Mill Company, who had bought the plant from J. R. Williams[on], the founder of Seabeck, and a shed, which still stands, was erected near the old mill site, and a number of piles were driven in the sand. Then suddenly the building operations ceased. The company found it could advantageously obtain a new town site at Port Haddock (sic) on the west side of Puget Sound. Thither they transported as many of their mill-hands as desired to go. Seabeck depended on the mill, when this industry ceased most of the inhabitants who did not follow the company to the new town, dispersed to other homes.

Most of the houses, which at that time were comfortable and even elegant homes, have been sold for a song or simply abandoned, many of them afterward being torn down and carted away, and a few occupied by whoever felt inclined to move in. The vast majority have stood vacant and uninhabited, becoming more and more dilapidated with the lapse of time.

The grounds, lawns, garden plots and orchards wrested from the woods by man long years ago at the cost of much arduous toil and strenuous labor are slowly, but surely, being reconquered by the wilderness.

Here around a doorstep, long since untrod, wild raspberry bushes have formed an impenetrable screen, and it is only after a second glance that one notices the climbing roses that once made the entrance to the home beautiful and lent their fragrance to perfume the air for its occupants.

In a large front yard where once children played under the apple trees during the long summer evenings, there is now no sign of a lawn. Everywhere is a tangled mass of raspberry and huckleberry bushes, with a few young balsam firs. The whole is flanked by rank ferns. The growth is so thick that a kitten would find it difficult to get through even where the walk once led up to the front door. The apple trees seem gnarled and old and ready to give up the struggle.

Here, frequently, lilacs bloom in a thicket of blackberry bushes, and roses are found almost concealed in the midst of ferns. The wisteria has interwove its slender twigs with those of the salmonberry, and the pure wax-like syringas seem to grow on the same stems as the wild but sweet-scented spirea, and flowing currant bushes set off the more sharply the red flowerets of the hawthorn.

In the orchards apple and plum and pear trees, gnarled and old, and with moss-covered and scaly limbs and branches, carry on a losing struggle for existence amid a vigorous growth of young firs and cedars.

Everywhere the growing trees and bushes, both of the garden and of the wood, seem bent on covering and concealing the unsightly, the tumble-down and sometimes picturesque houses with their broken steps and decaying, dilapidated porches.

Where some house is in an exceptionally good state of preservation the sight of the ferns and raspberry vines and salmonberry bushes growing among the roses and lilacs, and the young forest trees, that have taken root in the yard, growing as tall as the fruit trees, makes the scene all the more incongruous. It is an unmistakable indication that now the lawns and gardens are really a part of the wilderness.

The impression of desolation is deepened by a visit to the village cemetery, reached by a narrow road winding around among the trees which meet overhead. On a comparatively level spot on the hillside is this city of the dead, portions of it being even more neglected than the deserted village itself.

Young trees, tall and vigorous, are rooted in some of the older graves, and a younger growth is springing up over some of more recent years. Here, too, raspberry and huckleberry bushes flourish, half concealing moss-grown headstones and decaying wooden slabs. The rhododendron waves its tender, fragile flowers over the narrow beds, springing up near tame roses and lilacs which perfume the air. Portions of the cemetery, however, are well kept, showing that loving relatives of the departed are still living in the locality.

While change and decay has been going on in the village, the surrounding country has been slowly settled and the population increased.

Owing to this fact, Seabeck is again in some measure becoming a trading point. Steamers from Seattle stop there daily, bringing in supplies and carrying out to the Seattle markets fruit, eggs, poultry and other products.

Seabeck's future is bright and her prospects for becoming an important trading point in the products of the soil are increasing every day. This is largely due to her favorable location, which is on the west side of the peninsula which forms Kitsap County, and but twenty-five miles from Seattle in a direct line. It is nearly the same distance from Foulweather Bluff, the northernmost point of the peninsula which separates Hoods Canal from Puget Sound, making the distance to Seattle by the all-water route only about sixty miles.

Fork in the road, symbolic and necessary change for Seabeck.
(Author's collection.)

The population of the surrounding territory is growing at a rapid rate and the beautiful location of the town with its calm and peaceful surroundings is attracting tourists and summer visitors to the village itself.

Seabeck will come into her own, but is on the wrong side of the Sound for railroad connection with the East, and will never become a commercial or manufacturing center. A better and brighter future as the center of an agricultural community and a summer home for those seeking the calm, peace and contentment that can be found close to nature's heart awaits Seabeck and beckons from no great distance.

An idea was planted . . .

Seabeck Christian Conference

By Larry Hill

In the early part of the Twentieth Century there were few places for large groups to go where they could come together for a common purpose in a place of special and untainted beauty. As the century nears an end, these places are again becoming more and more difficult to find. The problem in the early years was the lack of developed property; the case now is that there is so much development and growth. Bridging this situation for nearly the entire century has been the facilities of Seabeck Christian Conference Center.

Since 1915 the Conference Center has been a significant provider of inspiration, spiritual growth, self renewal, and education to the people of the Northwest and beyond. Since opening it has been a haven to hundreds of groups and thousands of individuals who have come to find answers, guidance and knowledge within this setting of antique buildings, tall trees, and mountain vistas. It would be impossible to know how many lives have been changed by their experience in Seabeck, or how many other lives have been touched by those who have dedicated or rededicated themselves to service to others through that experience. What we do know is that Seabeck has remained steadfast in its mission to offer that so desperately needed renewal and inspiration from its inception to the present day.

One of the organizations frustrated in the early 1900s by the lack of suitable facilities in the Puget Sound area for youth and religious conferences was the Seattle YMCA. At that time they would hold conferences each summer at hotels and resorts on the Oregon coast. Arn Allen, General Secretary of the Seattle YMCA in those days, found that these facilities had too many distractions and interference from other hotel guests. It became his dream that the "Y" someday have a place of its own

where large groups could concenate on the task before them. A place that was surrounded by God's beauty but yet offered the necessary accommodations for lodging, meals, worship and meeting space. He and Mr. Stone of the Portland YMCA discussed this idea at the YMCA Conference in 1914 at Delano Beach. It was Arn's idea that if he could get ten men to give $10,000 each, they would have enough to buy some land and start their own conference center.

One of the first people he talked to about this idea was his friend, and member of the YMCA Board of Trustees, Laurence Colman.

Arn's wife, Julia, remembered later that it was one of his best ideas ever. Mr. Colman was interested at once in Arn's concept. *"Let's look around,"* he said, *"and see what we can find."* Thus began a search for the right place where these two men, one with a vision, one with the necessary resources, could establish a type of place that people from throughout the Northwest could use.

They spent many weekends on Mr. Colman's yacht, *Osprey,* looking at possible sites. They found several that they thought might be suitable. When they came to Seabeck Bay, they found the deserted mill town. The mill had burned 29 years earlier. Amongst the abundant growth of bushes and blackberries were a number of old houses, the old United States Hotel, and the abandoned cookhouse. Mr. Colman was impressed with the site at once. He especially liked the fact that there was a plentiful supply of water on the site from a free-flowing artesian spring located near the road. He told Mr. Allen, *"I will buy the land and develop what is needed for the conference grounds."*

Mr. Allen's dream of a conference center in the Northwest was about to become a re-

148

ality. Mr. Allen and Mr. Colman took a number of trips visiting other conference centers across the country including Asilomar in California and Silver Bay YMCA Christian Conference Center in upstate New York. They became convinced that the property at Seabeck could be developed into a more than adequate conference site.

Laurence Colman did buy the land. In fact, he and his brother, George, purchased several hundred acres of Seabeck waterfront and adjoining timber lands. One of his Seattle employees, Ben Berg, and his family moved to Seabeck to begin restoring those buildings that were still in reasonable condition and cleaning up the land. From the beginning, the Colman's were directly involved with the conference grounds. Mr. Colman financed the restorations. Many old buildings were torn down as they were not worth the effort or cost to recondition. The front of the old hotel had all but collapsed and had to be rebuilt. In the end, the hotel and ten of the old houses were painted, plastered and made ready for occupation. Mr. Colman's mother also got involved with this new project of her sons. It was at her insistence that each of the houses must have white sash curtains and white bed spreads. She wanted to provide a more *home-like* appearance to the simple furnishings and unadorned cottages. (Most of the old houses *still* have white sash curtains. A few of the old bed spreads remained in use as mattress pads until the 1960s.)

When all was ready, Mr. Colman said to Arn, *"The grounds are ready but I don't know anything about running a conference."*

Arn was deeply appreciative of what the Colmans had done. He said to Mr. Colman, *"I will manage it for a year or two."* Arn never dreamed that he would spend the next 29 summers at Seabeck. From that first summer in 1915 until the summer of 1943, Arn Allen assumed the management of Seabeck Christian Conference in addition to his regular YMCA duties. He never received any additional compensation for this responsibility. For him it was a labor of love. Furnishings were sparse and utilitar-

ian. Candles were used for light in the houses and gas lamps were purchased for use in the Administration Building. King county contracted Mr. Colman to refurbish the old ferryboat *Washington,* and he took the boat's old wicker deck chairs and brought them to Seabeck. Some of them are still being used by guests today.

The old hotel became the Administration Building. The cookhouse with upstairs community hall, built in 1864, was converted to the Chapel to be used for meetings and services. A couple years after the Conference started, that structure was barged across the lagoon where its reflection lured many photographers.

Arn brought to Seabeck his administrative skills, his commitment to serve all mankind, his deep religious and evangelical convictions. He remained always committed to the mission of Seabeck and he felt eternally thankful to the Colmans for this special gift to serve the YMCA, that he cared so deeply for, and all the people of the Northwest. Mr. Colman was glad to turn over the operation of Seabeck to Arn Allen. The two had been friends and colleagues in the YMCA movement for many years. Mr. Colman's only request of Arn was, *"I would like to see the cost to guests kept as low as possible so that ministers can come here and receive the inspiration that will last them throughout the year. Also students with little money will be able to attend the conferences."*

And so it began, the culmination of Arn Allen's dream. Seabeck Christian Conference was to become that special meditation place for renewal and retreat for thousands from the Northwest and throughout the world. Arn never found his ten men to give ten thousand dollars each. Instead he had convinced just one man that his vision was an important one. When the conference grounds opened in June 1915 for a YMCA Student Conference, no one realized that it would continue to serve groups until the end of the century and beyond.

. . . and grows.

Arnold Southwick Allen

Arn Allen (B. 1870 Waterloo Iowa; D. 1948 Seattle) came to the Northwest in the 1880s with his family. His father was a doctor on Fox Island. He was college-educated but also read widely on the subjects of history and the Bible. For years he taught a businessmen's Bible class at the Seattle YMCA.

Arn was dedicated to the YMCA movement and to his evangelical Christian beliefs. He served as General Secretary of the Seattle YMCA from 1898 to 1933. He was well respected in Seattle as a man of high principles and integrity.

He was married to Kathern Hubbard and had three daughters and two sons. When Kathern died, he married her sister, Julia. They had one daughter, Mary Jane. His granddaughter, Jean Allen Hanawalt, still serves on the Seabeck Board of Trustees.

From the very first days, Arn set about to run the type of operation that would not only serve the needs of the groups coming to Seabeck but also to operate as economically as possible so there would be some money at the end of the season to return to Mr. Colman. Arn is remembered as an inspiration to everyone at Seabeck. He was fortunate to have with him people like Ben Berg who re- mained as the caretaker at Seabeck for 32 years.

Joining Arn for many summers were his wonderful cook, Rachel Rose, and her assistant, Mrs. Fussel. Both women worked in the kitchen at Seattle Pacific University during the year. They saw summer employment at Seabeck as an extension of their Christian service.

"Mother Rose" became a fixture at Seabeck during those early years. She used local blackberries and raspberries for jam and apples from the aged trees around the grounds for cider and apple sauce.

Of all the meals prepared by "Mother Rose" and her staff, she is probably best remembered for her famous Corn Fritters. She would make these tasty delights once weekly in a huge iron pan with a heart- shaped handle.

The rest of the Seabeck weekly menu usually followed the same predictable pattern:

> **Monday**: Beef (usually chuck roast)
> **Tuesday**: Boiled Ham
> **Wednesday**: Salmon
> **Thursday**: Pork, veal, or lamb
> **Friday**: Beef (all guests were Protestants)
> **Saturday**: Salmon. *Again.*
> **Sunday**: Chicken.

Salmon was served twice each week because it was the cheapest food available. Local salmon could be purchased for ten cents per fish.

And so the dream that was Seabeck began to take on human forms with names and faces. With Mr. Colman's help and the support of loyal and hard-working, dedicated people, Arn Allen was ready to start holding summer conferences on the shores of Hood's Canal. He had much to be thankful for and it is certain that he raised up many a prayer of thanks for all the gifts he had received.

. . . and starts to bloom

150

**Mrs. Fussell,
"Mother Rose"
and
Arn Allen
. . . advocates of
Seabeck Corn Fritters.**

~ Seabeck Corn Fritters ~

Ruth DeRose was feature writer for *Seattle Times*. In 1975 she wrote an article about some of her fondest memories of childhood at Seabeck.

. . . But my strongest memory was of one particular breakfast which was the highlight of the week. It consisted of corn fritters served with sausage, scrambled eggs and lots of coffee.

These fritters were mouth watering, deep-friend morsels, served with syrup, the likes of which I haven't tasted since. The staff would service platter after heaping platter too each table in the large dining room until we couldn't hardly move.

When the recipe came across my desk, I immediately thought of those Seabeck fritters, and wondered if they were similar. They are.

The temperature of the oil is very important. I used a thermometer to maintain the oil at 375 degrees.

Corn Fritters (Yield about 18.)

1- 1/3 cups flour	3/4 t. baking powder
1 t. baking soda	1/4 t. salt
2 T. sugar	1 egg
2/3 cups milk	2/3 cup cream-style corn
1/3 cup drained canned whole kernel corn	

About 1 quart corn oil

1. In a medium mixing bowl, stir together flour, baking
        powder, baking soda, salt and sugar.
2. In a small mixing bowl, beat the egg and milk to
        blend, stir in cream-style corn and whole corn.
3. Make a well in the center of the flour mixture;
        add corn mixture and stir until dry ingredients are moistened.
4. Pour oil into a large iron skillet, filling 1/3 full.
        Over medium heat, heat oil to 375 degrees.
5. Drop mixture by tablespoons into oil, no more than 3-4 at
        a time. Fry until brown. Turn once. Drain on absorbent paper.
6. Serve at once with syrup.

Recipe may be doubled.

Every winter Mr. Berg would bring in sheep to help keep
the grass trimmed. In the spring, they would be butchered
and served throughout the season
to the conferees.
(Photo courtesy Seabeck Christian Conference.)

The first groups to come to Seabeck were students from the YMCA and YWCA. These summer conferences drew young men and women from all across the Pacific Northwest.

For a week at a time they would attend workshops and listen to well known speakers from the YMCA and the church. Another important part of every conference, however, was the fellowship that young people experienced while together amidst the natural beauty of Seabeck. Soon there were other conferences being held each year. Among them were YMCA Summer School, Girl Reserves of the YWCA,

Presbyterians, United Disciples of Christ, Congregational Church, Dutch Reformed Church (for some reason this was the only group that Arn permitted to smoke on the grounds), Interchurch World Missionary Movement Training Conference.

One of the early conferences that Arn started was the YMCA Volunteers. This was a chance for "Y" workers and volunteers and their families to get a chance to enjoy Seabeck and what it had come to mean to the YMCA. The conference always had a "Minister in Residence" who spoke each day at 11 a.m. in the *Cathedral in the Woods*.

Groups were usually regional in nature and came for a week at a time. Often Mr. Colman would bring guests to Seabeck on his yacht while others arrived on steamer *Potlatch* which offered daily service between Seattle and Union. Ferry service was available to Bremerton with an auto stage to Seabeck.

Arn was always very conscious of the support he received from the Colmans who continued to own the property and provided many of the goods and services that the fledgling conference center required. Arn's wife, Julia, recalls that he spent many hours in his little Seabeck office keeping track of every bit of food used for each conference, the number attending, and all that pertained to the staff and the grounds.

But still, on occasion, he would find time to sit at the edge of the ball field with Mr. Berg and watch the young people play a spirited game of baseball. Arn would return to Seattle once a week for meetings at the "Y". He was never far away from those responsibilities by phone. But he so enjoyed his time at Seabeck, teaching and serving those who came to find inspiration or fill some spiritual need. He loved to have his children and grandchildren come to stay with them, and it goes without saying that they grew to love those summers as much as he did.

One of the responsibilities of the manager was to hire the staff needed each summer to work at Seabeck in the dining hall, kitchen and on the grounds. College students from all over the Northwest would apply each year to come to Seabeck. In 1970, Julia Allen wrote in a letter continuing this interesting story about Arn:

"Much to the amusement of Mr. Stone and many of his friends, Arn had a habit of removing the backs of envelopes and using them for notes of all kinds, even notes for his Bible classes. One day I saw one on his desk in his little Seabeck office. When Arn came in I asked him if I might have it and he said 'sure'. So I put it in my scrap book and when I read it, it reminds me of the talks he used to give the staff as we sat at a table after a meal.

1. You are a 'picked' group, better than 100 had to be turned down in order that you might come.

2. You occupy exposed positions. What you do you do in sight of 100 to 250 people. You should, therefore, avoid extremes of dress, speech, and conduct.

3. You represent the management. What you do and how you do it reflects on the Colmans and myself.

4. You are all my 'favorites' else you would not be here. Now that you are here, I have no favorites."

Many people remember an expression that Arn often repeated to his staff: *"Keep your mind on the conference."*

Arn always remained faithful to his promise to Mr. Colman to keep the rates as affordable as possible so that all would be able to come. It would seem from some early brochures that exist that Seabeck was indeed as inexpensive as possible.

Arn began to feel frustrated by the practice of some conferences of adding an extra charge to the Seabeck rates in order to pay for speakers, etc. He felt somehow that this was taking advantage of the Colmans who continued to subsidize the conference grounds to a great extent.

Each year things at Seabeck improved and grew. Each year more groups came and more people were exposed to the wonders of worship, study and fellowship in Seabeck. And the Colmans continued to invest their time and talents in making this a successful venture. One day as Mr. Colman and Arn Allen watched a ball game on the field next to the Inn, a Model "T" car came along the road and forced the game to stop. Mr. Colman shook his head and said: *"This won't do!"*

Soon after one of his work crews arrived and began filling in the bay to connect the spit to the shore. He then traded the County a road right-of-way across the water where it is today. This also accomplished the enclosing of a small section of the bay behind the spit to form the lagoon which is still used for swimming and boating by Seabeck guests. This is when the old cook house on the spit was floated across the lagoon and resettled on the eastern shore.

Years later, in 1946, this building would be moved again. This time it was moved to dry land up the hill looking out over the bay with a spectacular view of the snow-covered Olympic Mountains.

Rates for Room and Board

Rates for the Conference period are:

For two in a bed, $1.50 each
For one in a bed, $2 per day

The conference period begins with the evening meal WEDNESDAY, July 28 and ends with the morning meal SATURDAY, August 7.

Rates for less than the Conference Period:

For two in a bed, $1.75 each.
For one in a bed, $2.25.

But in no instance shall the total charge exceed the Conference rates.

1920 Missionary Training Conference brochure.

A brochure produced by the Conference Grounds in the mid-1940s states: *"Accomodations are comfortable, clean, and not too fancy --- about half-way between a camp and a summer hotel. Bring your tennis racket --- there are four hard-surface courts. There are nine short but sporty holes of golf, so bring your golf clubs. And of course bring your bathing suit and fishing tackle and any other articles of sporting equipment. There's volleyball and horseshoes, too."*

In November 1935, Laurence Colman died. His contributions to the people of the Northwest had many monuments, both tangible and spiritual. His gift of Seabeck was both. The gifts he gave served both the bodies and souls of thousands. His legacy did much to further the spirit of citizenship and family values to those who were lucky enough to attend one of the many conferences at Seabeck.

Girls in period dress pose as part of the Missionary Education Conference, 1923. *(Photo courtesy Seabeck Christian Conference.)*

In 1946 original cook house moved a second time, from east side of lagoon to hillside. *(Photo courtesy Andy Olsen.)*

Laurence J. Colman

The eldest son of Northwest pioneer James Murray Colman, Laurence Colman (B. Sept. 25, 1859 Milwaukee, Wisconsin; D. Nov. 29, 1935 Seattle) devoted his life to the bettermen of his community. His father arrived in the Northwest in 1861, working at the Port Madison Mill, Bainbridge, until 1864 when he purchased the Port Orchard Mill at present-day Enetai Beach, East Bremerton. He later purchased Henry Yesler's Seattle mill and was instrumental in bringing the railroad to the Northwest.

Laurence came west in 1872 with his mother, Agnes (Henderson) Colman, and brother, George to join his father. He was educated in the schools of Milwaukee and Seattle and after graduation from the University of Washington, joined his father's many business enterprises. When J. M. Colman died in 1906, Laurence and his brother took over an already successful Seattle business empire. Not only did Laurence emulate his father's success, but he became even more successful and diversified with vast real estate holdings in downtown Seattle and a variety of other business ventures.

Joshua Green, long-time family friend and business associate of the Colman family, was quoted as saying: *"Laurence was even a better businessman than his father."*

Laurence married Ida May Burwell in 1892 and they became parents of four children: Agnes, Kenneth, Katherine and Isabelle.

During his life, he devoted time, energy and money to a variety of Seattle charities and causes. He was especially interested in organizations that furthered the character-building of young men and women. In addition to Seabeck Christian Conference, he was primary in establishment of Horse Head Bay Camp, now known as Camp Colman. He was a member of the Plymouth Congregational church and many civic organizations.

Laurence was once quoted as saying: *"If I couldn't afford to paint a car, I wouldn't have one."* This referred to a time he had purchased a perfectly good second-hand car instead of a new one. Laurence Colman was not a man who spent money foolishly.

He was also a man who believed strongly in principle and fairness for all. At one time he was the brains and financial support of the movement to recall Mayor Gill of Seattle. When Gill was indicted for alleged complicity with illicit liquor opertions, Colman believed that he was innocent and furnished his bond as a showing of his absolute fair-mindedness.

Laurence Colman

Kenneth B. Colman

Like his father before him, Kenneth Burwell Colman inherited a lot more than wealth. Ken inherited his father's sense of civic responsibility, philanthropy and a deep love of Seabeck Christian Conference.

Ken Colman was born in Seattle in 1896, the only son of Laurence Colman and grandson of Seattle pioneer, James M. Colman. He was graduated from the University of Washington with a degree in engineering and served as President of J. M. Colman Company and Smith-Gandy, Inc.

His civic memberships and awards included: Founding Trustee of the Seattle Foundation, Chairman of Citizens Committee for the Civic Center Bond Issue, member Seattle Park Board and chairman Seattle Policy Advisory Committee. He was active in the arts, Seattle YMCA as well as other "character-building organizations."

He won Seattle's *First Citizen* award in 1941 and the National Association of Christian and Jews Brotherhood Award in 1962. Mr. Colman was married three times and had four children.

Ken Colman, as much if not more than anyone else, is responsible for the Seabeck Christian Conference Center as it is today. One of the ways that his family had subsidized Seabeck over the years was to pay the property taxes. It was Ken who formed the non-profit Seabeck Corporation in 1936 and deeded the property to this non-profit corporation. This made the property tax exempt and also assured that it could not be used for any other purposes other than that which his father and Arn Allen had laid out in the preceding two decades.

Being incorporated meant that Seabeck would now be governed by a Board of Trustees. The Articles of Incorporation were filed Feb. 29, 1936 by prominent Seattle attorney Alfred Schweppe. The first Trustees were Constance Hamlin, Jane Carmody, Alfred Schweppe, Nancy Simpson and Edna Leslie.

These *Articles* stated the purpose and objectives of the corporation as: *"To function as a non-sectarian organization, and to be conducted primarily and chiefly for religious purposes, and not for profit; and to acquire, erect, equip and maintain buildings and grounds which shall be exclusively under the management and control of the Board of Trustees of this Corporation, and which shall be wholly used for the purpose of holding religious conferences and to promote the moral, social, educational, and spiritual welfare of all people who come under the organization's influence.*

At the first meeting of the Board on April 8, 1936 all Board members tendered their resignations and all were accepted with the exception of Schweppe who remained on as Secretary of the Board. The new Trustees and officers elected were: Frank Baley, President; Mrs. Arthur Worlund, Vice President; Walter Wyckoff, Treasurer; Kenneth Colman.

The first action of the new Board was to hire Arn Allen as Manager, *without* compensation.

Kenneth Burwell Colman

Over the next few years, under Ken Colman's direction and influence, the Board expanded to include many of the business and religious leaders of Seattle, executives of the YMCA and YWCA, representatives of the Washington-Idaho Council of Churches, and leaders of some of the groups that used Seabeck. Ken himself remained on the Board for the next 46 years. Some, like Patricia Donnelly who worked for Ken Colman and was very involved with his Seabeck operations, and former Managers and Board members remember that Ken was intimately involved with every aspect of Seabeck. He hired the managers and caretakers, he provided the services of architects and contractors. No part of Seabeck escaped his scrutiny or his care. He visited Seabeck as often as possible, often bringing with him items he had picked up that he thought might be of use to the managers. Much as the way it started, Seabeck continued to flourish with the obvious, and quite often, behind the scenes support of the Colmans.

Ken Colman died April 27, 1982. Ironically, this was the day of the Seabeck Annual Meeting of the Corporation. There had never been a meeting without Ken before. In the time since his passing, there have been many meetings and gatherings of the Seabeck members, but there is rarely an event where his name is not mentioned, his presence is not felt, or his love of Seabeck is not missing.

In the ten years between 1935 and 1945, Seabeck went through significant changes in the people who were responsible for her care and direction. Gone were those who had been there in the beginning: people who had seen it grow from an idea to a fully fuctioning conference center. Fortunately for Seabeck, Ken Colman was willing to step in where his father had left off in his support. In 1943, ten years after his retirement from the YMCA, Arn Allen passed on the management of Seabeck to his friend, Charles Norman. Ben Berg retired from Seabeck in 1945 and in his place came Andy Olsen. Three people who brought together a combination of vision, energy, enthusiasm, conviction, talent, money and principles to create a place of great beauty with a tradition of service. They shared many characteristics but most of all they, as well as those who stepped in after them, are all remembered as being fine *gentlemen*.

From a single seed a garden has grown . . .

Today as people drive through the growing community of Seabeck, the collection of buildings across the lagoon from the road seem somehow out of sync with the new homes and growth that is popping up everywhere. Driving over the rattling wooden bridge, guests often describe a feeling of *"stepping back in time."*

What seems to be a neat, New England-like village is sometimes quiet and serene and at other times bustling with activity. On the hillside behind the buildings, the cedars and firs that were non-existent at the end of Seabeck's mill period have regrown into a forest once again. Among the historic buildings of the long-gone timber town are more modern structures built in the 1950s and 1960s in addition to older buildings moved into this site from the Central Kitsap area.

Everywhere at Seabeck the new is blended with the old. In the administration offices is the most modern of computer equipment, while in the lobby, the old, giant iron kettle with the heart-shaped handle holds firewood to burn in the enormous stone fireplace. The two-wheeled wagon that the Bergs used to carry mattresses to winter storage and the days' garbage to the tidelands has been replaced with a fleet of trucks and electric carts, and *nothing* gets dumped into The Canal anymore.

Next to the large house built in the 1860s as the home of the mill manager, stands the new and modern Colman Center, built in 1979 as a meeting/program facility. Gone is the short, 11-week summer season and then the long winter rest. Seabeck is now a year-round conference and retreat center. People still come for inspiration, renewal, knowledge and fellowship. But now there are more than 10,000 guests each year belonging to a much wider range of organizations and religions.

It sometimes seems amazing that so many pioneer vintage buildings have survived into the last part of the Twentieth Century. Despite the constant repair or remodel, they have the advantage of being built from strong, quality materials and wood products that will never be available again. Like the old buildings that define its physical character, Seabeck will be forever grateful for the strength and quality of those who started and those who have guided this facility and its mission since 1915.

The legacy of leadership begun by these men has been continued through the years by the Managers and Directors who followed Arn Allen. (As it was often the case at Seabeck, the Board would hire the Manager and get the wife for free, many of the spouses of Seabeck Managers have served in positions of service to Seabeck and its guests.) Those who served long tenure at Seabeck included Charles and Ruth Norman, Louis and Elsie Fiscus, Kermit and Faye Franks, Dick and Sue Rose, Kenneth and Camilla Munson, and Larry Hill and Sandra Fowler-Hill.

There have also been a number of men who have had responsibility for the grounds and buildings at Seabeck and have achieved near miracles in keeping these aging buildings in usable condition. They include Andy Olsen, Everett Nordmark, Bill Cunningham, Wayne Purdham, Hearl "Buzz" Stice and John Loveless.

The Surviving Buildings

Drawing by Victoria Rowe.

The Historic Inn

The Inn is a genuine piece of Washington history. In 1992 it was designated as a *Building of Historical Significance in Kitsap County.* On the lobby wall are photos and reminders of the once thriving lumber town. There are several photos of conferences dating back to 1915 when the place called Seabeck was at the edge of Northwest civilization.

A wooden grave marker hangs by the door. the epitaph of Hiram Bryant tells us only that he was "about 47 years old" and was "killed in a dispute". (More on that story in the section on Seabeck's hotels.) Although he wasn't murdered in the present inn, he was murdered in the hotel that stood on this same ground.

The Inn was constructed in 1869 and appears today much as it was at the time it was built.

When Laurence Colman purchased the deserted mill site in 1914, many of the old buildings were decayed beyond repair. Of those that could be saved, the one that all agreed had to be preserved was the old hotel.

Mrs. Colman insisted that each room was furnished with a new dresser and a porcelain pitcher and basin. The porcelain sets and bedspreads are gone but those dressers are still in use. Each room was equipped with its own chamber pot.

Over the years, stories of ghosts in a couple of rooms have persisted. We are certain that they are friendly ghosts who have dropped in on the fun.

In the first years of the Conference, a tent was erected next to the Inn to serve as a dining room. Later an enclosed porch was built with canvas curtains that could be lowered if the rain was blowing in from the south. In the 1920s, the present dining hall was built with its characteristic arched windows and stone fireplace. Little by little, electricity and plumbing were provided for the cabins.

159

The Meeting House

The oldest confirmed structure on the Conference Grounds is the Meeting House. Completed during the winter of 1864-65, Marshall Blinn mentions in his diary on Jan. 12, 1865 that they'd just put the stove in the new hall. As mentioned previously, the Colmans moved this structure (originally known as the cookhouse and community hall) across the lagoon prior to 1920. In 1946, it was moved to its present location on the ridge above the cottages.

The Cottages

Many of the original cottages appear to be located at their historic site. There were a number of mill-owned homes near the Head of the Bay. Alder (Cottage #10) was located near this settlement (across from the present firehall) and Laurence Colman wanted it moved to the Conference Grounds. But Ben Berg was reluctant to move it. It wasn't worth the effort. Colman prevailed: *"If we can just get 15 years out of it, it'll be worth it."*

Andy Olsen wanted to tear it down in the 1950s. Ken Colman said, *"Let it be. Should get another ten years out of it."*

In 1990 Grounds manager John Loveless said, *"We've got to tear Alder down."* Larry Hill stopped him: *"Give it a couple more years."*

~

Conference Grounds Today
(Victoria Rowe, artist.)

Seabeck Cottages

Alder
Cottage Number
Ten

Madrona
Cottage Number Five

Juniper
Cottage Number Six

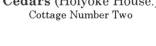

Cedars (Holyoke House.)
Cottage Number Two

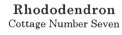

Rhododendron
Cottage Number Seven

Tamarack
Cottage Number Eight

Cypress
(Executive Director's House)
Cottage Number Three

Manzanita
Cottage Number Nine

Hemlock
Cottage Number Four

161

(A letter to early 1930s ' staff member Warren Flanagan.)

I have been wanting to write to you all year, and finally with less than a month to Seabeck, here I am attempting to write a note that has been due all year.

I have wondered whether you were having any difficulty keeping your weight down without lemon pie, chocolate cake, root beer, and blackberry jam. To say nothing of fried oysters and green apples.

Doesn't the thought of those Seabeck experiences make you impatient for the summer to come around? I was trying just now to think of the thing which I was looking forward to most. First, I thought it was the making of a dam, a lookout or some other constructive out-of-doors project. Then I thought of the swell swims in the lagoon and the bay on hot days. I thought of Mother Rose's cooking (and incidentally of the staff girls' salads.) But after all it's a combination of all of these which make Seabeck what it 'tis --- That delightful combination of old friends, new ideas and fresh air.

It begins to look like I would never grow old enough to desert Seabeck for some other summer activity. But in a few weeks, I'll be out of school and then I shall no longer qualify for my place at staff table. We who call Seabeck our own, owe much to the Colmans and to Arn for making it possible. It seems we shall never be able to pay the debt we owe them.

Sometimes I think I'm lazy when I want to come back to Seabeck again and again. Yet Seabeck is not a lazy place -- we are growing every minute we are there.

Seabeck was made for the study of new problems and the meditation of the bigger things in life --- a place for the finding of new Christian friends and the greater thrill of working with those friends. Yet Seabeck is, like all other places where we choose to stop in life, the product of our cooperation, our effort and our spirit. We can not break faith with those trusted to those grounds and this opportunity to us! God helping us, we of the staff can make Seabeck still a greater Seabeck.

(Unknown)

Ben Berg and His Family Leave Mark on Grounds and Comunity

Emanuel Olsen Berg

Ben Berg's (B. 1880 Norway; D. Feb. 18, 1965 Bremerton) real name was Berge Olsen. He shipped out of Norway at age 12 as a cabin boy, sailing to New York where he had a brother and

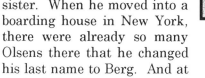

Ben Berg fixing horse mower.

Bergs' first home - the dynamite shack on old store dock.

sister. When he moved into a boarding house in New York, there were already so many Olsens there that he changed his last name to Berg. And at Seabeck for 32 years he was always known as Ben.

After a few years in New York, he moved west to Seattle and while living in Ballard he met, and married, Agnes Brown in 1908. They had four children, Alice, Berge, Kenneth and Albin. Berg worked for Laurence Colman in Colman's shipyard business in Seattle. His job was hewing the large wooden keels by hand with an adz. When the Colman's bought the land at Seabeck he was offered the job of caretaker. He was good with tools and machinery, skills that were needed to keep the aging buildings and equipment running.

During their years at Seabeck, all the Berg children worked in some capacity at the conference grounds. Working in the kitchen and washing dishes were just a few of the jobs that needed to be done during the busy summers. Mrs. Berg often canned pears from the trees on the grounds. After he retired in 1945, the Bergs moved to Bremerton where he worked in real estate. Mrs. Berg died April 18, 1953.

Berg Boys
Ken, Alben, Berge

Andy Olsen's
Symbolic Redwood Tree

**Andy and Clara Olsen accept their
retirement gift from long-time boss and friend,
Ken Colman.**

A growing monument to all those men and women who have made Seabeck Christian Conference a model retreat is a Redwood tree, not native to the Northwest, but planted on the grounds by Andy Olsen in 1947 when it was just a foot tall.

Andy was the last of the Seabeck-Brinnon ferryboat skippers, giving up the run in 1941. Ken Colman and Andy first became friends in 1939 when Colman asked him to take campers out for a cruise on The Canal. Andy agreed and for a minimum of 100 passengers (at 25 cents each) gave a two-hour run.

After pursuing work out of the area, Ken Colman offered Andy the job of Grounds' manager. He worked there from 1945-67 when he retired.

Andy's management spanned an active period in the growth of Seabeck Christian Conference. He was responsible for remodeling and restoring many of the old structures and special-ordered much of the material from Lofthus Lumber, Bremerton, especially siding so that it would match exactly the original mill-produced dimensions.

A major Olsen coup occurred when, as appraiser of the Emel estate, he suggested to the family that the property be turned into a park. Andy worked with the State and twisted enough arms to petition to a positive response from the State. The Emel family, according to Olsen, accepted $50,000 less that a private developer had offered. The property is now Scenic Beach State Park.

A retirement party was held for Andy and his wife, Clara, Jan. 19, 1967. Planned as a surprise, Andy knew about it but it didn't dampen his excitement nor give a clue as to his retirement gift. His long-time friend, Ken Colman, knew that he was saving to buy a table saw.

His retirement gift wasn't a gold watch or plaque to hang on the wall, but a saw which Andy and Clara and the boys used in building his Maple Beach waterfront home.

Linkletter Photos

Lloyd Garrison Linkletter (1879-1937) learned his profession in Michigan. When his minister father wrote that he could no longer support two sons at college, Lloyd returned home from Olivet College to take up book selling to rural households. He traveled by bicycle and was a good salesman. He read about the new dry plate process and its boon to photography and added family portraits to his offerings for his customers.

His older brother, Frank, wrote from Seattle that the market for photography looked good out West, so in 1906 Lloyd took the last of the colonizing trains ($10 westbound, $100 return trip) to begin his 31 year career here. He photographed the 1907 graduating class of the University of Washington in a giant "W" that he had laid out south of Denny Hall, shooting from the top of the next building.

Lloyd ("LG" to his fellow photographers) bid successfully for the summer photography concession at Rainier National Park and held that post from 1907 through 1916.

His big tent shielded many a tourist from "mists" while viewing his photos and his evening lantern slide shows were the only views of the huge mountain that many saw in a week long stay because of those mists.

His commercial business in Seattle's University District also prospered and customers included many businesses, University departments, student groups and public affairs. His skills and equipment he kept improving with training from Eastman Kodak representatives and with new cameras and enlarging developments. His 40" x 60" enlargements of Rainier scenery were a hit for business, hand colored in oil, using his

Lloyd Garrison Linkletter

excellent memory for colors, not exaggerated color as modern color film often yields.

The Hood Canal Scenes which interest the readers of this book he made on one of his many travels for good scenic views. He also made photos of the weekly gatherings at the Seabeck Conference Grounds in the 1920s. Groups taken on Mondays were shown proofs on Wednesdays for ordering and delivered finished prints on Fridays.

Smog was no stranger to The Canal: forest fires filled the sky with dense smoke, eliminating the blue light that was needed for the old color-blind films. He found his negatives blank when developed on one occasion and invested in the new Wratten Panchromatic Plates for a second try on a Tuesday, with success, despite the limitations of that red orange Sun.

He kept on with the ongoing rapid development of modern films and chemicals, but died just as color prints were making their debut. He is still remembered by older UW Alumni, and some recall their cry of *"Link, Let 'er go!"* while waiting for his final focus on their group.

Richard L. Linkletter

There is a Place

The young Marine was home on a two week's furlough. He bore marks upon his body which proclaimed: *"I have been through hell and yet, I live."*

"Mother," he exclaimed one morning, *"Before I return, there is one place I must visit."*

"Where is it, son?"

"Seabeck," he replied very quietly. *"You remember, don't you, that I was there with our church young people just before I went in? It meant a lot to me."*

And so to Seabeck they went --- Mother, father and the boy. The silent Olympics to the west, the rolling waters of the Canal at their feet, and the forest above them --- God's temple. They watched their boy disappear into the woods with head erect, eyes front, shoulders back! Straight to the *Chapel of the Firs* he went, up to the rustic cross, a spot made sacred by vows made between young people and their newly found Savior.

Soon he returned, his face glowing.

"Now," he exclaimed joyfully, *"I can take it again!"*

Taken from remnants of a
YMCA Student Conference newsletter
from the 1940s
found 40 years after it was printed,
under the floor of the
cottage known as Hemlock.

Book Four

Winter

The flood was sent because the people were wicked and it overflowed all the land except one mountain. The People fled in their canoes to the highest mountain in their country --- in the Olympic range --- and as the water rose above it they tied their canoes with long ropes made of cedar limbs to the highest tree; but the water rose above them.

While they were there some of the canoes broke from their fastenings and floated away, so far that they never returned which accounts for a few being left in the Twana tribe now.

Rev. Myron Eells,
T he Twana, Chemakum and Klallam Indians of Washington Territory.

Surrounding Communities

Little Beef Bridge circa 1910 with Frank Emel on wagon and his father, Peter, standing with white hat and sweater. *(Photo courtesy Darrel Emel.)*

Big Beef, Little Beef and Lone Rock

The names *Big Beef* and *Little Beef* refer to the creeks that flow into The Canal just north of Seabeck and were named for the headwaters where Jacob Hauptly kept cattle during the mill period. *Lone Rock* was named for a large rock that sets off shore just north of Big Beef and south of Anderson Landing. The areas are so closely related, that it is difficult to separate the information and often it is overlapping.

Two of the earliest residents of the area were Joseph H. Boyd and Tom Clark. Boyd wrote his reminisces of the area.[1]

---

[1]*Washington State Historical Quarterly.* Vol. 15, 1924, Pp. 248-249.

An Argonaut of 1857

"From Point Roberts I proceeded to Port Townsend where there were several sawmills. One Tibbals ran the hotel and the place might have had a population of 200. I stopped here for a few days to inquire about work and then went on to Port Ludlow, which is, as I recall, some 20 to 25 miles up the Sound through Hood's Canal. I found employment in a saw mill at Port Ludlow and worked there for about six months.

"One day a fellow workman, an Irishman named Tom Clark, asked me how I would like to take up a ranch in partnership with him. I was agreeable and we proceeded further up Hood's Canal to a place near Seabeck where we located our ranch. This land was the finest tract of

land I have ever seen and a fine place to live, especially in those days.

"We soon got up a comfortable cabin and cleared three or four acres of alder and maple growth and put in a crop of potatoes and some vegetables. We had a good boat and we passed our time in improving our farm or in hunting and fishing, as we felt inclined. We had always plenty of fish and fowl.

"One could wade into the creek and catch a good sized salmon by the tail. I have seen a square mile of ducks and geese in the inlet at one time. We had an old flintlock musket and could get all we wanted at any time. On the flat at the mouth of the creek we had a neighbor, an Englishman named Lile or Lysle, who possessed a dog named Caesar.

"I stayed on our ranch about six months. My partner, Clark, was very fond of whiskey and usually, when he drank he was very amusing.

"About this time, however, we went on a visit to one of our few neighbors, Clark became full, and we got at outs and came to blows. The next morning I said to him, 'Tom, you and I have been together about long enough. I have five dollars and I'll take the boat and you can have the ranch.'

"The next day I took our boat and left and after going to Seabeck and looking around some, I pulled thirty miles to Port Gamble and there sold the boat and secured employment from (Amasa) Miller in a logging camp at Squalwish Harbor."

This property later became the Fred Miller estate.

Perhaps it was this same property to which the following relates:

A Seattle newspaper reporter[2] stopped in Port Gamble to wait for the *St. Patrick* to take him to Seabeck. He encountered a Chinese farmer there and learned that he had purchased a small ranch three miles north of Seabeck for $800 and that his annual sales amounted to something like $1,400.

"With pole over his shoulder and a basket of vegetables at each end, (he) put in an appearance . . . (Having raised vegetables) I never see a nice lot of beans, squashes, cabbage, cucumbers, corn and such without feeling an irresistible desire to stop and have a chat with the producer.

"I found the John Chinaman above, equal to the average of his countrymen in intelligence and able to speak English well enough to be well understood. Examining his basket, I found a fine assortment of vegetables which I name with prices attached:

Cauliflower	3 cents a pound
Cabbage	1-1/3 cents a pound
String beans	3 cents a pound
Turnips	1 cent a pound
Potatoes	1-1/3 cent a pound
Sweet corn	25 cents a dozen
Celery	4 stalks, one *bit*

"All of these products would compare favorably with the best anywhere. He finds a ready market for all he produces. He employs four of his countrymen and takes his produce, except what he ships, to Seattle per steamer or in his own small boats. He uses as fertilizers such stable droppings he can get in Gamble, Seabeck and other places, besides the offal from a Chinese fishery nearby.

"There might perhaps be nothing specially noticeable in all this but for the fact that on my return to the Port Gamble hotel, I mentioned these facts and was informed by the landlord that three or four white men had starved to death (I use his own words although they were doubtless spoken metaphorically) on the same ranch. And the probability is that we would starve to death for vegetables up here if it were not for the Chinaman.

"Captain Macomber (of the St. Patrick) pointed out the ranch (as we headed for Seabeck) and with the aid of a good field glass, I saw that between the stumps every available foot of land seemed to be cultivated to capacity. Neither time, room nor labor seemed to be wasted. Nearby was the Chinese fishery from whence the Chinaman obtained his fertilizers or a portion of them."

[2]*Seattle Post-Intelligencer.* Sept. 20, 1882.

Fred Miller, Remittance Man

Puget Sound newspapers, starved for sensational news in August 1937, headlined the murder of an attractive 38 year-old Seabeck *housekeeper* and for several months reporters attended hearings, then the trial of the divorcee's employer.

Not many people in Seabeck wanted to believe that Fred Miller could be guilty of the murder. Wasn't he the one who pledged the most at fund-raisers, who gave one of his boats to a neighbor kid? He was a great sportsman, taking his female companion of many years on hunting and fishing trips. His looks were distinctive: he wore wide brim hats, was short and squat and spent money freely. Seabeck folk said he was a *"remittance man"*, meaning in the 1920s and 1930s that his income came from family in the east who'd pay well to keep him in the west.

He was the son of George F. Miller, associated with the First National Bank in Huntington, West Virginia who died in 1910.[3]

Fred Miller was the owner of a yacht, airplane and drove around in a Chrysler touring car. He entertained lavishly and many think that there were a lot of Hollywood people whooping it up with his imported spirits. It was said that the boats that sped into Little Beef Harbor were bringing booze from Canada.

All of the Northwest read each word of the newspaper coverage, from discovery of the body, through interrogation of Miller and his confession, then the trial.

Miller tried to convince sheriff's deputies that Jeanette Dunbar had taken her own life but *considerable evidence* prompted Sheriff Rush Blankenship to pursue the investigation. Miller insisted that she'd been despondent and took her own life with the 32-20 rifle which, indeed, had fired a single bullet.

The *luxurious* home was sealed off. Fingerprints were taken and photographers gathered evidence. (The home was torn down in 1991 to make room for several new homes on the north side of Little Beef Creek.)

The victim was the mother of a 17 year-old deaf mute child who lived in Port Angeles. Miller said that he found her body when he returned home from Bremerton shortly after 5 p.m. She was slumped in a chair. Miller called a neighbor to help move the body to a bed and Dr. Clifton Benson was summoned. He pronounced her dead and notified the coroner and sheriff's department.

Miller claimed to have left home at 10:30 a.m. and didn't return until he found her body. Floyd Lowe heard the shot and saw Miller leave shortly afterwards. Bertha (Brumm) Sibon was ironing clothes overlooking the Seabeck highway and saw Miller come home in a strange car. (Miller was generous when she had been collecting for the TB fund. He was a wonderful man, she said.) The car left a short time later.

Dr. H. A. Barner performed the autopsy. The bullet, his report noted, entered at an angle below the heart and shattered the liver, but did not strike the heart.

The rifle was found in a closet adjoining Mrs. Dunbar's room. Blood stains indicated that the woman had placed herself on the bed after being shot, then moved to the chair where she was found dead.

Dr. Barner reported, following the postmortem examination, that after suffering such a wound could have placed the rifle in the closet, placed herself on the bed and later moved to a chair. *"She might have lived an hour after the shooting,"* he wrote. *"BUT it is doubtful that she would have been able to move."*

Evidence indicated that the gun was fired from close range. And she'd been dead six or seven hours before Miller reported the death.

County Prosecuting Attorney Ralph Purves called a coroner's jury to determine the cause of death. Key witness was Miller. The six person jury heard evidence and brought back a verdict: *We, the jury, do not believe that the death of Mrs. Jeanette Dunbar was suicide. From a preponderance of circumstantial evidence, given before us by several witnesses, we find she came to her death at the home of her employer near Seabeck, Aug. 20, by reason of a gunshot wound*

---

[3]George S. Wallace. *Cabell County* (West Virginia) *Annals.* 1935.

unlawfully discharged by some unknown person."

At the hearing, Miller admitted that they lived together as man and wife, although not married. Mrs. Dunbar had wanted the security of marriage and they often quarreled about that. He refused to marry her.

Miller was arrested and charged, not with murder, but with co-habitating with Mrs. Dunbar. *"After being arrested and taken into custody and as he entered a First Street barber shop, Miller was spirited to Seattle by two officers. Arrangements had already been made to quiz the man about Mrs. Dunbar's mysterious death."*[4]

A month after the murder, Miller confessed. Murder charges were filed against him. His motive: self defense. He confessed to Purves, Seattle police detectives and a county investigator, Reynolds C. Cox. His confession was printed in all area newspapers. He said that they'd gotten into a disagreement. She grabbed the gun. They were both half drunk and he pulled the trigger. He put the gun in the closet and left to establish an alibi. *"I was pretty sure she was going to die."* He came home several hours later. After the confession he asked for a drink.

When he was booked into Kitsap County jail, his (almost) legal name was used: Charles Fred Miller (although it was Charles Frederick Miller.)

Miller posted a $20,000 property bond and was released to go home. Ray Greenwood became his attorney and when he showed up in court to plead not guilty to manslaughter, he smiled at friends as the charges were read.

The jury was given instructions by Judge H. G. Sutton stating there were only three verdicts from which to choose: guilty of second degree murder, guilty of manslaughter or not guilty. First-day testimony indicated that Miller had threatened to shoot Reynolds C. Cox, the special investigator, two days after the murder.

When Greenwood put his client on the stand, his first question was his age. Miller stated 37, then 36. When asked a third

time he said, 35. John J. Sullivan, the second attorney for the defense, tried to calm Miller and asked again. Miller stated that he was 55.

Miller said that he had come to Kitsap County in 1912. He had met the victim at the Seward hotel in Seattle ten years previously and they began living together at the Little Beef property. They didn't have any trouble until about two years before the murder when she wanted to get married. He offered her money if she wanted to leave, but she stayed. He'd never denied her anything that she asked.

Testimony was introduced about the disappearance of Mrs. Dunbar's son in Seattle and the successful search to find him. Miller financed the search.

Miller admitted that the victim drank heavily in recent years and often became ill. He sent her to Columbus Sanitarium in Seattle for treatment.

The next witness was Mrs. John Stanioch, a Seabeck neighbor of Miller's. She testified that she had heard Mrs. Dunbar, intoxicated, tell Miller that he would leave the house feet first if he insisted on sending her to the sanitarium for acute alcoholism treatment.

Miller said that when she was drunk she often threatened him, once chasing him with a butcher knife and he ran her out of the house.

Greenwood asked Fred about the day of the murder:

Greenwood: Remember the day of Aug. 20. The day of the tragedy?

Miller. Yes.

Greenwood: What did you do the forenoon of that day?

Miller: I got up and had breakfast; went to Seabeck for the mail and drove on to Bremerton.

Greenwood: What did you do in Bremerton?

Miller: Played cards at the barber shop.

Greenwood: Was Georgie (Mrs. Dunbar's nickname) drinking much that day?

Miller: Yes.

Greenwood: What time did you come home?

Miller: About 2 or a little later.

---

[4] *Bremerton Daily News-Searchlight.* Sept. 20, 1937.

Greenwood: What did you two say?

Miller: She said: 'What the hell you doing home so early?' And I said, 'Can't a person come in his own home any time he wants to?' She said, 'No. I'll show you you can't.' Then she went into the bedroom. She was pointing the gun at me. I grabbed it and we struggled. The gun went off and she fell onto the bed.

Greenwood: Were you separated when the gun went off?

Miller: I don't remember.

Greenwood: What did you do?

Miller: I shook her, but she didn't answer. I didn't know what to do so I drove in to Bremerton.

(Under cross-examination, he was accused of going to town, playing cards and drinking whiskey while she was lying out there dying. Miller's head dropped. He was silent.)

Greenwood: Did you know what you were going to do?

Miller: I was deciding on reporting it.

Greenwood: Did you think she was dead?

Miller: I knew she was dead.

Greenwood: Do you know why you didn't report it?

Miller: I don't unless I was half out of my mind.

Greenwood: Have you ever been arrested?

Miller: No.

Greenwood: Did you have any reason to shoot her?

Miller: No.

Miller admitted returning home and stopping along the highway to talk with Donald McLean, a friend and neighbor. Miller told McLean he was having his other car painted as a surprise to Georgie whom, Miller, later admitted, had been dead for nearly three hours. The two had two or three drinks.

Character witnesses for the defense were Mrs. Jesse Larkin, Mrs. Donald McLean, Mrs. John Stanioch, Mrs. L. A. Hutchins, Mrs. Earl Smith, A. G. Benbennick, Stan Reeve and Dr. Alexander Rock Robinson. All (except Robinson) testified as to Miller's kindness toward Mrs. Dunbar. Robinson testified in connection with the effects of narcotics and liquor and the probable effect of the bullet after it struck Mrs. Dunbar.

Testimony of the witnesses tended to show that Mrs. Dunbar had suffered a change in her attitude toward Miller because of her physical and mental breakdown due to the use of liquor and morphine.

The jury deliberated slightly more than four hours. Jury Foreman, W. H. Barber of Kingston, informed Judge Sutton that they had reached its verdict. He handed the printed copy to the judge who handed it to

Fred Miller home at Little Beef. *(Photo courtesy Joe Emel.)*

the court's clerk, Reina Osburn. She read the verdict: *"We, the jury, find the defendant not guilty."*

Miller rose slowly to his feet. *"My God. That's wonderful!"* His many Seabeck friends gathered around him and shook his hands. Some sobbed.

The jury foreman thought that the trial would make him a better man.

Less than six years later, on Aug. 23, 1943, Charles Frederick Miller died in Wenatchee. He had moved to Soap Lake the previous year for health reasons, seeking a dry climate.

He was born in Colesburg, Kentucky, Oct. 15, 1881 and was survived by a stepmother and a brother. The body was brought to Bremerton and services were handled by Lewis Funeral Chapel and then his body was shipped to Huntington, WV.

Stories abound about Miller.

Floyd Lowe and Melvin Hagen saw a sea plane coming in once. They rowed out toward it and saw people unloading whiskey boxes. Many people in the area contend that he was not a rum runner, but he sure enjoyed a good stock of private liquor.

When Lowe's nephew, Dennis Dibley, was six years old, he rolled a big snowball down the hill and it hit Miller's rowboat, damaging a board. When he got home and told his mother, she made him go back and tell Miller what he'd done. Miller said, *"If you can get that thing out of here, you can have it!"*

One of Marie Halvorsen's favorite people on The Canal was Miller, the flamboyant Easterner. Fred often confided in Marie. She liked him even though he'd tell terrible stories and had a bad mouth. Billie Barner, her daughter, remembers when

Miller insisted that she and one of her sisters ride in his airplane and both girls agreed but were petrified when they got up in the air. Miller's pilot was at the controls of the plane.

Another time Billie and her husband were trolling out in front of Miller's house and he insisted that they beach the boat and come to his house for a drink of "moon". Although they tried to resist his invitation, Miller insisted and the two of them sipped, once, from the jug. After that the young couple never boated anywhere near Miller's property.

Miller spent lots of money. He had a huge three-tier fountain for goldfish, as big as a swimming pool.

June and Hal Collier lived in the Miller house for a year. They'd heard stories about a tunnel from the house to the beach where booze was brought into the house although they never found it. They'd also heard that when Miller was picked up for questioning about the murder, he asked the sheriff if he couldn't have ten minutes to bury his valise of gold coins.

Helen and Stan Reeve were friends of Miller and she remembers that he had a big refrigerator in the living room so he could keep beer close at hand.

Walton Family Promotes Population Explosion

John Alexander Walton (B. July 15, 1855 St. Johns, New Brunswick, Canada; D. Sept. 29, 1937 Seabeck) was the village blacksmith, arriving at Seabeck around 1875.[5] He had crossed the continent on the Union Pacific Railroad and worked at a San Francisco shipyard before moving here.

He lived up Big Beef Valley where he built a home for his teenage bride. He owned at least three 1/4 sections. One piece of property adjoined Jake Hauptly's, a fence separating them. Only one mention of Walton is recorded by Hauptly: *"Nailed up my fence between Walton and me when a little altercation took place. He, Walton, insulted my wife yesterday and I called him to time about it. No one hurt."* [6] When reading this, one of the descendants said, *"Yes. Old John was hot-headed."* Prior to the fire, Hauptly took out a pre-emption claim near Camp Union with Big Beef Creek running through it.

Walton received his citizenship papers in May 1887 with final proof made in 1890.

After his marriage to Alice Nickels (B. 1865 Pittston, Maine; D. 1948) on April 8, 1885, the couple continued to live in his bachelor cabin and it was here that their

---

[5]*Bremerton News.* July 19, 1918.

[6]Hauptly. May 10, 1886.

first two sons, Edwin Augustus (1887-1953) and Albert Ernest (1889-1964) were born. It was after the birth of Al that the couple moved to the deserted milltown site, living in what is now known as Cottage #7. It is probable that many of the houses were occupied and probably by squatters. Several of the abandoned millworker cottages were torn down or moved.

Walton and Nathaniel Sargent logged the property at Scenic Beach. Nat used to give all the Walton kids haircuts and if the kids needed to take a bath, it was at Nat's house.

In 1900 Walton occupied the 37-acre waterfront tract, school land once owned by the State of Washington, cleared and improved it and built a three-story house, large barn and blacksmith shop. The actual contract was dated 1910 and was filed in 1917. The cost: $1,425.

Kitsap County commissioners had

The Walton House circa 1910
(Photo courtesy Ray and Shirley Walton.)

leased the property to Barnard E. Buell for six years at $10 annually and he was prohibited from cutting timber and any improvements should be left in place at the end of the term.

They moved into their new waterfront home in 1907. Much of the lumber and other materials was carried from the abandoned milltown. The three-story bannister is a relic of the original Cliff House or Con-

ference Grounds Inn. It is still known as the Walton House and has been occupied continually by Waltons. The current owners are Ray and Shirley. The three-story home

has been remodeled, tastefully redecorated in a turn of the Century motif and is run as a Bed and Breakfast. Annual taxes are many times the original purchase price.

Six more children were born: Lena May (Emel) (1892-1956 at Hadlock); John William (1895-1975); Irene Gertrude (County birth records state that her name is Gertrude Irene) (Brett) (1898-89); Herbert Ray (1900-82); Irvin Roosevelt (1902-1977); and Ernest Russell (1909-84). Only Ernest was born at the home now known as The Walton house.

Walton shod horses, did iron work for logging camps and was hired as a timber cruiser. He bought a 9 x 12 steam donkey engine and logged for several years. When Fred Miller wanted a yacht built, Walton bought mill equipment, hooked up his steam donkey for power and cut 3,000 board feet of lumber per day on the flat at Little Beef Creek.

After the Walton mill started, gypo loggers were towing in logs to be cut at $6 per thousand board feet. Or Walton charged $12 per thousand board feet if he furnished the logs. The mill, his son, Herb, was to say, started a building boom in the area. Walton retired from his mill during World War I. He also tried to sell lots, promoting the area and offering free hot dogs to those who came to look at the property. No one came.

John A. Walton's sister, Martha, was married to William Little in 1883. She came either with her brother or shortly afterwards as Hauptly's diary first mentions her in March 1879.

Herb Walton moved to the Walton home after his marriage to Gladys DeMoss but shortly after their first child, Ray, was born (1923), they moved to Camp Union where Herb worked for the West Fork Logging Company as a choker and a fireman on the locomotives.

Peter F. Emel

Old Peter F. Emel was quite a fellow. He had three wives and ten children, all boys except the two girls, one from his first wife, the other from his last. Peter (B. Dec. 25, 1853 Canada; D. Feb. 21, 1924) was married in Canada to Margaret Stroeder and they had three children (Frank, Peter E., and Elizabeth). Margaret died and Peter emigrated to Ada, Minnesota where he was married to Anna Lichen. They had four sons (Joe, Bill, Ed, John).

Anna and Peter and the boys moved to Seattle where he acquired the Duwamish Dairy. His son, Peter, delivered milk to town people by horse-drawn wagon while other customers came to the dairy with various containers and ladled out their milk. Peter thought he needed a bigger piece of property for his growing (and grown) family and he purchased property up the Big Beef valley. He still maintained a grocery in Seattle, two hotels and a beer hall.

When the Emels first came to the Big Beef area, the road from Silverdale wasn't much more than a trail. With a team of oxen, he brought his belongings over the trail, leading them single file. Son Frank carried a yoke and the other boys carried what they could of the family belongings. Emel purchased two homesteads. He employed a number of men to supply The Canal steamers with wood and worked as a logger. His sons also logged, hauling out old-growth logs on tram cars with an eight-

Peter F. Emel
(Photo courtesy Darrel Emel)

horse team, according to grandson Ernie Emel.

When Pete brought the boys to Big Beef, there were very few families who lived in the area. The John Johnsons lived on the Wade place and Jim Smith and family lived on Big Beef where the cabins are now. When anyone had to go to Seattle, they rowed out in The Canal and flagged down one of the steamers.

Beef Harbor was a popular area for fish traps and two traps there in 1901 took in 6,600 fish at one time and after that 2,000 were taken at one time. The traps were owned by the Rosaw Straits Packing Company. Other companies and individuals had traps throughout the Seabeck area and numerous fishermen were working with nets and seines.

Peter married Maud Gregory June 12, 1899 in King County. They had three children (Ernest, Alice and Jim).

"As more families moved to the area, Emel proposed that a bridge be built across both Big and Little Beef creeks. The neighbors guffawed and asked what good a bridge would do when there were no roads

to the bridges, but he convinced them if they had the bridges, the roads would come." [7]

When bids were opened for Little Beef Bridge, he was awarded the contract at $1 per foot and he was to furnish all the lumber for the 330-foot span. Emel cut and split the cedar planks from timber off his property. The planks fit so closely together they needed to use no nails. Bridge railings were four feet high and the bridge was 16 feet wide. Little Beef Bridge was completed July 4, 1896.

John Walton was the foreman on Big Beef bridge which was started when the first bridge was completed. Walton and John Simpson built the pile driver and Bill Emel tripped the hammer which weighed about 2,400 pounds. It was powered by a team driven by the senior Emel. [8] This bridge was used until 1916 when new piling was driven and it was replanked. It was then built over the spit and connected to land. The bridge was 1,170 feet long and built of number one creosoted piling and all lumber was number one quality. [9] It was also at this time that the Anderson Hill road was greatly improved, creating a complete circuit from Seabeck to Silverdale, then to Bremerton and back to Seabeck via Crosby.

The bridge was rebuilt again in 1942, about the time of the construction of the road in its present location. In the winter of 1965 the bridge was torn down and the present structure completed.

Pete, Sr. and wife number three, Maud, divorced in 1912 and some of the details of their marriage and later family problems are chronicled in property abstracts (and county records).

Briefly (from a Cliff House abstract) Peter purchased an additional 56 acres from John and Alice Walton in 1901 and deeded it to Maud the following year. The property included the original Cliff House and store. Emel thought of tearing it down, but then used it as a dairy store. Maud sold the property to Fred Miller for $4,500 in 1922

and he then platted the property as Cliff House View Tracts and built three homes in the tract, all designed by a Mrs. Dahl. One of the homes is owned by Helen Reeve.

In 1926, Sheriff John Stanioch, built the log house now occupied by June Collier, with jail house labor.

Maud later married William Halffman May 26, 1916 and ran the store and post office at Coyle, across The Canal.

Peter sold the large parcel of land up behind Big Beef Harbor to one of the Seattle Piggott family members.

Of the sons who stayed at Seabeck, Peter Ernest Emel (B. April 17, 1879), owned property on Pioneer road. The younger Peter caught the gold fever and his father "staked" him [10] and although never striking it rich, he earned a living packing in miners' supplies over Chilcoot Pass and brought back gold nuggets and other memorabilia.

Pete logged at Crosby and used to walk the five or six miles from Seabeck to Crosby to work and court Hattie Sacher. Then he got a bicycle *"And still I couldn't get anywhere with her,"* he told Adele Ferguson on their 53rd wedding anniversary. *"Finally after a year, off and on, I got a horse and buggy. The buggy had small high seats so she couldn't jump off. I says to her: 'You want me to take you out for a ride?' She said, 'Yes.' And I said, 'Well, what's the chance now? I've been out here often enough."*

He and Hattie lived in one of the mill houses while building their home on Pioneer Road. [11] The family boarded the local teacher and owned the Seabeck Dairy. He had the first *"for hire car"* in the Seabeck area, an open Model T touring car, transporting passengers to Silverdale or Bremerton.

"No matter how busy they were, there was always time for company and good times playing cards or dancing to the record of the day. [12]

---

[7] Kitsap County Historical Society, *Kitsap County: A History.* 1977. P. 49.

[8] Ibid.

[9] Floyd Lowe interview. 1992.

[10] Hazel (Emel) Louden interview.

[11] Ibid.

[12] Ibid.

They had three children (Ernest Peter, Ruby and Hazel) who were born on the property.

Hattie told Adele Ferguson, *"The country folk were a lot more neighborly then and they got together nearly every Saturday night for a dance. They thought nothing of dancing all night long, going home at dawn in their wagons and buggies. There was no problem about baby-sitters --- the children always went along. The little ones slept peacefully in their buggies, tended by their mammas and any mamma present who wasn't being whirled around the floor on the arm of her husband."*

Pete logged until he was 40 years-old when he was almost killed by a falling tree. After that he hauled, cut wood and farmed.

Ruby (1909-1911) is the only other person, besides the senior Peter, bearing the Emel name buried at Seabeck.

Ernest P. Emel became a logger as soon as he could swing an ax. He was the last of county loggers using a team of horses, *those prized Belgians.* He prided himself in later years (when others were plowing wide, rutted logging roads through the old growth timber) that he still used horses. While working a piece of land in the Seabeck area he told a *Bremerton Sun* reporter: *"If you came in here with a cat, you'd skin up the bark on the standing trees and smash down all the undergrowth. A horse can't do that. It does not have the same kind of power as a cat. It won't pull out the little trees or tear up the roots."* Ernie's son, Ivan, did all the felling and bucking with a chain saw and Ernie did the yarding and loading with the team. The horses could drag about 4,500 lbs. dead weight.

William logged, was a fire warden and sold fried chicken at the Seabeck dock. He owned a logging operation at Stavis Bay and invented *"The Galloping Goose"*, a rig which was set on the front of a tram and pulled the cable, eliminating the need for steel tracks as small logs were used. It was a short-lived project.

Peter, Sr.'s son Joe (he always went by Joe and not Joseph) owned both Scenic Beach and Miami Beach and at one time had both parcels up for sale. Miami Beach sold first and he retained the Scenic Beach

property. His brother, John, and he owned a fish cannery in Valdez, Alaska.

Joe's son, also Joe, says that Indians used to come to the Big Beef area and camp on the spit, harvesting and smoking salmon. They'd split the salmon and throw them up on poles and the only smoke used to cure the fish was from the campfire. Two Indians that Joe remembers hearing about were *Nose-No-Nose*, who had a problem with his nose, and *Pants-No-Pants* who wore cutoffs.

Frank (Francis Joseph) and his wife, Elizabeth, moved to Seabeck from Seattle in 1906. Daughter Florence Brumm was one year old and her brother, Frankie, was three. A half-sister, Lillian McLean, was eight, and Lillian's brother, Donald McLean, was 13.

Elizabeth ran the Cliff House Hotel and Frank farmed the Pete Emel, Sr. property. Later they moved to Big Beef Valley where her father continued farming. Once when the creek flooded and water ran under the house, Elizabeth was afraid, so they built a log house on top of the hill. In about 1913 they bought a place near Big Beef bridge.[13]

Frank trained a team of oxen to work (and used them) to build a road for the County and plowed and logged with them. Florence wrote:[14] "There were lots of salmon in Big Beef creek, steelhead, silvers and dog salmon. We caught them in the fall from the creek and smoked them and also salted them. There were lots of deer and bear and cougars in the area and solid timber for many miles.

John Mike Emel was the owner of Emel Packing Company and the family still retains their summer home, Emel Glade, between Little and Big Beef Creeks. He started in the business world when he walked to Silverdale with a silver dollar and a saw that needed to be filed. He bet the dollar on roulette and returned home with enough money to buy a fishing boat. He forgot the saw in town.

Other early property owners in Section 15 (Township 25N, Range 1 West) were Herod Wells, Cam Whitney, Albert Robinson, William Barry,

---

[13]Florence (Emel) Brumm correspondence.

[14]Ibid.

James Smith, Robert Wenborn, Abe Tharp, and Andrew W. Frisk.

Swedish-born Andrew and Annette (Grundstrom) Frisk purchased their property in August 1892 from Andrew Anderson, two government lots for $266. They were the parents of Olga (1888), Estelle (1891) and Edith (1893). Edith may have been born here. While Andrew farmed, Annette found work in Seattle to supplement the family's income. Photos from the family album show a cluster of farm buildings around their small home, a windmill and chickens. They left the area in the early 1920s.

John and Rosanna Norman
(Photo courtesy Brenda Haberlin.)

John Norman

Johannes Norman (B. Sept. 15, 1857 Malmo, Sweden; D. March 1935 Seattle) wanted land and as land was extremely expensive in his native Sweden, he opted for a trip to the United States, pausing in Michigan to log. He found a parcel on his trip West, up Big Beef, probably in 1883. In the 1889 census his listed occupation as farmer. Here he built a log cabin and that first winter, while he and a friend were sitting at the kitchen table, talking, a tree fell through the house, severing their conversation. The tree landed in the middle of the table. Norman cleared his land by hand. It was tough, tedious work but had its "exciting" moments. His daughter, Brenda Haberlin, says that once when John Norman was coming home on horseback, he found a bear in a tree and another time a bobcat sitting on his kitchen counter drinking milk.

To get out of the area, he walked or rode over the trail by Wild Cat Lake. It was while on one of these trips that he met Rosanna Spickard Evans (1869-1930) whose family lived across from The Mountaineers. (She was Seattle's first long distance operator.) They were married in 1898. Their first child, Carl, was born up the valley in 1900 and the delivery of the large baby was difficult. The couple, anticipating more children, ended the pioneering experience and moved "in town" to Chico

where Norman opened a blacksmith shop. Three more children were born: Brenda in 1902; Thomas (1903) and Rose. The Norman property was "proved up" in October 1895, that NW quarter of Section 34, Township 25N, Range 1 West.[15]

Lone Rock

There is, Myron Eells wrote, on the east side of The Canal, about three miles below the mouth of the Dewater (sic) a large stone of very hard conglomerate about 13 feet high and five to six feet in diameter, tolerably regular in its rounded shape. This was a woman previous to the coming of the Changer.[16]

Many people often refer to the Big Beef area in the same breath as Lone Rock, that area immediately north of Beef Harbor. The Lone Rock store is on the south side of Big Beef and the Lone Rock chapel on the north side.

Lone Rock school, District 43, was established in 1895 and the second school, with additions, is now the Lone Rock Chapel.

---

[15] Land Title records.

[16] *Seattle Post-Intelligencer.* Oct. 17, 1884.

**Lone Rock - Photo taken pre-1920
by member of Andrew Frisk family.**
(Photo courtesy Bob Nord.)

Because Peter Emel, Sr. realized the increase in value of his property if there was a school in the area, it is said that he donated the lumber to build the school. It's also true that he had enough kids to fill it. Some of the early students came from the families of Johnson, Wondersheidt, Prosch, Steffen, Peterson, Sisson, Mingnon, Creel, Risch, Taylor, Holmes, Woods, Perry, Simpson and Coffin. Early teachers were Miss Churchill (who later became Mrs. Al Walton), Miss Scheckles, Miss Gates, Mrs. Schold, Mr. Hart, Emma Lindsey Squier (author of *Wild Heart,* a nature book) and George Cady Johnson. Seabeck postmaster George C. Johnson taught at Lone Rock during the six month term ending November 1901.[17] Johnson retired from the postmaster job, selling out to Frederick Prosch. He then accepted a contract at Crosby.

The original school later became the home of Jean and Al Schold and it was here that they raised their four children John, Margaret, Genevieve and Betty. Jean first saw the school in about 1920 when Mrs. Lindgren and Mrs. Merrick asked her to

help in their emergency: the teacher they had hired quit the day before classes were to start. Jean explained that she had a year-old baby, but Mrs. Merrick, said that she'd care for the child if Jean would teach. *"So I went and stayed the full year and that was my last year of teaching."*[18]

Emma (Bowers) Brumm began teaching at Lone Rock in 1921:[19] Emma (1893-1975) and her husband, William (1888-1968) (both born West Point, Nebraska) moved to Goldendale after their marriage, then to Lone Rock in 1921. She became the community's teacher, earning $110 monthly. There were fewer than 20 students but the school began to grow and County superintendent, David Wolfle, said students would soon have to hang from the ceiling. Students used apple boxes for desks. Her students included those from the families of Emel, Hipp, Wesch, Anderson, Cameron, Wilson, Weaver, Hutchings, Compton and Briggs.

Her career in education continued and she taught at Chico, Franklin, Glenwood and Seabeck where she was also principal. She was awarded the Central Kitsap schools' Golden Acorn award at a retirement tea in 1960 which marked the end of 41 years as a teacher beginning in Randolph, Nebraska.

A tribute to Emma Brumm was written by Adele Ferguson summing up her long career in education:[20].

She remembers the times she was called out of the room and returned to find a cake and hear a jubilant "Happy Birthday" from her people -- she always calls her students her people -- and how she'd send out for soda pop and ice cream to make it a real party.

The little things. Like all the times she had to sew up a little boy's blue jeans when he burst them in a flying leap for second base. All the skinned knees, bloody noses and mashed fingers she has cared for. All the tears she has wiped away over every-

[17]*Bremerton News.* Nov. 2, 1901.

[18]*The Way it Was in Kitsap Schools.* Kitsap County Retired Teachers, Bicentennial Committee. 1977. Pp. 212-213.

[19]Ibid. Pp. 214-215.

[20]*Bremerton Sun.* May 26, 1960.

thing from broken hearts to failure in the spelling bee.

All the tears she herself could shed over the children who were hungry and neglected, the unwashed and the unwanted, the lonely and the lost, who needed love the most and reached out for it from a gentle-voiced gray-haired school teacher.

She taught her own children, many of her ten grandchildren and had three of her 14 great grandchildren in school.

William Brumm worked for West Fork Logging at Camp Union and started the Lone Rock Store and two-pump auto service center in 1937. They sold the store to Nellie Welliever in 1950 and it burned in 1952. Kerosene barrels and items in storage fueled the fire.

The couple were the parents of three daughters, all nurses: Bertha (Sibon), (1912); Marie (Olsen), (1914) and Clara (Perry), (1915).

From Emma's reminisces:

Teaching in a little one-room school of long, long ago, Lone Rock, about 1921, was far different from a day in our modern schools of today. All the grades were in the same room and all classes, from phonics in the first grade, through history and physiology in the upper grades, had to have a time for class recitations.

The days were happy ones though and we all worked together. The buildings were not modern and water had to be carried from the neighbor's home in pails. The pail was then put upon a shelf in the entryway. Beside it was a wash basin and on a nail in the hall hung a long-handled dipper which was used by us all. Under the shelf was a pail to be used for waste water. "Germs" did not seem to be a part of this arrangement and no one seemed to catch anything from each other.

There were two out houses, out under the trees: one for the boys and one for the girls. The toilet paper was made up of the contents of the wastepaper baskets. Coal oil lamps furnished light.

There were no hot lunches for many years but in my district we had a little neighborhood club which worked very closely with the school. We worked out a plan in which the mothers would take turns bringing lunch every day. Lunch usually

Original Lone Rock School
(Photo courtesy Darrel Emel.)

consisted of soup or hot cocoa which was very welcome on cold winter days.

The club and school also had programs and plays each month and on holidays and we had very good times together. I think the children enjoyed a very much closer relationship with the grownups than they do now.

The children got along very well on the playground. We all played together: the old games Hide and Seek, Blind Man's Bluff, Pull Away, Beckon, Bear, Run-Sheep-Run.

It was not hard to get the children back into the building and sitting in their seats quietly after play time in the morning and when noon was over. They were anxious to hear the next chapters of the interesting book being read for opening exercises. The books were chosen with care and we almost felt that we knew the characters in the books personally. We read Anne of Green Gables, Tom Sawyer, Beautiful Jo, Black Beauty, The Wild Heart and the Nancy Drew books.

To make the study of State history more interesting, we planned trips to other places of historical interest near us. We went without recesses and shortened our noon hours to make up for the time we would use. We went through the old hotel at Port Gamble with its many, many things of historical interest. It is too bad that it ever was torn down. It had so much of interest to contribute.

We also went through the old cemetery there and some of the old houses and the old church whose furnishings came from New England around The Horn. Another time we went to see Chief Seattle's Grave in Suquamish and the remains of the old Indian long houses. We went to the Capitol in Olympia and saw the many interesting buildings. We used the bus from one of the larger schools for some of our trips and all the children enjoyed these extra sightseeing trips very much.

Needless to say there were no discipline problems as these children, unlike the children of today, had had very little travel outside their own neighborhood. There were very few cars in those early days at Lone Rock.

Sometimes at home now a stranger knocks at the door and turns out to be a pupil of school days of long ago and they bring back so many happy memories of school days. Some bring along children and grandchildren of their own. Many have become teachers, others hold responsible jobs in big companies. Many work in the Navy Yard and it makes us old, retired teachers feel that being a teacher is our own small way in shaping the lives of our pupils into respected and useful citizens.

William Brumm's older brother, Charles, (1876-1944) and his wife, Lena, and their children moved to Crosby in 1921 and in 1929 built a home on Pioneer road. They had eight children: Ida, Emil, Emma (Snyder), Frank, Dorothy (Bush), Ella (Benson), Marie (Storey) and Edna (Erickson).

Another Pioneer Road family consisted of Robert and Margaret (Weimer) Compton who arrived in 1920. They were the parents of Robert, Fredrick and Margaret Elinor (Clark).

Daughter Margaret wrote about their life in the area:

"I recall that my folks owned one of the first sedans in the area. Ours was a 1923 Ford. Roads weren't geared for autos yet because I can remember a three-mile trip to the Seabeck store sometimes entailing fixing three flat tires.

"My mother (1886-1962) had worked at the Cliff House before her marriage (in 1910). Her sister, Mrs. Frank Emel, lived in the area.

"My father (1883-1953) earned his living as a carpenter. He took contract jobs and worked for McCormick Logging Company building bunk houses and stores. The folks raised chickens and, for a while, turkeys. They sold eggs, chickens, turkeys, some milk and garden produce.

They bought a home on less than ten acres: a two-story house with log barn and a large shed for $750 at $10 per month, five per cent interest. The house burned to the ground in March 1924. After the fire the neighbors were generous in helping by donating clothing and money to tide us over. They also gave us shelter until the shed could be made livable while building the new home.

One of the favorite pastimes was community dances. When I was a small child we

Lone Rock School 1927-28
Dorothy Bye Higgins, Harvey Carson, Carolyn Wesch, Marie Brumm, Kendall Carson. (Front) Elenor Compton, Elsie Keller, Hazel Emel, Cathryn Hipp, Hans Wesch, Dorothy Brumm.
(Photo courtesy Bertha Brumm Sibon and Dorothy Bye Higgins.)

occasionally had dances in the hayloft of our barn before the new hay crop was put in. Family, friends and neighbors joined in the fun and music was provided by Victrola, fiddle and harmonica.

The Comptons had one of the first radios and neighbors would come to hear Amos 'n Andy and Lum 'n Abner. The family also had one of the first closed cars, a 1923 Ford.

Elinor met her husband, Charles E. Clark, when he was teaching his first year at Seabeck. After their marriage, they lived in one of the houses on the Conference Grounds.

Another early Lone Rock and Seabeck teacher was Dorothy Bye, later Higgins. She attended Pacific Lutheran, then College, and after two years received a certificate to teach. The professor took the qualifying new teachers around to various schools to meet school board members. As a 19 year-old she was hired at Lone Rock, beginning her three year stint in 1927.

During her first year of teaching, she boarded with the Pete Emel family. The following year, Dorothy and the Seabeck teacher, Dorothy Peake, rented the Halvorsen's cottage and as one of the Halvorsen girls was also named Dorothy, it meant a lot of confusion. When Miss Peake left the Seabeck school, the then Miss Bye took it over, living at Miami Beach.

In 1928 she purchased a six year-old Ford coupe which made it easier to get home to Tacoma. Previous to that she would board the *Virginia V* in Tacoma, transfer to the Bremerton ferry at Seattle and ride in an old touring car (stage) to Seabeck.

In 1930 she bought a new Ford roadster with a rumble seat for $750.[21]

Today the Lone Rock chapel is still a viable part of the community. A manuscript was prepared giving the history of the Lone Rock chapel and it tells much of the early history of the area.[22]

It is impossible to separate the history of Lone Rock Chapel from that of the Lone Rock School/Schoolhouse. A one-room school was held in the Lone Rock area at the present site of the chapel from 1892-1941. At least two different buildings housed this early school, the latest being an add-on constructed in 1920.

The chapel still uses this structure although updates and modifications have been made, inside and out. During these early years it was not unusual for the school board to hire a different teacher for each school term. Teacher availability, weather and transportation were three of the biggest difficulties faced. This situation changed in 1921 when Mrs. Emma Brumm was hired to teach and stayed through 1926, returning to teach again 1932-1941.

In 1941 it was deemed prudent for Lone Rock to merge with the Seabeck School and this part of its history came to an end. The only remaining effects of the school are the school clock and pump organ which can still be seen in the sanctuary of the chapel.

During the early 1930s, the need was seen for a Sunday School for the children of the area. It was organized and started with the efforts of two ladies, Mrs. Emma Brumm and Gladys Merrick. We cannot pinpoint the exact date of this venture, but evidence exists showing the Sunday School was in existence during 1934. An article from the *Silverdale Breeze* reads:[23] *"Lone Rock Sunday School held its picnic Sunday on the beautiful grounds of Mrs. Merrick on Hood Canal (Lynmere). Over fifty children, fathers, mothers and friends were present. The lunch tables were lovely, being artistically decorated with produce from garden and orchard, ferns and flowers from the woods. Boating, swimming and games were enjoyed. A delightful and cooling surprise was given the gathering when Misses Merrick and Lockwood passed around the ice cream for all."*

Bertha (Brumm) Sibon relates her remembrances from this era:

"My mother would leave the roast, or pies in the oven of the wood stove. She would call up the stairs that she was leaving for Sunday School and Marie, my sister, was to keep the fire going or watch the pies. Gladys Merrick was always there, serving

---

[21]Dorothy Bye Higgins letter May 21, 1993.

[22]Steve Coffey and Bertha (Brumm) Sibon.

[23]*Silverdale Breeze*. Aug. 23, 1934.

as Superintendent, organist, and/or teacher. Others who attended during these early years were Mable Hutchings and sons, Mr. and Mrs. Fred Hart and family, Mrs. Bulette and Mrs. Boyer Halvorsen and daughter, Susan, from Seabeck, Mr. and Mrs. Floyd Calkins and family, The Ed Greeers, Mr. and Mrs. John Longfellow, Dr. and Mrs. Hendrickson, Mrs. Ernest Crosier, Mr. and Mrs. Schroeder and family, Mrs. Al Schold, Mr. Carl Jenne, Mrs. Frank Kirby, and Mrs. Warenstaf and children.

The Sunday School had very little money and janitor work was done on a volunteer basis. For several winters, Mr. and Mrs. Ray Hartt and family came early on Sunday mornings, from Silverdale, to start the wood heater and warm the building. Later Bobbie and Danny Greer were hired to do this and to clean the building.

The Lone Rock and Sunday School markers, along Seabeck Highway, were a project of the Lone Rock Community Club, the Ladies' Club and the Sunday School. Around 1940 a bachelor, Mr. Ransom (Deke) Bell was hired to carve these markers. It was winter and very cold. Mr. Bell became very sick with pneumonia and lived with Mr. and Mrs. George Radomski until his death. Mr. Radomski completed the carvings as verified by his son, Hank. These markers were dedicated on Easter Sunday, 1943.

In 1943 the process was started to acquire the deed to the property from the Central Kitsap School District. The transaction was not completed until 1948. The treasurer, Mrs. Bertha Sibon, paid Mr. Jenne, School District Superintendent and Sunday School trustee, $1 in pennies from the cigar box treasury.

It was also during this same time period that Lone Rock Sunday School affiliated with the American Sunday School Union. Missionaries Charles and Jessie Knautz made the trip over from Tacoma regularly to assist the Sunday School, teach Bible Study classes and arrange for Vacation Bible School. The Knautz's retired from the mission in 1959 but continued to teach Bible Studies for many years more. During these years, some building modifications were made, bringing changes to the entrance and adding classrooms.

Denny and Diane Huffman followed the Knautz couple, serving from 1959-1972. Wally and Clara Kippola served as leaders and teachers until 1984.

John Emel died in 1967 and left a $5,000 legacy to the Sunday School. Sanctuary, nursery and bathroom were added, completed in 1972.

Missionaries Steve and Barbara Coffey spearheaded a search for a full-time minister and during 1977 several candidates were heard and considered but the Coffeys accepted the position and moved to the area.

Samuel Merrick arrived in Lone Rock in 1915 with his wife, Carolyn Rebecca (Taber) because of its tranquilty and beauty. They were the parents of three children George (1878-1895), Jesse (1880-1967) and Grace (1887). They'd row to Seabeck daily to check the mail brought in by *Potlatch.*

Samuel was a promoter, builder and inventor, according to his late daughter, Gladys.[24] Grace was sickly and once her doctor suggested that she drink beer before her meals.[25] It was during prohibition and Mrs. Merrick didn't want any of the neighbors to know that there was beer in the house so she ordered it through a Bremerton drugstore thinking they would deliver the suggested commodity. The family was shocked when the beer truck parked in front of their home and brought in the lager.

Jessie was superintendent of physical education in Seattle schools and wrote the original course book for the School Patrol. She and the principal of John Muir school, Jessie Lockwood, were honored as pioneers of the national school patrol system. On the 25th anniversary of the school patrol in 1961, she was honored in a Washington, DC presentation but because of health problems, a Bremerton school patrol boy, Chuck Knight, was sent to the nation's capitol to pick up the honor.

The small, shingled cottage the sisters lived in at Lone Rock was dismantled and reassembled on the Conference Groups by members of the Seabeck Community Club.

---

[24]KCHS. Merrick family history.

[25]Dorothy Bye Higgins. 1993.

Head of the Bay

Norwegian Immigrants Settled And Created Population Boom

Look at any Seabeck school picture of the 1920s and there will be Dahls and Hagens. Today the two families gather for family parties, fill churches at weddings and funerals and dote over the new babies, whether they are Hagens or Dahls . . . but especially precious are those babies who carry the bloodline of both families.

The two sets of parents raised large families and provided them with the basics of life: a love of family, a deep sense of reverance for their Norwegian heritage, a belief in God and the ethics of hard work. Most stayed in the area, earning their living off the land and the water whether it was logging or milling, fishing or brushpicking.

The families are marked by longevity. Many of the first generation are now in the 80s and 90s and have clear skin, sparkling eyes, keen minds and few wrinkles. That generation can speak and understand Norwegian.

Peder and Karen Hagen

Peder Hagen[26] (B. Dec. 23, 1873 near Qualheim, Norway; D. Aug. 10, 1952 Bremerton) was struck by wanderlust. By the time he was 27, he had crossed the Atlantic two or three times going to Wisconsin, then to Seattle and up to the gold mines near Douglas, Alaska for three years. Each time he returned to Norway, he was drawn back to the United States by a sense of adventure. In Wisconsin Peder and Daniel Dahl worked at a tobacco farm. They were later to become neighbors at Seabeck.

While passing through Seattle, Peder came to Seabeck and bought 40 acres by paying back taxes. He left his property, at the head of the bay, for his final trip to Norway. It was here that he married Karen Vauge (B. Aug. 18, 1872 Norway; D. Nov. 24, 1959 Bremerton). Karen wouldn't leave Norway until her mother died, according to Ingie (Dahl) Cicelski. Other than being a close neighbor, Ingie says that the Dahls and Hagens intermarried at least three times: in Norway, Seabeck and about five years ago in Tacoma.

The first of their nine children, Ingvald, (B. March 27, 1902 Qualheim) was just six months old when they left Norway.

Most immigrants from this area came on the Dominion Line which ran a triangular route from Bergen to Liverpool to Montreal. It was apparently much less expensive than going through New York. It cruised at 11 knots and carried something like 100 in first class, 200 in second class and 1,000 in third class or steerage.[27]

They left Norway with their traditional name, Qualheim, but Peder changed the surname to Hagen.

When they arrived in Seattle, they took the old stern-wheeler *State of Washington* to Seabeck. Rasmus O. Qualheim, a cousin of Peder's, met the boat and took the young couple and infant, Ingvald, to his home at Crosby where they stayed for a few days until they had made arrangements to rent one of the old millhouses. Peder begin building their home and it stands today attesting to his skill as a carpenter.

They probably moved into the home on the south side of the Miami Beach road sometime in 1904. (By this time, they had two sons.)

---

[26]The Peter Hagen road is named after a Crosby man who was German, not the Norwegian Peder Hagen.

---

[27]Don Christensen letter. Oct. 28, 1992.

Peder Hagen's home that grew:
The original home was remodeled but still maintains some of its original character including the building to the right which still stands.
(Photo courtesy Invald Hagen.)

After the birth of Thoralf or "Tom" (B. July 26, 1903 Seabeck; D. June 7, 1969 Seabeck) Karen *thought* that she was busy. Some of Peder and Karen's children were delivered in Poulsbo at Watlands, friends from Norway. Perhaps assistance in this birth was offered by the Qualheims.

Tom later was a logger, fished in Alaska, built boats, worked at PSNS and as a furniture assembler with his sister, Mable, and her husband Wally Johnson in Arlington. He and his wife, Dena (Dahl), had four children.

Peder cleared trees, planted gardens and fruit trees, built a narrow and high smoke house down by the beach. They had cattle and chickens and he fished out of Neah Bay as well as Canal waters.

His avocation was building boats. He built several on the beach in front of their home and, Ingvald says, some are still used in the fishing fleets of the Pacific Northwest. All were fishing trollers: *Swallow* (30'), *Dove* (31' double ender), *Neva* and *Nellie Ann* (43') and others. He was also known on The Canal as a man who could repair boats.

But at home there were more children. Jacob was born in 1904 or 1905. His was the first grave marked with the Hagen name in the cemetery. He died when about two years old from pneumonia.

Another son was born and also named Jacob: (1909-1979). He was a fisherman, worked at PSNS and served in WWII when the US raided the Philipines. He lived in the family home at Seabeck until his death.

Laura (B. May 4, 1911 Poulsbo) worked in fisheries in Seattle and was married to Reidar Westeren and they had six children.

Karen Hagen really had her hands full now and when Peder's sister, Tomina, a recent widow, showed up with her five children, the house was really full. Tomina moved across the street and later moved to Tacoma. After Tomina Rasmussen (B. Sept. 20, 1882; D. July 30, 1959) arrived, more children were born to the Hagens.

Laurence (B. Aug. 7, 1912; D. Oct. 21, 1971) was a logger and worked at PSNS. He and his wife, Jean (Brinker), owned a drycleaning business in Brookings, Oregon and had twin daughters.

Klare (B. May 25, 1915 Seabeck) moved out of the area for 40 years living in Oregon and California, working at Penneys and for several pharmacists. She was married to

Richard Reynoldson and they had two daughters and one son.

Melvin (B. June 19, 1916 Seabeck; D. Jan. 18, 1955, Seabeck accident) was a logging truck driver, logged and was in WWII, serving in Italy. He was not married.

Mabel (B. Feb. 22, 1918) was married to Wallace Johnson and lives near Lake Stevens. Wally owns and operates Modern Furniture Manufactures, Inc. in Arlington. They had a son and daughter.

In 1935, after the children were raised, the Hagens remodeled and expanded their home replacing the outhouse and Saturday night washtub with a bath and a half. When they were finished, there were two bedrooms downstairs and three upstairs.

The siding for the main house and at least one of the out buildings came from Al Walton's mill at Little Beef Creek. One of the buildings was built from Port Gamble lumber and another from lumber from the original Seabeck school which Mr. Hagen bought, then tore down and removed to his property. Peder, according to his children, was always moving houses and buildings around. Most of the homes at the head of the bay were built by Peder Hagen.

Ingvald attended the old one-room school located on the south side of the fire station. It had a cloakroom, wood furnace and wood shed outside. Ingvald worked tugboats, as a gypo logger, and for West Fork Logging Company. For a time he worked on the log booms for Pope and Talbot in the bay in front of his home.

When they were young, there was a blacksmith shop on the spit. It was later moved near the intersection of the Miami Beach/ Holly Road. Archie Kellum would make ice skates for the kids out of old files and put them on a board. They'd skate on the pond below their property or up at Crosby on a lake they called "Mary's Lake."

Ingvald worked in logging camps and for Murray at Camp Union. He also ran tugboats for Pope and Talbot at Port Gamble and Port Ludlow and rafted logs on the Cowlitz River.

When the old logging railroad ran from Camp Union, the train tracks went through the Hagens' back yard, crossed the road and logs were dumped into the water at the head of the bay. You could hear the trains coming down the hill, blowing their horns whistles. There were four locomotives owned by Pope and Talbot that worked constantly. *"Logs came down on those cars that were 120' long,"* Ingvald remembered.

Ingvald began working at the Conference Grounds in the early 1920s. He'd prune and spray trees and worked on restoring the old cottages, putting in new floors or doing whatever had to be done. Huge piles of brush had to be burned.

None of the buildings were torn down after the Colmans bought the property, according to Ingvald. Those remaining were just fixed up. Virtually everyone agrees that prior to the purchase by the Colmans, old millhouses were stripped or moved entirely throughout The Canal region.

He and brother Tom cleaned out the old mill pond with a dredger and built up the land in front of the store. They found much debris in the pond including wood slabs.

He helped build the tennis courts up behind the fire station. Whatever had to be done, Ingvald was there.

He built roads in the area. The old Chico road went from Camp Wesley Harris to Chico down a steep grade and when it rained, the gravel would wash across the road making it difficult for the old stages to pass that way. Ingvald worked on the new road from Star Grocery (Northlake Way) to Camp Wesley Harris in the early 1920s. Later he worked on the road from Camp Wesley Harris to Big Beef.

Karen's brother, Abraham Vauge, built Klare's first house in 1932 (which still stands) for $500 in lumber and other materials. She totally furnished it with another $500.

Ingvald still lives in the original family home. Period wallpaper (hung by Klare in modern times), French doors leading off the diningroom, a large family kitchen (but not like modern familyroom/kitchen combinations) are reminiscent of another time, a time when neighbors would gather and kids would play parlor games. A wood-burning stove in the kitchen gives off a warmth not found in modern homes.

It was in this home that monthly religious services were held with a Lutheran minister coming from Seattle. Klare would play the piano while the older people in the community, at least older to her then, came for the sermon. Peder and Karen brought their children up with Christian principles. Organized church services weren't necessary in this home where the bible was read, and prayers were said. Lutheran services were also held at the old school, but much later.

Not many years ago, salmon were plentiful in the stream that flows through the Hagen property. Klare always had canned or smoked salmon and more wrapped in the freezer. Those days have changed and she admitted that there was no salmon in the house.

Of the original 40 acres, 28 acres are left. The property was divided at the death of the parents between the children.

A 1980 family history[28] states that Jacob Qualheim had a son named Thorstein who married Parnelle Blaksaeter. Most of their 11 children changed their name from Qualheim (or Kvalheim) to Hagen. Many of the children immigrated to the United States and raised families in Tacoma, Marysville and Seabeck. The 11 children, besides Peder, were Anders Hagen, Jacob Qualheim, Minert Hagen, Rasmus Hagen, Tomina (Rasmusson), Berent (Ben) Hagen, Sivert Hagen, Adolph Hagen, Samuelina (Gangeskar) and Didrick Qualheim.

Daniel and Didrikka Dahl

Daniel Dahl (B.Dec. 14, 1875 Raude-berg, Norway; D. Aug. 5, 1968 Bremerton) arrived in the United States on June 12, 1897 and returned to Norway in 1901 to marry Didrikka Refvik (B. July 10, 1874 Norway; D. May 14, 1948) in Raudeberg. They came to this country, settling in Crosby by the time their first child, Hjalmer was born (March 3, 1902). Didrikka took her maiden name from the town in Norway where she was born. Their first child was

The Hagen home after remodeling and much as it looks today. The building on the right was the original Seabeck School.
(Photo courtesy Ingvald Hagen.)

born in Bremerton where the young immigrants went to stay with the Qualheims.

Mrs. Qualheim served as midwife. A couple of weeks after the birth, the couple walked back to their Crosby home carrying their first child.[29]

Daniel purchased 40 acres and while he was building their first home they lived with the Myre family. By 1914 they were living in Seabeck, moved back to Crosby and eventually settled permanently in Seabeck at the head of the Bay near the Hagens. Daniel was a truck farmer, raising enough to keep his family well fed. He supplemented the family "table" by fishing. One of his first jobs in the United States was as captain of an Alaskan fishing boat owned by John Emel. He built commercial boats and finished his last vessel in 1960. He also was a commercial fisherman on his own boat and his last two trips were made during 1958-59 with his daughter, Ingie. He and his brother, Ivar, ran a sawmill at Seabeck when he wasn't fishing or building boats.

Hjalmer (B. March 3, 1902; D. May 21, 1986) was married to Hazel Carnes. He worked as a logger and picked brush. He bought the hull of a fishing boat from Peder Hagen and finished it, then made his living fishing.

The other children were born at home. Daniel was so adept at delivering babies

---

[28]Mrs. Arnold (Mary) Wennerberg

[29]Interviews at July 4, 1993 family gathering.

that he assisted in the delivery of Ingie's second child.

Ingeborg (Ingie) (B. July 10, 1904) married Jack Cicelski. A niece said that she worked as hard as any man. She fished, cut brush, was a seamstress, janitor and bus driver. In 1916 or 1917, Ingie worked at the Conference Grounds for Arn Allen and was a dishwiper. She and her husband had two sons and one daughter.

Anna (B. July 13, 1906; D. circa 1989) married Fred Foy, a logger, and they had three daughters. She worked for the Hagens, caring for Grandma Hagen. Anna worked at logging camps as a cook.

Borghild (B. circa 1908 and died at age 8) was the little girl everyone remembers sadly. She's buried in the Seabeck cemetery.

Dena (B. Nov,. 17, 1909) married Thoralf Hagen. She worked at Bremerton General Hospital. They had a daughter and three sons.

Haldor (B. July 12, 1912) married Lila Danielsen and they had two daughters. He was a logger, drove logging truck, worked at Camp Union and other northwest logging areas. He retired at Tillamook, OR.

Isaac (B. March 5, 1914 at Seabeck) married Pat Castle and they had a son and two daughters. He worked as a logger and lives at Port Angeles.

Martha (B. Dec. 7, 1916) married John Martin and they had one son and two daughters. She worked as an aid at a Bremerton nursing home and also in Arlington.

David (B. Dec. 21, 1918) married Mildred Rhodes and they had one son. He then married Freda and they had seven children. He lives in California.

The Dahl's home at the head of Seabeck Bay was built from lumber from the mill town. Many houses in the area used materials from the original milltown houses. Clayson's Bayview Hotel was on the Hagen property and as it was falling down, much of the material was used in "new" homes.

Norwegian was spoken exclusively in both the Dahl and Hagen homes. The children learned English at school. Grandma Hagen never spoke English but she could understand her grandchildren. The Dahls boarded Norwegian loggers at their home and the children would come home from school and teach them what they'd learned.

The Dahls and Hagens call Seabeck Creek a *"crick"*. Now the grandchildren and great-grandchildren and great-greats call it *"the crick"*. Ingie remembers vividly the smell of *"the crick"* each fall as spawning salmon died . . . hundreds and hundreds of them. *"Now we're lucky if we see ten salmon in the fall,"* Ingie says poignantly.

When Daniel Dahl died 25 years ago (1968) he was survivied by 25 grandchildren, 44 greatgrandchildren and one great-great-grandchild. The family has quit counting. Add that to the Hagen family's multiplication and you have a medium-sized city.

Miami Beach

Indians' Resort;
Henny's Oasis

No one is quite sure now why the area is called Miami Beach, but one look at the white sand washed for centuries by Canal waters gives a fairly good clue.

It was here that Twana Indian families summered, leaving tell-tale mounds of clam shells, Indian trade beads, ancient charcoal and at least one skeleton exhumed during a building project.

Today all signs of a former time are gone except the three-story home Ben Cade built beginning in the summer of 1911. Over the years the entire property was raised until the house looked like it was two stories.

Henny Aarts, a later owner, made friends with one of the early participants in building the home. Angus McMillan gave the family his recollections of the area with photos.[30]

"As nearly as I can remember, Charles Hall bought all the waterfront between the Seabeck oyster beds and Stavis Creek for delinquent taxes about 1905. He subsequently sold that portion you now own to one Ole Gifford. Ole died in Hoodsport about 1955.

"In early 1911 he sold the property to Ben Cade who built the house you now occupy. We worked all that summer of 1911 making the cement blocks, clearing the lagoon of logs, cutting firewood and clearing out the brush immediately back of the lagoon. We also put in the flood gate at the outlet of the lagoon.

"At that time the creek kept the lagoon filled with fresh pure water. All the creeks in that region seem to have dwindled to mere trickles.

"The house was built in 1912 tho I believe it was not finished until later.

"The Cade tent home was located about 100 feet west of your present home. It was built early in 1911, March as I recall it. The floor was about three feet above the sand. About 100 feet west of the tent was a tool shed.

"Just east of the lagoon entrance is where Anton Anderson and I made the cement blocks (for the foundation and house) We carried fresh water from the creek which ran into the lagoon. This creek also supplied fresh water for the Cades household uses.

"There were no roads and as far as we knew no one lived between your beach and Bremerton. It was all cut-over land with many down trees as a result of a bad wind storm about 1904."

(The Cades built a tent house and lived in it until the house was built. McMillan photographed the bedroom and living room of the tent house.) *"Mrs. Cade wouldn't let me take a picture of the kitchen, insisting that it was too messy. She was, however, a stickler for neatness and the place was always very neat and livable."*

"Piecing together the tales we heard around Seabeck, Dewatto and Brinnon, it seems that a tribe of Indians were wiped out by smallpox some time about the turn of the Century. Numbers varied from over a hundred to just one family. The truth probably lies somewhere in between. We had heard that they were buried out on the sand spit, but tho we did a lot of digging, we never found a trace of a grave. It's reasonable that they would have buried the bodies where the digging was easier."

While digging up on the bank, at the site of the lagoon flood gate, McMillan uncovered an Indian skeleton. The body had

[30] Angus M. McMillan. Correspondence Sept. 28, 1968 and July 25, 1969.

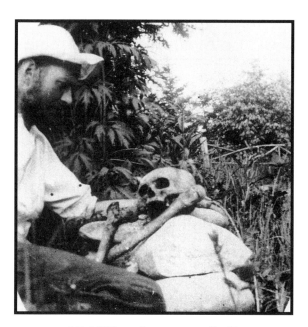

**McMillan dug up an Indian
skeleton in the 1920s.**
(Photo courtesy Roger and Norman Anderson.)

despondent. The next day he had soaked the place with gasoline, set it afire and died in the ruins. According to the Seattle paper, nothing but the foundations were left.

"Hall had done all of the rock work, built the bridge as well as a dam about 30 feet above the bridge. The place was at the site of the present park reserve. I couldn't find a trace of any of the old landmarks."

~

Adrian Aarts was a logger and then owned heavy equipment, working in construction. He put in bunkers at the Kitsap County airport, worked on West Park and East Park and made improvements to the road to Seabeck. When Adrian and Henny (Skagen) Aarts purchased the property in September 1945, they built a boat house and remodeled the main house. There were 18 small cabins, each with a wood stove. And with a small grocery and restaurant, the complex was complete as a summer resort. Dwight and Thela Sullivan ran the grocery and later Serine and Ed Munger.

Because the property was lower than sea level, rain and high winter tides would flood the property and wash over the bulkhead. The Aarts would secure driftwood and logs, preventing damage to the bulkhead. During a period when they leased the property, such care wasn't taken and much damage was done to the cabins and property. The Aarts' leased the property for a short time beginning in September 1948 but Henny was happy when they had to repossess it and she could resume her work.

Henny (B. June 25, 1911 near Bergen, Norway) and Adrian (B. Nov. 17, 1904,

been buried by covering it with cedar shakes.

Hall put in an immense amount of work including rock walls and trails and planted an assortment of trees including a palm.

"Hall (worked hard) *making the place attractive. Yet he lived like a pig inside the house until Anderson and I moved in.*

"Hall sold property to Joe Bacher in 1911. Bacher lived in tents for a couple of years while his lovely chalet was being built. I couldn't find a trace of Joe's place but perhaps I didn't get to the right place.

"In 1924 or 1925, I've forgotten which, my wife and I called on Joe. His wife had just died and he was very

**Harrison Eastman
sketched two Indian
village scenes in the
Seabeck area in 1873.
Sharon Barney
identified this one as
Miami Beach.**
*(From the photo collection
at the Washington State
Historical Society.)*

Holland) were the parents of three daughters, Penny (Lovelace), Connie (Coons) and Norma (Anderson). Adrian wanted to buy a farm but Henny saw potential in Miami Beach and she loved living there. The Canal reminded her of home by Norway's fjords. Summers were idyllic for the daughters even though they worked along with their parents.

When they bought the property, there was no road to the area. The property was a virtual island with a large pond or lagoon behind the buildings. A bridge was built by Roger Anderson, a son-in-law. They remodeled the five bedroom house which also had an attic and in the attic was an old trunk filled with photos, letters, an old lamp shade with beads and a set of false teeth! The trunk is still there: the attic was finished around it and there's no way to remove it.

The main house had been used as a hotel, of sorts, and at times even the attic was full of renters. Although it is said that "sea captains" stayed here, the home was built long after sailing ships called on the Seabeck area.

Three of the cottages were sold to a logger who moved them all around the Seabeck area. There were 30 boats and 23 cabins and thousands of families who spent part of their summers here.

Improvements were made to the property but fire destroyed many of Henny's dreams on June 18, 1957. The boathouse and restaurant and one cabin were destroyed by fire at a loss of more than $100,000 and although the structures were

covered by insurance, the boats that were stored for other owners were not. Mrs. Aarts was determined to pay for the losses out of her own pocket and it was the beginning of a change in the community. Harry Jeffs who lived in the cabin lost not only his personal possessions but his boat.

Jeffs worked for Henry Broderick in Seattle and was an ardent fisherman. He kept a diary noting cloud formations, temperature, tides and used the knowledge to become known as the best fisherman at Miami Beach. He never came back without at least one fish, according to Anderson.

The answer to the financial dilemma was to sell some of her beloved property. She never listed the properties nor advertised. Most of the sales were to neighbors or summer patrons who loved the area. Shipyard derby officials vowed to make no changes in derby plans for later in the summer. But because of the loss, Henny announced the following year that she would have to charge $100 per day for the two weekend event. Shipyard officials balked and moved the traditional Miami Beach event to Hansville. She had not charged for launching boats nor parking and profits to her during the four-day run were minimal. And she was hurt.

It was then that she began thinking about expanding the resort, but first she needed a rezone to Business General. neighbors fought her bitterly and the commission tabled her request to allow her to present a planned unit development proposal. It was then that she hired Keith Garrison of Branch, Branch and Garrison to design a new complex. These plans called for 100 motel units, restaurant, conference center and heliport on a five-acre tract with 600 feet of waterfront. The commissioners turned her down and asked that she come back with a scaled down version. Which she did amidst continued protest by the neighbors. Approval was granted for two 20-unit motel structures and five duplex cottages. It was a long, uphill fight. The cost, her age and other factors won out and the resort was never built. The property was sold to many people who had summered there.

Shipyard Derby time at Miami Beach.
(Photo courtesy Norma and Roger Anderson.)

An early (and only partial) history of Miami Beach south to Scenic Beach can be traced through an abstract owned by Raymond and Barbara Berglind. John Lantz received a patent on 153.25 acres on July 5, 1882. Lantz knew his share of tragedy. A fisherman, his six year-old son, Richard, drowned out in front of their home in 1878. Within 18 months, his wife died leaving John the care of the two little girls.

Jacob Hauptly has many diary entries for Lantz, [31] the first July 10, 1878 when "the Dutchman Lantz" went to work for him at the Beaver Valley ranch. Hauptly fired him. When the little boy died, Hauptly built the coffin, raised money and gave the mother $35.50, a gift from the community, and employed Maggie Davis for $12 to make some clothes for the other Lantz children. Hauptly wrote: "Husband no count."

Hauptly doesn't mention him again until August 1885 when he writes: "Someone put a head on Lantz last night." Hauptly paid Lantz' property taxes in December 1885 and sent the $28 to the County auditor. Hauptly's diaries and the abstract show that Lantz deeded the property to his sister, Emma Johnson, as trustee for his daughter, Sarah, in 1882 and then tried to sell the property to Oscar Lundberg, landing Lantz in legal hot water. The last mention of Lantz in Hauptly's diaries was when he filled out an application for Lantz on his coal claim and writes: "I fixed them up and also settled with the *brute.*"

Lundberg sold the land to Jacob Hauptly in 1890 and when Hauptly failed to pay his taxes, R. O. Qualheim purchased the 50 acres for $47.98. Qualheim sold this acreage and beach front to Charles R. Hall in 1904.

---

[31] Jacob Hauptly diaries. Kitsap County Historical Society.

Scenic Beach State Park

Scene from Front Porch

Charles Hall and friends,
pre-1920
(Photo courtesy Scenic Beach State Park.)

Sitting on the porch of Grandpa Joe's cabin and gazing at the Hood Canal with glimpses of the Olympic Mountains peeking through the maples, one can truly understand why this magnificent place has come to be called Scenic Beach.

The primary reason for its existence as a state park is due in large part to the efforts of Andy Olsen who in the early 1960s was able to convince the director of state parks, John Vanderzicht, to purchase the land. The property became available for sale in 1962 when Joe Emel (Sr.) passed away. Andy was the executor of Mr. Emel's estate and he felt that the property should be shared with the public as a state park. Circulation of early petitions sent a message to the park commission that indeed there was a great deal of interest in developing the property into a state park. In 1963 the State paid $98,000 for 31 acres, the Emel House and 950 feet of beachfront on Hood Canal. The area was operated as a primitive camp ground with camping sites located in the east side of the present-day use picnic area. The ranger's residence was in the Emel House with picnic sites located in the present west picnic area.

During those early years (from 1963-70), the State employed caretakers Herb and Dorothy Potts to collect camp fees and keep the pit toilets tweaked. Forty acres was added in 1970 of Department of Natural Resources property for $20,000. That 40 acres today encompasses the present campground. During a budget crunch in 1971, State Parks turned the park over to Kitsap County for operation. Greg Voigt, who was working out of Wildcat Lake and a Seabeck resident became the county ranger for a year.

Development money became available during the 1973-75 State budget. Construction started in April 1973 by Commercial Builders of Bremerton. The contract was for $450,000 and work progressed from April 1973 until dedication in June 1975.

The wrecking ball was poised for demolition of the Emel House in 1973 when once again local residents made their collective voices heard. Sharon Barney and the ranger's wife, Elsa James, gained support from neighbors and started on the trail to save the Emel House from destruction. They accomplished this feat in 1974 when the State allowed the revitalized Seabeck Community Club to use the house as its community clubhouse.

Today the Emel House is a very well-respected addition to the overall flavor of the park. It hosts numerous weddings and family reunions throughout the year.

Another 17 acres of property and an additional 500 feet beachfront were added to the park in 1981. State Parks purchased the Dupar family campsite from the Seattle chapter of Camp Fire Girls. This area was originally the home of Joe Bacher, owner of Seattle's "Our House" saloon before prohibition. He died on the site in 1923 when a fire destroyed his home. The Scenic beach site has been restructured into a 50-site group camp area and the only remaining building remodeled, it from the Dupar camp and made into an adirondack shelter.

During an average year, 175,000 day-use visitors from throughout the United States and from around the world visit.

Another 16,000 park patrons camp overnight at Scenic Beach.

Central Kitsap School District utilizes the park for students in a wide range of activities from environmental education classes to school picnics.

Many visitors from Scandinavian countries compare The Canal to the fjord areas of their lands. A glance at this majestic view is available while resting on wooden benches nestled in the forest.

Our visit along the history trail of Scenic Beach has brought us back to the park's newest show piece, Grandpa Joe's cabin. Originally built by Joseph E. Emel in 1936 when he was 16, the cabin was destroyed in the wild winds of 1991. The cabin was reconstructed by Pat Halford and his crew from Mission Creek Youth Camp.

This unique building is a tribute to grandfathers all and once again enables us to sit on the cabin porch and look out at The Canal to visualize what life was like at this beautiful place 100 years ago.

(Contributed by Mike James, Scenic Beach State Park ranger, 1993.)

Dupar Property, one of several cottages owned by the family, this one, Dorothy Lynch's.
(Photo courtesy Scenic Beach.)

Maple Beach

Depenheuer Laughter
Echoed Across Canal

On a still night, one can still hear echoes of John and Elisabeth Depenheuer. Their laughter is something that Maple Beach friends, neighbors and guests will never forget.

Neighborhood children couldn't pronounce John's surname, so they became Mr. and Mrs. Johnnie. John (B. Sept. 1, 1887 Schuld, Germany; D. Sept. 22, 1981 Bre-

merton) served 1903-1908 in the German Navy and in the Merchant Marine until 1911. While his ship was anchored at Philadelphia, he and two others slipped overboard with their seabags and swam for a big light which they assumed was a pier. As the river carried them closer, they realize it was a dredge and they cried out for help and the captain sent a boat. He was

Mr. and Mrs. "Johnnie" were a familiar site in their 1913 Model-T pickup.
(Photo courtesy Sharon Barney)

able to communicate with the Scandinavian crew members and when the night crew left in the morning, the three deserters left with them and disappeared into the world.

Johnnie worked coastal steamers between Boston and Jacksonville and in 1912 rode the rails to San Francisco, finding employment on a ship going to Seattle. It was in Seattle that he met a German crew member who was building a house at Miami Beach. It sounded intriguing and in 1913 he bought part of Maple Beach: 5 acres for $100 down, monthly payments of $10 on the balance of $400, interest at 7 per cent. He added to his property in 1920, buying an additional tract from T. H. O'Brien for $1,200. Tidelands were included.

Depenheuer's closest neighbor was Otis Brinker and Brinker fenced his property including 14 feet of Johnnie's parcel. Johnnie consulted several attorneys contemplating a suit but was advised by Judge James Bryan that although he had a good case finding an attorney to represent him would be difficult: Brinker was Superior Court Judge for Kitsap County. Johnnie settled with his neighbor and it was determined that the fence would be the property line.

Back in Germany, an orphaned seamstress and spinster, Elisabeth Weber, (B. Feb. 17, 1899 Hoengen, Germany; D. Feb. 8, 1983 Bremerton) was encouraged by her employer, Johnnie's mother, to correspond with Johnnie in America. Correspondence developed into courtship and Johnnie returned to Germany where they were married Dec. 29, 1929. They returned to Maple Beach. It was The Depression. He did what he could to make a living. He built roads on both sides of the Canal, raised chickens and produce.

He felled trees from his original ten acres and towed them to Quilcene behind a dory, returning a week later for fresh milled lumber. From this they built the Maple Beach resort in the early 1930s consisting of four cabins and two day cabins, the latter more like changing rooms. Wainscotting, trim and knotty pine that covered cabin walls came from timber on the property, milled at Quilcene. The cabins were modern: wood-burning stove and ice box on the porch. Each cabin had a living and dining room, kitchen, two bedrooms, commode and

cold water. They charged $5 a night. Families were allowed to picnic on the grounds for 50 cents a carload.

Mr. and Mrs. Johnnie were a darling couple, each measuring less than 5' tall. They were devoted and worked hard for common goals. Elisabeth moved into his bachelor cabin and then he built her a larger home. He planted a grove of firs in a row, above the high tide line. They worked together moving the house with a stump-puller to a location up away from their beach-front home site when the opened the resort. After the resort closed, their last home was created by combing two cabins. They revered the earth, and replaced that which they took. Elisabeth loved all of nature, people and children. She nurtured 30 hummingbirds and watched from her window as black fish frolicked and listened to the loons. Salmon sold for five cents each and Mr. Johnnie fed them to the chickens. Smelt were so thick in front of their home that they couldn't clean their lines.

Sea lions swam through their landscape. Like so many others in the area, they were self-sufficient. They raised chickens, ate clams and fish, grew fruits and vegetables. She washed clothes by hand, scrubbed the cabins, washed the bedding and curtains. They made their own tools and scooted around the area in the only vehicle they ever owned, a 1913 Flivver or Model-T pickup which was later traded to the mailman, Bob Josephsen for a load of horse manure and dirt. Josephensen prizes the Model-T, not only because he collects old vehicles but because he cherishes those memories of Mr. and Mrs. Johnnie.

The Depenheuers would hold big picnics for everyone on the beach. They'd dig pits, filling them with gravel and the corn, beans and fish would bake all day.

Elisabeth liked to serve *fresh* corn. Sharon Barney remembers hearing Elisabeth say that she'd blow her whistle for John to come home from his work, then pick the corn, shuck it and put it in the pot. *"That way, she figured, if she fell between garden and house, she'd still have time to go back and pick more corn so that it would be fresh."*

Elisabeth worked on the Election Board and School Board, traveling to special meetings in Port Orchard and Seattle. They both worked at PSNS during World War II, he as a machinist, a trade he learned in the Germany Navy.

Elisabeth was also one of the first women in the Nation to test packaged cake mixes. The Fishers, of Fisher Flour Company were summer guests, and they sent her products to test.

Childless, the couple adopted neighborhood children as their own. There used to be as many as 30 kids up and down the beach and the Johnnies knew all of them.

When Orin and Laura Ruehle bought just down the beach in 1939, it was the Ruehl's two little girls, Sharon and Lois, who became quite special. Each contributed to this story along with Bill Card, Ted Peterson and Maxine Strong. Each has fond memories of the Johnnies.

In 1901 C. A. Spriggs purchased the Maple Beach property for $128.42 in back taxes. In 1927, he .was selling part of his 50-acre parcel. Hugo W. Berglind, a Bremerton native, met with Spriggs to look at the 150 feet of waterfront just north of Maple Beach and expressed a genuine interest in buying it.

"I'm sorry, Hugo," Spriggs told him, *"this gentleman just made me an offer."*

As Berglind turned to leave, the apparent buyer pulled a flask from his pocket to celebrate his purchase. Mr. Spriggs, a teetotaler, turned to Berglind and said: "Hugo. It's yours." The property was purchased for $15 a front foot, or $25, according to Ted Peterson. The Berglinds and Petersons purchased 150' while a Mr. White purchased an additional 150'. The Berglinds and Petersons still retain ownership while the White parcel has been sold many times.

The Berglind family and friends tent-camped on the property to the north of The Johnnie's for many years, eventually building a home there. Hugo's father was one of the early Bremerton settlers, arriving in 1893 from Sweden.

Maple Beach during the Johnnie's Resort Days.
(Photo courtesy Sharon Barney.)

Stavis Bay

Staves or St. Ives?
No One Knows Now

If the word for the bay is an adaptation of an Indian word, no records remain except that Thomas Talbot Waterman said the Indians called the lagoon just north of Stavis Bay *Cte'u.*[32] If we could pronounce it and put on "S" on it, perhaps it would sound something like Stavis.

Kate Marie (Hobbs) Bartlow said that her father who staked his claim on the bay in 1889 named it after a place near his home in England, St. Ives.[33] Yet Jacob Hauptly's diaries, written long before Hobbs arrived, refers to *Stavis Bay.* And Marshall Blinn refers to Stavis Bay in his 1864 diary.

Was it named Staves Bay as one of the meanings of stave as *"to smash a hole in"* or *"to crush or break inward"* each descriptive of the geography?

Perhaps we'll never know. We do know that the settlers here were hearty souls and led lives of isolation, excited by passing steamers or the appearance of fishermen, hunters or loggers.

William and Mary Hobbs

William S. Hobbs (B. March 10, 1866 Enfield, England; D. Jan. 21, 1932 Seattle) arrived on his Stavis Bay claim in December 1889. A fine carpenter, he was able to quickly construct a cabin and eight years later bring his bride, Mary Watkins (B. July 12, 1870 Hanswell, England; D. Feb. 26, 1959 Seattle). She arrived in 1894 but put off marriage for three years. Five children were born to the couple while they lived at Stavis: Joseph William (1898-1971); Cecilia

Mary (B. Nov. 14, 1899; D. Nov. 25, 1899); Ellenora Violet Martenson (1901); Herbert Edway (1903-1967); Kate Marie Bartlow (1905).

They left the area in 1906 for Seattle as accessibility to the Seabeck school was an impossibility. Their fifth child, Ralph Watkins (1907) was born in Seattle. They returned to the area, living in Silverdale, where the final child, Christina Brown (1910) was born.

Hobbs worked for the Colman family in Seattle and took a special interest in the development of the Seabeck Christian Conference Center because of his love of the Seabeck area and his interest in the Colman family.

Letters written to his mother in England were preserved by his daughter, Kate, and made available to the Kitsap County Historical Society.

> 15 Spring
> Seattle
> December 25, 1889

My dear mother,
I have taken up a claim out here of about 150 acres (situated on Hoods Canal a large natural body of salt water several miles long and 100 miles or so from N to S) about 50 miles from Seattle. I had first to take the oath of allegiance, so Her Gracious Majesty has one less. I went to see the land four weeks ago, came back to Seattle and filed on it at the land office costing me three pounds, and then returned and stayed nearly three weeks building me a cabin and planting out some fruit: 50 apple, 33 pear which if all is well will at the end of five years when I get my title be bearing somewhat.

I was pretty lucky in getting out fruit so quick, as most of the land in Western Washington is covered with dense forest, requiring very hard and incessant work to clear but most of the

---

[32]Thomas Talbot Waterman. *Ethnographic notes on Puget Sound. (Unpublished.)*

[33]Kitsap County Historical Society. *Kitsap County: A History.* 1977.

timber had been stolen off this piece and it had been burned over too, so I managed to find enough clear on which to plant and I can continue to do more and improve it while they are growing.

I can land right off the steamer on the claim at high tide having over a mile of waterfront and if I build a (float) 50 feet out, I can land at any time. The land lays about 100 to 150 feet above the Canal, but once you are on the top, it is pretty level. This steep cliff makes it almost impossible to land in many places but to get the timber out they built several shutes down to the water's edge, which would make good roads up.

All the land around is taken up. This place was not open to settlement, being reserved by government for sale when the territory became a state (which it is now) for University purposes, therefore called University reserve. It was abandoned as such and thrown open to settlement doubtless because the timber had been stolen off. It was quite an experience with me to have three weeks all alone (except now and again to see a boat) and to do my own cooking and was pretty lonesome at times and the way seemed decidedly rocky.

I must tell you about it for our mutual edification. The Steamer Josephine which leaves Seattle twice weekly for Hoods Canal started that Wednesday morning at 9:30, three hours late and with numerous delays at her stopping places, landed me at my destination at midnight. (Actually) about a mile from it on a piece of land from which I could not get to my claim without a boat on account of the tide. There was a large freight house that someone had built on a long neck of land, almost tide land, which was on my claim, and that was where I had figured on spending the night but I had to be content with the spacious beach, my blankets and the soft side of a stone and get what sleep I could. Rather out of common and uncomfortable, eh? On the other hand, it was a beautiful, moonlight night and on the other or western shore, the snow capped peaks of the Olympics glistened prettily in the softened light.

Next morning I had to wade a piece and get me a boat to take me and mine to my destination. This freight house was too roomy to be comfortable and without any door to the opening. But there was plenty of driftwood and I could have as good a fire as I wished in the wooden fireplace lined with stones. But on Saturday evening I was rather cold and so left a small fire burning and about 3 on Sunday morning was awakened by a great roar which I at first thought was the tide but instead found the place was on fire. The thin wood of which the chimney was built having caught and being about 12 feet high, there was plenty of it to burn and the roof was already

alight. However I managed to tear the whole chimney down apart from the rest and the tide being high got the fire on the roof out, though I had to hustle to do it. All I lost was my apron and my pants which I had hung by the fire to dry. So that left me only a thin pair of overalls which going through the wet brush absorbed the water in anything but a comfortable manner.

The next event was the visit of a skunk, an animal with a very offensive smell or odor but as I had finished my cabin on the hill I was able to retire in his favor. I was not able to build me a good house at all, not being able to find any good cedar out of which to split my boards and when a most terrific windstorm came last Saturday, I thought she would have blown down but I had braced it well (it having blown very hard while building it) and so it stood.

I had repaired the roof and rebuilt the chimney on the Sunday it burned, a drenching rain coming on which I was obliged to work in before I could again build a fire to dry by. I also built a chimney in my own cabin, but you can guess I was careful to have the fire low as well as large. The fir bark makes a splendid fire, burning almost like coal with intense heat and lasting a considerable time.

As my provisions were running short I had concluded to go to Seattle on a ways and means committee, and so built me a raft on which to cross a small piece of water to get to Seabeck about four miles distant from whence I could take the steamer. But I was not up in raft building and so had a free bath with my clothes on after which it was in order to climb up the hill to my cabin, a sadder and wiser and wetter man and evaporate for the rest of the day.

Monday I left but hurrying with my tools I lost the track in the woods and after an hour or so found myself (as many before me, I suppose) coming out very near where I started. But the second time I made it all right but had lost the steamer of course. Anyone who had not been in these woods can hardly imagine the difficulties in places. For instance, where this track left the beach, it was a good road, somewhat grown over with brush through which you could push your way, down which they had hauled the lumber to the water but about every 10 feet for a considerable distance. Gigantic firs lay square across. No chance to get around or under and just about as much as you could do to climb over especially with a load.

But there are compensations in everything. The sun shining as bright as possible and the sky blue overhead with the mountains covered a little lower down than before with snow glistening in the strong sunlight made a scene in which difficulties were forgotten.

So I had that night at the hotel at Seabeck another compensation, a chance to evaporate once more and a couple of good meals and a bed. After the fare I had had on the ranch, it was really good. And the fare at these country hotels is good, much better than that you get in the city restaurants. Ham and beefsteak with crisp homemade rolls, fresh butter, plenty of vegetables with cake and preserves made a meal which I enjoyed after my walk that frosty morning.

Then next morning another walk of eight miles through the woods on a somewhat better trail (though I got off that once) to Silverdale where I took The Mountaineer and arrived in Seattle about 5:30, glad to get back into civilization once more.

April 18, 1890

Thank you for your kind letter received on my return from my second visit to the claim. They did not land me this time at midnight, but would not land me at all only on their return trip from Union City to Seattle so I had a trip of 30 hours on the water.

Things went better with me this time and I found everything all right and my trees all alive. I stayed 17 days there and built a float which I can anchor out in The Canal at which a steamer could stop at low tide, dug about eight feet of a well, cultivated all the trees and helped a neighbor, Veldee, a Norwegian, for two and a half days as he gave me a hand with the float and took me about six miles towards Seattle in his boat on my return.

He has not been on his claim much longer than I have, but as he is married he has to make that his home and stay there all the time, so he has improved his place quite a bit. He had just planted out strawberries, gooseberries, rhubarb and potatoes (of which I also planted some) and I helped him get some land ready for grass as he is going to buy a cow this Fall.

The next time I go out, about June, the blackberries will be ripe and as he shipped some last year to Seattle we agreed to work together and see what we could do as they fetch a pretty high price. You get a rather small saucer full for five cents.

July 16, 1890

There is talk of a steamer making the trip daily from Seattle to Union City and return. At present the two boats running take a day each way. As the country settles, the steamers are sure to run oftener and cheaper too so that if I could start a poultry farm, there would be no difficulty in getting to a market.

December 10, 1890

Yes. I have quite a comfortable place here now. Quite watertight and warm. I have just been papering it with the C.W.'s I have saved and that of course makes it look still more like home.

My neighbor, Veldee on one side, is married with three children and just expecting a new arrival. On the other side is Kaison (another Norwegian). Kaison wishes me to find out the dividing line between our claims and then we could build close together and help one another and one could be there while the other was away for a time working and so everything would be safe as there are some thieves on The Canal (Kaison having just lost some blankets and cooking things while working on the other side of the Canal.)

Last week I had my first long row, going to Seabeck (the nearest post office) and back about nine miles altogether. Today I am in Seattle buying some tools and provisions as the three of us are going to work together for six weeks or two months getting out firewood at which we can earn I think 8s or 10s a day which will pay us in Winter as it will not cost much to live there with the salmon we have smoked and other things. Some salmon here over 2 ft. 6 long. Very fine fish. Fine eating salted and smoked.

January 21, 1891

Since writing to you last, I have been over my land more with my next neighbor, Mr. Kaison, and we found a piece of about 30 acres much better than any I thought I had on my claim. It lays nice and level about 150 to 200 feet above the water, but we are making a very easy road up a small valley that will not be too steep to walk up. I had made up my mind to build up there.

This piece of land is very fine clay soil and I have bought 4 sacks of potatoes which we will plant so that we will have vegetables this next winter. Kaison is a good man to have for a neighbor. Straight in all cases.

Feb. 5, 1891

Seabeck is quite an old town as towns go in the West, older I guess than Seattle with a very large sawmill, but it was burnt down a few years ago and the company paid by a timber trust not to start a mill again there for a certain number of years. The term is now expired and the town may begin to grow. I am between four and five miles from there. By starting from home here at 9 a.m., rowing eight miles, walking four more and then taking the steamboat to Seattle, I get there about 3:30 p.m. at the cost of 2s. In time I think they will get a tram car across that four miles as that is the most direct way from Seattle to the greater part of the Canal. To go all the *way to Seattle by water costs from 8s to 10s as it is a long way round.*

I have 151 acres in my claim with about one mile waterfront. I have all I can use of good land, the greater part would be good for fruit and grass and only a small part too rough and hilly to use at all. For chickens, it would be just the place.

Peder and Severine Velde

Norwegian immigrants, Peder (B. July 2, 1858 Norway; D. July 21, 1933) and Severine (Salvesen) Velde (B. July 28, 1861; D. Jan. 20, 1919) were lured to the Puget Sound region and especially The Canal because of reports of its similarities to their native Norway.

In October 1889, Peder found a man who was willing to row the couple and their three children from Seattle, around Kitsap's upper peninsula and down The Canal to Stavis Bay. It took four days. Peder built a 12' x 18' cabin of plank and cedar shakes taken from the abandoned mill site at Seabeck. The family, like the other early settlers around Stavis, dug a well, grubbed out tree stumps and planted a vegetable garden and fruit trees.

Peder supported his family by selling eggs to Cooper and Levy, a Seattle *supermarket-of-the-day* through the Seabeck store. Another source of support was selling cedar shakes.

Once the eldest children, Conrad and sister, Solvieg, were sent in the rowboat to Seabeck and trolling on the way back, they snagged a salmon so large that they couldn't get it into the boat. They clubbed it, then after beaching the boat, drug the fish home.

The Veldes spent 15 years at Stavis. Both had been trained as teachers and not for the hard physical labor and isolation of life on The Canal.

As the eldest daughter, Solvieg assisted in delivering her younger brothers and sisters and was responsible for keeping the boys in hand knit socks. The boys learned the carpenter's trade, a skill each put to use later. Odd jobs were sought for there was little cash and that was earmarked for the necessities of daily living like flour, sugar and shoes.

When Peder became a citizen in 1897, he added a second "e" to his name to make it easier to pronounce and anglicized his first name.

The children were daughter Solvieg (B. 1883 Norway); Conrad (B. 1886 Minnesota); Will (1888 Minnesota); Milton (1890); Martha (1893); Ida (1894) and Harry (1897); Pearl Irene (B. 1900; D. Jan. 17, 1903). The last five children were born at Stavis.

Conrad began school at age 10 and two years later he was working at a logging camp, greasing skids. When they moved to Bremerton, he was able to go to school and with two others were the first graduates of Bremerton's Union High School in 1907.

Conrad and Milton graduated from the University of Washington and Milt attended three years. Milt went on to receive a medical degree from Harvard and developed the scarlet fever streptococcus antitoxin.

Jacob and Ella Baer

Jacob and Ella Baer were living at Stavis before 1909 (their property appears in the 1909 plat book under Ella's name.) Jacob was better known to Canal folk as *"Silvertip"* and he was considered one of the characters of The Canal.

He maintained a camp at Stavis with boats for rent and furnished entertainment, *The Bremerton News* reported to most of the sportsmen of the vicinity. *"Baer's a good hunter and splendid shot and can always locate fish and game."* He was from Oklahoma, according to *The News*, which also said that he had been shot in the ankle bone while on the Cherokee strip participating in fights with Indians and outlaws. Dr. Schutt of Bremerton amputated his foot due to that bullet wound and several years later, Jacob died on April 22, 1929.

Frances and Albert Rogers

Frances Rogers arrived in the Seabeck area a full 70 years late to be considered a true pioneer but her life typified many in the isolated communities of the Puget Sound area. Her Stavis Bay diaries cover the period January 1922 through January 1936 and paint a vivid panorama of the hardworking class of people who carved a niche in the early 20th Century wilderness.

Her son, Andy Rogers, is the last of a generation of men and women who have lived off the natural resources of Hood's Canal country He, his brother, Almanza, and sister, Rosemary, were bathed in the waters and browned by the sun, nurtured by fresh air, taught by the common sense and industry of their mother.

Andy is a conservative, a believer of Constitutional rights and defender of even those large landowners who clear-cut half century old trees surrounding the Conference grounds: *"They own the land. They should do what they want with their land."* It's not that he agrees with what they did. He defends their right to do it. No one loves Canal country more than Andy.

His mother was born in Iowa and came to Entiat (on the Columbia River) with her family. It was here that she met an Okanagon doctor, Albert Rogers, 25 years her senior.

Albert was educated at Starling Medical College and came west in 1900 to practice medicine in Okanogan where he stayed until 1915. When his office burned, he moved to Lopez Island in the San Juans. Two years later the couple was married and it was on Lopez Island that their first child, Andrew J. Rogers, was born Nov. 1, 1917.

Albert convinced his reluctant wife that they should move to Stavis Bay where he retired from medicine except for pulling neighbors' teeth (while Frances held chloroform over the patient), treating minor injuries and delivering babies..

The couple and their two young children (Andy and infant Rosemary) arrived in Seabeck in March 1919 on a passenger boat from Seattle and then were transported by launch to Jake and Ella Baers' house on Stavis Bay. While their cabin was being built, they lived with the Baers.

They burrowed themselves into the isolation as had Henry Baker and his Indian wife, the first homesteaders on Stavis Bay who proved up on thier property in November 1884.

At high tide, saltwater lapped up and under their home located on Stavis Creek. In the winter, the cold north wind blew and the wood pile grew slimmer. Nearly every diary entry began: *"Cleaned and cooked".*

Frances Rogers
(Photo courtesy Andy Rogers.)

But other chores never stopped. There was churning and mending and tatting, reading and playing games in the winter, the daily bread making. She chopped wood and split kindling and rolled logs with Albert as he cleared the land.

Albert worked every day in those early years on his tile ditch. By the time he finished, he had more than a mile of underground drains on three acres.

He cut trees, dynamited stumps and burned them. He kept the creek clear and stacked wood and worked on building the Stavis Bay Road.

An amazing bartering system developed. Frances' bread was in demand and she exchanged bread for eggs or flour . . . whatever the family didn't have. Once she even convinced a traveling salesman to give her a magazine subscription in exchange for a cowhide. Her customers included people as far as Hite Center. She raised geese and ducks and took those that didn't sell at her home to the stores in Seabeck, sometimes in the wheelbarrow. When the neighbors came for eggs, butter, milk or produce, Frances would induce them to play games: caroms, 500, whist, and flinch. After a hard day's work, Frances would read classics to the children or articles from magazines.

The Baers were nearly daily diary entries. Interestingly Frances never mentioned either by anything other than "Mr. and Mrs. Baer." It was at the Baers that Frances first heard a radio and mentioned in her diary listening to two Dempsey fights and Sunday night religious shows.

The *"kiddies"* worked alongside their parents from the time they were toddlers. Rosemary was baking by the time she was five; Andy cutting wood and pulling thistles at the same age. Almanza, who was born while they lived at Stavis, seems to have been more protected and rarely did Frances mention that he was doing anything until he was school age.

All helped in the garden. They grew apples, beans, beets, cabbage, carrots, cauliflower, cucumbers, gooseberries, lettuce, onions, parsnips, peas, potatoes, raspberries, rhubarb, squash, spinach, strawberries, tomatoes, even peanuts and popcorn. There were chickens, ducks, geese, hogs, cattle, goats, rabbits. They picked wild mushrooms, huckleberries, Oregon grape, blackberry and Albert hunted grouse.

October was deer hunting season and every one of Frances' diaries tells of either Albert or Andy *"out hunting"*. Not once did they bag a deer although neighbors often shared their venison. Once Andy went in the boat with his gun *"and all he shot was the boat"*, according to Frances' diary. The Canal provided geoduck, clams, crab, shrimp, sole, flounder, salmon, and an occasional red snapper. Albert caught 31 trout in the creek on Oct. 5, 1922. *"Hurrah"*, Frances wrote.

Potato harvest was in October, carrots in November. In 1933, Frances harvested 50 sacks of carrots in one week. Andy built a smoke house where he smoked salmon during winter months.

Albert's health deteriorated. By July 1, 1930 he had grown weak from the ravages of cancer. Neighbors stayed with him while Frances delivered produce and worked in the gardens. Albert had given her some training in medicine, so when the pain became unbearable, she administered a hypodermic injection, probably morphine. He died several days later on Aug. 4. The following day Frances went to the cemetery where there *"was a large crowd. Lots of flowers."*

Andy walked old trails to the two-room Seabeck school which was nearly new when he started. School started at nine o'clock. He'd hear that bell ringing and he'd still be walking. In 1926, for the first time, a schoolbus picked Rosemary and Andy up a short distance from the house, along with Margaret, Elizabeth and Richard Hennicke, the Rogers' closest neighbors.

When Almanza first started school, he missed the bus the first few days and Frances would walk with him to school.

The first three grades got out at 2:30, the older students at 3:30. Only one of the two rooms was used. *"They can say what they want about graded classrooms, but kids can go a lot faster and get more out of class in that atmosphere. You're not held back by slower kids."*

Andy's school, identical in design to those at Crosby and Holly, was moved to Brownsville where it has served as a church.

Kids aren't much different today, according to Andy, than back then. Kids get away with what they can get away with. *If he'd gotten in trouble at school, he'd really have to pay when he got home.*

The daily mailboat continued running on the Canal until 1925. When it stopped, life changed on The Canal as most post offices were closed. The freight boat continued service long after the mail boat stopped, delivering to logging camps along the beach or any other place that had a gathering of residents.

After Albert's death, Andy, as eldest son, became head of household. The family moved to Entiat to live with Frances' family but they returned to the Seabeck area a couple years later.

For Andy the Depression wasn't bad. He did what he could. He trapped, logged and picked brush. The old piling along the Seabeck waterfront was torn out in 1933 and Andy helped rebuild the new one, driving piles, putting in planks and backfilling with dirt. As the Depression ended, he was drafted to serve in the Army, doing a tour in Europe with a railroad outfit.

As a teenager, Almanza worked for the forest service, then became a logger in Randall. Andy too followed logging nine months of the year, the other three as a trapper, considered among the State's best. Andy was trapping by the time he was eleven. As a novice, he was good at catching skunks and civit cats, later the prized mink. Besides trapping surplus beaver for the State, he trapped otter, mink, bobcat, muskrat, raccoon and an occasional coyote. He doubled as State beaver control trapper. Although beaver were protected by the State, in some places they were too abundant and Andy helped control the surplus.

Anyone could be a trapper, Andy believes, by use of scent to attract them. Catching the furbearing animal was only a small part of the job. Many trappers ruined choice pelts through carelessness, mostly in the process of skinning.

Andy would strip down to his long johns to go under water to retrieve a trapped beaver. Beaver traps had drowners attached to a wire extending from a post on the beach to an anchor in deep water. The traps were set near the beach and when a beaver got caught, it could only slide toward the anchor and drown. After a day's trap line check, Rogers spent another day skinning, fleshing and sewing pelts on a three to four foot hoop allowing the skins to stretch and dry. He admitted he could make more money elsewhere, but he enjoyed the out

doors and trapping was in his blood. Each beaver pelt, ready for market brought $7 regardless of size even though the State received around $30 on the open market. Other pelts only brought $5. Otter brought $30, mink, $15, raccoon $2.50 and muskrat, 85 cents.

Andy's produce has been the talk of the area. Huge cabbages and squash were a result of commercial fertilizers and Conference Grounds' leaves. *"Organic gardening is great. But we're living in the latter part of the 20th Century, not the 17th Century. Why not use something that has been scientifically developed. Use the best of what's available. If it weren't for chemical fertilizers we'd all be starving. "*

Andy's namesake grandson, a tall, handsome boy, was working at the Conference Grounds in the summer of 1993 before entering college. His interest in the history of the area and the preservation of the natural resources is a reflection of the ideals instilled by the modern pioneer Rogers' family.

Camp Union

Glory Days of Logging;
Vestiges Still Visible

There are few old families in the greater Seabeck area who weren't associated with the logging operation out of Camp Union. Those old-timers contributing to this book always mention the nearly 100 miles of railroad track and the four big locomotives which sped through the woods, their whistles distinguishable, their types memorable. There were a big and little Shay, Baldwin and Porter.

Children would watch from across Seabeck bay as the cars dumped loads of logs or they'd run along the tracks waving to the engineers. Homes along the route would shake as the huge engines and cars bumped along the tracks, their brakes squealing, their whistles piercing the otherwise silent countryside. Occasional pieces of track are found, buried under half century old growths of blackberry brambles, salal and huckleberry.

In the early 1920s Westfork Logging Company began an operation that gave employment to hundreds of men and women *and* children. Kids were expected to do a man's work but more often than not they were given employment in the less dangerous jobs like following the locomotives with a bucket, putting out fires along the tracks.

Dozens of small logging outfits supplied Westfork, each having its own brand. Westfork was bought out in 1928 and Charles R. McCormick took over the operation.

Camp Union was called *Westfork* until McCormick began its operation and it was then that it became known as Camp Union. Retaining the flavor of those glory days of logging, the Camp Union Cookhouse, a restaurant, is decorated with old photos and memorabilia of those days.

The operation had its own store, company cookhouse, cottages and later a tavern. There were stills in the woods during Prohibition and once there was an erroneous story in a Bremerton newspaper announcing the destruction of the still of one prominent Crosby family. The newspaper printed a retraction the following day, saying that a disgruntled neighbor had given the paper the story. That didn't mean, however, that the family and others didn't have a still. It just indicated that law enforcement officials hadn't found any. The tavern was moved to the Chico/Erland's Point junction where it now is the Nineteenth Hole Tavern.

The logging operation was a relatively short-lived enterprise and ended operations in the mid-1930s but it offered employment in one form or another to virtually every family in the area. The McCormick Lumber Company was dissolved in June 1938.

Logging Brands

At the Kitsap County Courthouse, there is a small book with hand-sketched logging brands used by various Seabeck logging companies in 1923. The following are those reproduced by computer but nearly identical to the hand-drawn brands that were stamped on logs for identification.

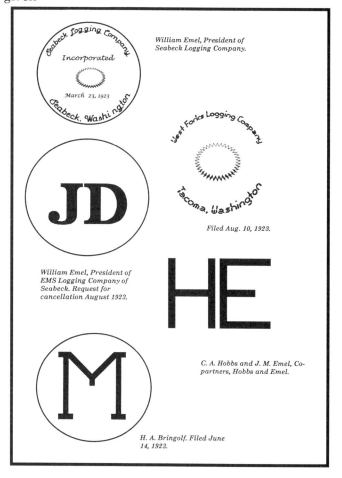

Seabeck Logging Company. Incorporated March 23, 1923. Seabeck, Washington.

William Emel, President of Seabeck Logging Company.

West Forks Logging Company. Tacoma, Washington. Filed Aug. 10, 1923.

William Emel, President of EMS Logging Company of Seabeck. Request for cancellation August 1923.

C. A. Hobbs and J. M. Emel, Co-partners, Hobbs and Emel.

H. A. Bringolf. Filed June 14, 1923.

One of the abandoned cabins during 1940s.
(Photo courtesy Seabeck Christian Conference Center.)

Starvation Flats

Although various stories exist as to the origins of what was once ramshackle shacks on the hillside behind the Conference Center, few are true.

There weren't 30 cabins built of hand-hewn logs and rough cedar shakes and the Chinese, during the mill's heyday, weren't forced to live away from the rest of the community in this isolated area..

There were just four families up there trying to make a living, according to the consensus of most of Seabeck's old-timers.

They didn't make it according to an interview Seabury Blair, Jr. had with Berge Berg.

The first house was built around 1908 by a family named Hanby, according to Berg, and three more families followed: Stone, Watson and Iman. They were loggers and worked the woods or anyplace they could find a job. One family raised cattle but cattle couldn't survive on salal and brush.

Stone was a well digger, according to Berg and he dug all over the area trying to find water.

Cabins were built of hand-hewn logs and rough cedar shakes. Residents didn't remain long. Lack of water and the difficulty of bringing in food and materials drove them away.

Peter Emel hauled in much of the food and building supplies.

The cabins stood for many years even though not occupied with their little picket fences falling in around them..

The area has been called *The Lost City, Haunted Village or Poverty Flats.*

Appendix

Faustina Blinn
Daughter of Samuel Blinn
Spent Seabeck money but only
rarely visited.
(Photo courtesy Olanie family.)

Legends Unfounded

Seabeck, Maine

Seabeck was named after Seabeck, Maine, the birthplace of Marshall Blinn or one of the other owners. Truth: Sebec, Maine is the only town in Piscataquis County, Maine with an Indian name origin. The word means "big lake."

Marshall Blinn was from Dresden Mills, Maine, south of Augusta. None of Seabeck's settlers was from Sebec, Maine.

Ah Fong

Poor Ah Fong. Probably killed in the woods up above the village for all the gold he had hidden. At least that's the way the story goes.[1]

"Ah Fong was, in the early days, cook for the mill hands. Like most Cantonese, he was both skilled in the culinary art and frugal in his habits. He lived in a tiny shack back of the town meeting house, ate his meals from cook house leftovers and was reputed to be still in possession of the first American dollar he had ever earned.

"Proceeds from the sale of lumber cargoes were, at that time, deposited in a San Francisco bank to the credit of the mill company. A coastwise ship, heading north at about the time a payroll was due at mill and shipyard, would carry the required amount of cash to Seabeck.

"If the ship carrying a payroll was delayed by storms, calms or late sailing, the mill management was in the habit of securing a temporary loan from the thrifty Ah Fong. When the pudgy Chinese saw the mill manger approaching the cook house, he would meet him with the smiling question, 'How muchee?'

"The reply was usually, 'Five thousand, if you can spare it.' Ah Fong would nod happily, wipe his hands on his apron and trot off toward the forest. He would soon return with the required amount in twenty dollar gold pieces.

"But one fatal day Ah Fong trotted off to his private bank in the woods and never returned to the cook house on the beach. Legend has it that he was murdered for his money, most of which is probably still buried somewhere on the hill behind the town. To this day campers and tourists sometimes wander off to the Seabeck woods in search of Ah Fong's vanished hoard of gold."

Gordon Newell had a marvelous imagination. Conference Center directors have had the same wild thoughts. A lot of Newell's version is inaccurate. Quite a lot. First of all, Ah Fong was the town washerman. As such he didn't earn a whole lot, but what mattered that considering he lived in the most beautiful place in the world and there were many of his countrymen with whom he could spend his leisure hours.

Payroll of $5,000? If the average millworker/shipbuilder made $50 per month, there would be 100 employees. But mill employees and those engaged in shipbuilding received credit on the company books and out of their salary, the rent was paid . . . to the mill company.

And why wasn't there a body found? And doesn't it seem logical that whoever followed Ah Fong through the woods would see where he held his cache of cash?

What really happened to Ah Fong?

Last heard, he was languishing in a Seattle jail cell. In January 1886 he applied for a writ of Habeas Corpus, claiming that he was illegally held in jail.[2]

Ah Fong was accused of violating a certain ordinance of the City of Seattle known as Ordinance Number Seven hundred and five entitled "An Ordinance to license and regulate auctioneers, hawkers and peddlers." He was ordered to pay a fine of $5 and costs of $11.85. Unable to come up with the gold (probably left it in the woods at

---

[1] Gordon Newell. *Town Where Time Stood Still, The Story of Seabeck.* Seabeck Christian Conference. 1958.

[2] King County court, Case No. 4784. Regional Archives, Burien.

Seabeck) Ah Fong was thrown in the slammer.

Ah Fong claimed Ordinance 705 was unconstitutional, illegal and void. When signing the writ, he acknowledged that he understood the contents and signed with his Chinese mark.

Various legal documents passed back and forth. Ah Fong was accused of unlawfully engaging in the business of peddling without having obtained a license. He went from house to house offering vegetables for sale. This, one of the affidavits said, was against the peace and dignity of Seattle.

He was to be confined in the jail of Seattle at hard labor for 16 days .

"And said Ah Fong is a subject of the Emperor of China and one who has not declared his intentions to become a citizen of the United States and to whom a license to peddle is not grantable under the ordinances of the City of Seattle."

The court denied Ah Fong's petition, sent him back to jail and said that he had to pay for the costs of the hearing, plus the fine of $5 plus the other costs of $11.65.

That was the last we heard of Ah Fong. We question his memory. He forgot where he hid the gold in the Seabeck hillside.

Seabeck, Territorial Capital

That Seabeck was to have been the Territorial capital. Now really. Look at a map. It's pretty hard to get here from anywhere.

Tramp Steamer to Orient

That people from Seattle wanting to go to the Orient would come to Seabeck for transport. (Most ships leaving Seabeck were lumber-laden and headed for California.)

Seabeck Booming Metropolis

Seabeck was once bigger than Seattle. Wrong. Check the census. Even Port Gamble, Port Madison and Port Blakely were larger and they were all in Kitsap.

Murder of Hood
Gives Canal a Name

An early settler who was murdered by the Indians was named Hood. Thus the name. He must have been very early as The Canal was named by Capt. George Vancouver in 1792. The early settler theory is wrong, according to Edmond S. Meany.[3]

Hudson Bay Company
Entrenched at Seabeck

Hudson Bay Company had an outpost at Seabeck. This assumption was pursued by Dawn and Bob Hansen. From a letter from the Hudson's Bay Company, dated Sept. 9, 1980: "As you will note from the enclosed article,[4] The Hudson's Bay Company did not operate posts on the Pacific Coast until 1821, when the H B C was amalgamated with the North West Company. At that time it took over control of Fort George (Astoria) until Fort Vancouver, the Company's headquarters in the Columbia District, was established in 1825. To my knowledge Fort Nisqually, the headquarters of the Puget's Sound Agricultural Company, was the only H B C post on Puget Sound.

"The Company did trade with Indians throughout this area, and there are references to the Hood Canal in some of its published records. It is possible that H B C men camped in Seabeck Bay during the period of the Company's operations south of the 49th parallel. However such an arrangement would probably have been quite temporary, and would not appear in the records as a post.

[3]Edmond S. Meany. *Vancouver's Discovery of Puget Sound*. Binfords & Mort, Portland. 1942, P.109.

[4]*The Beaver*, Spring 1963.

Ernest Riddell
History of Seabeck

(Compiled for the Kitsap County Good Roads Committee.)

**Lunch Break
at the Mill - 1883**
*(From Seabeck panorama
as seen on end pages.)*

Seabeck's first settlers were from Maine. They settled on the little bay called by the Indians *L-Ks-bsk-hu.*[5] They named the place after one of the towns they had come from, which there was pronounced *Saybock.*[6]

A mill of considerable capacity, for its time, began to be built in the fall of 1856[7] and in July 1857 they began to cut timber and manufacture lumber. The boilers and machinery for this mill were bought at second hand in San Francisco for $20,000.[8]

The company owning the mill was composed of Wm. J. Adams, Marshal (sic) Blinn of San Francisco and Hillman Harmon and W. B. Sinclair of the Sound.[9]

This was the fourth lumber town to be established in Kitsap County. It was rather isolated in the territorial days. Township 25 N, Range 1 West, was one of the first Government surveys made in this part of Washington Territory.

In 1858 the Territorial Legislature passed an act to located a Territorial road or trail to Seabeck. By 1861 a trail was located and viewed out from Seabeck to the head of Hood Canal. In 1862 a law instructed the Board of County Commissioners to establish a territorial road from the head of Port Orchard Bay to intersect the road to Seabeck.[10]

In 1858 the Seabeck Mill had a daily capacity of 15,000 feet and in 1859 it was enlarged to

---

[5]Various spellings.

[6]None of the original settlers were from Seabeck, Maine although several were from Maine. Wilkes named the bay *Scabock.*

[7]In the spring of 1857.

[8]The value of the mill and property was $20,000 according to Kitsap County assessor.

---

[9]See mill chapter for partners and correct spelling of names.

[10]More precise information available elsewhere in this book.

meet the demands of foreign trade. But due to trouble between the partners the mill was in a very unsettled condition during the first eight or ten years. Settlement was finally made and the mill firm became Adams & Blinn.[11]

In 1859 Joseph H. Boyd selected a piece of land near Seabeck and near him at the mouth of a creek was an Englishman named Lysle. The tax roll of 1859 for Kitsap County shows personal property tax of the Washington Mill Company (Seabeck Mill) was $27,362, including one mill at $15,000. In 1861 the boat fare from Seabeck to Port Gamble was $3.00 (16 miles). In 1864 the daily capacity of the mill was again increased to 50,000 feet.

In 1865 Seabeck embarked upon the ship-building business and the Steamer Colfax, 83T. was built for Marshal Blinn. From that time until 1884 when it became difficult to find suitable boat-building material, the shipyard was very busy and turned out the following ships and boats.

Richard Holyoke - In 1872 for Capt. John Connick who ran her as passenger & tow boat between Seabeck & Pt. Gamble.

*Cassandra Adams** - 3 million foot lumber capacity.

Georgia (steamer) -

State of Sonora - a steamer built for the Mexican government.

American Boy - Barkentine christened by Mrs. J. A. Walton

Louise - Sternwheeler.

*Olympus*** - Large sailing vessel built for The Washington Mill Company.

Retriever - Steamer. So named as she was expected to retrieve what *Olympus* lost.

Edward Clayson was one of the early (came 1865) settlers and took up land at the head of the Bay. He built a hotel there. He had a sloop in which he carried passengers and freight up and down the Canal. In 1868 the Post Office Department established a post office at Seabeck.

*Frank Libby said she was a clipper ship and the largest single deck ship on the coast when she was built.

**Frank Libby says there were three vessels built in 1880. The *Olympus* had an 11-foot keel enabling her to sail against the wind. But, on her first return trip from San Francisco she was destroyed by fire. She was replaced the next year by the steamer *Retriever*.

Marshal Blinn was appointed as first postmaster with mail service twice a week from Port Gamble. Clayson obtained the contract to carry the mail on his sloop named *Biddy*. That sloop was the sole mail system for the district. Clayson was the whole crew and would sail or row according to the weather. It would take him a week to go the 80 miles of his route, but there was no set time for the mail to arrive. It just got there when it could. Mrs. Clayson was the eighth woman to arrive at Port Gamble.[12] All rejoiced because they now could have two full quadrille sets. Previously one poor man always had to act "the perfect lady" with a handkerchief tied over one arm to designate the role. Clayson's daughter, Dr. Esther Pohl Lovejoy, who was born and raised in Seabeck, later because famous as president of the Medical Women's International Association of London, England.

In 1878 Edward Clayson started the little newspaper, *The Rebel Battery* at Seabeck. It had little value as a newspaper since its sole purpose was to wage war on the Washington Mill Company.

In 1874 the mill manufacturer some 14,000,000 feet of lumber. The mill was thoroughly repaired in 1878 -- new foundations and new engines. With these improvements the mill was able to turn out 150,000 feet of lumber in 24 hours. In 1883 the Company was busy erecting a new mill and trying to reduce expenses. They employed Chinese laborers but abandoned the ideas as unprofitable in 1884. In 1886 the mill was destroyed by fire and was never rebuilt although a new foundation was started. Because the men struck for higher wages and the loss of the *Olympus* several years before, the Company was short of money. They decided to buy the mill at Hadlock and moved there.

Samuel Nichols[13] located at the head of Seabeck Bay in 1871. Their daughter, who became Mrs. J. A. Walton, still resides here. She was educated in Seabeck common schools.

A school district was formed November 3, 1860 as District No. 3 but was renumbered "4" at the first Board meeting. The first Board of School Directors were J. H. Williamson, Hill Harmon, James Clark and S. S. Harmon, clerk. Marshal Blinn was elected clerk soon afterward. Harmon resigned.

Among old-timers on the school board were E. C. Lindsay, 1864; Nathaniel Harmon and E. L. Miller, 1866; Michael Fredson and Nathan Bucklin, 1867; D. B. Jackson and Richard Holyoke, 1877.

The first schoolhouse was completed August 6, 1866. A special tax was levied on the district

---

[11]Not totally accurate. The name of the lumbering firm was Washington Mill Company. Adams, Blinn & Company was the San Francisco lumber dealers who sold Seabeck lumber

---

[12]Seabeck.

[13]Nickels.

to pay the building cost of $367.98. Marshal Blinn donated the lot on which the building was erected -- the present school house is on that lot. Mr. Hanford of the Seattle firm of Lowman & Hanford was the first teacher in Seabeck.

A second and larger school house was built in 1877. It was paid for by the Washington Mill Company to amount of $1,267.43. The big snow of 1893[14] (Mrs. Walton said 1881) broke the roof down. School was held in the original building until the new one was repaired. J. A. Walton came to Seabeck and took up a homestead in 1874 about a mile north and east of town. He worked in the mill and shipyard and took an active part in community affairs. He was school clerk for several years. About 26 years ago, he bought the waterfront property on which he and Mrs. Walton now reside. They still retain the old homestead. Mr. Walton was 83 years old in 1937. The present school building was erected in 1911. In 1877 Mr. S. A. Green and his family arrived overland from California with several items and two prairie schooners.

Seemingly the prohibition question is forever with us. Marshal Blinn was a strong Prohibitionist. He devoted much time and money trying to make Seabeck a model Prohibition Town. He tried to keep Collins, Jameson & Warin from obtaining a liquor license and presented a protest to the fall term of Kitsap County Commissioners at Port Madison, signed by a majority of the voters at Seabeck. The license was granted in spit of the protest. So Blinn at once put up notices that a new hotel would be finished and opened which would be run on Prohibition principles; and that if any one else opened a saloon in the neighborhood, the would stock the new hotel with wines, liquors and cigars free of charge. Bill Waren[15] had not been idle. He was full of resources. He obtained a liquor license for himself and sold liquor for a little while at his shanty upon the hillside just back of the hotel. But this location was not suitable so he secured a new location down on the beach. He built the first Cliff House.

Marshal Blinn was defeated for Delegate to Congress and in his whole aims at Seabeck. He sold out to his brother, Samuel, of San Francisco. Samuel and Marshall were very different sort of men.

The old, original Cliff House burned down. It was rebuilt above[16] the road and later burned and was rebuilt by Mr. Bergman. Recently it

was bought by Colman, the building moved across the road where it remains, empty. Richard Holyoke's residence still stands a short distance from the present YWCA building. The old cookhouse for the Mill Company was originally on the waterfront across the pond from where it now stands. It served also as a hall and church for many years and today is used for community purposes. The Pond which has been made into an attractive swimming pool, by the present owners, used to be used for floating a reserve supply of logs for the mill's use. Flood gates were erected at the end of the pond and when the tide was full and flooded the pond, the gates were closed, retaining the water in the pond. The old boiler now rusting beneath the store was formerly in the steamer *Richard Holyoke*. In early Seabeck, pigs were so numerous that they ran wild through the town. Mrs. Walton, as a little girl, was scared to go to the store. The arrival of a large boat to load lumber was an event of the day. As soon as it came in sight, it was announced by three long blasts of the mill whistle. Then everyone ran to the dock to get the latest news from the outside.

The present YWCA building was formerly a hotel, owned by the Washington Mill Company. A. L. Hoskins[17] bought the old store of the Washington Mill Company and ran it for several years. When Halvorsen's came to Seabeck in 1914, they started a small store on the beach in front of their present residence. After two years Halvorsen's bought out Hotchkin and moved their stock into the present store building where they continue to operate a general merchandise store.

The first stage between Seabeck and Bremerton was started in 1910 by George Edgar. He sold to Thompson & Green. They continued for some time and sold to Arthur Kellum. Arthur Kellum later sold to the Puget Sound Navigation Company, who now operate the stage line in connection with their ferry to Brinnon. The ferry between Brinnon and Seabeck was in 1917 operated by the Nichols[18] brothers. They borrowed a log float from Ben Berg and operated it as the first ferry. It was soon replaced by a scow which the brothers towed by a launch. Later a small ferry boat was built and operated for some time.

Catholic priests, Episcopal, Methodists and Baptist ministers came regularly to early Seabeck and held services. Rev. Damon began services in 1870. In 1876 Rev. Eells began visiting Seabeck. A church was organized in 1880.

---

[14]1880.

[15]Warin.

[16]Below.

---

[17]Hotchkin

[18]Nickels

In 1883 D. K. Howard purchased the *Phantom* and operated her as well as the steamer *Patrick*[19] between Seabeck and Port Gamble.

In 1870 Seabeck had a population of 150 - - - in 1876, 400; and two stores, two hotels and four saloons. It was reported to be the liveliest place on the Sound. During 1877 new dwellings for mill employees were erected and grounds were being cleared for a cemetery. In 1878 Seabeck had, for amusement, a library, baseball, a brass band, traveling shows and several saloons. In 1882 the hotel was enlarged.

The English explorer, Captain George Vancouver, discovered and named Hood Canal in 1792, thus honoring the Right Honorable Lord Hood.

The store, run in connection with the Washington Mill Company occupied the building used as a store by the Halvorsen's. It has been moved a few feet north of the original store's location. The Halvorsen Store burned in 1933. It has since been rebuilt.

Account books from the Mill Company's store give some interesting items of the cost of articles in early Seabeck.

Sugar (not the refined white sugar of today) $20 per sack; Coal oil - per 5-gallon can, $5; Flour - per barrel - $9; Nails - per keg - $12.50.

Other items differed little from today's prices (1930), e.g. Coffee - per pound - 40 cents; Beans - per pound - 5 cents; Potatoes - per 100 pounds - $1.75; Dressed lumber sold for $18 per thousand feet. Labor brought $2.25 per day with board for $4.50 per week.

Colman, well known as owner of Seattle Colman Dock, bought up 800 acres around Seabeck Bay. From Point Misery, opposite Seabeck on the West to the Cliff House on the north. Colman has developed the beautiful YWCA camp, where hundreds of people hold meetings during the summer.

During Seabeck's early days, native Indians were numerous. Their shacks along the waterfront were occupied by natives bearing such English names as Old Pete, Cultus Pete, Saddle Sam, Sally Smash Rocks and others very familiar in their day.

The first Chinese laundry in Kitsap County operated at Seabeck when the mill company employed Chinese for awhile.

Ferryboat
Pioneer.

*(Photo courtesy
Dennis Dibley.)*

---

[19]*St. Patrick.*

215

Olympus Lost

Seabeck's finest home-built ship, *Olympus,* burned at sea in latitude 47 degrees 10', longitude 132 degrees 25' on Sept. 14, 1881 while enroute from San Francisco to Seabeck in command of Capt. W. F. Edwards, despite efforts of officers and crew to extinguish the flames.

All 26 on board took to the boats and were picked up the same day by the Ship *War Hawk,* Captain Hinds. They were taken to Port Discovery. The three passengers aboard were Guy C. Phinney and Thomas and Agatha Marie (Olanie) Lewis. The newlywed Lewis couple were moving all their worldly belongings to Seabeck where Tom had secured employment at the mill.

Phinney wrote a concise account of the loss, while years later Agatha Marie wrote a fictionalized version of the same event.

Phinney wrote: *"About half past six on the morning of the 14th, I was standing near the aft hatch when I heard the cry of fire. The captain appeared immediately on deck and gave the order to close the fore hatch, get buckets ready and the pumps to work. The order was promptly obeyed. A portion of the aft hatch was then taken off and water pumped into the hold.*

"The fire ran over the hay and oakum like a brush heap and in a moment was coming out of the hold. The hatch was then closed with difficulty, the first and second mates getting their eyebrows singed in doing it.

"When the fire burst through the main and after hatches, the Captain gave the order to clear away the boats and all on board safely embarked, taking their most valuable effects. Together with the master and crew, there were three ladies: the Captain's wife and daughter and Mrs. Lewis.

"Fortunately we fell in with the ship War Hawk *a few hours after bound for Port Discovery which came to our assistance and took us on board after which we were well cared for by Capt. Hinds and his estimable wife.*

"Too much praise cannot be given to Capt. Edwards for his coolness and bravery under the trying circumstances. He was the last to leave the ship and his orders throughout were carefully obeyed by the crew, thereby saving the lives and a good part of the property of those on board.

"Before night fell, nothing was seen of the ship Olympus *but a black, charred hulk. All united in praising the conduct of Capt. Hinds and his wife who did everything they could for the unfortunate party and landed them at Port Discovery.*[20]

Ironically a year later the *War Hawk* caught fire and was scuttled and sunk at Port Discovery. Then in 1884[21] she was towed about 300 yards from where she sunk and beached.

Years later Agatha Marie Lewis wrote a *fictional* version of the events. All names were changed, but the events of the burning of the ship and their rescue are said to be true. The story is an excellent example of a Victorian romance novel.[22]

Making up our minds to begin our new life in a new country and grow up with it, Mr. Sewall was fortunate in getting passage for us on a sailing vessel to a sawmill town on Puget Sound.

White Wings deserved her name, with all her sails set, she looked very roomy and comfortable for a lumber ship. Captain Jenkin's wife, daughter and son accompanied him on his voyages and as they did not carry passengers as a rule, we were fortunate in being on board.

I was sad at leaving a place that had been home to me all my life, marrying against my parents wishes, there were no loving hands to wave farewell to one that they might never again see, but their hearts

---

20 *Daily Intelligencer.* Sept. 20, 1881.

21 *Seattle Post-Intelligencer.* Oct. 16, 1884.

22 Lewis family manuscript donated to Kitsap County Historical Society.

were hard and I had him who must be henceforth all in all to me.

So, no wonder my heart was sad in leaving dear Frisco with all its beauties and the beautiful homes. As it recedes from my longing gaze, with eyes so dimmed with tears that I could scarcely see the Cliff House. Many a happy hour had I walked the sands with my lover at my side and now with him near me I left, equal for all hardships that might come to us.

My husband! How the name thrills me even as I write after a quarter of a century. Of fair height with dark waving hair and hazel eyes, which looked black in moments of passion, olive skin and bright red lips. I often wondered why my parents failed to see why I loved him. Of course he was poor. All nice looking young men are! Equally, of course, they wanted me to marry one man older than my father, just because he had plenty of gold.

I chose the one gladly and let the other go. How could I do different for when his arms were about me and his eyes looking into mine, I would not change with an angel from heaven.

Now the die was cast, for better or worse, going out into the world, just we two to make a home. Perchance to meet many troubles that would try this love of ours and show what it was worth.

How many have cried "What is this mighty love that conquers and makes us slaves?" No. Not slaves, but masters of our own destinies for poverty and troubles only draw us nearer when the love is from God, which is true of all pure love. It is of Divine Origin. No man can truly love a pure woman and not believe in an Almighty God. So my husband has said reverently many times to me and my heart answers likewise.

Now we are on the open sea and every hour takes us further away. Will I ever see thee again and I still ask it.

Captain Jenkins is a bluff, hearty man of perhaps 50 years, beloved by his crew, a man that could be master and friend as his men knew. His wife was insanely jealous of him, tho he never seems to give her any reason to be.

She was heard to remark of a certain lady friend of hers that *she* was the only woman she could trust not to make love to

her Captain. She was very amusing in her ways. Of Irish parentage and very little education, she was very careful of her manner. In fact so much so that she made queer mistakes at times and as she thought, to be a lady one must have plenty of jewelry and she had a profusion of it. Mostly solid gold.

Their daughter Molly was so sweet and refined in looks and manners that made one think that there was good blood and breeding in some bygone ancestors. Sweet Molly. How I learned to love her and she returned the love thousand-fold.

On board I noticed the first mate, a fine manly fellow. One that you felt that you could trust. It could be plainly seen where his heart lay. How his eyes would light up when our Sweet Molly came on deck and how the minx heeded him not. She just tossed her pretty head and went on, sometimes just stopping for a few words. She had just come from a grand finishing school and was airing graces for his benefit. Poor fellow. He would look downcast when she passed with just a merry nod and a *"How do."*

How terribly blind and stupid some men are. They never understand a woman. Why can't they see that half the charm of wooing would be gone if a girl were to meet their advances half way. Modest and shy as a wild flower was she. Her wavy brown hair and such beautiful blue eyes I never saw but once before and they are closed forever these many a day.

But Molly's eyes were shaded with black lashes that made them look dark. When I was introduced and she looked up at me with those wonderful eyes, my heart went out to her as she put out both of her pretty hands to clasp mine and said, *"Oh. I am so glad you are coming with us. We can have oceans of fun for you haven't been married long enough to be staid and prim yet, have you?"*

"No," I said, *"just six months, that's all."* My hubby is only a boy in spite of his 25 years. Why I must be a girl still and we can have a good time and no mistake.

"There, there," said Captain, *"run away, you scalawags. Of course you both will be into all sorts of mischief. There's one consolation though,"* he continued, *"it's bed*

you two will have to go soon as we cross the bar and she will be pitching and tossing into it. Then we'll have peace for at least three days or more, perhaps."

"Oh dear," I said, "Will it be that bad? I'm sure I won't be seasick for I've often been out on the bay in heavy weather."

"Oh that's different to what you'd catch pretty soon," he laughed.

Sure enough, we began to feel the vessel pitching as he spoke and I will leave the next three days to your imagination.

The steward having failed to come and Mr. Sewall took his place for the trip up to Puget Sound, so I was left alone most of the time. When we were up on deck again, Captain Jenkins brought a gentleman to us and introduced him: a Richard Jenkins, a very distant connection of his. He had been brought aboard the night before sailing in an intoxicated condition and as he had been going the pace in Frisco all summer, it took him a few days to recover.

That was why we had not see him before. About 28 years of age, tall with dark hair and eyes, he certainly was handsome, of a type that some women love and others turn away from, according to their temperaments. He could sing and play very well and certainly knew women's ways, having had a great deal of experience by his own say so.

He had a way of looking at women, young or old, as though they and only they occupied his heart and mind and I firmly believe that he deluded himself in that belief.

As for Molly, she teased and tantalized him on every turn. The little witch would not take his love-making seriously. When I reasoned with her, she clasped me around the waist and began waltzing around the deck.

"There. There, dearie. Don't get serious. You don't look a bit nice and besides it won't hurt Rich a little bit to be played with. He's had his own way so much with women that he thinks I should be easy game. Besides he's spent two fortunes already and he thinks it's time to settle down and be good and chooses me for a settler. No, thank you! I don't want the situation. As I heard a servant say once when a lady wanted her to mind the baby on her afternoon out," said Molly.

"But dear. Remember that you might wound another by your thoughtlessness," I said.

But she danced away. Soon I heard her playing the piano and singing in the cabin and Rich was bending over her and turning the music, looking so devoted and hanging on to every word she sang as though his love would not be still.

Then he sang that old, old song, *"Speak to Me, Speak. Why Turn Away When I Draw Near."*

I could have shaken her to see how interested she seemed, knowing what I knew. Oh my lady. You will pay for this some day. Loving one man and playing with another, for I had guessed the secret she tried so hard to conceal for she would not see how Will Dutnon loved her. Oh. The perversity of some of these young girls, of breaking a good man's heart and ruining their own lives just to show their power. But the reckoning day came for her, as it comes to us all.

Among the crew was an old German, carpenter of the ship. He was a queer character, always giving advice where none was needed or desired. No one seemed to know his real name for *Chips* he was called and answered to it. Although he said *Sheffs* wasn't a very nice name but it would do. Tommy, the Captain's son, was a great favorite with Chips and of course the dog, Jack, was too, for as the boy and dog were inseparable, it was a case of *"love me, love my dog."*

I could never understand why Chips loved the two so much. For there was no doubt of his affection for them. Tommy would hide his tools in such out of the way places as the bread and flour bins. He certainly was a great trial to the old German. But he would shrug his shoulders and with such a comical grin would say, *"That's all right. Boys will be boys."*

The only one aboard that held any terror for Tommy was the cabin boy. A Swede with hair like flax and pale blue eyes that bugged out of his head, as Tommy would say, and those eyes scared him. If he would steal into the galley and beg cookies and then Joe would sneak up on him and pretend to duck him into the flour barrel. *"I wouldn't mind that,"* Tommy would say, *"but them eyes of his scares me. They look like they would fall out."*

So the days came and went, each one taking us nearer to our future home. When evening came, Mr. Sewall would be at liberty and we could walk the deck or stray into the cabin where we could always find Molly and Rich playing and singing. One moonlit night we were all amusing ourselves in different ways. Captain and Mrs. Jenkins had retired. The mate was on deck in charge. *"Come out in the moonlight, Molly,"* said Rich. *"It's too nice to stay indoors on a night such as this."*

"Oh yes," said she, *"I want to dance. Will you play a waltz, Marie dear?"* she said to me. For it was so with us, first names. Just two girls. So I played several pieces and between pauses I could hear her merry laughter and sometimes just the murmurs of his voice.

"Oh do be serious, Rich," I heard her say. *"Come, Mr. Dunton. Won't you dance with me?"* I did not hear his answer but she told me afterward he came very reluctantly and put his arms about her as though he were afraid she would bite him. She laughingly said, *"But he was so clumsy I sent him off."*

With merry goodnights all around, we retired. I could not sleep, but for awhile lay in my bunk looking out the port window at the moon. It was at its zenith and looking so grant I felt awed at the vastness and beauty of the heavens. The sea was quite clam. Just a long rolling swell and the vessel seemed to glide along so silently. Everything seemed so still, only the creaking of the rigging and the stamping of feet overhead as the sails had to be tended.

I lay thinking of God's goodness to me and thanking Him for His mercy. I prepared to sleep and it was time as I heard 8 bell ring. That is midnight at sea and they change the watch so that those who were on deck could go below and others take their places until 4 o'clock A.M. when they change again.

Mr. Sewall always had to get up at 5 o'clock . After he left me that morning, I lay thinking of many things and feeling grand. That my dear parents would have none of

me because I chose my own mate. For why should parents deny us the rights they themselves claimed. For they confessed that in all things my dear one was worthy of me but he was poor.

My father was poor when he married mother and they loved each other and worked together until now they were independent and why could they not have faith that it would be so with us? When I said so to them, they said conditions were different. I who had had every advantage was not fitted to be a poor man's wife, that I knew nothing whatever of household affairs, who had never sewed a stitch, nor cooked a meal. Well, I could learn. Besides my lover could cook and so teach me. He ran away from his home in England when a mere boy. He was always craving to go to sea and as his people would not hear of it, he took matters into his own hands and ran away, shipping on a trading vessel. He had to help the cook and in that way learned things that came in good stead afterwards.

It was the old story over again. My father stormed and threatened to lock me up. My mother wept but I stood firm. At last they consented to a quiet home wedding. Just our people and two friends of his. Then as my father expressed it: *"Now young people. You have made your bed and must lie on it though it be filled with thorns."*

But little cared I for his preachings for some poet says, *"Hope shines ever eternal in the human breast."*

As I lay musing, I heard a shouting and tramping of feet on deck. My door burst open and Molly, wild-eyed and pale, cried *"Get up. Quick. Quick. The ship is on fire."* And wringing her hands she sank in a heap on the floor weeping.

"Be still, dear. Don't give up until we have to," I said as I quickly robed myself, forgetting parts of my apparel in my nervous haste. An omission I did not find out until afterwards.

Shoes on. Stockings I just put in my pocket. Then I looked around for my dearest treasures: a small bundle of love letters and a few pieces of jewelry that my dear mother had give me . . . only a few but every piece with a history. I put on my long coat and into the pockets placed these, my most valued treasures.

Molly had recovered her calmness by this time and Mr. Sewall came to our door and said, *"Come Marie. You and Miss Jenkins must come with me while I place you in a safe place until the boats are gotten ready. Yes. We must leave,"* he answered my questioning look. *"She's all afire and we can't put it out. The hatches had not been off since we left Frisco. That is ten days ago. Until this morning and when there was need of a few things brought up, we took a hatch off and in a few moments the man below shouted FIRE! And when we looked, it seemed a seething furnace. He had to run for his life. We put the hatch back on and they are going to take off the after hatches to try to put out the fire. Come now. Quick, before out way may be cut off."*

As we were going through the cabin, Mrs. Jenkins was putting on all her jewelry, tho but partly dressed. She would not complete her toilet until she put it on.

Molly wanted to stop and help her but she said to go on *"I'll be there soon."* When we got to the cabin door, the flames were pouring out of the hatches, clear to the top of the mast.

My husband shielded us the best he could and got us past the fiery furnace and placed us in safety near the galley while he went back to assist them in replacing the hatches for with that we were certainly lost as the fire was gaining great headway. After struggling with the hatches in vain by hand, they put ropes through the rings and after a great deal of trouble, they replaced and battened them down.

The men's hands and faces were terribly burnt, but none of them seemed to feel it for what was a few burns to our lives. After every effort was made to control the fire, Captain Jenkins concluded to leave the vessel, for she was loaded with hay, oakum, kerosene and powder and not knowing how near the fire was to the powder, the men became panic stricken and before the Captain could interfere, they had thrown a boat overboard and their dunnage into it and were proceeding to follow.

"Hellow there!" shouted the Captain, *"Quit that. The first man that steps into that boat loses his life."*

They turned, terror stricken, to gaze into the mouth of a revolver held by the Captain.

"Take the dunnage out of that," he sternly commanded, *"and be men, not cowards. Wait your turn. Can't you see that the boat is leaking like a sieve and could not float five minutes in this swell and look overboard you idiots and see who is along side."*

We all crowded over at his words and there was a terrible sight: a shark that was lazily lying near the ship, waiting for its prey. The men shuddered and there was no more trouble just then.

"Stand by the ropes and lower the life boats," called the Captain in stentorian tones. The men, mostly Danes and Swedes who could scarcely speak English and understood less, came running in a body to obey orders.

"Come back some of you lubbers and man the two boats at once." They all turned and ran back to the other boat just like a flock of sheep.

Then Molly sprang to one of the ropes: *"Come some of you and help or else we shall be burned."*

The men seemed calmed at her words and part came back to her and did as she directed. When at length they were settled in the water, we could hear the flames roaring beneath us and the pitch stuck to our shoes as it boiled out between the cracks. We had had no breakfast and no one thought of any.

"Put up the Danger signal, Dunton," said Captain Jenkins. As it went up I saw the Union Jack upside down. That is the signal that we needed help. With the aid of field glasses, the Captain had seen the tops of masts of some vessel, but was uncertain as to her heading towards us, but thought it best to go into the boats and steer for her as it was not safe to stay longer. The boats were small and would barely hold us all without carrying a thing else. Had it been a choppy sea, we could not have lived in it, but the long rolling swells made it possible for us to make the attempt to reach the other vessel.

So one by one we women were lowered into the life boats. Just imagine the ship dipping into it. So we had to wait until the boat came level with the ladders, hanging down the side. Then the first mate would lower us down to the second mate and he would catch us just at the right time, else we should have to wait for another swell.

When it came Mrs. Jenkins turn, she screamed and hung on so long that Barnett, the second mate, had to fairly tear her down. She still was only partly dressed with all her jewelry on. She looked a strange sight.

At length we were all in but the Captain. He stood on the rail as if loath to leave his ship. Heaving a heavy sigh, he at last came down, put his head between his hands until Molly crept to his side: *"Don't grieve, Daddy dear. You couldn't help it and if we only come safely out of this, we still are together and we can work."*

"Oh, yes," cried her mother, *"it's easy enough for you to talk. Al our clothes and furniture gone and your lovely new piano. Oh dear. Why did I ever marry a seafaring man. They are never easy on shore, but to sea must go.*

Oh she cried as we dipped in the trough of the sea. Nothing but a wall of water on each side. It was frightening for it seemed as though it would break right into the boat.

"Father of mercies," she screams, *"I'll dig clams on the beach before I'll ever go to sea again."* And so she continued lamenting. No one paid any attention to her for we were anxiously looking for the vessel and in the meantime thinking our own thoughts.

The boat was leaking some and my feet were wet. Barnett, the second mate, was a very large man and had hip rubber boots on. Noticing my feet being wet, he took off his boots and insisted on my putting them on. I did so and no one seemed to think it at all strange which shows how circumstances can change us.

It seemed five days instead of hours when the Captain said, *"I believe she is heading for us."* Thank God for His mercies. Yes, she did seem to be coming nearer and a cry of thankfulness went up from both boats for they had kept together. The first mate had charge of the other one. Sometimes our hearts sank for it seemed as

though the vessel was heading away from us.

Rich tried to be funny, but soon quit as no one responded for it was serious to most of us. Out on the ocean 400 miles from land and nothing to eat. But Captain's plans were that of the coming ship failed us we would have to go back for food and water and make a raft of the spars to carry provisions and take our chances of the ship blowing up when the fire reached the powder.

Molly and I were silently praying. Her eyes following the mate's boat whenever she could see it. I could see how great the suspense was when we were down amid the walls of water and could not see his boat. Then when it appeared, how fervent was I. *"Thank the Lord"* in a whispered tone.

"Do you think if we have to go back whether his men will leave him and head back?" she asked me. *"They are so frightened of the thought of the ship blowing up. I heard one of them whispering to the other before we left the ship that you bet once he left he wouldn't set foot on deck. I know the others will follow him as he seems their leader."*

"Don't worry, Molly. Look up," I said, *"God is good to us for that vessel is unmistakably coming straight for us."*

At last she did come near enough to hail us. Then I had to learn the courtesy of Life at Sea, even in disaster. It was the old ship *War Eagle*, one of the old time steamers turned into a sailing vessel.

Old Captain Howard, an old war veteran, was her commander and a grander one never lived despite his 70 years. He stood on the poop-deck of his vessel, tall and dignified. Captain Jenkins stood up and saluted, *"Good morning, Captain Howard. I crave your hospitality for a few days as our ship is afire and seeing your vessel heading our way, came to meet you."*

"You are welcome to all that we have," he returned, *"although we are on short rations ourselves as we are overdue and have run short of both food and water, but you are welcome to what is left."*

They had a bosun's chair rigged for taking the women aboard and as it seemed a curious contrivance to me, I will describe it. Just a common arm chair rigged with a rope at each corner which came together over our heads and fastened to one strong line that was run through a block to the main yard. My Molly went up smiling but her mother as so frightened, for fear that she would fall out though tied in securely, that she screamed all the way up and promised many gifts to her Patron Saint if she arrived safely on deck.

Then it came my turn. I got in and held on to those immense rubber boots and as I neared the deck could hear an audible laugh among the men.

"*Never mind, my dear,*" said Mrs. Howard, a dear white haired lady, to me. I don't wonder at their laughing. They do look immense but they kept me nice and dry and I hardly realized how comical they must look to others.

After we were all on board, Captain Howard said: "*Now this question of food and water is a serious one as we are still about four days from land and with 28 more we should soon be striving unless we can get more.*"

"*I've figured that all out,*" said our Captain and calling his men to him he called for a volunteer crew to go back to the burning vessel for food and water. "*You understand that having battened down the hatches and closing every outlet into the hold, the fire was still confined there,*" he said.

As we laid to, we could see her, about five miles away. None of the sailors would go. Will Dunton stepped forward: "*I'm with you, Captain,*" he said.

Count me in," said Rich.

"*Well,*" said old Barnett, "*I've no one waiting so I won't be missed if she blows up.*"

"*You had better take me,*" said John Sewall, "*for I know just where to lay my hands on the stores and the passage way heading into the lazeretti is only four feet high, I could go easier than a tall man.*"

My heart stood still for a moment when I heard his offer to go. I could not say "*Stay*" and I dare not say "*Go*" but turned away into the cabin and dropped on a lounge, burying my head in pillows and began to weep for the first time that awful day. I felt his loving arms around me. "*Dear, don't make it any harder for me than*

you can help, for all our lives may depend on our getting food and water, for they are really on the verge of starvation on this vessel now and the fresh water is nearly gone also and dearest I don't think God has permitted us to be happy just to part us now. Have faith, sweetheart, and pray for me, for us all. For we may need it. God bless and keep my darling," he prayed and with a fond caress he was gone. I seemed to lose consciousness for a time.

Molly came running in, throwing herself at my feet in a frenzy of weeping, saying "*Oh what shall I do? He's gone and not even a loving look or word for me. I may never see him again and my dear old Dad. Oh what shall I do?*" I gathered her in my arms and we wept and prayed for those we could do naught else for.

Mrs. Howard came by us in silent sympathy, just a soothing word and touch, but it meant so much to we two young creatures.

"*Come,*" she said. "*Dry your tears and come on deck ready to welcome them back.*"

"*No,*" said Molly. "*I cannot endure the sight of the vessel. I must stay here and close my ears for fear to hear an explosion.*"

We went on deck and stood by the rail watching the other vessel. You could see a faint line of smoke arising from her and the masts seemed to be loosening. She looked a grand sight with all her sails set. She seemed almost human to me. Mrs. Howard got the glasses for me so I could watch the vessel but my trembling hands could not hold them and the tension at last grew too much for me and I had to go back to Molly.

So together we sat saying very little. Trying to be brace and cheer one another. How long we sat there, I'll never know. At last we heard a great joyous shout from Tommy and at about the same time we heard a noise like thunder.

"*Oh what can that be. It's White Wings blowing up,*" cried Tommy in terror.

We rushed up on the deck not knowing what to expect. Captain Howard came hurrying towards us. "*They are safe,*" he cried. "*I saw them leave the ship just before the explosion.*"

For a time we could see nothing owing to the smoke.

"Oh I see her," cried Molly. "There they are. Oh my darling Daddy is safe. Oh, Marie. God has heard and answered our prayers." And we both sank on our knees on deck in thanksgiving.

"They are coming," Tommy screamed, "and they got lots of grub and barrels of water."

We ran on deck and with thankful hearts watched the approach of the loaded boat. But whose form is it which lies in the boat? At first we could not make out. Then I saw through a misty haze . . . my husband! Was he dead? No. No. Thank God. He seems me and feebly waves his hand.

They got him on deck and into a bunk in the stateroom where I could tend him. "I'm all right. Only inhaled that smoke," he said. And indeed he smelt as though he had stepped into hay smoke. He was quite ill for 24 hours, but soon recovered, much to our thankfulness.

Later my brave lad told me all about it. "You see no one else knew as well as I just where to lay their hands on the things we most need," he said. "I got a Turkish towel out of the cabin, wet it and tied it over my mouth and nostrils and before I went in I told the Captain to wait 20 minutes and if I didn't come out to come in after me. I went in closing the door after me. I could hardly see for the smoke, so got down on hands and knees and crept to where the food was, about 40 feet.

"I carried load after load to the door and piled it all up there. I worked as fast as I could for the smoke was stifling and I knew that I could not stand it very long. But I took a peek into the hold and you talk of Dante's Inferno. It isn't in it with what I saw. The flames were all colors. It looked grand. You may be sure that I did not stay there very long.

"Just as I went with the last load I heard the Captain calling 'Come Sewall. I'll open and come to you if you don't answer.' I could not answer as the smoke was overcoming me.

"I sank at the door but not before I heard it burst open. Then all was blank. When I came to, I was in the boat and we were pulling for our lives. For there was a rumbling noise like distant thunder. Then the whole upper works of the vessel went straight up and settled hissing into the water and fragments all around us. It was a miracle that we were not hurt for a great spar just grazed the side of our boat."

"I am so glad to be with you again, my darling," I said. "Even though all our clothes and furniture are gone, we still have each other and with brave hearts, we will make a home. For where there is true love, we can overcome poverty."

We had a pleasant time for the four days aboard the *War Eagle*. Captain and Mrs. Howard were most kind but we were all happy when we finally dropped anchor at the end of our voyage.

Mill owned house lived in by Walton family after fire.
(Victoria Rowe, artist.)

1857 Kitsap County Territorial Census Annotated

The author's real interest in Kitsap History is the Territorial History, that history prior to Statehood in November 1889. The 1857 Kitsap Territorial History for Seabeck has been corrected and additions made to some individuals' personal history. There were other Territorial census records in 1871, 1879, 1881, 1883, 1885, 1887 and 1889. These contain excellent material usually overlooked by serious students of history and genealogy. The entire Kitsap 1857 census is available through the author or at the Kitsap County Historical Society.

Name	Age	Birthplace	Occupation	Annotated Remarks
J. R. Williamson	27	New York	Blacksmith	Arrived Port Gamble

1854 and during the following decade assisted in establishing mills at Seabeck, Port Madison and Freeport. He was a machinist and mechanic and operated sawmills, foundries, machine shops, steamboats, vessels. He was one of the original minority partners at Washington Mill Company, Seabeck.

Name	Age	Birthplace	Occupation	Annotated Remarks
Woodbury B. Sinclair	28	Maine	Lumberman	Owned minority interest in Washington Mill Company

at Seabeck and sold out in 1861. Married one of the Alki settlers, Mary E. Low. Elected to Territorial Legislature representing King and Kitsap counties. Later moved to Snohomish County.

Name	Age	Birthplace	Occupation	Annotated Remarks
William Jefferies	25	Sweden	Lumberman	
Henry Jackson	28	New York	Lumberman	
Charles Bachelder	30	Vermont	Lumberman	Sailed into Steilacoom

December 1850 and joined Alfred A. Plummer in a timber venture and finding it nonprofitable, paddled a canoe to Port Townsend the following spring where he staked a claim but failed to prove his title. In business enterprise with Plummer, Francis W. Pettygrove and Loren B. Hastings but sold his interest soon afterward and moved to Port Ludlow where he died.

Name	Age	Birthplace	Occupation
J. W. Bates	23	Massachusetts	Lumberman
Robert Gardner	29	Indiana	Lumberman
Andrew J. Young	34	Maine	Seaman
John Witty	35	Edgebard Ille (?)	Teamster
William Jenden	22	England	Cook
Julius Henerky	24	Denmark	Lumberman
William Kingsley	25	Massachusetts	Lumberman
Samuel Higgs	27	New York	Lumberman
Supply Woods	34	Massachusetts	Blacksmith
Charles Bruinard	29	Jamaica	Mason (Negro)
Hill Harmon	34	Maine	Lumberman. One of the original minority millowners.

Was maintaining home on Whidbey Island at time of this census.

Name	Age	Birthplace	Occupation
William Hutchins	30	Virginia	Lumberman
Jackum Rushum	42	Genoa	Cook

Thomas Browning	26	Norway	Lumberman
James Davis	33	New York	Blacksmith
William Bayley	23	England	Lumberman
A. P. Howe	37	NewHampshire	Lumberman

A. P. Howe who was captain of the Washington Mill Company's *Oregon*. If so, he was still living at Seabeck in 1885 when his daughter, Louisa, in anticipation of her death, all her personal property for the benefit of her son, Frederick William Weston of Seabeck. This included jewelery, gold watches, $50 watch chain, silver Waltham watch chains, gold finger rings, gold lockets for a total value of $399 plus two cows (one named Molly who was give years old) and the other, Bess, seven years old, and their calves and about nine head hogs. She was married to George Weston at Seabeck April 20, 1875 and less than two years later sued him for divorce.

J. H. VanWinkle	23	Illinois	Farmer
Henry Dealand	25	Vermont	Lumberman
George Abraham	40	Norway	Farmer
Charles Bayley	40	SouthCarolina	Farmer
J. H. Yackett	42	Pennsylvania	Lumberman
B. B. Stevens	31	Maine	Lumberman
Francis Moran	40	Maine	Lumberman
B. Goodridge	44	Maine	Lumberman
Otis Wilson	56	Maine	Lumberman
William H. Littlewood	32	New York	Lumberman

Had a contract to keep the trail open between Hood's Canal and Dye's Inlet. Died at Silverdale April 24, 1895. Was a logger. Considered the Silverdale area's earliest settler.

Frank Wood	24	Ireland	Seaman
Peter Smith	30		Seaman
J. W. Pierce	37	Rhode Island	Lumberman
J. W. Balch	38	Maine	Teamster.

Balch was a long-time resident of Seabeck and a logger.

William Sackett	35	New York	Cook
Charles R. Drew	47	England	Steward
R. Fawcett	59	Pennsylvania	Wheelwright
Ewell Brinnon	30	Ireland	Fireman.

Logged at Tahuya. He was an early settler on The Canal. Later lived across The Canal where the town is named after him.

Thomas King	25	England	Lumberman
William Roach	23	Ireland	Carpenter
Jacob Patterson	40	Norway	Seaman
Thomas Herald	35	New York	Mason

NOTE: It appears that the census was taken prior to start-up of the mill as the "lumbermen" are all loggers and the others appear to have occupations necessary to building the mill.

1860

House Number	Name	Age	Sex	Occupation	Birthplace
342	Harmon, Hill	33	M	Lumberman	Maine
	Harmon, Bathaline	32	F		Maine
	Harmon, Edwin	12	M		Maine
	Harmon, Olive	11	F		Maine
	Harmon, Ella	5	F		WT
	Harmon, Emma K.	3	F		WT
	Harmon, Ida F.	1	F		WT
343	Wallace, J. M.	28	M	Lumberman	Maine
	Conant, Alv.	39	M	Lumberman	Maine
	Burke, John	25	M	Lumberman	Maine
	Dunbar, J. T.	27	M	Lumberman	Maine
344	Clark, James	27	M	Lumberman	Pennsylvania
	Clark, Lavina	25	F		Pennsylvania
	Clark, James, Jr.	11	M		Pennsylvania
	Clark, Ellen	6	F		Pennsylvania
345	Pierpoint, D. L.	35	M		New York
	Keller, M. N.	21	M	Lumberman	Maine
346	Blinn, Marshall	33	M	Lumber Merchant	Maine
	Blinn, Julia E.	29	F		Maine
347	Williamson, J. B.	30	M	Engineer	New York
	Williamson, Julia	27	F		Ireland
	Williamson, William	1	M		WT
348	Harmon, L:S.	27	M	Lumberman	Maine
	Harmon, Augusta	24	F		Maine
	Harmon, Theodore P.	4	M		Maine
349	Ludington, H.	29	M	Bookkeeper	New York
	Ludington, Louisa	25	F		Maine
350	Longfellow, John	24	M	Lumberman	Maine
	Galvin, Catherine	25	F	Housekeeper	Massachusetts
	Galvin, Hannah M.	2	F		WT
	Wenborn, F.	31	M	Gardener	England
	Wenborn, Emma	29	F		England
	Wenborn, Mary A.	4	F		WT
	Wenborn, Robert J.	2	M		WT
	Wenborn, Robert	27	M	Lumberman	England
351	Young, A. B.	37	M	Lumberman	Maine
	Young, Hulda	35	F		Maine
	Young, Frederick A.	9	M		Maine
	Young, Horace H.	6	M		Maine
352	Newell, Joseph A.	36	M	Lumber Merchant	Maine

There are 55 additional men engaged as lumbermen, seamen, blacksmith (2), sawyers, baker, carpenters, ship carpenters, lumber planers, saw filer, fireman, mason, sparmaker and watchman. There are eight additional structures which housed the 55 men, the largest grouping of men at 14.

1870

Pg No.	House No.	Name	Age	Sex	Color	Occupation	Birthplace
1	4	Miller, Charles	35	M	W	Hotel Cook	Norway
		Miller, William	9	M	W		WT
		Miller, Charles	4	M	W		WT
		Miller, Josephine	5	F	W		WT
	5	Pitman, Solon	35	M	W	Machinist	Maine
		Pitman, Kate	27	F	W	Keeps House	Maine
		Pitman, Elizabeth	21	F	W		England
		Pitman, Katie	5/12	F	W		WT
	6	Blair, William	27	M	W	Laborer	Maine
	7	Nichols, Samuel	26	M	W	Saw Mill	Maine
		Nichols, Ella	24	F	W	Keeps House	Maine
		Nichols, Alice	5	F	W		Maine
		Nichols, Augusta	1	F	W		California
	8	Calligan, Robert	30	M	W	Saw Mill	Maine
		Calligan, Augusta	28	F	W	Keeps House	Maine
		Calligan, Mary	8	F	W		Maine
		Calligan, Ada	1	F	W		WT
	9	Morrison, Michael	27	M	W	Saw Mill	England
		Morrison, Anna	27	F	W	Keeps House	Maine
		Morrison, Edna	4/12	F	W		Maine
	10	Vrooman, Edgar	50	M	W	Bookkeeper	New York
		Vrooman, Jane	48	F	W	Keeps House	New York
		Vrooman, Rosie	6	F	W		WT
2	30	Warin, William	36	M	W	Retail Liquor Dealer	France
		Warin, Hattie	9	F	W		WT
		Warin, Julie	12	F	W		WT
		Flynn, Robert	36	M	W	Hotel Clerk	Canada
		Moren, William	37	M	W	Lumberman	Canada
		Carrigan, William	26	M	W	Lumberman	Sweden
		Peterson, Isreal	27	M	W	Lumberman	NewBrunswick
3	32	Misner, George	36	M	W	House Carpenter	Canada
		Misner, Harriet	31	F	W	Keeps House	Canada
		Misner, Hattie	4	F	W		BritishCol.
	33	Craig, Charles	25	M	W	Saw Mill	Scotland
		Craig, Annie	27	F	W	Keeps House	England
	34	Dagnin, Thomas	33	M	W	Cook	Ireland
		Dagnin, Joanna	32	F	W	Keeps House	Ireland
		Dagnin, Mary	37	F	W		Massachusetts
		Dagnin, John	5	M	W		WT
		Dagnin, Willie	3	M	W		WT
		Dagnin, Walter	1	M	W		WT
	35	Owens, Herman	42	M	W	House	

					Carpenter	Ohio
	Owens, Nancy	28	F	W	Keeps House	Missouri
	Owens, Wallace	6/12	M	W		WT
36	Little, Gilbert	38	M	W	Saw Mill	Scotland
	Little, Ellen	37	F	W	Keeps House	Scotland
	Little, Archie	12	M	W		Chili
	Little, Belle	10	F	W		WT
	Little, Willie	8	M	W		WT
	Little, Clara	2	F	W		WT
37	Farnham, Edward	37	M	W	Lumberman	Maine
	Farnham, Ella	31	F	W	Keeps House	Maine
	Farnham, Alice	4	F	W		WT
38	Butcher, Thomas	31	M	W	Blacksmith	England
	Butcher, Christina	24	F	W	Keeps House	Scotland
	Butcher, Jane	6	F	W		Vancouver Is.
	Butcher, Isabella	4	F	W		Vancouver Is.
	Butcher, Fred	6/12	M	W		WT
39	Clayson, Edward	30	M	W	Seaman	England
	Clayson, Ann	24	F	W	Keeps House	England
	Clayson, Edward	5	M	W		England
	Clayson, William	2	M	W		WT
	Clayson, Esther	6/12	F	W		WT
40	Barker, William	33	M	W	Keeps store	Maine
	Barker, Addie	31	F	W	Keeps House	Maine
	Barker, Fred	13	M	W		Maine
	Gart, Oscar	40	M	W	Saw Mill	Denmark
	Oliver, Lewis	26	M	W	Saw Mill	Maine
52	Balch, William	57	M	W	Farmer	Maine
	Balch, Sarah	50	F	W	Keeps House	Maine
	Balch, Frank	24	M	W		Maine
	Balch, Sarah	22	F	W		Maine
	Balch, Augustus	18	M	W		Maine
	Balch, Laura	14	F	W		Maine
	Balch, Minnie	11	F	W		Maine
	Balch, Willie	9	M	W		WT

There were 59 men not mentioned above who were employed as laborers, seamen, lumbermen, cooks, sawmill employees, farmers, and one hotel waiter.

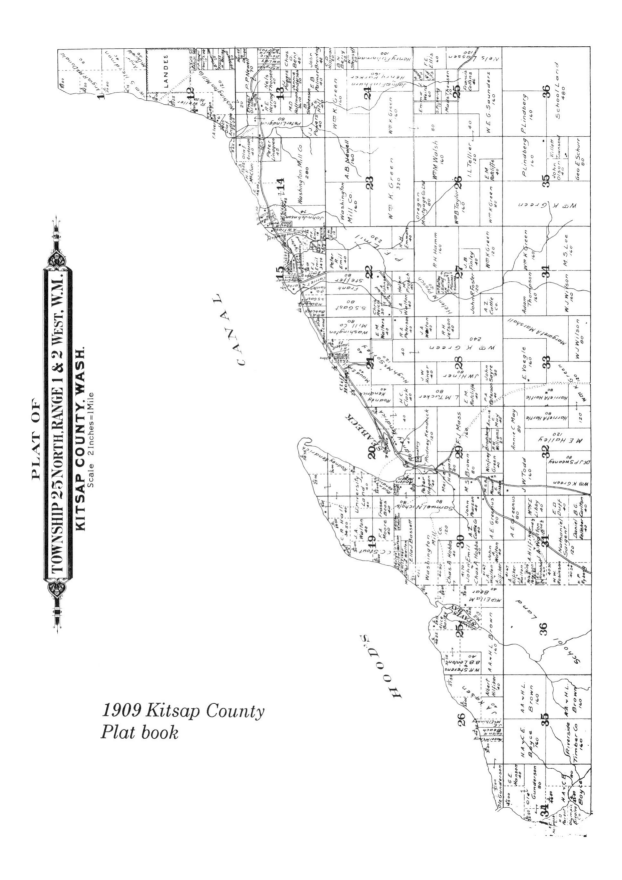

PLAT OF
TOWNSHIP 25 NORTH, RANGE 1 & 2 WEST, W.M.
KITSAP COUNTY, WASH.
Scale 2 Inches = 1 Mile

1909 Kitsap County
Plat book

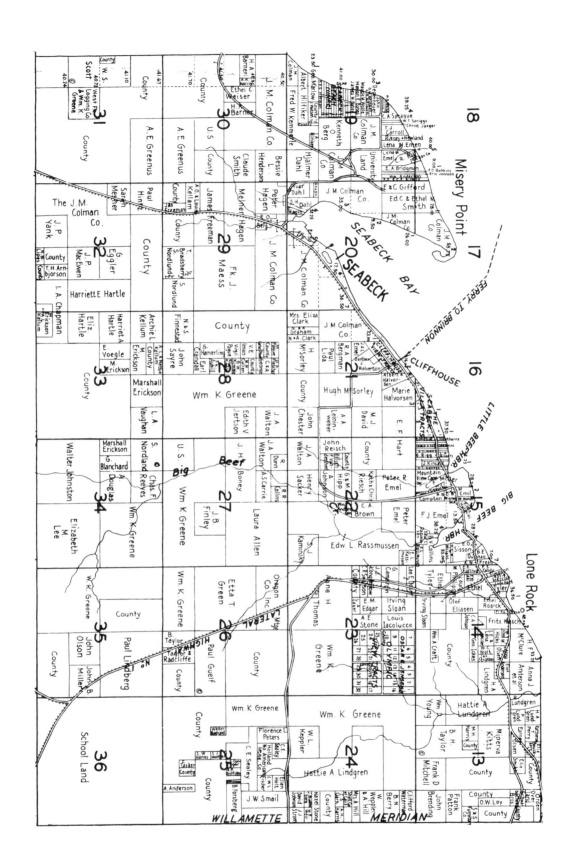

1930s Kroll map

(Used with permission of Kroll Map Company, Seattle.)

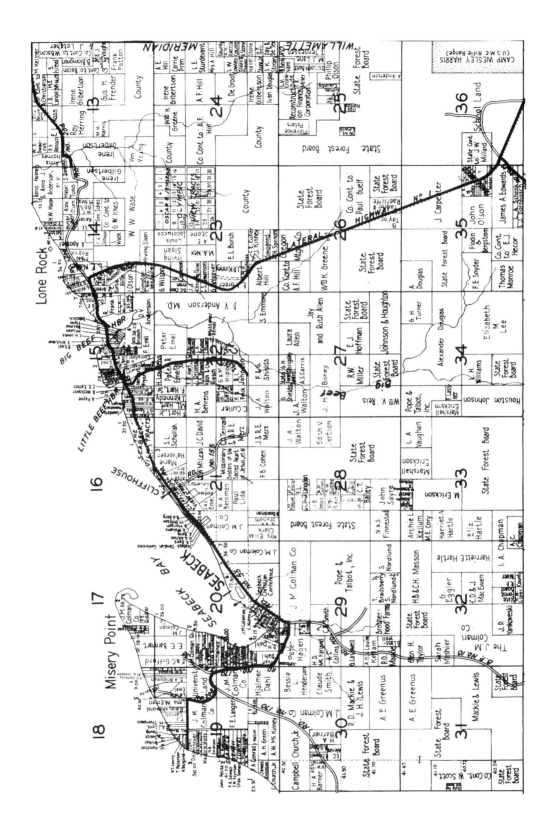

1955 Kroll Map

(Used with permission of Kroll Map Company, Seattle.)

**A typical family at
Seabeck Christian Conference
during 1920s.
WHOOPS!**

(Photo courtesy Seabeck Christian Conference.)

Index

A

Aarou, Switzerland, 31
Aarts, Adrian, 191, 192
Aarts, Connie Coons, 192
Aarts, Henny (Skagen), 190-192
Aarts, Norma Anderson, 192
Aarts, Penny Lovelace, 192
Abraham Lincoln, 83
Abraham, George, 45
Acorn, 92, 95
Ada, Minnesota, 176
Adams, Ansel, 44
Adams, Blinn & Company, 40, 46-47, 51-53, 77
Adams, Cassandra (Hills), 44, 66, 71
Adams, Cassandra (daughter), 44
Adams, Charles, 44
Adams, Glenn, 22
Adams, Olive, 44
Adams, Sarah, 44
Adams, Taylor & Company, 52, 73
Adams, William J., 40, 44, 46, 47, 48, 52, 53, 55, 59, 66, 70, 73, 74, 75, 79, 82
Adams, William L., 55
Addie (steamer), 87
Ah Fong, 210
Airey, Jane, 59, 108
Airey, Robert, 33, 59-60, 83, 88, 114
Airline (ferry), 92
Alaskan, 91
Albee, ?, 45
Albion, 91
Alexander, Samuel, 83, 103
Alexandre, Capt. Louis, 136
Alida, 35
Alki Point, 42-43
Allen, Arnold Southwick, 148-154, 157-158, 162, 189
Allen, Jim, 99
Allen, Julia (Hubbard), 148, 150, 153
Allen, Kathern (Hubbard), 150
Aloha, 91
Althof, Harold A., 119, 122
Althoff, Vivian (Cramer), 119
American Boy (2-masted schooner), 66, 76
Amherst, Nova Scotia, 60
Anderson Landing, 96, 169
Anderson, Andrew, 179

Anderson, Anton, 190
Anderson, Roger, 192
Appletree Cove, 86
Arronson, Mr., 106
Arvil, 19
Arvil Pilot, 16

B

Bacher, Joe, 191, 195
Baer, Jacob and Ella, 202- 203
Bagley, Mrs. Daniel, 47
Bagley, Rev. Daniel, 47
Bailey, Ida, 49
Bain, Capt., 88
Bainbridge Island, 17, 21
Baker, Arthur J., 84
Baker, Charles, 100
Baker, Clara E. (Little), 84
Baker, Gilbert Little, 84
Baker, Henry A., 84, 203
Baker, Isabelle (Little), 62
Baker, Isabelle May Shibler, 84
Baker, Jasper Gage, 59. 61-62, 84, 114, 120
Baker, William West, 84
Balch, Billy, 45, 46
Balch, Capt. Lafayette, 40
Baley, Frank, 157
Barber, W. H., 173
Barner, Billie (Halvorsen), 92, 117-120, 122, 174
Barner, Dr. H. A., 119, 171, 174
Barney, Sharon (Ruehle), 91, 191, 195-198
Barry, William, 178
Bartlow, Kate Marie (Hobbs), 199
Barton and Gooding, 106
Barton, Euphemia, 117
Barton, William, 106, 117
baseball, 109
Battle of Port Gamble, 39
Battle of Seattle, 39
Bay View Hotel, 8, 23, 76, 101-102, 109, 126, 189
Bayley, Charles, 45
Beaver Valley, 193
Bee, 83
Belgian horses, 178
Bell, Ransom "Deke", 184
Bell, William, 74-75, 136
Bellingham, 53-55
Bellingham Bay Route, 90
Benbennick, A. G., 173
Benbennick, Clarence, 97
Berg, Alben, 130-131, 163

Berg, Alice, 163
Berg, Ben, 129, 149-150, 153, 158, 160, 163
Berg, Berge, 163, 208
Berg, Emanuel Olsen (see Ben Berg)
Berg, Kenneth, 163
Bergen, Norway, 191
Berglind, Hugo W., 198
Berglind, Ray and Barbara, 193
Bessamart Inn, 92-93
Biddy (sloop), 121
Big Beef, 10, 2, 169-184
Big Beef Bridge, 96
Big Beef bridge, 177-178
billiards, 102
Billie (tug), 118
Black Ball Line, 94
blacksmith shop, 98
Blair, Bill, 99
Blair, Seabury Jr., 208
Blakefield, Frank, 122
Blaksaeter, Parnelle Qualheim, 188
Blanchard and Company, 53
Blanchard, W. C., 23
Blankenship, Sheriff Rush, 171
Blinn, Faustina, 44, 209
Blinn, Frank Lincoln, 44
Blinn, Fred, 44
Blinn, Gilmore and Hannah, 43
Blinn, Helen (Goodwin), 44, 125
Blinn, Ida May, 42-43
Blinn, Julia (Baker), 42, 47
Blinn, Marshall, 24, 39-40, 42-43, 45-49, 51-53, 69, 83, 99, 101-103, 113-114, 119-120, 122, 124, 160, 199
Blinn, Peter, 43
Blinn, Samuel, 40, 43
Blinn, Samuel Preble, 40, 43-44, 46, 51-52, 125
Blunt, 48, 78
Blythe, Robert C., 63
boat building, 186
Boise Basin gold rush, 47
Boreson, Stan, 95
Boston, 62
Bowker, Francis, 50
Bowker, Frank, 50, 128
Bowker, Joseph, 50
Bowker, Martha, 50
Bowker, Simeon C., 50, 60, 137
bowling alley, 102
Boyd, Joseph H., 169

Bradley, Mrs. Dennis, 136
Branch, Branch and Garrison, 192
Brandon, Mississippi, 115
Brass Band, 108
Bray, George, 33
Bremerton Union High School, 202
Brinker, Bob, 131-132
Brinker, Chester, 132
Brinker, Jean Hagen, 131, 186
Brinker, Otis, 197
Brinker, Roy, 131-132
Brinnon, 32, 45, 89, 91, 96
Brinnon, Ewell, 5, 3245, 49, 103
Brinnon, Kate, 5
Brisbane, John M., 121
Broderick, Henry, 192
Brodigan, Vivian, 119
Brontes (bark, ex-ship) 39, 43, 48-49, 70, 77-78, 82
Brooklyn, New York, 116
Brown, Addie, 128
Brown, Agnes, 163
Brown, Amos, 32, 46
Brown, Charles, 100
Brown, Harry, 128
Brown, Hattie, 128
Brown, P., 48
Brown, Richard, 46
Brown, Sarah B., 117
Brown, William H., 48, 100
Browne, J. Ross, 6
Brownlee, Bill, 100
Brumm, Bertha Sibon (see Bertha Sibon)
Brumm, Charles, 182
Brumm, Clara Perry, 181
Brumm, Dorothy, 182
Brumm, Emma, 180-181, 183
Brumm, Florence (Emel), 178
Brumm, Lena, 182
Brumm, Marie Olsen, 181-183
Brumm, William, 180, 181
Brunswick, Maine, 79
brush picking, 204
Bryan, Judge James, 197
Bryant, George, 99
Bryant, Hiram, 99, 159
Buckeye, 91
Bucklin, Eben, 46
Bucklin, Edward Sanford, 46-47
Bucklin, Nathan, 46-47, 124
Budd, Lt. Thomas A., 20
Buffum, F. G., 86
Bulette, Mrs., 184
Bulger, Martin, 74, 75
Bunker, E. F., 51
Burgess, Mrs., 34
Burkell, Tom and Nondis, 119
Burr, Theodore, 48

Burtt, Asahel R., 50, 128
Bushwacker (sloop), 83, 103
Butcher, Amie, 50
Butcher, Bessie, 50
Butcher, Frederick, 50
Butcher, Isabella, 50, 125-127
Butcher, Mary, 50
Butcher, Mrs. Thomas, 137
Butcher, Thomas, 50

C

Cade, Ben, 190
Calais, Maine, 41
Caledonia (sidewheel steamer), 69-70
Calhoun, Dr. Rufus, 60
California Gold Rush, 64
Calkins, Floyd and family, 184
Calligan, R. H., 51, 57
Camp Fire Girls, 195
Camp Union, 33, 59, 98, 174, 176, 181, 187, 189, 206, 207
Camp Union Cookhouse, 207
Campbell, Martin, 48
Campbell, William, 106
Capitol Point, 91
Card, Bill, 198
Carlotta, 78
Carmody, Jane, 157
Carpenter, George, 83
Carrick, W., 51
Carson, Harvey, 182
Carson, Kendall, 182
Carswell, 83
Case, Lt. Augustus L., 15, 21
Cass, Charles, 122
Cassandra Adams, 54, 66, 71-73, 78-80
Castle, Pat Dahl, 189
cemetery, 49-50, 135-139
Census
    Hadlock 1889, 60
    Jefferson County, 1900, 84
    Seabeck, 1857, 45, 224-225
    Seabeck, 1860, 60, 226
    Seabeck, 1870, 227-228
    Seabeck, 1871, 84
    Seabeck, 1880, 228-232
    Seabeck 1889, 60
Central II, 95
Chadwick, Fred, 65
Chadwick, Nellie (Nickels), 65
Chapel of the Firs, 166
Charles Nelson Company, 59
Charles R. McCormick Company, 206
Chatham, 11
Chatham, New York, 116
Chehalis, 91
Chilcott, Capt., 106
Chillman, Gertrude, 128

Chillman, Nellie, 59
Chillman, William, 59
Chinese, 57, 208
    Ah Fong, 212
    Census 1889, 60
    farmers, 57, 170
    fisheries, 57, 170
    Grand Jury, 58
    Hadlock 1889, 60
    laundrymen, 57
    mill workers, 57
    pay scale, 57
    Port Gamble explusion,   58
    railroad workers, 57
    Seattle riots, 57

Cicelski, Ingie (Dahl), 185
Cicelski, Jack, 189
circus, 108
City of Angeles, 91
City of Kingston, 94
City of Quincy, 109
Civil War Relief fund, 51
Clark, Charles E., 183
Clark, Ellen, 124
Clark, H. W., 128
Clark, James, 48, 124
Clark, Tom, 169
Clarke, H. W., 61
Clarke, Harry, 122
Clarke, James, Jr., 124
Clatawa, 94, 96
Clayson, Edward, 8-9, 22-30, 32, 42, 45-46, 54, 57, 75-76, 83-84, 99-102, 109, 111, 120-121, 125- 126
Clayson, Edward, Jr., 23
Clayson, Esther Lovejoy Pohl, 23, 25-26, 62, 75
Clayson, Frederick, 23
Clayson, Annie (Quinton), 23
Clayson, Ted, 23
Clayson, William, 23
Clement & McDonald, 46
Clements, Mrs. John, 136
Clench, B. W., 51
Cliff House, 81, 87, 89, 91, 96-97, 102-104, 106-107, 117, 119, 123, 175, 178, 182
    abstract, 177
    store, 104, 177
    View Tracts, , 107, 177
Clifton (Belfair), 34
Clifton, John, 102
Clifton, Mike, 102
Clinton, 95
Coffey, Steve and Barbara, 184
Coffey, Wanda and Robert, 119
Coffin family, 180
Coleman, Tom, 100
Colesburg, Kentucky, 174

Colfax, 32, 35, 46, 51, 53, 57, 59, 63, 69, 71, 72, 74, 78, 82, 83, 84, 114, 121
Colfax, Schuyler, 69
Collier, Hal, 174
Collier, June, 174, 177
Collins, John, 103
Collins, Luther, 40
Colman Center, 158
Colman family, 199
Colman, Agnes (Henderson), 118, 56, 159
Colman, George, 149, 156
Colman, Ida May (Burwell), 156
Colman, Isabelle, 156
Colman, James M., 111
Colman, James Murray, 58, 156
Colman, Katherine, 156
Colman, Kenneth Burwell, 118, 129, 156-158, 160, 164
Colman, Laurence J., 148-150, 153-156, 159, 163
Colvocoresses, Lt. George M., 21
Columbia, 112
Commercial Builders, 195
Compton, Elinor Clark, 182-183
Compton, Robert and Margaret (Weimer) and family, 182
Condon, John, 42, 120
Connick, Capt. John, 83
Connick, Capt. John T., 70, 83-85, 114, 120
Conover, C. T., 55
Cook, Capt. James, 11
cook house, 28, 58, 111, 114
    moves, 154-155
corduroy road, 98
corn fritters, 150-151
Corns, Miss M., 34
Cotes, Louise, 128
Cottle, Ham, 45
Cox, Reynolds, 172
Coyle, 177
Craig, Charles, 50, 55, 111, 137
Craig, Mrs. Charles, 111
Creel family, 180
Crosby, 188
Crosby school district, 128
Crosby, Oscar, 34
Crosier, Mrs. Ernest, 184
Crosus (brig), 43
Cunningham, Bill, 158
Curtis, Asahel, 89, 104
Cyrus Walker (steamer), 69, 78

D

Dabob Bay, 7, 12, 17
Dagnin, Johnny, 63
Dagnin, Minnie, 63, 75
Dagnin, Thomas, 33
Dahl, Alf, 131-132

Dahl, Andrew, 131
Dahl, Anna Foy, 189
Dahl, Borghild, 189
Dahl, Daniel, 185, 188-189
Dahl, David, 130, 131, 189
Dahl, Dena (Hagen), 130, 186, 189
Dahl, Didrikka (Refvik), 188
Dahl, Haldor, 130, 189
Dahl, Hazel (Carnes), 188
Dahl, Hjalmer, 188
Dahl, Ingeborg Cicelski (Ingie), 188-189
Dahl, Isaac, 130, 189
Dahl, Martha Martin, 130-131 89
Damariscotta, Maine, 42
Damon, John F., 35, 105
dance hall, 108
Dancing school, 111
Danielsen, Lila Dahl, 189
Dashing Wave, 75
David Crockett, 80
Davis, Betty, 130
Davis, Margaret (Ninemire), 35, 59, 193
Davis, Phyllis, 130
Davis, Simon H., 35, 59
DeCarty, Biddy, 33, 57, 109
DeCarty, Fred, 57
Deception Pass, 95
Deception Pass route, 95
Deception Pass/Utsalady route, 95
Delany, John L., 79
Delta, 88-89, 144
Demaris Cove, 40
Denny, Arthur, 100
Department of Natural Resources, 195
Depenheuer, Elisabeth (Weber), 196-198
Depenheuer, John, 196-198
DeShaw, William, 143
Deverol, William, 35
Dewatto, 88, 89
Dibley, Dennis, 98, 174
Dickey, Sylvanus A., 128
Dickins, Arnot G., 122
Discoverer (mailboat), 91, 121-122
Discovery, 11
Discovery Bay, 50
Dispatch Line, 80
Doane, J. K., 51
Dode, 89
Donato's comet, 47
Doncaster, Ensley James, 50, 60, 72, 76
Doncaster, Hiram, 55-56, 60, 66, 71, 73, 75-76, 79, 102

Doncaster, Jennie, 56
Doncaster, Lloyd, 60
Doncaster, Martha (Bowker), 50, 60, 108
Doncaster, Ruth, 60
Donnelly, Patricia, 157
Doyea, Frank, 64
Dresden Mills, Maine, 39, 42, 44, 210
Dublin, 53, 62, 79, 80-81
Duckabush, 32, 49, 50, 99
Dunbar, Jeanette, 171, 172
Dunsmuir, Diggle and Company, 80
Dupar, Dorothy Lynch, 195
Dupar, Frank and Ethel, 195
Durgin, Teddy, 100
Duwamish Dairy, 176
Dye's Inlet, 88

E

Eagle Hotel, 28, 48, 65, 99, 101, 136
Earnest (Survey Schooner), 57
Earthquake (1949), 119
East Machias, Maine, 40-41, 49
Eastman, Harrison, 10, 191
Ebey, Col. Isaac, 41
Ebey, Eason, 51
Edwards, Capt. William, 79, 81
Edwards, Joseph, 102
Edwards, May, 75
Eells, Cushing
Eells, Edwin, 3
Eells, Myra, 3
Eells, Myron, 3, 6, 60, 108, 179
Eliza Anderson, 78
Ella Francis (bark), 49
Ellis (steamer), 88
Emel estate, 164
Emel Glade, 178
Emel, Alice, 176
Emel, Anna (Lichen), 176
Emel, Darrel, 176
Emel, Ed, 176
Emel, Elizabeth, 176, 178
Emel, Ernest, 176, 178
Emel, Florence Brumm, 178
Emel, Frank, 176, 178
Emel, Hattie (Sacher), 177
Emel, Hazel, 178, 182
Emel, Ivan, 178
Emel, Jim, 176
Emel, Joe, 44, 92, 132. 143, 173, 178
Emel, Joe (Sr.), 194, 195
Emel, John, 122, 176, 178, 184, 188
Emel, Margaret (Stroeder), 176
Emel, Maud (Gregory), 176, 177

Emel, Peter Ernest, 176-177
Emel, Peter F., 106, 143, 169,
    176-178, 180, 208
Emel, Ruby, 178
Emel, Russell, 130
Emel, William, 176, 177
Enfield, England, 199
Englebrecht, Gustav, 39
Erminia Alvarez, 136
Estados de Sonora - see *State of
    Sonora*, 74
Eva (3 mast schooner), 54, 73-74
Evangel, 87
Evans, Daniel Jackson, 24, 103
Evans, Samuel, 100

F
Fairfield, George, 129
Fanny Lake, 109
farming, 204
Ferguson, Adele, 136, 138, 177-
    178
fire, 58-59, 66
Fiscus, Louis and Elsie, 158
Fish Harbor, 45
fish traps, 92-93, 176
Fisher Flour Company, 198
fishing, 186, 188, 193
Flanagan, Warren, 162
Florence, 78
Forest Queen (bark), 71, 75, 79
Fort George (Astoria), Oregon,
    213
Fort Kitsap (Suquamish), 48
Fort Nisqually, 6, 213
Fort Steilacoom, 41
Fort Vancouver, 213
Fourth of July, 109
Fowler-Hill, Sandra, 158
Foy, Anna (Dahl), 189
Foy, Fred, 189
Francisco, Joe, 48
Frank Jones (full-rigged ship),
    73
Franks, Kermit and Faye, 158
Fraser River Gold Rush, 47, 48,
    55
Fraser, Robert and James, 102
Frasier, Angus, 46
fraternal organization: Knights
    of Good Templar, 111; Lodge
    of the Champion of the Red
    Cross, 111
Frazier, H. P., 106
Frazier, Robert, 101
Frederick Funsten, 94
Fredson, Michael, 51, 124
Freeport, 42
Fremont, 78
Friday Harbor, 94

Frisk, Andrew W., 178, 180
Frisk, Annette (Grundstrom),
    179
Frisk, Olga, Estelle, Edith, 179
Fulton, Bill, 46
Fulton, William, 100
Fussel, Mrs., 150-151

G
Gale, E. L., 107
Galloping Goose, 178
Galvin, Catherine (See
    Catherine Condon), 42
Galvin, Johanna, 42
Gardner, Maine, 43
Gardner, William, 83
Garland, 89, 94
Gassey Charley, 99
Gates, Miss (teacher), 180
Geddes, Annie, 128
Geddes, Willis, 128
Gem (steamer), 25, 83, 86
General Cobb, 79-80
Georgia, 91
Georgie (screw steamer), 83-84,
    70
Germania (bark, ex-ship), 53, 80
Gibbs, George, 3-4
Gifford, Ole, 190
Gilbert, Roxanna, 130, 131
Gillespie, Capt. H., 87
Glory of the Seas, 80
Gold Dust (propeller), 88
Golden Gate, 73
Goliah (tug), 73
Gordon, John, 51
Gove, Capt. George W., 86
Gowan, George, 86
Grant, President Ulysses S., 70
Green, Adelbert, 63, 64
Green, Christina (Peterson), 64
Green, Ella, 34, 64
Green, Franklin, 63-64, 111
Green, John Willis, 64
Green, Joshua, 156
Green, Lilla or Lillie, 64
Green, Lucinda Melvern (Lee),
    60, 63, 108
Green, Mary or Mayme, 34, 64
Green, Samuel Starr, 60, 61,63,
    110
Green, Stephen Rupert, 64
Greenwood, Ray, 172
Greer, Ed and family, 184
Greer, Bobbie and Danny, 184
Griffin, Miss, 34
Grizzly Williams (see John R.
    Williamson)

H
Haberlin, Brenda (Norman), 179
Hadlock, 35, 59, 61-62, 73, 83-
    84, 96, 115-116, 128, 143
    Census 1889, 60
    depression, 59
    production, 59
Hagen, Adolph, 188
Hagen, Anders, 188
Hagen, Berent (Ben), 188
Hagen, Dena (Dahl), 186, 189
Hagen, Ingie (Dahl), 188
Hagen, Ingvald, 124, 185, 187
Hagen, Jacob (1), 186
Hagen, Jacob (2), 186
Hagen, Karen (Vauge), 185-187
Hagen, Klare Reynoldson, 130,
    186
Hagen, Laura Westeren, 130,
    186
Hagen, Lawrence, 130, 186
Hagen, Mable Johnson, 130-132,
    186-187
Hagen, Melvin, 98, 130-131 174,
    187
Hagen, Minert, 188
Hagen, Peder, 124, 185- 188
Hagen, Peter, 185
Hagen, Rasmus, 188
Hagen, Samuelina Gageskar,
    188
Hagen, Sivert, 188
Hagen, Thoralf (Tom), 186, 187,
    189
hairdresser, 111
Halffman, William, 177
Halffman, Maud Emel, 107
Hall Brothers, 97
Hall, Charles R., 190-193
Hall, Harrison, 51
Hall, Henry, 73
Haller, Granville O.,, 49
Halvorsen, Albert, 106, 117, 118
Halvorsen, Billie (see Billie
    Barner)
Halvorsen, Boyer, 92, 117
Halvorsen, Dorothy, 117, 183
Halvorsen, Hazel Margaret, 117
Halvorsen, Marie, 97, 106, 117,
    119, 122, 174
Halvorsen, Mrs. Boyer, 184
Halvorsen, Sig, 117
Halvorsen, Susan, 184
Hamlin, Constance, 157
Hanawalt, Jean (Allen), 150
Hanby family, 208
Hanford, Frank, 125
Hansen, Bob and Dawn, 15, 213
Hanson & Ackerman, 52
Hanswell, England, 199

236

Harmon, Bathalina
  (Clendennin), 41
Harmon, Edward G., 41
Harmon, Edwin, 124
Harmon, Ella Keller, 41
Harmon, Emma, 41
Harmon, Fred, 40-41
Harmon, H. W., 51
Harmon, Hill, 40-41, 48- 49, 51,
  124
Harmon, Ida F., 41
Harmon, L. S., 124
Harmon, Lincoln L., 41
Harmon, Nanina, 41
Harmon, Nathaniel, 124
Harmon, Olive, 41, 124
Harmon, Olive (wife), 41
Harrington & Smith's wharf, 87
Harrison, L. S., 48
Hart, Mr. (teacher), 180
Hart, Mr. and Mrs. Fred, 184
Hartt, Mr. and Mrs. Ray, 184
Hatch, H. R., 51
Haunted Village, 208
Hauptli, John and Frances, 31
Hauptly, Cleveland C., 34
Hauptly, Ethel (Crosby), 34
Hauptly, Harry, 34
Hauptly, Jacob, 24-25, 31-35, 45,
  48, 50, 59-65, 83-86, 88, 101-
  102, 104, 108-110, 112, 114,
  135-136, 169, 174, 176, 193,
  199
Hauptly, Lena (Mickelson), 34
Hauptly, Louise (Reid), 34, 63-
  64
Hauptly, Mary (Hester), 34
Hawkes, Miss, 34
Hayter, Bill, 114
Hazel, 118
Hazel Point, 12
Head of the Bay, 9, 37, 59, 101
Hearst, George, 34
Heath, Agnes, 61
Henderson, Bess (Nickels), 65,
  91-93
Hendrickson, Dr. and Mrs., 184
Heneke, Julius, 48
Hennessey, Capt. James, 87
Hennicke, Elizabeth, 130
Hennicke, Margaret, Elizabeth
  and Richard, 204
Hennicke, Margret, 130
Hennicke, Richard, 131-132
Hewitt, William, 54, 119
Higgins, Dorothy (Bye), 132,
  182-183
Hill, Capt. John, 47
Hill, Larry, 158, 160
Hills, Dr. Cyrus, 44
Hinds, Capt. S. B., 48, 81

Hipp, Cathryn, 182
Hirsch, Robert, 59
Hobbs, Cecilia Mary, 199
Hobbs, Christina Brown, 199
Hobbs, Ellenora Violet
  Martenson, 199
Hobbs, Herbert Edway, 199
Hobbs, Joseph William, 199
Hobbs, Kate Marie Bartlow, 199
Hobbs, Mary (Watkins), 199
Hobbs, Ralph Watkins, 199
Hobbs, William S., 199
Hoengen, Germany, 197
Holbrook, Capt. R. B., 90
Holly, 89
Holmes family, 180
Holton, Charles F., 114
Holyoke Block, Seattle, 53
Holyoke, Annie (Hammond), 53-
  54
Holyoke, Marion, 53
Holyoke, Mrs., 108, 126
Holyoke, Richard, 22, 48, 53-55,
  72, 84, 102, 109, 119, 122,
  124, 136
Holyoke, Richard, Jr., 53
Hood Canal Bridge, 96
Hood, Lord Samuel, 14
Hood, Thomas, 121
Hood's Channel, 14
Hoodsport, 89, 94
Hope, 83
Hopkins, Solomon, 51, 136
Hoppe, John, 131
Hoppe, Leslie, 131
Hoppe, Ray, 131
Horse Head Bay Camp, 156
Hotchkin, Albert L., Sr., 115-
  116, 119, 122
Hotchkin, Albert, Jr., 117, 119,
  122
Hotchkin, Blanche Macfarlane
  (See Blanche Macfarlane),
  115
Hotchkin, Harry, 116
Hotchkin, Irene N., 122
Hotel Howard, 102
Hovey, Steve, 120
Howard, Catherine Mootz, 106
Howard, D. K., 109
Howard, Dennis K., 24, 85- 88,
  101-106, 110
Howard, Dennis K., Jr., 106,
  128
Howard, Lucy, 99
Howard, Nellie (Lyons), 105,
  119, 122
Howard, Samuel, 99
Howard, William C., 106
Howard, Willie, 128
Howe, Capt., 102

Hoy, Tom, 121
Hudson Bay Company, 3, 6-7,
  11, 15, 211
Huffman, Denny and Diane, 184
Hufnagle, Hutoka, 106
Hultgren, Claes, 144
Huntington, Charles, 52
Huntington, West Virginia, 171
Hutchings, Mable and sons, 184
Hutchins, Mrs. L. A., 173
Hyland, Rev. P. E., 84

I

Iman family, 208
Indian Island, 96
Indians:
  Big Beef, 178
  burial, 7, 190
  Chetzamoka (see Duke of
    York)
  Chief Chilewatched, 103
  Chimakum, 3
  Chinook jargon, 5, 8, 22-23
  Du-hle-lips, 4
  Duke of York, 5-6
  ethnobotany, 4-5
  Hudson Bay Company, 213
  Indian uprisings, 1855-56, 43
  Indians, 3-10
  Jack Clams, 8
  Jennie Linc, 5-6
  King George, 6
  Kolsids, 4
  liquor, 99
  Nose-No-Nose, 178
  Old Jenny, 9
  Old Sam and Betsy, 8-9
  Owato, 5
  potlatch, 8-9
  Pants-No-Pants, 178
  Princess Angeline, 64, 143
  Queen Victoria, 5-7
  race with Clayson, 121
  Sally Klanbish, 103
  Sally Smashrocks, 8
  S'klallam, 3, 5, 17, 21
  Skokomish, 3-4, 13, 17, 19
  smallpox, 190
  store order, 114
  Suquamish, 3, 16
  Toando, 3, 16-17, 19-21
  trail, 96
  Twana, 190
  Vancouver, Capt. George,
    11-15
Inland Flyer, 91
Insane Asylum of Washington
  Territory, 41
Irondale, 60
Isaac Jeans, 78
Isabella (steamer), 83

J

J. M. Colman Company, 135, 156
J. M. Griffith (barkentine), 68, 76, 82
Jackson, Capt. Sam, 47
Jackson, D. B., 24, 46, 103
Jacksonville, Maine, 49
Jacobs, John, 101
James McNaught (steamer), 57, 83, 86
James Mortie (steamer), 83, 88, 121
James O'Hara, 94
James, Elsa, 195
James, John, 106
James, Mike, 195
Jameson, Winfield Scott, 103
Jamestown, 3
Janes, Charles, 83
Jefferson County Historical Society, 114
Jeffs, Harry, 192
Jenne, Carl, 184
Jenny Pitts, 78-79
Jensen & Smith, 88
Jerome, Canada, 106
John Kentfield and Company, 75
Johnson, Capt., 112
Johnson, Emma, 193
Johnson, George Cady, 116, 122, 129, 180
Johnson, John, 176
Johnson, Mabel (Hagen), 187
Johnson, Wally, 186-187
Johnstone, Master James, 11-15
Jones, Martha, 128
Josephine (sternwheel steamer), 74, 83, 85, 87-88, 200
Josephsen, Danny, Dick, Bob, 122
Josephsen, Robert, 122, 197
Just, Andrew II, 135

K

Kaiser, Ben, 106
Kaison, Mr., 201
Kate Alexander (sailboat), 65, 83
Katie (tug), 67
Keller, Arlene, 130
Keller, Elsie, 182
Keller, J. P., 40
Keller, Lonnie, 130
Kellum, Archie, 98, 187
Kellum, Arthur, 97-98
Kellum, Louise (Bailey), 97
Kellum-Benbennick stage, 97
Kelson, Ramone, 130
Kendrick, F. P., 60

Kendrick, Iva (Jones), 59-60, 115
Kendrick, Rodney, 55, 59- 60, 97, 110, 115-116
Kendrick, Sarah Edith Macfarlane, 115
Kennedy, Cornelius, 59, 62
Kentfield, John, 74
Kidder (sloop), 83
King, George, 138
King, J. A., 45
King, Miss (teacher), 125
Kingsley, C. W., 48
Kingston, 89, 91
Kinnear, Joseph, 120
Kippola, Wallace and Clara, 184
Kirby, Mrs. Frank, 184
Kitsap County Commissioners, 48
Knautz, Charles and Jessie, 184
Knight, Chuck, 184
Knights of Labor, 59
Koch, Sharon, 135
Krom, Jacob, 122
Kvalheim (see Qualheim and Hagen)

L

Ladonna, 122
Lake Constance (ex-*City of Kingston*, 94, 96
Lake Tahoe, 60
Lantz, John, 193
Lantz, Sarah, 193
Larkin, Mrs. Jesse, 173
Larry, Robert, 47
lath mill, 51, 57
Laurel Hill Cemetery, San Francisco, 44
Leif Erickson, 88
Leithead, Robert, 91
Leonard, Joseph, 51
Leslie, Edna, 157
Lewis, Agatha Marie (Olanie), 55, 60, 67, 81, 216-223
Lewis, Thomas J., 55, 60, 67, 81, 216-223
Libby, Frank, 61
Libby, Mary (Green), 61
library, 58, 111, 124
Lilliwaup, 13, 87, 89
Lindgren, Mrs., 180
Lindsay, Edmund, 51
Lindsey, E. C., 124
Linkletter, Frank, 165
Linkletter, Lloyd Garrison, 165
Linkletter, Richard L., 165
Little Beef, 9, 96, 169-184
Little, Albert H., 62
Little, Anna, 62

Little, Archibald, 61, 62
Little, Clara, 61, 136
Little, Edward, 62
Little, Frank, 59
Little, Gilbert, 61, 84
Little, Helen (Walker), 61
Little, Isabelle, 61, 84
Little, Isabelle (see also Isabelle Baker), 84
Little, Martha (Walton), 59, 62, 176
Little, Mary, 59
Little, Nellie, 62
Little, William, 59, 61, 62
Lizzie Horner, 88
Llewellyn, Billy, 120
Llewellyn, D., 51
Lockport, New York, 63
Lofall/Southpoint crossing, 96
logging, 45-46, 50, 58, 88, 176-178, 187, 189, 202, 204, 208
logging brands, 207
logging railroad, 187, 206
Lombard, Clara, 127
Lone Fisherman (steamer), 87-88
Lone Rock, 169-184
Longfellow, Mr. and Mrs. John, 184
Lost City, 208
Louise (sternwheel steamer), 55, 57, 59, 76, 83, 88
Loveless, John, 158, 160
Low, Mary (see Mary Sinclair), 41
Lowe, Anna Lee, 97
Lowe, Archie, 97, 130-131
Lowe, Arthur (see Arthur Kellum), 97
Lowe, Bernard, 97, 131
Lowe, Chauncey, 97, 131
Lowe, Floyd, 97, 130, 171, 174
Lowe, Lucille Peck, 97, 130-131
Lowe, Mae Raymer, 97
Lowe, Myrtle Davis, 97, 131
Ludlow, 79
Lundberg, Oscar, 193
Lydia Thompson, 94
Lynch, Dorothy (Dupar), 195
Lynch, Potlatch Holbrook, 90
Mable, C. A., 48
Macfarlane, Blanche (Hotchkin), 115
Macfarlane, Rev. Peter, 115
Macfarlane, Sarah Edith (Kendrick), 115
Macfarlane, Walter Rodney, 115, 122
Machias, Maine, 84
Macomber, Capt. Julius, 85, 170
mad house, 38, 104, 108

Madison County, Illinois, 31
Madison, R., 51
mailboat, 83, 85, 87-88, 120-121, 204
Maloney, David, 59, 62
Maloney, Hannah, 59, 62
Maloney, Margaret, 62, 128
Maloney, Mary, 62
Maloney, Michael David, 62
Maloney, Minnie, 128
Maloney, Nora, 62
Maloney-Dixon house, 108
Manchester, Daniel, 100
Maple Beach, 91, 95, 164, 196-198
Maples, Jacob, 40
Maples, Samuel, 40
Maps:
    Kroll, (1930s), 234
    Kroll, (1955), 235
    Plat, (1909), 233
    U.S.Coast & Geodetic Survey, 56
    Vancouver, 13
    Wilkes, 18
Mare Island, 49
Maria, 83
Marrowstone Point, 11
Marshall, C. M., 48
Martin, John, 189
Martin, Martha (Dahl), 189
Martin, Wally, 119
Mary Winkleman (barkentine), 76, 82
Mary's Lake, 187
masquerade ball, 111
Mathews, J. F., 48
Maynard, Dr., 100
McAlpine, Capt., 90
McCallum, Nelson, 60
McCormick Logging Company, 182
McCoy, Newton, 127
McCurdy, William, 73
McDermoth, Charles, 125, 127
McFaddin, Gordon, 50
McKenzie, W. W., 89
McLean, Donald, 173, 178
McLean, Lillian, 178
McMillan, Angus, 190, 191
McMillan, Donna, 122
McQuillian, H. C., 47-48

McQuillian, Mrs., 108
McReavey and Purdy, 46
McReavy and Latham, 86
McReavy Brothers, 86
Meigs, George Anson, 48
Mercer girls, 127
Mercer, Asa, 127
Merchant's Tow-Boat Line, 79

Merrick, Carolyn Rebecca (Taber), 184
Merrick, George, Jesse, Grace, 184
Merrick, Gladys, 183, 184
Merrick, Samuel, 184
Merwin, Miss (teacher), 125
Messenger, 86
Metropolis, Illinois, 129
Miami Beach, 7, 92, 96, 178, 183, 190-193
Middlemas and Boole, 60, 71
Middlemas, George, 71, 73
Midnight Cry, 83
midwife, 63
Milborn, John, 51
Milford, Maine, 136
Miller Machinery Company, 59
Miller, "Apple", 83
Miller, Amasa, 46, 121, 170
Miller, Capt. George, 83
Miller, E. L., 124
Miller, Fred, 107, 121, 170- 175, 177
Miller, George F., 171
Milwaukee, Wisconsin, 156
Mingnon family, 180
Minor, J. J., 51
minstrels, 109
Misery Point, 7, 92, 121
Mjelde, Michael Jay, 68-82
Montgomery, S. T., 48
Moore, Laura, 128
Moran, Mrs. Thomas, 137
Morelock, Emoreah, 130
Morton, Bernice (Winsor), 98, 129
Moses Taylor (steamer), 46
Moses, Col. Simpson C., 99
Mosquito Fleet, 83
Mother Rose (see Rachel Rose), 150-151, 162
Mountain View Cemetery, Oakland, 44
Mountaineers, 106, 179
Mulhern, Frank, 128
Mulhern, Mrs. Thomas, 125
Mulhern, Thomas, 48, 65, 126, 128
Muller, Alphonse, 64
Munger, Serine and Ed, 191
Munson, Kenneth and Camilla, 158
murder, 99, 104, 108, 159, 171
Murray, Charles, 73-74

N

Nantucket, 62
National Bank of Commerce, 53
Naygard, Emil, 119

Nellie, 74
New Brunswick, 53
new year's eve, 109
Newell, A. B., 97
Newell, Gordon, 212
Newell, Joseph A., 51-52
Newell, Joseph H., 49
Newell, Mrs. E., 51
Newell, Oscar, 51
Newland, Alexander, 107-108
Newland, William Y., 107
Newlands Dance House, 108
Nibbe, Capt. John, 88
Nickels Brothers, 90-93
Nickels, Alice Walton, 65
Nickels, Arthur (Art), 65, 91-93
Nickels, Augusta, 65
Nickels, Bess (see Bess Henderson)
Nickels, Clara, 60, 65
Nickels, Edward, 67
Nickels, Frank, 65
Nickels, Nellie, 65
Nickels, Sam (Jr.), 65, 91
Nickels, Samuel, 60
Nickels, Samuel T., 65, 67
Nickels, Samuel (Sr.), 92
Nickels, Sarah, 92
Nickerson, Rev., 108
Ninemire family, 34, 63, 108
Ninemire, Belle, 34, 109
Ninemire, Ellen, 34
Ninemire, George, 34, 62
Ninemire, John, 34, 59
Ninemire, Margaret, 34
Ninemire, Mary, 34, 59
Ninemire, Will, 62
Nordmark, Everett, 158
Norman, Brenda, 179
Norman, Carl, 179
Norman, Charles, 158
Norman, Charles and Ruth, 158
Norman, Johannes (John), 179
Norman, Rosanna Spickard (Evans), 179
Norman, Rose, 179
Norman, Thomas, 179
North Pacific, 85
North West Company, 213
Northerner (steamer), 47
Nova Scotia, 55

O

O'Brien, T. H., 197
O'Green, Charles, 104
O'Toole, Martin, 125
Oak Harbor-Utsalady, 92
Oak Head, 83
Oakland (Shelton), 48, 87
Ohio (steamship), 40
Olanie family, 43-44, 107, 117

Olanie, Agnes, 67
Olanie, Eliza (Rounds), 67
Olanie, Ella, 49, 62-63, 127, 135
Olanie, Francis X., 67
Olanie, Henry, 63, 67
Olanie, Henry J. F. X., 67
Olanie, Howard, 67
Olanie, Irene Eliza, 67
Olanie, Samuel A., 67
Oliver, Capt. J. L., 80
Olsen, Andy, 95-96, 155, 158,
    160, 164, 194
Olsen, Clara, 164
Olsen, Marie (Brumm), 181
Olson, Agaton, 95
Olson, Berte, 95-96
Olympia, 43
Olympia, Pacific Hotel, 41
Olympic, 91
Olympic Motor Transit
    Company, 98
Olympus (barkentine), 54-55, 66,
    72-73, 80, 82, 102, 216-223
orchard blight, 55
Ordway, Elizabeth M., 127-128
Oregon, 40, 53-54, 77, 79-80
Oregon City, Oregon, 40
Oriental (brig), 40
Osburn, Reina, 174
Osprey (yacht), 148

P

Pacific Foundry, 73
Pacific Mail, 74
Pacific Mail Line, 40
Pacific Pine Manufacturers'
    Association, 52
Palmer, John, 5
Parker, Capt., 88
Patriarch (newspaper), 22
Patterson, Dave, 63
Patterson, Frank, 33
Pawtucket (tug), 67
Peabody, Capt. Alexander, 94-96
Peake, A. J., 129
Peake, Dorothy, 131, 183
Peiser, Theodore E., 64-65
Pennell and Newland's saloon,
    107
Pennell, J. W., 107-108
Perdita, 89, 90
Perry family, 180
Perry, Clara (Brumm), 181
Peterson, Christina Green, 64
Peterson, Joyce, 132
Peterson, O., 38
Peterson, Ted, 198
Peterson, Veborg, 64
Phantom (steamer), 57, 74, 83,
    86, 88

Phillips, John, 84
Phinney, Guy C., 55, 81, 83
Pickford, Mary, 97
Pierce, Annie, 50
Pierce, Clinton, 50
Pierce, Josie, 50
Pierce, Mary Ellen (McCabe),
    49-50
Pierce, Thomas, 46, 49-50, 99
Pierpont, Daniel T., 42, 124
Pike, John, 102
Pilot, 20
Pinnace, 11
Pioneer, 91, 95, 215
Pioneer Society, 43
Pitt, Joseph, 61
Pittston, Maine, 42, 65, 174
Plaskett, P. L., 86
Pleasant Harbor, 91
Point-No-Point Treaty, 3
Point Discovery, 11, 14
Politkofsky, 106
Poor Farm, Port Orchard, 93
Pope and Talbot, (See Port
    Gamble)
Pope, Andrew, 40
Port Blakely, 42, 51-52, 55, 58,
    106
Port Gamble, 7, 32, 39-43, 46,
    48-49, 51-52, 55, 57, 61, 65,
    67, 83-89, 96, 99-100, 102-
    103, 108-109, 120-121, 127,
    170, 187
Port Gamble/Shine route,   95
Port Hadlock (see Hadlock)
Port Ludlow, 37, 39, 46, 55-56,
    60, 71, 89, 96, 169, 187
Port Madison, 33, 41, 48-49, 51-
    52, 55, 86, 111, 127- 128, 135,
    156
Port Orchard, 42-43, 48, 111,
    126, 156
Port Townsend, 5-6, 11, 32-3347,
    51, 62, 97, 99, 108, 169
Port Washington (Dye's Inlet),
    48, 88
Portland YMCA, 148
Portland, Oregon, 42
post office, 113, 117, 119
postmasters, 122
Potlatch, 119, 153, 184
Potts, Herb and Dorothy, 195
Poulsbo, 95
Prenatt, J. A., 97
Prescott, James M., 40, 53
Preston, Alexander, 99
Preston, Margaret, 99
Primrose, Capt. William Henry,
    106
Primrose, Peter, 48
Prosch family, 180

Prosch, Charles, 116
Prosch, Frederick, 110, 116, 119,
    122, 143, 180
Prosch, Helen (Elder), 119, 122
Prosch, Susan, 116
Prosch, Thomas, 116
Puget Sound Navigation
    Company, 89, 90, 92, 94, 96
Puget, Lt. Peter, 11-15
Pulk, James, 47
Purdham, Wayne, 158
Purdy and McReavy, 83
Purvis, Ralph G., 98, 171
Putman, S. F. 105

Q

Qualheim, Didrick, 188
Qualheim, Jacob, 188
Qualheim, Norway, 185
Qualheim, Rasmus O., 185, 193
Qualheim, Thornstein, 188
Quilcene, 91, 197

R

Radomski, Hank, 184
Radomski, Mr. and Mrs. George,
    184
Ragsdale, J. R., 119
Rainbow, 95
Rainier, 91
Raisback, E., 86
Ranger (sidewheel steamer), 69
Rasmusson, Tomina, 186, 188
Raudeberg, Norway, 188
Raymond Shoe Company, 55
Raymond, Annie, 54
Raymond, Celia (Hammond), 54
Raymond, Charles, 54
Raymond, Chester, 54
Raymond, Frederick R., 54
Raymond, George F., 54-55
Raymond, Harrison, 54
Raymond, Laurence, 54
Raymond, Willie, 54
Reagan, John, 51
Reeve, Helen, 174, 177
Reeve, Stanley, 96, 173
Renton, Capt. William, 42, 43
Restless, 83
Retriever (barkentine), 58, 76,
    82
Reynoldson, Klare (Hagen), 186-
    188
Reynoldson, Richard, 187
Rhodes, Mildred Dahl, 189
Rice, J. B., 97
Richard Holyoke, 72-73, 75, 79,
    81-82, 85
Riddell, Ernest, 212-213
Ried, Charles, 111

Rip Van Winkle, 83, 88
Risch family, 180
roads, 48
Robinson, Albert, 178
Robinson, Dr. Alexander Rock, 173
Rockland, Maine, 78
Rogers, Almanza, 203-204
Rogers, Andrew J. (Andy), 130-131, 202-205
Rogers, Dr. Albert, 202, 204
Rogers, Frances, 202-204
Rogers, Rosemary, 131, 203-204
Rosalie (steamer), 88, 94
Rosaw Straits Packing Company, 176
Rose, Dick and Sue, 158
Rose, Rachel, 150
Rosenfeld, John, 80
Rounds, Eliza Francis (Olanie), 62-63
Rounds, Eliza Olanie, 63
Rounds, Fannie Blythe, 62-63
Rounds, Frank, 62
Rounds, George, 62
Rounds, Howard, 62
Rounds, Marcella Luke, 62, 128
Rounds, Samuel A., 62-63, 65
Rounds, Sarah, 62-63
Ruehle, Lois, 198
Ruehle, Orin and Laura, 198
Ryan, R. E., 127

S

Samish Logging Company, 53
San Francisco, 44
Sarah M. Renton, 91
Sargent, Nathaniel, 114-115
Scenic Beach, 91, 164, 178, 194-195
Scheckles, Miss (teacher), 180
Schenectady, New York, 41
Schold, Al and Jean, 180
Schold, John, Margaret, Genevieve, Betty, 180
Schold, Mrs. (teacher), 180, 184
school, 61, 65-66, 111, 124-134, 187, 204
school patrol, 184
schoolbus, 204
Schroeder family, 184
Schuld, Germany, 196
Schweppe, Alfred, 157
Scoland, James, 86
Sea Nymph (bark), 136
Sea View, 92-93
Seabeck (barge), 118
Seabeck Christian Conference Center, 97, 99, 148-166, 184, 187, 199, 203, 205, 208, 212

55
Seabeck Community Club, 184, 195
Seabeck Corporation, 157
Seabeck Creek, 189
Seabeck Dairy, 177
Seabeck stage, 97
Seabeck stage schedule, 98
Seabeck, Maine, 210
Seabeck, Territorial Capital, 211
Seabeck-Brinnon ferry, 93, 95-96
Seattle YMCA, 148, 150
Sebec, Maine, 210
Severence, William, 48
Seward, William Henry, 43
Seymore, William B., 104
Shaffer, Harry, 136
Shark, 83
Shelton, Mary, 125
Shibler, Peter, 84
shipbuilding, 54, 55, 60, 68-76, 121
Shoo Fly (steamer), 83, 88, 100, 121
Sibon, Bertha (Brumm), 93, 171, 181, 183-184
Sidney, 135
Silverdale, 88, 128
Simpson family, 180
Simpson, Nancy, 157
Sinclair, Mary, 41
Sinclair, Woodbury B., 41, 19, 119, 122
Sires, Rev. David, 108
Sisson family, 180
Skokomish, 5, 13, 31, 34, 59, 121
Skokomish Indians (see Indians, Skokomish)
Sloan, Capt., 80
Smith, George, 48, 51
Smith, James, 178
Smith, Jeff, 51
Smith, Jim, 176
Smith, Mrs. Earl, 173
Smith, Ned, 100
Smith-Gandy, Inc., 156
snowstorm (1880), 111
Sovereign of the Seas, 80
Spaulding, Henry, 48
Spear, Isaac, 47
Spriggs, C. A., 91, 198
Sprout, H. W. , 32
Squamish Harbor, 104
Squier, Emma Lindsey, 180
St. Johns, New Brunswick, 174
St. Patrick (steamer), 32, 35, 57, 62, 65, 74, 83, 85, 86, 88, 106, 114, 170
stage, 153, 183
Stanioch, Mrs. John, 173
Stanioch, Sheriff John, 177

Stanley, H. A., 143
Stark, Thomas, 100, 114
Starvation Flats, 208
State of Sonora (steamer), 74-75
State of Washington, 90, 94, 185
Stavanger, Norway, 95
Stavis Bay, 9, 26, 129, 178, 190, 199-205
Steffen family, 180
Steilacoom, 40-42, 116
Stevenson, John, 51
Stice, Hearl "Buzz", 158
Stone family, 208
Stone, William S., 51
storm (1990), 123
Stowell, Charley, 46
Strickland, Isaac, 51
Strong, Maxine, 198
Sullivan, Dwight and Thela, 191
Sunday, Billy, 95
Sutton, Judge H. G., 172-173
Swanson, Walter, 130
Sweat, John, 46

T

Tacoma (steam tug), 67, 73
Tacoma Mill Company, 73
Talbot, Frederic, 40
Talbot, William Chaloner, 40
Tanner, 78
Tart, James, 102
Taylor, Harry, 83
Taylor, Peter, 52, 53
Teapa, 94
telephone poles, 97
Temple, H. C., 45
Temple, W. K., 51
ten pin alley, 8
Tharp, Abe, 178
Theobalds, Mary, 125-126
Thomaston, Maine, 44, 47
Thompson Steamship Company, 90
Thompson, James, 49
Thorn, Bill, 125
Thorndyke Bay, 47
Thornton, Bill, 94
Thornton, Capt. William P., 94-96
Thornton, Frank, 94-96
Thornton, Phil, 94
Thornton, Phyllis, 94
Toander, 49
Toby (tug), 62
Tolmie, William Fraser, 3
Totten, George M., 20
Tramp Steamer to Orient, 213
trapping, 204
traveling troupes, 109
Treen & Raymond, 55
Troutman, Capt. Daniel, 88-89

Troutman, Dora (Wells), 89
Troutman, H. A., 51
Troy, New York, 115
Turner, Ben, 46
Turner, Robert, 106

U

U.S. Coast and Geodetic survey, 135
Ungren, Jack, 132
Union City, 59, 83, 85, 87- 89, 121
Union City Wilson, 121
United States Hotel, 99, 100, 148
University Land Grants, 47

V

Van Asselt, Henry, 40
Van Winkle, James, 45
Vancouver, Capt. George, 11-15
Vanderzicht, John, 194
Vauge, Abraham, 187
Veitch, Christiana (see also Christiana Butcher), 50
Veitch, Isabelle (see also Isabelle Airey), 83
Velde(e), Peder, 201-202
Velde(e), Severine (Salvesen), 202
Veldee children, 129
Veldee, Conrad, 202
Veldee, Harry, 202
Veldee, Ida, 202
Veldee, Martha, 202
Veldee, Pearl Irene, 202
Veldee, Solvieg, 202
Veldee, Will, 202
Vickery, Mr. and Mrs. F. C., 86
Victoria, BC, 51, 85, 99
Virginia, 74
Virginia V, 183
Voigt, Greg, 195
Vrooman, Edgar, 122

W

Wa Chong, 34, 57
Wade family, 176
Walker, Jennie, 125
Walker, John, 46, 100
Walker, Mrs. (teacher), 125
Wall, Jack, 131-132
Wallace, J. B., 51
Walter L. Wyckoff Company, 135
Walton House (Bed & Breakfast), 175
Walton, Alice (Nickels), 58, 60, 65-66, 76, 83, 106, 174, 177
Walton, Capt. Al, 91, 122, 187
Walton, Ernest Russell, 175

Walton, Gladys (DeMoss), 176
Walton, Herbert Ray, 175-176
Walton, Irene Gertrude Brett, 175
Walton, Irvin Roosevelt, 175
Walton, John Alexander, 60-61, 65, 106, 121, 129, 174, 176-177
Walton, John William, 175
Walton, Lena May Emel, 175
Walton, Marie, 122
Walton, Martha Little, 176
Walton, Ray, 175-176
Walton, Shirley, 175
Wanderer, 83
War Hawk, 81
Ward, Dillis R., 47
Wareham, England, 121
Warenstaf, Mrs. and children, 184
Warin, Brinnon & Company, 105
Warrin, Harriet (Hattie), 34
Warin, Jessie, Katherine, William, Jr., 103
Warin, Sally, 103
Warin, William, 51, 85-86, 99, 101-103, 108, 117, 121
Warren, Maine, 46
Washington (ferry), 149
Washington Mill Company, 39-67, 40, 45-46, 59, 62, 69, 116, 120
Washington-Idaho Council of Churches, 157
Waterford, Washington, 85
watering trough, 117
Waterloo Iowa, 150
Waterman, Delos, 34
Waterman, Thomas Talbot, 9, 199
Watson family, 208
Watson, William, 103
Wayland, Rex, 143
Welch, Maude A. Baker, 84
Welliever, Nellie, 181
Wells, Herod, 101, 103, 178
Wells, Josephine, 103
Wenborn, Robert, 45, 51, 178
Wenham, Robert, 48
Wesch, Carolyn, 182
Wesch, Hans, 182
West Fork Logging Company, 92, 176, 181, 187, 206
West Point, Nebraska, 180
Westeren, Reidar, 186
Westeren, Laura (Hagen), 186
Western Mill and Lumber Company, 59
Whatcom, 94
Wheeler, B. E., 51

Wheeler, Emma, 127
Whidbey Island, 41, 49, 61, 95
Whiskey Spit, 32, 104
Whitney, Cam, 45, 46, 136, 178
Whitney, Hank, 46
Whitneyville, Maine, 61
Whittaker, Jane, 131
Whittaker, Jim, 131
Wiggins, Charley, 46
Wild Cat Lake, 179
Wild Irish Rose (plunger), 83
Wilkes, Lt. Charles, 15-21
Willey, Capt. S. H., 88
Willey, E. S., 51
William J. Bryant (schooner), 89
Williams, James, 85
Williams, Walter J., 135-136
Williamson, John R., 41-42, 47-49, 87, 124
Williamson, Julia (Flynn), 42
Wilson G. Hunt (steamer), 43
Wilson, G. B., 51
Wilson, H. C., 43
Wilson, Union City, 121
Winser, Miss (teacher), 108, 125, 126
Winsor, Minnie, 98, 129
Wirth, Rev. Mr. A. T., 63, 108
Wisker, Rev. Mr., 108
Wissell, Al, 88
Witwer, Betty J., 122
Wolfle, David, 180
Wondersheidt family, 180
Woodstock, New Brunswick, 54
Worlund, Mrs. Arthur, 157
Wyatt, Capt. Cyprian, 88, 89
Wyckoff, Walter, 157

Y

Ye Galleon Press, 22
Yesler's wharf, 87
Yesler, Henry, 46
YMCA, 28, 55, 148, 149, 150, 157
Young America, 80
Young, A. B., 48, 124
Young, Charles or John N., 99
Young, Enoch, 33
Young, Frederick A., 124
Young, Horace H., 124
Young, O. S., 45
YWCA, 157

Z

Zaspel, Jerry, 119

Patrons

Julia (Baker) Blinn
Wife of Mill owner Marshall Blinn
(Photo courtesy Olanie family.)

Keith Lovell
WALLPAPER INN

9468 Silverdale Way NW
Silverdale, WA 98383
698-4817

Alice S. Myhre

In honor of
Agnes and Alfred Blomlie
and in Memory of
Norman A. Blomlie.

Sharon O'Hara

To those who made Seabeck's history
possiible:
Andrew Workosky
Dorothea Workosky Speed
Arthur Bates
Lincoln Perry

Garry and Cynthia L. Thompson
Kimberly, Sierra and Tiffany

In Memory of our parents,
William J. Brumm,
1888-1968
Emma F. Brumm
1893-1979

Bertha, Marie T. and Clara Brumm

Robert and Lois Catterall

William and Mary Jane
Cunningham

Victoria Rowe

In Memory and appreciation to
the Emels and Brumms:
You've bettered the lives of
hundreds of descendants by
settling near Seabeck.
Darrel Emel
Emel's Tree & Lawn Service

PAMELA E. PERRY

*Thanks for letting us be a
part of this community.*

*Larry, Sandy,
Spencer and Whitney*

*In Honor of our
Grandmas and Grandpas
We love you.*

Andi, Arlan and Alanna

KEN
AND
THERESA PERRY

Michael Jay Mjelde

Hood Canal Sustains Life;
Body and Soul.

Ed Arness and family

Land
Title
Company

Serving Kitsap County since 1968.

To T. J. Lewis, F. X. Olanie
and
Nathan Bucklin:

They saw a future for all of us.

Warren & Shairon Lewis

---

*Rev. Kit England Dietrich
and
Capt. (Ret.) Frederick P. Dietrich*

Parker & Company

CERTIFIED PUBLIC ACCOUNTANTS

9222 Bayshore Dr. NW
Silverdale, WA 98383

Office: 692-8808
FAX: 692-3620

---

*In Memory of my parents,
Frances and Albert Rogers,
who provided me the
opportunity to live in
happiness on Hood Canal.*
Andy Rogers

---

*In loving memory of
Harold Collier
whose dream of living on the water
brought our family to Seabeck.*

June Collier

**J. Michael Koch
and
Sharon L. Koch**

In memory of C. W. Howard
whose research of records from the
1850's maintains a family memory
of his grandparents,
Hill and Bathalina Harmon,
in Washington Territory.

Phyllis and Bradley Jones